The Spirit throughout the Canon

Journal of Pentecostal Theology Supplement Series

Editor in Chief

John Christopher Thomas (*Pentecostal Theological Seminary, Cleveland, and Centre for Pentecostal and Charismatic Studies, Bangor University*)

VOLUME 48

A former Deo Publishing series

The titles published in this series are listed at *brill.com/jpts*

The Spirit throughout the Canon

Pentecostal Pneumatology

Edited by

Craig S. Keener
L. William Oliverio Jr.

BRILL

LEIDEN | BOSTON

All articles in this volume, with the exception of the Afterword, have been published in Brill's journal *Pneuma* 43.3-4 (2021).

Library of Congress Cataloging-in-Publication Data

Names: Keener, Craig S., 1960- editor. | Oliverio, L. William, Jr., editor.
Title: The Spirit throughout the canon : Pentecostal pneumatology / edited by Craig S. Keener, L. William Oliverio, Jr.
Description: Leiden ; Boston : Brill, 2022. | Series: Journal of Pentecostal theology supplement series, 0966-7393 ; volume 48 | Includes bibliographical references and index.
Identifiers: LCCN 2022018250 (print) | LCCN 2022018251 (ebook) | ISBN 9789004518711 (hardback) | ISBN 9789004518728 (ebook)
Subjects: LCSH: Holy Spirit–Biblical teaching. | Pentecostal churches–Doctrines.
Classification: LCC BT121.3 .S667 2022 (print) | LCC BT121.3 (ebook) | DDC 231/.3–dc23/eng/20220624
LC record available at https://lccn.loc.gov/2022018250
LC ebook record available at https://lccn.loc.gov/2022018251

Typeface for the Latin, Greek, and Cyrillic scripts: "Brill". See and download: brill.com/brill-typeface.

ISSN 0966-7393
ISBN 978-90-04-51871-1 (hardback)
ISBN 978-90-04-51872-8 (e-book)

Copyright 2022 by Craig S. Keener and L. William Oliverio Jr. Published by Koninklijke Brill NV, Leiden, The Netherlands.
Koninklijke Brill NV incorporates the imprints Brill, Brill Nijhoff, Brill Hotei, Brill Schöningh, Brill Fink, Brill mentis, Vandenhoeck & Ruprecht, Böhlau and V&R unipress.
Koninklijke Brill NV reserves the right to protect this publication against unauthorized use. Requests for re-use and/or translations must be addressed to Koninklijke Brill NV via brill.com or copyright.com.

This book is printed on acid-free paper and produced in a sustainable manner.

To Gordon Fee and the other pioneers of biblical studies in the global Pentecostal-Charismatic tradition, and to Patrick Mastrobuono and the other Pentecostal-Charismatic faithful who have heard the voice of the Spirit in these texts

Contents

Acknowledgments XI

Introduction. Pentecostal Biblical Scholarship and Pentecostal Pneumatology 1
    Craig S. Keener and L. William Oliverio Jr.

The Spirit in the Pentateuch: From Creation to Supernatural Empowerment 6
    Michael L. Brown

The Spirit in Numbers 11: God's Pentecostal Plan 12
    Roger D. Cotton

The Spirit in the DtrH/Former Prophets: "And the Spirit Came Upon Him" 16
    Brian Neil Peterson

The Spirit in 1–2 Chronicles, Ezra-Nehemiah, and Esther: Transforming the Spirit Traditions for New Contexts 23
    Emma M. Austin and Jacqueline Grey

The Spirit in the Book of Psalms: Creating, Saving, Sanctifying, Guiding, and Judging 28
    Lee Roy Martin

The Spirit in Isaiah: God's Might and His Charismatic Presence on the Elect 37
    Wonsuk Ma

The Spirit in Ezekiel: The Presence of Yahweh with His People 45
    Alicia R. Jackson

The Spirit in Daniel and The Twelve: When Divine Winds Blow 52
    Rick Wadholm

The Spirit in Matthew: Righteousness and Obedience 59
    Blaine Charette

The Spirit in Mark: Power and Suffering   67
   Blaine Charette

The Spirit in Luke-Acts: Empowering Prophetic Witness   75
   Robert P. Menzies

The Spirit in the Gospel according to John, 1 John, and 2 John: "Rivers of Living Water"   106
   John Christopher Thomas

The Spirit in Romans: God's Community and Life in the Spirit   134
   Finny Philip

The Spirit in 1 Corinthians: Spiritual Formation and Giftedness   148
   J. Ayodeji Adewuya

The Spirit in 2 Corinthians: A Glorious Covenant and Consummation   158
   Jacob Cherian and Joe Thomas

The Spirit in Galatians: The Holy Spirit in Paul's Soteriological Arguments   163
   Roji Thomas George

The Spirit in Ephesians and Philippians: Together by Divine Enabling   169
   Daniel K. Darko

The Spirit in Colossians and Philemon: Love, Understanding, and Unity   181
   Holly Beers

The Spirit in 1 and 2 Thessalonians: The Function of the Spirit in Paul's Earliest Letters   183
   Roji Thomas George

The Spirit in the Pastoral Epistles: Inspiring, Gifting, Sanctifying Presence   190
   Kenneth J. Archer

The Spirit in Hebrews: Guiding the Community to Further Truth   195
   Cynthia Long Westfall

The Spirit in 1 Peter, 2 Peter, and Jude: Transformation and
Transcendence   204
    Rebecca Skaggs

The Spirit in John's Apocalypse: Vision, Prophecy, Discernment   208
    Melissa Archer and Robby Waddell

Afterword. From Bare Life to *Labash* Life: A Tribute to the Holy Spirit   222
    Nimi Wariboko

Subject Index   227
Biblical Index   229

Acknowledgments

All serious scholarship is a work of collaboration that stands on the shoulders of others and joins in a much larger and longer dialogue than what appears in the text. *The Spirit throughout the Canon* is not the work of merely the editors and authors. Many contributed to the text that we hope will further the study of biblical pneumatology for decades to come.

As the dedication indicates, this text represents the work of a whole generation of biblical scholars in the Pentecostal tradition, exemplified by Gordon Fee, who forged paths through which current and future ones travel and on which they expand and construct yet new ones. Behind the past, current, and emerging guild stand many educational institutions, churches and fellowships, families and friends, and more. The tradition of biblical pneumatology among Pentecostal scholars that is presented here has been a communal effort that has been brought to fruition by the recent labor of the leading scholars from around the world who have composed the chapters found in this book.

Standing behind the composition of these chapters are not only those referred to above but a number of other persons who especially contributed to the production of this text, which first appeared as a double issue of *Pneuma* (43.3–4) in 2021. The editorial staff at *Pneuma: The Journal of the Society for Pentecostal Studies* produced this text from the inside. Immense thanks goes out to Nimi Wariboko, Alex Mayfield, Anthony Roberts, and Nancy de Flon, along with our partners at Brill, including Tessel Jonquière, Dieuwertje Kooij, and Noralyne Maranus. The dozens of anonymous peer reviewers of what are now the chapters in this book made a special contribution to this volume. They read and criticized the chapters in ways that did not merely vet the quality of their work but pushed the authors (and the editors) in many helpful directions in both broader considerations and minute details. Their investments have significantly contributed to this text, though they are not responsible for any remaining errors or weaknesses in it. We are grateful to Julie Quackenbush for producing the biblical index and to Nicholas Oliverio for producing the keyword index, which will help students and other readers find their way around the many biblical references and ideas that run across the varied chapters.

We are also grateful to those who supported us in our day-to-day lives as we worked on the project that became this book.

I (Craig) thank *Pneuma*'s regular editors for inviting me to participate as a guest editor for the journal volume that became this book. I also thank my wife Médine and my seminary colleagues for their patience with my various publication projects.

I (Bill) am grateful for the support of my wife Rachel and our sons Nicholas and Joshua, my friends and colleagues at Northwest University's College of Ministry, along with the overall support which I receive at the university for my editorial and scholarly work.

INTRODUCTION

Pentecostal Biblical Scholarship and Pentecostal Pneumatology

Craig S. Keener and L. William Oliverio Jr.

This volume was first published as a double issue of *Pneuma: The Journal of the Society for Pentecostal Studies* and is now produced here in book form for use by students, scholars, and all those interested in how some of the leading biblical scholars from the global pentecostal tradition understand the appearances of the divine Spirit throughout the biblical canon. This work was birthed out of a moment of opportunity in the history of pentecostal biblical scholarship. Across the globe, a generation of pentecostal biblical scholars has generated new layers of scholarship and interpretation of the canonical texts, and this work is on display in this volume, among other works, of course. Over the past several decades, the authors who have contributed to this issue, along with many others, have provided thick strata of material upon which contemporary pentecostal scholarship of the Scriptures now stands. This book, then, presents a summarizing concert of this material as it locates the Spirit in the biblical texts. These critical summaries offer up an assembly of biblical scholars from all over the world accounting for the presence and work of the Spirit from Genesis to the Apocalypse. The authors who contributed to this volume are natives of Australia, Canada, Ghana, India, Korea, Nigeria, and the United States of America, and many of them have lived on multiple continents due to their educational and ministry journeys. This project thus represents many of the significant scholarly voices of pentecostal communities from across the world. Because only a limited number of slots existed for authors, we could include only a small proportion of pentecostal biblical scholars and could not represent all regions, but we hope that overall this work reflects the general tenor of pentecostal biblical scholarship concerning the Spirit's role throughout the canon.

As such, this volume allows many witnesses to the Spirit found in the biblical texts, each declaring the wonders of God in their own scholarly tongue. Like Handel's *Messiah* narrates the story of Christ in a sequential oratorio, this issue is thus a series of solos and duets that accounts for the appearance of the divine Spirit throughout the Scriptures. Each of our performer-scholars has done so in her or his own voice, in their own style, with their own convictions, and as the fruit of his or her own scholarship. Readers may note the stylistic as well as methodological and substantive differences among our authors. These reveal our editorial sense not to force conformity on the authors so that many of the best scholars in our tradition might freely communicate their convictions in the style and substance of their choosing.

The space that has been allotted to various authors is not meant to reflect differing levels of respect for different parts of the canon. Rather, word counts were assigned based especially on the proportion of references to the Spirit in various books or sections of the canon. Therefore, larger space has been given to the New Testament than the Old, and then, again, for works such as Luke-Acts than for 1–2 Thessalonians. Limitations of space precluded fuller engagement that might have been possible in a larger volume, but also allowed us to provide a more affordable sample of insights from some of our leading scholars.

Many continuities appear throughout the chapters of this volume, though we will note two key characteristics among them. First, all of the authors who have written here, as members of global pentecostal traditions, recognize the divine Personhood of the Spirit even as they have sought to faithfully reflect the historical moments reflected in the composition of the portions of the canon on which they have written. Secondarily, and to no surprise to those familiar with Pentecostalism, they have also stressed the theme of empowerment, whether for life, worship, or ministry for God. Together, this text produces a pentecostal pneumatology that witnesses the Spirit throughout the canon through some of the best of contemporary pentecostal biblical scholarship. They have come from leading doctoral institutions and are engaging wider scholarship far beyond specifically pentecostal emphases in biblical studies.

As we introduce this volume, we will note the authors' current affiliations at the time of publication as well as their doctoral institutions. Here, we will note our own as editors. Craig S. Keener (PhD, Duke University) is the F.M. and Ada Thompson Professor of Biblical Studies at Asbury Theological Seminary in Wilmore, Kentucky, USA. L. William Oliverio, Jr. (PhD, Marquette University) is Associate Professor of Public Theology at Northwest University in Kirkland, Washington, USA and Co-editor-in-chief of *Pneuma: The Journal of the Society for Pentecostal Studies*.

In the Old Testament, the Spirit acts as divine agency and empowers God's people. Michael L. Brown (PhD, New York University), founder and President of FIRE School of Ministry in Concord, North Carolina, USA as well as host of the Line of Fire radio show, and Roger Cotton (ThD, Concordia Seminary), Professor of Old Testament at The Assemblies of God Theological Seminary in Springfield, Missouri, USA address God's *ruach* in the Pentateuch, with observations that include the Spirit's activity in creation and empowerment for leadership, prophecy, and artistry. Brian Neil Peterson (PhD, University of Toronto), Associate Professor of Old Testament and Hebrew at Lee University in Cleveland, Tennessee, USA, explores God's Spirit in earlier narrative works about Israel in the land, emphasizing prophetic inspiration and miraculous empowerment. Emma Austin (PhD cand., University of Sydney) and Jacqueline Grey (PhD, Charles Sturt University), respectively Associate Professor of Old Testament Studies and Professor of Biblical Studies at Alphacrucis College in Sydney, Australia, discuss God's Spirit in postexilic narratives, including the Spirit's role in worship. Lee Roy Martin (ThD, University of South Africa), Professor of Old Testament and Biblical Languages at Pentecostal Theological Seminary in Cleveland, Tennessee, USA, as well as Co-editor-in-chief of *Journal of Pentecostal Theology*, addresses God's Spirit as agent of God's life-giving power in the Psalms. Wonsuk Ma (PhD, Fuller Theological Seminary), Dean of the College of Theology and Ministry and Distinguished Professor of Global Christianity at Oral Roberts University in Tulsa, Oklahoma, USA discusses the Spirit empowering God's chosen people in Isaiah. Alicia R. Jackson (PhD, University of Birmingham), Assistant Professor of Old Testament at Vanguard University in Costa Mesa, California, USA addresses the Spirit as God's presence also involved in restoring and transforming God's people. Rick Wadholm (PhD, Bangor University—Wales), Associate Professor of Old Testament at The Assemblies of God Theological Seminary, discusses the Spirit's role as life, witness, judge, and gift in Daniel and the so-called Minor Prophets.

Most of the Spirit's activity described in New Testament books flows naturally from the Spirit's activities already evident from the varied essays on sections of the Old Testament canon. Blaine Charette (PhD, University of Sheffield), Professor of Bible and Greek at Northwest University in Kirkland, Washington, USA, addresses Matthew's distinctive depiction of the Spirit, including in relation to the kingdom, and addresses the Spirit's empowerment to face suffering in Mark. Robert P. Menzies (PhD, University of Aberdeen), Director of the Asian Center for Pentecostal Theology, explores especially the dimension of prophetic empowerment in the pneumatology of Luke-Acts. John Christopher Thomas (PhD, University of Sheffield), the Clarence J. Abbott Professor of Biblical Studies and Director of the Centre for Pentecostal Theology at Pentecostal Theological Seminary, treats this and other aspects of the Spirit's work in the Gospel and Epistles of John.

These observations continue in the epistles. Finny Philip (PhD, University of Durham), Principal of Filadelfia Bible College in Rajasthan, India, addresses God's gift of the Spirit to Gentiles in Paul's letter to the Romans, as also Roji Thomas George (FFRRC, Senate of Serampore), Professor of New Testament at South Asia Institute for Advanced Christian Studies in Bangalore, India, does in

Galatians. Ayodeji Adewuya (PhD, University of Manchester), Professor of New Testament and Greek at Pentecostal Theological Seminary, explores the Spirit's role in the lives and worship of believers in 1 Corinthians. Jacob Cherian (PhD, Princeton Theological Seminary) and Joe Thomas (MTh, South Asia Institute of Advanced Christian Studies), respectively Dean of the Faculty and a member of the faculty at Southern Asian Bible College in Bangalore, India, address the Spirit as seal, deposit, mark of the new covenant, and member of the Trinity in 2 Corinthians. Dan Darko (PhD, King's College—London), Professor of New Testament at Gordon College in Wenham, Massachusetts, USA, discusses the Spirit's role in Ephesians and Philippians; Holly Beers (PhD, London School of Theology), Associate Professor of Religious Studies at Westmont College in Santa Barbara, California, USA, the Spirit's role in Colossians and Philemon; and Roji Thomas George, again, the Spirit's role in 1–2 Thessalonians. Kenneth J. Archer (PhD, University of St Andrews—Scotland), Professor of Theology at Southeastern University in Lakeland, Florida, USA, explores the Spirit's trinitarian role in salvation, holiness, and empowerment in the Pastorals. Cynthia Westfall (PhD, University of Surrey), Associate Professor of New Testament at McMaster Divinity School in Hamilton, Ontario, Canada, addresses the Spirit's work, including in speaking in and through Scripture, in Hebrews. Rebecca Skaggs (PhD, Drew University), who served for many years as Professor of New Testament and Greek at Patten University, Oakland, California, USA, discusses the Spirit's varied activities, including transformation and OT prophecy, in the Petrine epistles and Jude. Concluding our survey of the Spirit throughout the canon, Melissa Archer (PhD, University of Wales—Bangor), Professor of Biblical Studies and Chair of the School of Divinity, and Robby Waddell (PhD, University of Sheffield), Professor of New Testament and Early Christian Literature and Director of the Global Pentecostalism Center, both of Barnett College of Ministry and Theology at Southeastern University in Lakeland, Florida, USA, skillfully address the Spirit in John's Apocalypse, including the Spirit's role in inspiring prophecy. Nimi Wariboko (PhD, Princeton Theological Seminary), the Walter G. Muelder Chair in Social Ethics at Boston University and Co-editor-in-chief of *Pneuma*, provides readers with a winsome Afterword that offers an interpretation of the Spirit as the lifegiving Spirit.

To synthesize this concert of many scholarly tongues, a concluding chorus would ring out that the Spirit often empowered prophets and leaders in the Old Testament (for example, Num 11:17, 24–30; Judg 3:10; 1 Sam 19:20–24), and such empowerment, which Moses desired for God's people (Num 11:29), would also mark the promised time of future restoration (Joel 2:28–29 [MT 3:1–2]). Less commonly, we read of the promise of eschatological spiritual transformation (Ezek 36:24–27), related to the Spirit's role giving life (Ezek 37:1–14) and perhaps also in creation (Gen 1:2; Ps 104:30). Both of these prominent motifs also flourished in early Judaism, although the latter motif (of spiritual transformation) seems to have flourished in a more limited circle, especially among Essene or related movements.

Not surprisingly, then, these motifs resurface in a variety of ways in the New Testament, which depicts an already but not yet eschatological fulfillment. The Spirit both transforms (as in John 3:5–8, echoing Ezek 36:25–27; 37:9, 14) and empowers (for example, Acts 2:17–18, adapting Joel 2:28–29). To Paul, for example, everything in the Christian life—salvation, ethics (the fruit of the Spirit), ministry to others (by gifts of the Spirit), and so forth comes from the Spirit—from dependence on God. The essence of the Christian life, as Gordon Fee so copiously documented in his now classic *God's Empowering Presence*,[1] is life in and by the Spirit. Moreover, just as God's Spirit marks the restored, eschatological people of God in the Old Testament prophets, Paul, Luke, and some other New Testament writers highlight the Spirit's work among Gentile believers as a sign that Gentiles who embrace Israel's king are grafted into the covenant people.

Pentecostals continually affirm the authoritative role of the Scriptures in governing human understanding of divine revelation and current experience of the Spirit. Pentecostal pneumatology springs from the biblical texts and is understood in light of our communities, languages, educations, and all of our formative experiences. It is the Scriptures, though, to which Pentecostalism has held itself to account, as the chorus of the many movements which constitute our young tradition has become a major witness to the Spirit in the modern world. This volume is intended to help that witness and scholarship concerning it and its continued formation. We hope that it will bear much fruit for decades to come.

---

1 Gordon D. Fee, *God's Empowering Presence: The Holy Spirit in the Letters of Paul* (Grand Rapids, MI: Baker Academic, 2009).

The Spirit in the Pentateuch: From Creation to Supernatural Empowerment

Michael L. Brown

The noun *rûaḥ*, meaning breath, s/Spirit, or wind, occurs 378 times in the Hebrew Scriptures, with an additional eleven in the Aramaic portions of Daniel.[1] Within the Pentateuch, *rûaḥ* occurs a total of thirty-eight times.[2] The semantic breakdown of *rûaḥ* in these books is as follows: breath, five times (Gen 6:17; 7:15, 22; Exod 15:8, 10—although Yahweh's "breath" here is the equivalent of the blowing "wind"); spirit, meaning either the human spirit or the divine Spirit but distinguished from mere breath, twenty-seven times (Gen 1:2—on listing this under "Spirit" rather than "wind," see the discussion below; 6:3; 26:35; 41:8, 38; 45:27; Exod 6:9; 28:3; 31:3; 35:21, 31; Num 5:14 [twice], 30; Num 11:17, 25 [three times], 26, 29, 31; 14:24; 16:22 [plur.]; 24:2; 27:16 [plur.], 18; Deut 2:30; 34:9); wind, six times (Gen 3:8; 8:1; Exod 10:13 [twice], 19; 14:21).[3] The principal texts that will concern us are Gen 1:2; 6:3; 41:38; Exod 28:3; 31:3; 35:31; Num 24:2; 27:18; and Deut 34:9.

Starting in Gen 1:2, we read that in the beginning of God's act of creation, when the earth was yet "formless and empty," the *rûaḥ ʾĕlōhîm* was hovering over the face of the deep. Some Jewish traditions see a hidden reference here to the "spirit of the Messiah,"[4] but that is an overtly homiletical (midrashic) interpretation. Instead, Jewish scholarship, along with some modern critical scholarship, primarily views God's *rûaḥ* in Gen 1:2 as his wind (cf. NJPS, with "wind from God"; so also the NRSV; NJB has "a divine wind"). As Nahum Sarna

---

1 See S. Tengström and H.-J. Fabry, "*rûaḥ*, spirit, wind," in G. Johannes Botterweck, Helmer Ringgren, and Heinz-Josef Fabry, *Theological Dictionary of the Old Testament*, Vol. 13, trans. David E. Green (Grand Rapids, MI: Eerdmans, 2004), 365–402 at 372; other counts vary slightly.
2 Eleven times in Genesis, eleven times in Exodus, none in Leviticus, fourteen times in Numbers, and twice in Deuteronomy; especially noteworthy is the fivefold occurrence of *rûaḥ* in the important pneumatological passage in Numbers 11, specifically in vv. 17–29.
3 Note that the plural forms in the phrase "God of the *rûḥôt* of all flesh" (Num 16:22; 27:16) could also refer to human breath (contrast "the God of the spirits of all flesh" in KJV, NKJV, NRSV, NASB, and ESV, among others, with "the God who gives breath to all living things" [NIV] and "Source of the breath of all flesh!" [NJPS]). This points to the close semantic connection between breath and spirit, especially when speaking of the *ruach* of people (as opposed to the divine *ruach*).
4 See *Yalkut Moshiach v'Geulah al-haTorah*, Vol. 1, *Bereshis* (Brooklyn, NY: Kehot Publication Society, 1996), 49–55.

notes, "Wind often functions as a divine agent in the Bible."[5] Later, he adds, it "reappears as the agent by means of which the water is separated—that is, blown back—as in Genesis 8:1 at the conclusion of the Flood and in Exodus 14:21 at the crossing of the Sea of Reeds."[6]

Yet, while this is certainly possible, it is unlikely here in Gen 1:2, since in every other instance in the OT, a total of sixteen times, *rûaḥ ʾĕlōhîm* always means "S/spirit of God"; cf. Gen 41:38 (the Spirit of God is in Joseph; or, in Pharaoh's mind, it is the "spirit of the gods"); Exod 31:3; 35:31 (God fills Bezalel with the Spirit of God); Num 24:2 (the Spirit of God was upon Balaam); see also 1 Sam 10:10; 11;6; 16:15–16, 23; 18:10; 19:20, 23; 2 Chr 15:1; 24:20; Ezek 11:24. As the NET notes (to Gen 1:2), "Elsewhere in the OT the phrase refers consistently to the divine spirit that empowers and energizes individuals." Additionally, while the verb "hovering" (*mĕraḥeppet*) could potentially refer to the activity of God's wind, it is better to take it in a more personalized sense, just as the mother eagle "hovers" over her young in Deut 32:11. This would connect better with "Spirit" than with "wind."

Jack Levison rightly observes that, while "the border between wind, breath, and spirit is porous … the phrase *rûaḥ ʾĕlōhîm* (*rûaḥ* of God) cannot easily be construed as a wind from God in light of the many other occurrences of the phrase in the Jewish Scriptures that are not casual references to a wind from God. To take *rûaḥ ʾĕlōhîm* in Genesis 1:2 as a wind from God, then, is to deviate from the basic connotation of the phrase in every other occurrence in the Jewish Scriptures."[7] All the more does this hold true in one of the Bible's most foundational theological and cosmological statements.

Still, he adds, "Yet *Spirit* may not be quite right either. In every other instance of the phrase *rûaḥ ʾĕlōhîm*, an individual is mentioned on whom or in whom the spirit exists. The context of Genesis, by contrast, is cosmic, with waters and presumably winds." Thus, he concludes, "Another possibility, too, rears its head: *rûaḥ* as breath … So *rûaḥ* in Genesis 1:2 may reflect the impending reality of divine breath. Is *rûaḥ* wind? Spirit? Breath? Yes, and perhaps something more than each."[8]

On balance, however, given the scope of OT usage, it seems best to concur with Myk Habets, who wrote, "What is clearly stated in Genesis is that God's

---

5 Nahum M. Sarna, *Genesis*, The JPS Torah Commentary (Philadelphia, PA: Jewish Publication Society, 1989), 6.
6 Sarna, *Genesis*, 6.
7 Jack Levison, *A Boundless God: The Spirit according to the Old Testament* (Grand Rapids, MI: Baker Academic, 2020), 158.
8 Levison, *Boundless God*, 159.

presence is active in the *ruach* and that the *ruach 'elōhîm* is superintending the work of creation and also, linked to verse 3, bringing creation about through the W/word. As Hildebrandt states, 'The passage is emphasizing the actual, powerful presence of God, who brings the spoken word into reality by the Spirit.' In this sense then the Spirit of God is not merely the 'wind' of God blowing across the cosmos, but rather the personal, creative, and very active presence of God awaiting the proper time to begin the creation process."[9] In short, the Spirit of God is "the Creator Spirit and the sustainer Spirit (cf., Gen. 1:2; 8:1; Ps. 104:29; Job. 33:4; etc.),"[10] meaning that an important pneumatological statement is being made in this foundational passage of Scripture.

Further support for understanding *rûaḥ 'ĕlōhîm* in Gen 1:2 as "the Spirit of God" is found in John Sailhammer, who points to "the parallels between the creation account (Ge 1) and the construction of the tabernacle in Exodus. Many lines of comparison can be drawn between the two accounts, showing that the writer intended a thematic identity between the two narratives." Thus, "in both accounts the work of God (*mᵉlā'kâ* Ge 2:2; Ex 31:5) is to be accomplished by means of the 'Spirit of God' (*rûaḥ 'ĕlōhîm*). As God did his 'work' (*mᵉlā'kâ*) by means of the 'Spirit of God' (*rûaḥ 'ĕlōhîm*), so Israel was to do their 'work' (*mᵉlā'kâ*) by means of the 'Spirit of God' (*rûaḥ 'ĕlōhîm*)."[11] (For the Spirit of God in the building of the Tabernacle, see below, to Exod 31:3; 35:31.)

The next usage of *rûaḥ*, found in Gen 6:3, is also important theologically, but the precise meaning of the text is disputed, primarily due to the accompanying verb *yādôn* in the phrase *lō'-yādôn rûḥî bā'ādām le'ōlām*, "my *rûaḥ* will not *yādôn* with [or, within] mankind forever." This, the text states, is because the human race is merely flesh. The verb *yādôn* is normally rendered with either "strive, contend" (for example, KJV; NKJV; NASB; NIV) or with "abide, remain" (for example, RSV; NRSV; ESV; CSB; NET; NJPS; cf. LXX; Peshitta; Vulgate). If "strive, contend" is correct, then this would point to the personal aspects of God's Spirit, in keeping with verses found elsewhere in the Bible, where it is the Spirit of God which is grieved or angered; see Ps 106:32–33; Isa 63:10; Mic 2:7; in the NT, see Eph 4:30.[12] Here, the Spirit is striving with sinful human nature (as indicated by the context), characterized here as *bāśār*, flesh, which speaks of

---

9   Myk Habets, *The Progressive Mystery: Tracing the Elusive Spirit in Scripture & Tradition* (Bellingham, WA: Lexham Press, 2019), 25.
10 Levison, *Boundless God*, 20–21.
11 John H. Sailhammer, "Genesis," in Tremper Longman III and David E. Garland, eds., *The Expositor's Bible Commentary*, rev. ed. (Grand Rapids, MI: Zondervan, 2008), 55–56.
12 See further Michael L. Brown, *Answering Jewish Objections to Jesus*, vol. 1, *Theological Objections* (Grand Rapids, MI: Baker, 2000), 52–59.

human weakness. There is a time limit to the Lord's patience. He will contend with sinning humans for only so long before bringing severe judgment.

If "abide, remain" is correct (this is the majority view), it would speak only of God's enlivening breath, which will not forever indwell human beings, given their fleshly limitations. As noted by Gordon Wenham, "it seems much more likely that [my spirit] denotes the life-giving power of God, on which every creature is entirely dependent for its life. It is called the 'breath of life' (2:7) or 'the spirit of life' (6:17; 7:15) and the phrase 'my spirit' is used again in Ezek 37:14."[13] See also Num 16:22, where the Lord is referred to as "the God of the *rûḥôt* [spirits] of all *bāśār* [flesh].*"

The final pneumatological reference to *rûaḥ* in Genesis is found in 41:38, where Pharaoh, astounded by the revelatory wisdom given to the Hebrew prisoner Joseph and recognizing him as the perfect man to lead the nation through a difficult season, exclaims, "Can we find anyone like this man, one in whom is the spirit of God?" (NIV). While we can debate whether we should translate with "s/Spirit of God" or "spirit of the gods" or "divine spirit," there is no question that Pharaoh recognized Joseph's supernatural gifting. Surely this man is divinely empowered!

This would be in harmony with the usage of this term in Exod 31:3; 35:31. There, for the building of the tabernacle, God fills Bezalel "with the Spirit of God, with ability and intelligence, with knowledge and all craftsmanship, to devise artistic designs, to work in gold, silver, and bronze, in cutting stones for setting, and in carving wood, to work in every craft" (Exod 31:3–5, ESV). This is above and beyond the *rûaḥ ḥokmâ* in Exod 28:3, the spirit of wisdom or skill, which the Lord gave to others involved in this building process (cf. also below, to Deut 34:9). The gifting of Bezalel seemed to be on another plane, an even more supernatural plain. He could do what was humanly impossible, understanding just how to craft the specific items of the tabernacle that the Lord had revealed to Moses (cf. Exod 25:9, 40; Num 8:4).

Thus Joseph, endued with the Spirit of God, could interpret Pharaoh's dreams and come up with a nation-saving food distribution plan, while Bezalel, endued with that same Spirit, could both conceive and construct the items of the tabernacle with divine precision and beauty. This would be in keeping with the Holy Spirit's gifting and empowering in both the OT and NT. The divine wisdom and power are at work in and through human vessels.

Interestingly, as we continue to survey references to God's Spirit in the Torah, the word *rûaḥ* does not occur a single time in Leviticus, not as wind or breath or

---

13   Gordon J. Wenham, *Genesis 1–15*, Word Biblical Commentary (Dallas, TX: Word, 1987), 141.

s/Spirit. Accordingly, there are no references to the Holy Spirit in Leviticus. This, however, is more than compensated for in the book of Numbers, which features the single most important pneumatological passage in the Torah, found in Num 11. Also of note is Num 24:1–2, which states, "When Balaam saw that it pleased the LORD to bless Israel, he did not go, as at other times, to look for omens, but set his face toward the wilderness. And Balaam lifted up his eyes and saw Israel camping tribe by tribe. And the Spirit of God came upon him" (ESV; lit., "the Spirit of God was upon him"). And it was by this Spirit, the same Spirit that came upon the seventy elders in Num 11 (which means the same Spirit that was upon Moses) and the same Spirit that enabled Israel's prophets to utter God's word, that this hireling prophet now spoke.

Baruch Levine noted, "The 'spirit' may rest upon a person, a thought conveyed by the verb *nûaḥ* (Num 11:25–26), or it can clothe a person (Num 6:34 [sic; should be Judg 6:34]), or alight upon him (Judg 14:6), or, as here, simply 'be' upon him ... (cf. Judg 3:10; 11:29). This is the first time it is said of Balaam that he prophesied with God's spirit, and this statement clearly reflects a changing perception in Balaam's role. No longer a pagan prophet, he has become a prophet."[14] To be sure, in the eyes of the biblical authors, Balaam remained a sinner, the personification of a mercenary prophet (see Num 31:8; Deut 23:4; Josh 13:22; 24:9; Neh 13:2; 2 Pet 2:15; Rev 2:14). Yet he spoke by divine revelation and inspiration, since the Spirit of God was upon him. This is reflected in Targum's rendering, "and the spirit of prophecy rested upon him."

The last three references to *rûaḥ* as "spirit" refer to Caleb and Joshua, beginning in Num 14:24, which states that Caleb, Joshua's colleague in resisting the faithless report of the ten other spies, had a "different spirit" within him. While this could refer to the Holy Spirit, it more likely speaks of a different attitude or mindset. Otherwise, if Caleb had a "different spirit," what "spirit" did the ten spies have? Phillip Budd also sees this as a reference to "a psychological use of רוּחַ," but, in my view, wrongly compares this to Num 11:17, which speaks of the Holy Spirit.[15]

In Num 27:18, Moses is instructed to set Joshua apart as the next leader of Israel because "*rûaḥ* is in him." The Targum, once again, sees this as the "spirit of prophecy," in contrast with the other ancient versions, which translate literally. But what, exactly, does it mean to have *rûaḥ* inside someone? The NJPS translates with "an inspired man," while most modern Christian translations render more literally "a man in whom is the spirit" (or, "Spirit"), but even here,

---

14   Baruch A. Levine, *Numbers 21–36*; Anchor Bible (New York: Doubleday, 2000), 191.
15   Phillip J. Budd, *Numbers*, Word Biblical Commentary (Dallas: Word, 1984), 159.

the definite article is added, while it is missing in the Hebrew text. The NIV renders with "in whom is the spirit of leadership," but this is overly interpretive. Rather, as explained by C.F. Keil, *rûaḥ* here refers to "the higher power inspired by God into the soul, which quickens the moral and religious life, and determines its development; in this case, therefore, it was the spiritual endowment requisite for the office he was called to fill."[16] It would also appear that, by using *rûaḥ* without the article, emphasis is placed on the quality and nature of the enduement rather than simply stating that "the Spirit" was in him.

Joshua's standing is further enhanced in Deut 34:9, which states that Joshua was "full of the spirit of wisdom" (*rûaḥ ḥokmâ*), just as certain Israelites were endued with this spirit according to Exod 28:3. In the case of Joshua, this enduement of the Spirit would enable him to lead Israel into the promised land; in the case of these Israelites, it was to enable them to construct the articles for the Tabernacle. In the future, this same "spirit of wisdom" will be active in the Messiah himself (Isa 11:3, where this is only one of six expressions of the Spirit of Yahweh that is upon him) as he leads the entire world into an era of peace and harmony. It is the divine Spirit which enables God's servants to carry out the impossible tasks assigned to them.

---

16 Carl Friedrich Keil and Franz Delitzsch, *Commentary on the Old Testament*, Vol. 1 (repr., Peabody, MA: Hendrickson, 1996), 799–800.

The Spirit in Numbers 11: God's Pentecostal Plan

Roger D. Cotton

In Numbers 11, God revealed through Moses some very important truths about his purposes for the Spirit in the ministries of his people. This is foundational Old Testament pneumatology. Throughout the Old Testament, God empowered leaders to fulfill his purpose and mission. The event here shows that God planned that for all believers once Christ had come.

The event of Numbers 11 was a response to the first challenge to God's people Israel, as they began their journey to the place of his mission for them in the Promised Land. Moses responded to the people's craving for meat with desperation because he assumed he was responsible for providing it. God's answer was to expand the leadership team by empowering seventy elders with his Spirit.

God said he would take of his Spirit that was on Moses and put it on seventy other leaders. This made it evident that Moses, as a leader appointed by God, had had the Spirit of God upon him all along, even though that was never stated in the Scriptures before this. In observing the use of the Spirit with leaders in the Old Testament, it is clear that the reader is expected to know that God's leaders, particularly his prophets, are enabled and empowered by his Spirit when he has authorized them, so this will not always be stated, nor the Spirit mentioned.

The Numbers 11 event of God putting his Spirit on the expanded leadership team was a public authorization of them to assist Moses. This confirmed their authority to the congregation and to the leaders themselves. The description of the event indicates that it was an observable vocal and perhaps otherwise physical experience. This is shown by the choice of the form of the verb for prophesying. Numbers 11:25 says that they prophesied when the Spirit rested upon them. The verb form there is not the usual niphal stem of the root *naba'*, which is normally used to describe delivering prophetic messages; rather, it is the rarely used hitpael stem of that root. The hitpael is used here and in several places in 1Samuel for very demonstrative physical responses to contact with the Spirit, such as Saul experienced when he lay disrobed on the ground for a day and a night (1Kings 19:24). These contexts say nothing about communicating a message; rather, they are publicly observable, at least vocal, events caused by the Spirit of God. Gordon Wenham suggests, "As with Saul, the prophecy described here [in Numbers 11] was probably an unintelligible ecstatic[1] utterance, what the New Testament terms speaking in tongues."[2] That event in Numbers 11 and the tongues in Acts 2 are each described as a kind of prophetic speech. Biblically, genuine Yahweh-originated prophetic speech is always enabled by his Spirit. Prophetic speech is intended to communicate a message from God to the audience. However, in a few places, such as here in Numbers 11, the hitpael is used and the prophetic speech does not deliver a verbalized message but is a sign-demonstration of God authorizing or working in the person/people. This supports pentecostal doctrine and practice in relation to speaking in tongues as an observable event accompanying the empowering experience by God's Spirit, referred to as being baptized in the Spirit.

What happened next set the stage for a major revelation through Moses of the pneumatological plan of God for his people. For some unknown reason, two of the chosen and registered seventy did not come to the Tent of Meeting to receive with the other sixty-eight but remained out in the camp. When the Spirit came upon the group of leaders at the Tent of Meeting, however, the Spirit came on these two as well, and they too prophesied. Joshua asked Moses to stop the two in the camp, but Moses, now having returned to humble faith, responded by declaring the plan of God after he asked Joshua if he was jealous for Moses's sake. He implied that there was no need to see this as a challenge to his leadership, which God had authorized. On the contrary, Moses said, "I wish that all the LORD's people were prophets and that the LORD would put his Spirit on them!" (Num 11:29 NIV 2011). Moses's wish expressed the plan of God that would later be prophesied by Joel and finally declared by Peter to have begun to be fulfilled at Pentecost in Acts 2. The two prophesying in the camp pictured what God would do for all his people in the messianic age.

Numbers 11 is, therefore, programmatic[3] and paradigmatic for God's working by his Spirit in and through his people. Programmatically, Numbers 11 is significant for God's pneumatological intentions for humanity. Those who come into a relationship with Christ by faith are born again by the Holy Spirit and are expected to receive the empowering release of the Spirit from within them. As Israel was rescued out of Egypt and established with the presence of God among them, and as their leaders were empowered by the Spirit of God, so

---

1   I do not agree with the use of ecstatic here. I believe it could be speaking in tongues, which is not what I would call ecstatic speech but Spirit-enabled speech.
2   Gordon J. Wenham, *Numbers: An Introduction and Commentary*, TOTC (Downers Grove, IL: InterVarsity Press, 1981), 109.
3   As designated by Roger Stronstad, *The Charismatic Theology of St. Luke* (Peabody, MA: Hendrickson, 1984), 17; and Wilf Hildebrandt, *An Old Testament Theology of the Spirit of God* (Peabody, MA: Hendrickson, 1995), 110.

God's people today may all receive an empowering experience after they are saved and have received the indwelling presence of the Spirit. The Spirit comes upon all believers who ask, in order to become witnesses and ministers for God—the priesthood and the prophethood of all believers. Numbers 11 is a very significant passage for biblical pneumatology and therefore should be studied by Pentecostals.

Paradigmatically, as a pattern, Pentecostals have pointed out that God wants all his people to have an experience like the seventy had. In the Old Testament, Saul prophesied on the very day that the Spirit came upon him at his anointing as king. Then, in the New Testament, particularly in Acts, God showed that he wants all to have the Holy Spirit flow out of their lives, in their ministries, especially enabling them to witness for Christ. When this release of the empowering of the Spirit happens for the first time, it is accompanied by the person prophesying in tongues as a prayer and praise language to God. Numbers 11:25 reports that they did not continue to prophesy after the event. However, in the New Testament, it is clear that believers may choose to continue to pray in tongues in their private lives. This is the same in essence but not in purpose as the gift of tongues, which the Spirit also chooses to use some Christians to minister while in their worship gatherings (1 Cor 12:4–11; 14:18–19). It seems that the Lord gave a taste of various supernatural experiences that he wants for all his people in the New Testament era.

One more observation on the wording of this event is that the Spirit is said to "rest on" the seventy. The Hebrew verb here is *nwch*, which is often used for something gently settling down upon a place for the indefinite future. The same is said of the Spirit resting on the Messiah in Isaiah 11:2. God's Spirit doesn't come and go from his people, though his presence cannot always be outwardly demonstrated.

There are many lessons and principles here for God's people, both leaders and followers. God cares about the physical needs of his people and the practical details of how they are to function together in fulfilling his purposes. The answer to challenges on God's journey and mission for his people and the answer for the burdens of leadership is the Holy Spirit. Leaders can and should depend on the power and wisdom of the Spirit, and they should delegate responsibilities to others in the church, as the Spirit leads. That should not be a threat to leaders but a blessing. The Spirit does not concentrate all his empowering on one person. He democratizes the gifts and ministries of Christ throughout his Body. All Christ's followers are to be prophets for God and experience Spirit-enabled, prophetic, speech. When people receive God's empowering there is an experience of prophetic speech that is observable by others. The book of Acts shows this to be speaking in tongues. God is not legalistic or ritualistic about how his people are to receive his empowering experience and his gifts. All may have the power of God's Spirit to enable them to do what he calls them to do. The experience of the Spirit of God is both corporate and individual. The person filled with the Spirit, like Moses, looks ahead in the plan of God to how God wants them to minister to the lost world. The people of God should want all that God wants for them, beginning with this experience of the Spirit.

The Spirit in the DtrH/Former Prophets: "And the Spirit Came Upon Him"

Brian Neil Peterson

As a Pentecostal, when I read the Bible, admittedly I tend to be more attuned to the appearance of the presence and the working of the Holy Spirit than perhaps the average casual reader of the text. Likewise, as a teacher of the Hebrew Bible, I am particularly interested when I see unique ways in which the Spirit moves in the "First Testament." I am regularly intrigued by the way the authors of the Former Prophets—what scholarship labels the Deuteronomistic History (DtrH hereafter)—have presented the Spirit's moving among leaders and lay people alike in this important pre-exilic history of Israel and Judah, a history that stretches from the settlement of the land in 1406 BCE (1220 for those of the "late-date" persuasion) until the destruction of Jerusalem in 586 BCE at the hands of the Babylonians. The roughly 820-year time span makes giving a detailed assessment of the Spirit's movement throughout this period impossible in such a short essay. At the same time, it is important to remember that the ancients no doubt saw the Spirit of God as an extension of the presence and working of YHWH rather than from our modern trinitarian perspective, which regards the Spirit as a separate Person of the Trinity.[1] Such a conclusion would be to import too much theological baggage into the text of the Hebrew Bible. Nevertheless, post-cross, one can recognize the parallels, and as such, I will move forward with the designation of the Spirit as a distinct Person of the Trinity. Indeed, there is one thing that remains consistent both in the DtrH and the New Testament, that is, the reality that, like Jesus, one can say that the Spirit of the Lord is the same yesterday, today, and forever (Heb 13:8) when it comes to his empowering presence in the lives of those who are used by God.

The term *ruach* (רוח), which is used to denote "spirit" in the DtrH, appears no less than forty-eight times. While *ruach* has a wide range of usages in the DtrH, such as for one's emotional state (nine times),[2] for an evil, enticing, or

---

[1] Tremper Longman III, "Spirit and Wisdom," in *Presence, Power, and Promise: The Role of the Spirit of God in the Old Testament*, ed. David Firth and Paul Wegner (Downers Grove, IL: IVP Academic, 2011), 95–110 at 95.

[2] As a loss of hope/discouragement (Josh 2:11; 5:1); used for one's stirred emotions and physical strength (Judg 8:3; 15:19; 1 Sam 1:15; 16:23; 1 Sam 30:12; 1 Kgs 10:5; 21:5).

discomfiting spirit from God (twelve times),[3] as a designation for the meteorological phenomenon of wind (five times),[4] or poetically for God's breath (two times),[5] the most frequent occurrence of the term (twenty times) is when it is used to address the presence or the working of what today we would identify as the Third Person of the Trinity.[6] In the latter case, *ruach* commonly appears in the phrase "and the Spirit came upon x" for some important purpose.

In light of this diverse usage of *ruach* in the DtrH, and for the sake of focus, in this essay I will primarily address the role of the Spirit in the last category of the above list. But this certainly does not exhaust the way the Spirit appears in these books. As such, I feel it is important to provide a brief overview of the way the "gifts" of the Spirit, specifically the gifting of prophecy, miracles, and discernment, are evidenced in the lives of individuals (note also the Spirit's role to convict of wrongdoing). I will begin this essay, however, by tracing how the Spirit empowers select leaders and rulers for the purpose of ministry and leadership for the nations of Israel and Judah in the DtrH.

1   The Spirit's Empowerment for Service

A cursory handling of the DtrH vis-à-vis the empowerment of the Spirit quickly reveals that the way the Spirit comes upon people/leaders in the DtrH shows that the Spirit cannot be placed in a proverbial box. He is vibrant and alive and manifests in different ways in different situations for the express needs of the individual. Of interest, however, is the fact that none of the specific prophets noted in the DtrH are explicitly said to have had the Spirit enter into them in the way the Spirit enters, for example, Ezekiel (Ezek 2:2; 3:24).[7] Instead, it is assumed in the DtrH that the prophets have the Spirit working within them when they speak the words of God (cf. Deut 18:18). It is also important to note that after the judges' period and the reigns of Saul and David, the authors of the DtrH never explicitly mention the Spirit coming upon kings for the pur-

---

[3] Cf. Judg 9:23; 1 Sam 16:14, 15, 16, 23 (2x); 18:10; 19:9; 1 Kgs 22:21, 22, 23; 2 Kgs 19:7.
[4] Used in the Elijah narrative 1 Kgs 18:45; 19:11 (3x); 2 Kgs 3:17.
[5] As in the last words of David recorded as a psalm (2 Sam 22:11, 16; cf. Ps 18).
[6] See Judg 3:10; 6:34; 11:29; 13:25; 14:6, 19; 15:14; 1 Sam 10:6, 10; 11:6; 16:13, 14; 19:20, 23; 2 Sam 23:2; 1 Kgs 18:12; 22:24; 2 Kgs 2:16. It is also likely that the author of the DtrH is referring to the working of the Spirit of YHWH when Elisha asks for a double portion of Elijah's spirit in 2 Kgs 2:9 and 15.
[7] In these verses in Ezekiel, the verb בוא ("to enter in") accompanies the more fluid ב preposition, which can mean "in, against, with," etc.

pose of leading. Some of this may have more to do with style and authorship issues than anything else, or it may reflect the rhetorical intent of the author pointing to the downward slide of the kings as Israel and Judah moved toward exile. Having noted these anomalies, what we do find is the Spirit empowering specific rulers in a variety of ways.

There are six key terms used to describe the Spirit's working on leaders of Israel during the period covered in the DtrH. I will address the appearance of these terms in their canonical ordering, not according to their frequency. The first two appear before the book of Joshua begins in the Torah but deal specifically with his leadership in the DtrH. Joshua is said to have both the Spirit "in/upon him" (בו; Num 27:18; cf. Num 11:29 where the Spirit comes "upon" [על] the elders) as well as being "full" (מלא) of the Spirit of wisdom (Deut 34:9).

The third term appears in Judges. Othniel (as with Jephthah) has the Spirit come "upon him" (עליו; Judg 3:10; 11:29). Throughout the DtrH this is the most frequent way the Spirit is said to encounter a person. It also is a common way Pentecostals today speak of the empowerment by the Spirit when someone is moved to deliver a message in tongues, to give an interpretation, to prophesy, or simply to react to the Spirit's moving in general.

The fourth term appears in the Gideon narrative. Gideon is "clothed" (לבש) with the Spirit (Judg 6:34). Apart from its frequent use in poetic texts to speak of clothing metaphorically,[8] the idea of being clothed by the Spirit appears in only two other places: once related to a person being spiritually equipped for battle (1 Chron 12:19), and once for empowerment to minister (2 Chron 24:20). In Gideon's case, the Spirit envelopes him like a garment of protection, which he certainly needed when he went into battle with only three hundred men against the innumerable Midianite horde. Interestingly, the first appearance of the verb לבש is when God clothes Adam and Eve with garments of skins to protect them from the elements and to hide their nakedness. And the priests were to be clothed in special garments representing their holy status when they ministered before God in the tabernacle/temple.[9] In Gideon's case, the Spirit is his covering for protection *and* for ministry as a judge.

The last two terms are used in tandem. Several times in the Samson narrative, the Spirit both "stirred"/"impelled" him (פעם; Judg 13:25) and rushed upon

---

8 Poetically לבש is used for clothing someone with shame, dishonor, cursing, or horror (Ps 35:26; 109:18, 29; 132:18; Ezek 7:27). God is clothed with majesty (Ps 93:1; 104:1) and Job is clothed in righteousness (Job 29:14; cf. Ps 132:9, 16). God also speaks of people clothing themselves with splendor and honor and salvation (Job 40:10; Isa 61:10), as well as with strength and vengeance (Isa 51:9; 52:1; 59:17).

9 See Exod 29:5, 8, 30; 40:13–14; Lev 6:3–4; 8:7, 13; 16:4, 23–24, 32; 21:10; Num 20:26, 28.

him (צלח; 14:6, 19; 15:14). The latter is the same language that is associated with the Spirit's moving upon Saul (1 Sam 10:6, 10; 11:6) and David (1 Sam 16:13). Sadly, the reader is also alerted to the fact that the Spirit later "departed"/"turned aside" (סור) from Saul (1 Sam 16:14).

This brings me to one of the more interesting accounts in the DtrH related to the working of the Spirit. In 1 Samuel 19, the Spirit "comes upon" both Saul and his messengers in such a powerful way that they are diverted from their task of capturing David while he is staying with Samuel at Ramah. Instead of seizing David, three different contingents of messengers (cf. 2 Kgs 1:9–15), with Saul being among the fourth, begin to prophesy. Although against his will, Saul even ends up having an experience with the Spirit akin to being "slain in the Spirit," as Pentecostals are wont to say, as Saul tries to accost David, whom the Spirit is obviously protecting. While commentators have interpreted this event in various ways (for example, it merely duplicates the events in 1 Sam 10:10–12[10]), it seems clear that the Spirit in fact has come upon Saul and his men to prove to them that God is in control, not the wayward King Saul. Two points can be made about this event. First, the actions of Saul and his men are often likened by commentators to an "ecstatic experience" outside of the usual conduct of the person.[11] This certainly reflects the moving of the Spirit as often typifies pentecostal encounters with the Spirit. The second point is more sobering for anyone used by the Spirit in the prophetic or other spiritual gifts. This event in the life of Saul intimates, proleptically at least, a concept taught by Paul to the Romans that the spiritual gifts are without repentance (Rom 11:29).[12] Earlier the Spirit had departed from Saul (1 Sam 16:14), but here the Spirit comes once again upon him in a prophetic manner. It is a stark reminder that displays of the Spirit's moving in the lives of people do not guarantee their spiritual state before God. That is why the gift of the discerning of spirits and discernment in general are vital for the believer, pentecostal or otherwise (1 Cor 12:10).

---

10   Hans Wilhelm Hertzberg, *1 & 2 Samuel* (OTL; Philadelphia: Westminster Press, 1976), 167.
11   Walter Brueggemann, *First and Second Samuel* (Interpretation; Louisville: John Knox, 1990), 145. There is some debate on the use of the hithpael stem with the verb נבא ("to prophesy") and the interpretation of this event as "frenzied" or "ecstatic" in nature (see John R. Levinson, "Prophecy in Ancient Israel: The Case of the Ecstatic Elders," *CBQ* 65, no. 4 [2003]: 503–521). While a similar use of the hithpael and this verb appears in Num 11:25 and is often rendered as only prophesying in most English translations, in the context of 1 Samuel 19, something more than a simple prophetic event is going on when Saul strips naked and lies on the ground all night long! As such, I follow the Tanach and render this event as an "ecstatic experience," which reflects a more intensive nuance, which can be reflective of the hithpael stem.
12   Space does not allow for me to develop this concept beyond this simple observation.

Before completing this first portion of my essay, I would like to point out an interesting manifestation of the work of the Spirit in the DtrH that finds parallels with the NT book of Acts. In the period of Elijah there was an understanding among certain God-fearing people that the Spirit, unlike a visionary experience (such as Ezek 8:3), could literally translate or "carry" (נשׂא) people from one place to another. We first see this mentioned by Obadiah, the godly assistant of Ahab, when he is worried that the Spirit would whisk Elijah away to another land after Elijah had arranged a meeting with Ahab (1 Kgs 18:12). This is a similar concern voiced by the school of the prophets after Elijah was translated into heaven via the fiery chariots and a whirlwind. They thought the Spirit had taken him up into heaven and deposited him on one of the mountains or in one of the valleys (2 Kgs 2:16). This experience was not unique to Elijah. During the period of the early church, Philip was also snatched away and carried by the Spirit from the road between Jerusalem and Gaza to Azotus (Acts 8:26, 39–40).

2   Prophecy, Miracles, and Discernment

The pentecostal movement has long been noted for the gifts of the Spirit. While certainly not exhaustive of the way the Spirit has moved in the past and presently, three of the gifts of the Spirit, apart from the gift of tongues, that are hallmarks of the pentecostal movement of the Spirit from Azusa onward are prophecy, miracles, and the gift of discernment. There can be little doubt that in many cases the Spirit moves in the OT through these three gifts as well. This is particularly true in the DtrH. Prior to the period of the classical writing prophets, the prophetic office coupled prophecies with the miraculous as a way of vindicating the prophets. This was no less true of the work of the early church and is exemplified by Jesus's ministry (cf. Matt 24; John 4:24).[13]

One of the earliest presentations of the coupling of the prophetic and the miraculous in the DtrH is by Joshua, when God vindicates his leadership and prophetic word by drying up the Jordan River at flood stage (Josh 3:13–17). To be sure, Joshua begins the narrative by gathering the people to declare the word of God in a prophetic manner (Josh 3:9). While this event is a fine example of prophetic forthtelling (immediate future events), we see a good example of foretelling (distant future events) when Joshua prophetically declares God's

---

[13] See Brian Neil Peterson, *John's Use of Ezekiel: Understanding the Unique Perspective of the Fourth Gospel* (Minneapolis: Fortress, 2015).

punishment on those who would ever attempt to rebuild the cursed city of Jericho (Josh 6:26). The prophetic portion comes to pass hundreds of years later during the period of the kings (1 Kgs 16:34).

This being noted, the prophecy-fulfillment motif punctuates the entire DtrH. While the Spirit may not be explicitly noted in the DtrH and the rest of the OT when a prophecy is given, Peter notes that this was indeed the pattern (2 Pet 1:21; cf. Rev 19:10). This is the reason the Hebrew tradition identifies these books as the Former Prophets. After Joshua, Deborah is one of the earliest examples of this phenomenon (Judg 4:9//4:15–23). Samuel's early ministry is also marked by this motif (3:11–14, 18//4:11, 18). This was no less true of his interaction with Saul (1 Sam 13:14; 15:23). What is more, Nathan's prophetic word to David after David's sin with Bathsheba (2 Sam 12:10–12) drives the remaining narratives of 2 Samuel–1 Kings 1–2.[14] This pattern is also found in the book of Kings, in which the prophecy-fulfillment motif can be found in practically every chapter, specifically in 1 Kings 12–16.[15] This also happens in what is known as the Elijah-Elisha cycle (1 Kings 17–2 Kings 13). Throughout the ministries of Elijah and Elisha the reader is alerted to the numerous prophecies and miracles they performed. Of interest is the fact that the double portion requested by Elisha from Elijah prior to Elijah's translation plays itself out in the cycle.[16] This also has implications for the Spirit as the One who inspires Scripture itself. A quick analysis of the lives and miracles of Elijah and Elisha show striking parallels with the lives of John the Baptist (the NT "Elijah"; cf. Mal 4:5; Matt 11:14; Luke 1:17) and Jesus in the NT.[17] Finally, the prophecy-fulfillment pattern continues to the end of the DtrH in Isaiah's ministry to Hezekiah (2 Kings 18–20). Isaiah delivers prophetic words concerning both Hezekiah and Sennacherib that are fulfilled in the immediate context.

Two final concepts related to the role of the Spirit in the DtrH are evinced in the power of spiritual discernment and the faithfulness of the Spirit to convict of sin. One of the best examples of the gift of discernment can be seen in the life of Elisha. Elisha walked by the Spirit and saw into the spiritual realm, which is contrasted to the average person, in this case, Elisha's servant. First, when Gehazi tried to hide his interactions with Naaman, Elisha discerned his

---

14 Brian Neil Peterson, *The Authors of the Deuteronomistic History: Locating a Tradition in Ancient Israel* (Minneapolis: Fortress, 2014), 254–255.
15 Cf. 1 Kgs 11:29–39//12:15; 12:22–24a//12:24b; 13:1–5//2 Kgs 23:15; 14:12–16//14:17–18, and 2 Kgs 9–10; 16:1–4//16:12. Peterson, *The Authors of the Deuteronomistic History*, 276–281.
16 For a complete chart outlining the numbers of miracles and prophecies, see Rickie Moore and Brian Neil Peterson, *Voice, Word, and Spirit: A Pentecostal Old Testament Survey* (Nashville: Abingdon, 2017), 114.
17 Cf. 2 Kgs 4:8–36//Luke 7:11–15; 2 Kgs 6:5–7//Matt 14:25–29; 2 Kgs 13:21//Matt 27:50–53.

duplicity (2 Kgs 5:26). While it is true that the "Spirit" does not appear in this text, the fact that Elisha notes that his "heart went with" Gehazi seems to imply that the Spirit of God and the heart of Elisha were in unison, a fitting picture of the close communion of the Spirit and the prophet. Later, when Elisha and his servant were encircled by the Syrian army, Elisha could see into the spiritual realm and see the heavenly chariots and army of God (2 Kgs 6:15–17; cf. 1 Kgs 22:19–23). Elisha prays for his servant's eyes to be opened in a similar fashion.

As for the Spirit's role to convict of sin, two examples will suffice. First, when David cut the hem of Saul's garment at Engedi, his conscience immediately convicted him (1 Sam 24:5). While not attributed explicitly to the Spirit, it is obvious that as a man of God, David was attuned to the Spirit's conviction. This is no less the case later with his sin with Bathsheba (cf. Ps 51:13).[18] In an ancient context, the Mari texts (see also the Alalakh texts) note that the cutting of the hem was a means of immobilizing the prophet's authority.[19] Here David had thus usurped the authority of Saul and the Spirit convicted him of it. As a second example, when Elijah prophesied that Ahab would die, Ahab immediately repented, and God granted him an extension of life (1 Kgs 21:27–29; cf. 2 Kgs 20:1–7).

3   Conclusion

The Spirit's presence in the DtrH, while muted in some cases, is nonetheless present throughout. Whether explicit in the Spirit's moving upon, or empowerment of, individuals or whether it is more implicit in the prophetic voice or spiritual discernment, the Spirit is clearly at work to bring about the greater plan of salvation history while demonstrating the power of God. In many ways, even though we have the Spirit within us since the events of Acts 2, as I noted in my introduction, it is safe to say that the Spirit, like Jesus, is the same yesterday, today, and forever.

---

18   David fears losing the Spirit's presence/conviction in Psalm 51 but also seems to reject that conviction at other times when he commits what today are viewed as atrocities (e.g., 2 Sam 1:15; 4:12; 8:2).

19   Gary N. Knoppers and J. Gordon McConville, *Reconsidering Israel and Judah: Recent Studies on the Deuteronomistic History* (Winona Lake, IN: Eisenbrauns, 2000), 334.

The Spirit in 1–2 Chronicles, Ezra-Nehemiah, and Esther: Transforming the Spirit Traditions for New Contexts

Emma M. Austin and Jacqueline Grey

When examining the presence and activity of the *ruach* within the Old Testament (or Hebrew Bible), the complexities in precisely identifying the divine *ruach* or "Holy Spirit" become readily apparent.[1] This study explores the divine *ruach* in the postexilic texts of 1–2 Chronicles, Ezra-Nehemiah, and Esther. First, the six clear (and one ambiguous) references to the divine *ruach* in 1–2 Chronicles and Ezra-Nehemiah are discussed, followed by a theological reading of more ambiguous allusions across the scope of these postexilic texts. This article demonstrates that the retrieval of previous *ruach* traditions found in the Torah and Judges, such as military empowerment and creative inspiration, are adapted by the biblical writers to apply to prophetic speech and thereby affirm that God's Spirit remains with his covenant people in this new context of the Second Temple period.[2]

Within 1–2 Chronicles there are arguably four clear (and one ambiguous) references to the divine *ruach* that draw on and adapt the charismatic tradition of the spirit empowering military leaders in Judges. The first clear instance occurs in 1 Chronicles 12:18 (MT 12:19), with the *ruach* clothing (*labash*) Amasai, which results in prophetic speech. This reference draws on the tradition of the Judges: as the *ruach* had clothed Gideon and prepared him for battle (Judg 6:34), now the *ruach* clothes the battle-proven Amasai. However, the result is not military activity but spontaneous prophetic speech announcing peace. The threat overcome through the Spirit's power is not external oppression but internal disunity. Amasai's words are beautifully poetic as he expresses his loyalty in an oath to David, acknowledging God as the source of David's success. Amasai's

---

1 This includes determining when the term *ruach* refers to the divine Creator or the finite creation, such as wind, breath, or a created spirit. See Anthony C. Thistleton, *A Shorter Guide to the Holy Spirit: Bible, Doctrine, Experience* (Grand Rapids: Eerdmans, 2016), 3–5; David Firth, "The Historical Books," in Trevor J. Burke and Keith Warrington, eds., *A Biblical Theology of the Holy Spirit* (London: SPCK, 2014), 14.

2 Louis C. Jonker, "Chronicles in an (Un)changing World: The 'Persian Context' in Biblical Studies," *Journal for the Study of the Old Testament* 42, no. 3 (2018): 281; Andrew E. Hill, *1 and 2 Chronicles* (Grand Rapids: Zondervan, 2003), 206.

inspired speech ingratiates him with the future king, resulting in the acceptance of Amasai and his warriors into David's service. His words prove both "inspired and shrewd," thus reinforcing, as Jack Levison asserts, that "politics is the natural habitat of the spirit."[3]

The "Spirit of God" (*ruach Elohim*) comes upon Azariah in 2 Chronicles 15:1, resulting in a prophetic speech delivered to King Asa (15:2–7). Again, the Spirit inspires the delivery of Yahweh's word in the political arena.[4] The account echoes the *ruach* tradition in Judges—not to rescue God's covenant people in a physical battle, as with Jephthah (Judg 11), but for the purpose of inspired speech. The Spirit "comes upon" Azariah, using prophetic words to motivate the king to rescue the land from idolatry. The lengthy oracle speaks of God's conditional favor on the king, promised restoration if the covenant people turn back to God, and instruction for Asa to remain loyal to God. As a result, Asa takes courage and publicly purges the land of idolatry, conducts temple repairs, and leads a covenant renewal ceremony. This outcome of cultic reform reflects the priestly interests evident throughout the Chronicler. Similarly, in 2 Chronicles 20:14 the "Spirit of the Lord" (*ruach Yahweh*) comes upon Jahaziel, a Levite, amid the ritualized assembly of Judeans facing threat of invasion by a coalition force (20:1–4).[5] The *ruach* inspires Jahaziel's prophetic instruction for King Jehoshaphat to take courage and provides a creative strategy for the military campaign. This public speech (20:15–17) follows the pre-battle formula of priestly instruction described in Deuteronomy 20:2–4, reminding the people of God's presence and help.[6] Jahaziel's priestly role here nods to three other earlier biblical traditions: the language of Moses' speech prior to the victory over the Egyptians (Exod 14:13), the *ruach* coming upon the Judges (such as Othniel in Judg 3:10), and David's declaration prior to his victory over Goliath (1 Sam 17:47).[7]

The final clear reference to the "Spirit of God" (*ruach Elohim*) in the Chronicler occurs in 2 Chronicles 24:20. As with Amasai and Gideon, the *ruach* clothes (*labash*) Zechariah, a priest. His inspired prophecy is a terse, precise, and stinging challenge to the idolatrous Judean community, particularly the political

---

3 Jack Levison, *A Boundless God: The Spirit according to the Old Testament* (Grand Rapids: Baker Academic, 2020), 48.
4 Firth, "The Historical Books," 21.
5 Levison also connects the public setting "in the middle of the assembly" to Ezekiel 8:1, with "the hand of the Lord" coming upon him to reveal a vision. See John R. Levison, *The Holy Spirit before Christianity* (Waco: Baylor University Press, 2019), 194.
6 Levison, *A Boundless God*, 49.
7 Levison, *A Boundless God*, 49.

officials. However, Zechariah's words are rejected by the Judean leaders, resulting in his betrayal and execution. Though God sent the prophets to bring the people back to covenant faith, they do not listen. Zechariah's dying words point to the coming exile: "May the Lord see this and call you to account" (22). These four direct references to the *ruach* in 1–2 Chronicles transform the military focus of the charismatic tradition of the Judges to the empowering of prophetic voices to address Israel's political leaders and battle the endemic idolatry of Judah. It emphasizes the public function of prophetic speech to fulfill God's purpose and mission.[8] Azariah, Jahaziel, and Zechariah are each connected to the priesthood, which suggests a shift from the earlier empowerment of military figures with questionable morals to an emphasis on the piety of recipients of the divine *ruach*.

A significant, albeit ambiguous, reference to the divine *ruach* is found in 2 Chronicles 18:23.[9] In this account Jehoshaphat and Ahab are retrospectively seeking prophetic guidance before the Aramean campaign (2 Chr 18:1–34//1 Kgs 22:1–40).[10] Ahab's four hundred prophets ingratiate themselves to the kings with promises of success. In contrast, Micaiah, a prophet of Yahweh, arrives and shares his vision of the heavenly council in which Yahweh had called for one from the company to entice Ahab to war. The volunteer ("the *ruach*") offers to be a "lying" *ruach* in the mouths of Ahab's prophets. While the spirit is sent by Yahweh, it is not a clear reference to the divine *ruach*. Zedekiah, one of the exposed false prophets, strikes Micaiah and self-declares that his message originated from the "Spirit of the Lord" (*ruach Yahweh*). Ahab's subsequent death proves that these four hundred prophets (including Zedekiah) did not hear from the "Spirit of the Lord." This text emphasizes that a true prophet does not speak for political expediency but speaks the word of Yahweh.

Within Ezra-Nehemiah there are two direct references to the divine *ruach*, found in Neh 9:20, 30. Following the chaos and destruction of the Babylonian exile, the Spirit works to restore both community and temple worship. The public prayer of Nehemiah 9:5–37 begins by offering a condensed history of the covenant community. It includes a recitation of their deliverance out of Egypt, emphasizing the provision in the wilderness (Num 9), in which God's "good Spirit" is given to instruct them (9:20)—clearly connecting the law with

---

8   Thiselton, *A Shorter Guide to the Holy Spirit*, 4–6.
9   As David Firth discusses, this text is ambiguous in reference to God's spirit (Firth, "The Historical Books," 14).
10 Steven S. Tuell, *First and Second Chronicles* (Louisville: Westminster/John Knox Press, 2001), 177.

the Spirit.[11] Yet, despite the presence of the Spirit among them[12] and the warnings of the prophets "by your Spirit" (9:30), the people rebel, which ultimately results in their captivity. Nehemiah links the Spirit with "instruction on the basis of Torah," which by extension connects Ezra and the priests to Moses as Spirit-inspired teachers and interpreters of the law as they also instruct the people and apply Torah in this new postexilic context (Neh 8:8, 13; 9:13–14).[13]

In addition to these explicit references, two significant allusions can also be discerned through a theological reflection on these postexilic texts that arguably point to the presence and activity of the divine *ruach*, even though the divine Spirit is not explicitly mentioned. The first allusion pertains to the creation and re-creation of the temple. While the Chronicler describes how David gave to Solomon all the plans he had in mind (*ruach*) for the creation of the temple (1 Chron 28:12), the temple design is attributed to the Lord's hand upon David (28:19). This text alludes to earlier traditions of the Spirit-filled artisans skilled to create the tabernacle (Exod 31:3; 35:31). The Spirit's presence in the re-creation of the temple is further implied in Ezra 6:14, which suggests that the successful completion of the house of the Lord was enlivened by the prophesying of Haggai and Zechariah. A second theological reflection concerns the possible activity of the divine *ruach* in the book of Esther. Although Esther lacks explicit reference to God, the activity of the Spirit can arguably be discerned through divine providence or "hidden causality" orchestrating human events to protect and deliver the covenant community.[14] The remarkable coincidences in Esther, such as the king's insomnia, can be theologically read as evidence of God's guidance.[15] More specifically, there is an allusion to the divine *ruach* empowering Esther to fulfill God's purposes. The Talmud makes a direct connection between Esther putting on (*labash*) her royal robes (5:1) and the

---

11 Mark J. Boda, "Word and Spirit, Scribe and Prophet in Old Testament Hermeneutics," in *Spirit and Scripture: Exploring a Pneumatic Hermeneutic*, ed. Kevin L. Spawn and Archie T. Wright (London: T & T Clark, 2012), 31.

12 There is a suggestion here of the hypostatization of the Spirit in this text reflecting an evolving pneumatology in the biblical canon. This is also suggested by the parallels with Isa 63:10–11. As Levison notes, "one can only grieve or afflict the spirit when it is understood to be a hypostasis." See Levison, *The Holy Spirit before Christianity*, 89, 91.

13 John R. Levison, *The Spirit in First-Century Judaism* (Leiden: Brill, 1997), 196.

14 Jon D. Levenson, *Esther: A Commentary* (Louisville: Westminster John Knox Press, 1997), 21; see also Michael V. Fox, *Character and Ideology in the Book of Esther: Second Edition with a New Postscript on A Decade of Esther Scholarship*, 2nd ed. (Eugene: Wipf and Stock Publishers, 2010).

15 John Webster, "On the Theology of Providence," in *The Providence of God: Deus Habet Consilium*, ed. Francesca Aran Murphy and Philip G. Ziegler (London: Bloomsbury, 2009), 162.

spirit clothing Gideon, Amasai, and Zechariah (*b. Meg.* 14b). Grossman suggests the Talmud uses these prooftexts because "Esther's situation is reminiscent of Amasai's confrontation with King David, when the king had to decide whether to accept Amasai into his ranks or have him executed."[16] Divine providence and echoes of the spirit's activity in the Chronicler could suggest the Spirit's orchestration of events in the fulfillment of God's mission in Esther.

In conclusion, the direct references to the Holy Spirit in the books of 1–2 Chronicles and Ezra-Nehemiah point to the activity of the Spirit in inspiring prophetic speech and reorienting the community toward covenant faithfulness centered on the priestly concerns for the Temple and Torah obedience. Further allusions in these books and in Esther suggest that the Spirit is involved in the creation and re-creation of the temple and in orchestrating human events to accomplish God's purposes. Each of these references to the divine *ruach* utilizes earlier traditions, particularly from the Torah and book of Judges, adapting them to affirm the continued presence of God's Spirit with his covenant people in this new postexilic context.

---

16   Jonathan Grossman, *Esther: The Outer Narrative and the Hidden Reading* (University Park: Penn State University Press, 2011), 124.

The Spirit in the Book of Psalms: Creating, Saving, Sanctifying, Guiding, and Judging

Lee Roy Martin

1 Introduction

This study surveys the Spirit's[1] activity in the Psalms and suggests theological implications that emerge from that survey.[2] The Psalter witnesses unambiguously to the Holy Spirit's role as the agent of God's life-giving power and as the administrator of God's moral authority. As the agent of God's life-giving power, the Holy Spirit creates all life and sustains all life. As administrator of God's moral authority, the Holy Spirit saves, guides, sanctifies, and enacts judgment.

The Hebrew word for "spirit" (*ruach*, רוּחַ), found thirty-nine times in the book of Psalms, poses difficulties for translators. It can refer to the Holy Spirit (Ps 51:11 [13]),[3] the human spirit (Ps 76:12 [13]), the wind (Ps 1:4), God's breath (Ps 33:6), the breath of all living things (Ps 104:29), or a disposition (Ps 78:8). As a metaphorical extension of "wind," it can also signify transience or emptiness (Ps 78:39).[4] The New Revised Standard Version of the Psalms translates the Hebrew רוּחַ with three different English words: "spirit" (eighteen times), "wind" (sixteen times), and "breath" (five times). There is no scholarly consensus regarding how many of these thirty-nine texts refer directly to the Holy Spirit, but I would identify the following eight as such: 18:15 [16]; 33:6; 51:10, 11, 12 [12, 13, 14]; 104:30; 139:7; 143:10.[5]

The biblical text does not always clearly distinguish רוּחַ as "wind" from רוּחַ as "breath" or from רוּחַ as "spirit." Christopher Seitz, commenting on Ezek 37:1–14,

---

[1] Whenever referring to the Spirit of God, the phrases "the Spirit" and "the Holy Spirit" will be capitalized according to Christian convention.
[2] For a brief pneumatology of the OT, see Lee Roy Martin, "The Spirit and the Old Testament," in *T&T Clark Handbook of Pneumatology*, ed. Daniel Castelo and Ken Loyer (London: T&T Clark, 2020), 75–88.
[3] Verse numbers of the English and the Hebrew versions do not always match. In this study, the English verse number will be listed first, and the Hebrew verse number (if different) will follow in square brackets.
[4] Cf. John Goldingay, "The Breath of Yahweh Scorching, Confounding, Anointing: The Message of Isaiah 40–42," *Journal of Pentecostal Theology* 11 (1997): 25.
[5] Constraints of space will not allow for the discussion of all thirty-nine texts. We will focus on the most prominent ones.

where רוּחַ is first the Spirit of Yahweh (v. 1), then breath (v. 5), then wind (v. 9), and finally is the Spirit again (v. 14), insists that "a clean separation of 'spirit' in some more theological sense from the concrete manifestations of 'breath' or 'wind' would be unwarranted. Yahweh's spirit is at once Israel's breath and at the same time a wind gathered from the four compass points."[6]

2   The Holy Spirit Creating and Sustaining

2.1   *Psalm 104*
Psalm 104 is a hymn of praise to Yahweh that celebrates his creative power and majesty. In this song, the motive for blessing God takes the form of a lengthy description of God's role in creating and maintaining all of creation. God's authority over creation includes his control of the waters, the clouds, wind, and fire. God "goes forth"—that is, interacts with creation—by riding the "wind" (רוּחַ, v. 3, cf. Ezek 1:12, 20). Furthermore, God uses the winds (רוּחַ) as his messengers (v. 4). Both uses of רוּחַ are symbolic, inasmuch as God neither travels from one place to another, nor does he send messages in the winds. These symbols represent God's omnipresence and his mysterious activities (such as his revelatory work), which are carried out by the Holy Spirit.[7]

The creative role of the Spirit is stated more directly in vv. 29–30. First, from a negative perspective, when God removes the Spirit (or breath, רוּחַ), the creature dies and returns to dust.[8] Second, from a positive perspective, when God gives his Spirit (also רוּחַ) the creature is "created" (ברא). In the OT, the verb "create" (ברא) is used only with God as the subject.[9] Humans can "make" (עשה) or "form" (יצר) things (Isa 22:11), but only God can "create" (ברא). The giving of the Spirit recalls Gen 2:7, when the Lord breathed into Adam and he became a "living soul" (cf. Gen 7:22; Job 33:4).[10] The removal of the Spirit recalls Gen 6:3,

---

6   Christopher R. Seitz, "Ezekiel 37:1–14," *Interpretation* 46, no. 1 (1992): 53. Cf. A. Rebecca Basdeo Hill, "Sights and Sounds of Death Valley: A Close Reading of Ezekiel 37:1–14," *Old Testament Essays* 31 (2018): 547; and Goldingay, "The Breath of Yahweh," who observes the similar creative use of רוּחַ in Isaiah 40–42.
7   Other texts that link "spirit" with creation are Ps 33:6; 135:7, 17; 147:16–18; 148:7–8.
8   The Qumran manuscript reads "your spirit" rather than "their spirit" in v. 29, thus removing any ambiguity about the identification of רוּחַ. See James A. Sanders, *The Dead Sea Psalms Scroll* (Ithaca, NY: Cornell University Press, 1967), 163.
9   David J.A. Clines, ed., *The Dictionary of Classical Hebrew* (Sheffield, UK: Sheffield Academic Press; Sheffield Phoenix Press, 1993–2011), II, 258 (hereafter, *DCH*).
10   However, the OT does not teach pantheism; see Lloyd R. Neve, *The Spirit of God in the Old Testament*, Centre for Pentecostal Theology Classics Series (Cleveland, TN: CPT Press, 2011), 69, who writes:

when, because of human corruption, the Lord decided to shorten the human lifespan; and the shortening of life was accomplished by removing the Spirit. The removal of the Spirit continues to be the cause of death for all living things (cf. Job 27:3; 34:14–15). Indeed, the spirit "belongs to God and can be taken away according to his discretion … Human breath is always at the disposition of God's grace and must continually be renewed by a creative act of grace."[11] Taken together, these two verses declare that God's Spirit is both the creator of all life and the sustaining life-force of all living things (cf. Isa 42:5).

Three other points should not be overlooked. First, this psalm is concerned not with human life alone but with all created life. "God does not just stand outside and over against his creation. Through the Spirit he enters into it and already 'dwells' in it."[12] Second, this psalm associates the creating spirit with the "face" (פנה) of God, which signifies God's immediate presence.[13] Third, these references to the "spirit" appear in a hymn; and, therefore, they offer significant motives for praising God.

2.2 Psalm 142

In Psalm 142, the "spirit" (רוּחַ) of the psalmist is "faint," because his enemies have "hidden a trap" (v. 3 [4]) for him; therefore, he must cling to God as his "refuge" (v. 5 [6]). The weakening of the psalmist's spirit demands that he call on the Lord for strength. Although we may feel obliged to distinguish between the spirit of the psalmist and the Spirit of God, the Psalter does not draw a sharp distinction. If the Holy Spirit is the life-force of all created beings, as we have argued above, then the spirit of the psalmist is dependent on the Holy Spirit in some sense.[14] Therefore, in response to the psalmist's prayer, the Spirit of

---

In carefully distinguishing the creative spirit of God from the life-breath in the nostril of every creature, the Psalmist has precluded that concept of the spirit of God which would make of it a substance or a life force which emanates throughout the universe and exists in the nostrils of all creatures. Such a concept would make every creature the possessor of a portion of the divine and would contradict the strict separation between God and his creation which the Old Testament so frequently and so vividly describes.

11   Neve, Spirit of God, 69.
12   Jürgen Moltmann, "The Spirit of Life," in The Spirit in Creation and New Creation, ed. Michael Welker (Grand Rapids, MI: Eerdmans, 2012), 67. However, the spirit of the creature and the spirit of God are "not identical" (70).
13   See Anthony C. Thiselton, The Holy Spirit—in Biblical Teaching, through the Centuries, and Today (Grand Rapids: Eerdmans, 2013), 4.
14   Other texts that link "spirit" to the inner life of humanity are Ps 31:5 [6]; 32:2; 34:18; 77:3, 6 [4, 7]; 143:4, 7; 146:3–4.

God—which is "strong and transcendent, not frail and feeble" like humanity—will renew the spirit of the psalmist.[15]

3   The Holy Spirit Guiding and Sanctifying

3.1   *Psalm 51*

Psalm 51 is an individual prayer of repentance. The psalmist understands the severity of his sin and suffers its distressful consequences. The psalm begins with a solemn and earnest confession of sin and a plea for forgiveness (vv. 1–9 [1–11]), followed by a prayer for inner renewal and restoration of joy (vv. 10–12 [12–14]). The pain of broken fellowship is registered throughout the psalm, and it finds unique expression in the psalmist's prayer, "Do not cast me away from your presence, and do not take your Holy Spirit from me" (v. 11 [13]). To be cast away from God's presence and to be void of God's Spirit would surely signify utter abandonment.

The Hebrew word for "spirit" (רוח) appears three times in Ps 51:10–12 [12–14]. The psalmist desires a "steadfast spirit" (v. 10 [12]), the "Holy Spirit" (v. 11 [13]), and a "generous spirit" (v. 12 [14]). Scholars are divided over the identification of the "spirit" in these three verses. On the one hand, John Goldingay argues that all three verses refer to the Holy Spirit. He writes, "The psalm draws our attention to the fact that the Holy Spirit is also the steadfast or persistent spirit and the generous spirit."[16] On the other hand, W. Creighton Marlowe insists that none of these verses refers to the Holy Spirit; rather, they all point to the spirit of the psalmist.[17]

---

15   Thiselton, *The Holy Spirit—in Biblical Teaching, through the Centuries, and Today*, 8.
16   John Goldingay, "The Holy Spirit and the Psalms," *Journal of Pentecostal Theology* 27, no. 1 (2018): 11. Cf. Marvin E. Tate, *Psalms 51–100* (Dallas, TX: Word Books, 1990), 25, 31.
17   W. Creighton Marlowe, "'Spirit of Your Holiness' (רוּחַ קָדְשְׁךָ) in Psalm 51:13," *Trinity Journal* 19, no. 1 (1998): 30. Cf. Daniel J. Estes, "Spirit and the Psalmist in Psalm 51," in *Presence, Power and Promise: The Role of the Spirit of God in the Old Testament*, ed. D.G. Firth and P.D. Wegner (Downers Grove, IL: IVP Academic, 2011), 122–134, whose lengthy argument fails to convince. Along with the Aramaic Targum, a few writers suggest that while "steadfast spirit" is a human attitude, both "Holy Spirit" and "generous spirit" are references to the Holy Spirit. See, for example, Charles A. Briggs and Emilie Grace Briggs, *A Critical and Exegetical Commentary on the Book of Psalms*, ICC (New York: C. Scribner's Sons, 1906–1907), II, 8. Still other commentators interpret only the middle verse ("Holy Spirit") as a reference to God's Holy Spirit. Cf. James Luther Mays, *Psalms*, Interpretation (Louisville, KY: John Knox Press, 1994), 202–203.

In the first reference to "spirit," the psalmist prays, "Create in me a pure heart, O God, and renew a steadfast spirit within me" (v. 10 [12]). God alone has the power to create (ברא); therefore, the psalmist seems to be asking not for the cleansing of the old heart but for the creation of a new heart, one that is free from contamination (cf. Ezek 36:26–28 and Jer 31:31–34).[18] Along with a pure heart, the psalmist asks for "a steadfast spirit." Because "a steadfast spirit" stands in parallel to "a pure heart," the word "spirit" has often been interpreted to be the human spirit of the psalmist. However, if a pure heart is created and a steadfast spirit is renewed, how might that work be accomplished if not by the Holy Spirit?

The presence of God is mediated by the Holy Spirit; therefore, the psalmist prays, "and do not take your Holy Spirit from me" (v. 11 [13]). Despite the scholarly consensus that "Holy Spirit" (רוח קדשך) in Ps 51:11 [13] refers to God's Holy Spirit, W. Creighton Marlowe argues that it is the psalmist's spirit and should be translated "a spirit that desires your holiness."[19] He suggests that if the psalmist had intended to say "your Holy Spirit," the word "holy" should have been an attributive adjective; and because the Hebrew "spirit" (רוח) is feminine, the adjective "holy" would also be feminine (קדשה). On the surface, this makes sense; but the argument does not hold up, because the feminine form of the adjective "holy" does not exist in biblical Hebrew.[20] In biblical Hebrew, whenever an adjective is needed but is not available, the adjectival function

---

18 Cf. Scott A. Ellington, "The Face of God as His Creating Spirit: The Interplay of Yahweh's *Panim* and *Ruach* in Psalm 104:29–30," in *The Spirit Renews the Face of the Earth: Pentecostal Forays in Science and Theology of Creation*, ed. Amos Yong (Eugene, OR: Pickwick Publishers, 2009), who writes, "Restoration in verse 10 requires a fresh act of creation. Neither the heart nor the spirit marred by sin can be rehabilitated. They must be created anew" (8); and "Every breath of every creature is a new act of God's creation, an act which is only sustainable before the face of God as he breathes out new life" (11). Cf. Stanley M. Horton, *What the Bible Says about the Holy Spirit* (Springfield, MO: Gospel Publishing House, 1976), 50.

19 Marlowe cites John Calvin as support but misrepresents Calvin's view. While it is true that Calvin translates רוח קדשך as "*Spiritum sanctitatis*" ("Spirit of holiness"), his commentary on the verse, along with his capitalization of "Spirit" throughout, makes clear that he interprets the phrase to be a reference to the Holy Spirit. For example, he states that David is praying "that he might continue in possession of the Spirit" (*maneat in possessione Spiritus*). David's fear of losing the Spirit is real but unfounded, Calvin goes on to say, because the elect cannot lose the Spirit, even if they sometimes feel that they can; John Calvin, *In Librum Psalmorum* (Geneva: Excudebat Nicolaus Barbirius & Thomas Courteau, 1564), 340–341. It should be noted that the translators of the English edition cited by Marlowe do not accurately represent Calvin's capitalization of "Spiritus."

20 Cf. Ernst Jenni and Claus Westermann, *Theological Lexicon of the Old Testament* (Peabody, MA: Hendrickson Publishers, 1997), 1106 (hereafter *TLOT*).

is fulfilled with a different grammar, the construct–genitive. The noun "holiness" "replaces the adjective as a genitive attribute."[21] This usage is paralleled throughout the Hebrew Bible. The Hebrew קָדְשְׁךָ occurs twenty times in the Hebrew Bible, and nowhere does it mean "your holiness"; it is always translated "your holy ..."[22] Without an available feminine adjective, the genitive construction "spirit of holiness" (in which "holiness" functions as an adjective) is the best way to convey the English phrase "Holy Spirit."[23]

Another important indicator that רוח קדשך refers to God's Holy Spirit is the use of the pronoun "your." The psalmist is addressing God, and both the word "presence" and the word "spirit" are spoken of as "your presence" and "your spirit."[24] The pronoun "your" refers clearly to God.[25]

Because he views the Spirit's presence as incompatible with the presence of sin, the psalmist fears the loss of the Holy Spirit. At the initial anointing of David, the Spirit had come upon him "from that day forward" (1 Sam 16:13), that is, as a permanent endowment. However, considering the Spirit's departure from King Saul (1 Sam 16:14; 18:12), it appears that the Spirit can be lost.[26]

---

21 W. Kornfeld and Helmer Ringgren, "קדש," *Theological Dictionary of the Old Testament*, ed. G. Johannes Botterweck and Heinz-Josef Fabry, trans. Douglas W. Stott (Grand Rapids, MI; Cambridge, UK: Eerdmans, 2003), 528. Cf. Jackie A. Naudé, "קָדֵשׁ", in Willem VanGemeren, ed., *New International Dictionary of Old Testament Theology & Exegesis* (Grand Rapids, MI: Zondervan, 1997), III: 879, who writes, "the genitive, instead of the adj., is used most frequently after another nom., but is rendered like an adj., holy"; also, Wilhelm Gesenius, E. Kautzsch, and A.E. Cowley, *Gesenius' Hebrew Grammar* (Oxford: Clarendon Press, 1910), §128p; and A.B. Davidson, *Hebrew Syntax* (Edinburgh: T & T Clark, 1902), §24 (c).
22 The translation "Holy Spirit" in Ps 51:11 [13] is confirmed by the LXX (τὸ πνεῦμα τὸ ἅγιόν σου) and by the Latin Vulgate (*spiritum sanctum tuum*). The Aramaic Targum, using a construct–genitive phrase, conforms to the Hebrew.
23 BDB, 871. Cf. David J.A. Clines, ed., *The Dictionary of Classical Hebrew* (Sheffield, UK: Sheffield Academic Press; Sheffield Phoenix Press, 1993–2011), II: 200 (hereafter *DCH*); *TLOT*, 1111. However, the feminine adjective "holy" does appear much later. For example, the Qumran sectarian document *The Rule of the Community* has "by the Holy Spirit" (וברוח קדושה, 1QS 3:7). Cf. Florentino García Martínez and Eibert J.C. Tigchelaar, *The Dead Sea Scrolls Study Edition* (Leiden; New York: Brill, 1997–1998), 75. Oddly, the attributive adjective קדושה was misinterpreted by noted DSS scholar Geza Vermes, who translated the phrase as "spirit of holiness," probably due to the influence of the Hebrew Bible. Geza Vermes, *The Dead Sea Scrolls in English* (Baltimore, MD: Penguin Books, 1995), 56, 72, 75.
24 In an attributive genitive, a pronominal suffix is attached to the genitive but usually modifies the whole construct chain; Bruce K. Waltke and Michael Patrick O'Connor, *An Introduction to Biblical Hebrew Syntax* (Winona Lake, IN: Eisenbrauns, 1990), 149.
25 Thiselton, *The Holy Spirit—in Biblical Teaching, through the Centuries, and Today*, 13.
26 See Leonard P. Maré, "Psalm 51: 'Take Not Your Holy Spirit Away from Me,'" *Acta Theologica* 28, no. 1 (2008), 99. Goldingay remarks, "[I]t seems to me obvious that God" might take the

Although the NT frequently refers to the Spirit as the "holy" Spirit, the phrase "Holy Spirit" is found in the OT only three times (Ps 51:11 [13]; Isa 63:10, 11). The naming of the Spirit as the "Holy Spirit" emphasizes the "ethical element"[27] and indicates that holiness is an attribute of the Spirit. Inasmuch as holiness is essential to God and to the Spirit of God, the sanctification of God's people is a crucial work of the Spirit.[28]

In his third reference to the "spirit," the psalmist prays, "and sustain me with a generous spirit" (v. 12 [14]). The Hebrew סמך means "support, uphold, sustain."[29] Thus, in prayer, "the lamenter hopes for [Yahweh's] support"[30] through the giving of a "generous spirit." The translation of "generous" (נדיב) is debated. The Hebrew can signify "inclined, generous, noble ... willing."[31] Goldingay remarks that there is an "intrinsic link between the human spirit and the divine spirit ... God breathes into us his steadfast or persistent, holy, generous spirit, to make us steadfast, holy, generous people."[32] Erich Zenger adds, "And when God causes the divine '*holy spirit*' (v. 13b) to work in him, he can live a 'holy' life."[33]

3.2 Psalm 139

Psalm 139 stands out among the psalms as a powerful statement of trust in God. The emphasis of this psalm is upon God's complete knowledge of the psalmist from the beginning to the end of the psalmist's life (vv. 1–6). Not only does the Lord know the psalmist, but the Lord is present with the psalmist at any place in heaven, on earth, in the sea, or in the darkness (vv. 7–12). Obviously, this passage assumes the omnipresence of the Holy Spirit;[34] but, more than that, the parallel between "your spirit" and "your presence" is a powerful expression

---

spirit away from us ("The Holy Spirit and the Psalms," 11). Cf. John Rea, *The Holy Spirit in the Bible: All the Major Passages About the Spirit: A Commentary* (Lake Mary, FL: Creation House, 1990), 64.

27 Neve, *The Spirit of God in the Old Testament*, 86.
28 See Martin, "The Spirit and the Old Testament," 80–82.
29 *BDB*, 702. Cf. *DCH*, VI:168.
30 *TLOT*, 804.
31 *BDB*, 622.
32 Goldingay, "The Breath of Yahweh," 11.
33 Erich Zenger, "Psalm 51," in Frank-Lothar Hossfeld and Erich Zenger, *Psalms 2: A Commentary on Psalms 51–100*, ed. K. Baltzer; trans. L.M. Maloney, Hermeneia (Minneapolis, MN: Fortress Press, 2005), 21 (emphasis original).
34 Wilf Hildebrandt, *An Old Testament Theology of the Spirit of God* (Peabody, MA: Hendrickson Publishers, 1995), 82.

of God's relationality.[35] Furthermore, "The Lord's presence is essential to the psalmist's expression of hope in the face of personal challenge and crisis."[36]

3.3 Psalm 143

In Ps. 143:10, the "holy" spirit is called the "good" spirit, and just like the "Holy Spirit" of Ps 51:11 [13], the good spirit teaches the believer to perform God's will. Psalm 143 begins with a prayer for deliverance from enemies (v. 3), which is followed by a recounting of God's interventions in "days long past" (v. 5) and a word of appreciation for God's "faithful love" (v. 8). The last section of the psalm, the psalmist prays, "Teach me to do your will." The request to be in God's will is paralleled by a further prayer that God's "good spirit" would "lead" the psalmist on "level ground" (v. 10). The combination of terms in Ps 143:10 ("teach" and "good spirit") recalls the prayer of Nehemiah, who, in reference to the exodus generation, says to God, "You gave your good Spirit to instruct them" (Neh 9:20).

Just as holiness is central to the moral attributes of the Spirit, so is goodness (Exod 33:19). Because God is good, the Spirit is good (Pss 106:1; 107:1; 118:1; 136:1), and because the Spirit "is good, it leads on level ground."[37] Goldingay comments, "At the moment, the suppliant walks treacherous, uneven ground, and is in danger of falling. The plea for rescue asks for the journey to involve level ground instead of this."[38] The OT knows of lying spirits (1 Kgs 22:22–23) and bad spirits (1 Sam 16:14–23), which corrupt the individual, disrupt the community, and wreak havoc; but the "good spirit" can be trusted to teach and to lead according to God's will.

4 The Holy Spirit Saving and Judging

4.1 Psalm 18

This psalm is a jubilant celebration of God's victory, and its salvific symbolism is expanded into one of the most eloquent and moving narratives of deliverance in all the Psalter (vv. 3–21). The narrative is rich with figurative rhetoric in which God's mighty deeds are described in "theophanic and cataclysmic terms

---

35 Ellington, "The Face of God as His Creating Spirit," 3–16.
36 Jamie A. Grant, "Spirit and Presence in Psalm 139," in *Presence, Power and Promise: The Role of the Spirit of God in the Old Testament*, ed. D.G. Firth and P.D. Wegner (Downers Grove, IL: IVP Academic, 2011), 139.
37 Goldingay, "The Holy Spirit and the Psalms," 12.
38 John Goldingay, *Psalms*, Baker Commentary on the Old Testament, 3 vols. (Grand Rapids, MI: Baker Academic, 2006), III: 677.

in answer to the cry of the petitioner."[39] The Lord "came swiftly upon the wings of the wind" (v. 10 [11]), and his salvation was on the same order as the Red Sea deliverance. At the "blast of the breath of his nostrils" the sea was removed, and the "foundations" of the earth were uncovered (v. 15 [16]). Moreover, the psalmist's enemies will be "beat" into a fine powder "like dust before the wind" (v. 42 [43]). The Spirit as "wind" often represents God's power that is displayed in judgment and in salvation. The wind is "God letting forth divine power in the world, in order to achieve something."[40]

5 Conclusions

This study has shown that "spirit" (רוּחַ) represents the nature, actions, and attributes of God. The Spirit brings both blessing and judgment, life and death. The Spirit upholds the righteous and scatters the wicked.

Taken together, these "spirit" texts show that God's Holy Spirit is active in two broad theological arenas: purity and power. In the arena of power, the Spirit creates all life and ends all life. Whatever lives has Spirit; whatever is dead does not have Spirit; and the life-giving Spirit is derived solely from God. In this role, the Spirit acts not just upon humans but upon the whole creation (Ps 104:28–30). In the arena of purity, the Spirit is the administrator of God's moral authority. The Psalms show that the Spirit is "holy," even as God is holy; and the "good Spirit" is God's agent engaging humanity for "good." God rules over his creation, and that rule is administered by the Holy Spirit. Finally, the Psalter is a songbook of prayer and worship; therefore, its references to the Spirit must be considered as worship texts that affirm the role of worship in theological formation.[41]

---

39   Hildebrandt, *An Old Testament Theology of the Spirit of God*, 78.
40   Goldingay, "The Breath of Yahweh," 4.
41   According to John Goldingay, "The Holy Spirit and the Psalms," "the existence of the Psalms suggests" that the Spirit was active in Israel's worship. The psalms "were written by people who were inspired by the Spirit and they could be used only by people who were full of the Spirit" (13). Cf. George T. Montague, *The Holy Spirit: Growth of a Biblical Tradition* (New York: Paulist Press, 1976), 69–70.

The Spirit in Isaiah: God's Might and His Charismatic Presence on the Elect

Wonsuk Ma

1   Introduction

The book of Isaiah contains a high number of references to God's Spirit (approximately sixteen; cf. fourteen in Ezekiel per NIV) in a wide range of usages concerning the nature and work of the Spirit.[1] For this reason, the Spirit of God in the book of Isaiah has received more attention than in the rest of the Old Testament. There are at least two monographs on the subject[2] with a large amount of research on various aspects of the Spirit in Isaiah.

This study employs an "elect" concept to frame the diverse nature and work of the Spirit in Isaiah. God created humans in his image and enlivened them by his breath (Gen 1:26–27; 2:7) to "rule over" the whole of creation. This special status allowed them to relate with God and perform their God-given tasks. The same pattern is repeated in the calling of Israel. It was chosen from the nations to be God's own possession with a mission to the nations (for example, Ex 19:3–6). God's presence, either through the pillars of cloud and fire or God's Spirit among them (Isa 63:11), was the hallmark of this status and mission. The same elect pattern operated in Israel among the political leaders, including the judges, kings, and prophets. They held an extraordinary status granted by God with a specific task to perform for the nation and people. In this "elect" pattern, God grants something of his own existence to the elect: God's image and breath to the first couple, his presence for Israel, and his Spirit upon the leaders and prophets.[3]

---

1 For an excellent survey of the various usages of the Spirit, see Daniel I. Block, "The View from the Top: The Holy Spirit in the Prophets," in David G. Firth and Paul D. Wegner, eds., *Presence, Power and Promise: The Role of the Spirit of God in the Old Testament* (Nottingham: Apollos, 2011), 175–207.
2 For a forthcoming title, Lian Sian Mung, *Spirit from On High: The Function and Significance of the Prophet's Eschatological Vision in Isaiah 32* (Eugene, OR: Wipf & Stock, forthcoming) in addition to Wonsuk Ma, *Until the Spirit Comes: The Spirit of God in the Book of Isaiah*, JSOTS 271 (London: T & T Clark, 1999).
3 The "extension of God's personality" by Aubrey R. Johnson, *The One and the Many in the Israelite Conception of God* (Cardiff: University of Wales Press, 2961), 2.

This makes God's elect a "charismatic" figure: chosen or called to be his possession and to stand between God and the recipients of the elect's ministry, and to perform God-given tasks with his enduring and equipping presence through the Spirit. For the "tasks," the Spirit equips or empowers the elected entity. However, the book of Isaiah also contains references to the Spirit without a human agent, revealing God's character and work. This study will examine key passages of the Spirit in Isaiah to identify the Spirit's role over the recipients with a focus on its "charismatic" function upon the "elect."

2 The Spirit as the Core of God's Existence: In Creation, Judgment, and Salvation

The first discussion is on the Spirit of God in operation mostly without human agency. The Spirit signifies various aspects of God's being, character, or work, but all refer to the core of his existence. This usage is seen in creation and God's work of judgment and salvation, which are frequently related to each other. In First Isaiah, the message of judgment dominates.

Chapter 30 may describe the Assyrian crisis (701 BCE) during Hezekiah's reign. The prophet strongly objects to the king's plan to seek Egypt's help: "But the Egyptians are mere mortals and not God; their horses are flesh and not spirit" (30:3a). Although the passage does not contain a direct reference to God's Spirit, the statement reveals the "spirit" as the distinguishing element between "mere mortals" and God, and Egyptian horses and God's army. God rejects the Pharaoh's long-standing claim to be the incarnation of the sun god. The passage also denies any claims of the deification of Egyptian horses, which refers to the Egyptian notion of its deities often depicted with animal faces or bodies. The "S/spirit" is the core element of divinity, here denoting God's supreme power and his lordship over all nations (thus, creation).

Isaiah 34 is another passage of judgment, this time against the nations. After the complete destruction and desolation, the populated cities and towns become the haven for wild and exotic animals (34:1–15). The certainty and completeness of God's judgment are assured: "Look in the scroll of the Lord and read: None of these will be missing, not one will lack her mate. For it is his mouth that has given the order, and his Spirit will gather them together" (34:16). The occupation of the land by the animals instead of people is ordained by God through his word and Spirit, referring back to the creation: God's Spirit hovers above the pre-creation waters (Gen 1:2; cf. 2:5), and God's act of speaking brought the creation into being (for example, 1:3, 6, 9, 11, 14, 20, 24, 26). In this reversed act of creation, God's Spirit executes his judgment upon the nations.

Isaiah 63 contains a historical prayer that surveys the early history of Israel. Against God's election, redemption, and love, God's people rebelled and "grieved his Holy Spirit" (v. 10). As a result, he also "turned and became their enemy," now fighting against them. The Spirit here refers to the core of God's personality, the seat of his will, strength, and emotion. The "Holy" Spirit may refer to God's demand of obedience and reverence, as well as God's otherness. By implication, the Spirit played a significant role in God's fighting against the enemy nations (vs. 1–6) and in electing and showing kindness to Israel (7–9) until its rebellion. Then the people recalled "the days of old, the day of Moses." His care for the people during the wilderness period is described as the time when God "set his Holy Spirit among them" (11). At the end of their wandering, the people "were given rest by the Spirit of Yahweh" (14). All three occurrences of the Spirit in this passage can be substituted by "God," making God's Spirit almost indistinguishable from God. However, the Spirit accentuates certain aspects of God's being or action.

Similar usage is found in the context of God's argument against the nations (and their idols) for his supremacy with creation as an example: "Who can fathom the Spirit or instruct the Lord as his counselor?" (Isa 40:13).[4] In this dispute with the unidentified audience, the Spirit, which some versions translate as "mind," refers to the very core of God, as the parallel line uses the "Lord" as the parallel word. The Spirit particularly points to God's supreme wisdom and might displayed in creation.

In Isa 32:15–18, the pouring of God's Spirit upon his people ushers in the new era of restoration: "... till the Spirit is poured on us from on high, and the desert becomes a fertile field, and the fertile field seems like a forest" (v. 15). The land's fruitfulness is followed by the establishment of an ethical order ("justice" and "righteousness," v. 16) and culminates in the complete wholeness of life (vs. 17–18). Similarly, God will restore the land and people: "I will pour water on the thirsty land ...; I will pour out my Spirit on your offspring, and my blessing on your descendants" (44:3). Through the life-giving and renewing Spirit, they will multiply and flourish until the nations voluntarily come to acknowledge Yahweh and become his people (44:4–5).

The Spirit represents God's radical otherness from humans and other gods. As the creator and Lord of the nations and Israel, therefore, he has the right and power to judge and save his creation, Israel, and the nations. His Spirit is a dynamic concept: displaying power over the nations, their army (or horses), and gods/idols, executing judgment upon his own people and their enemies,

---

[4] Scripture quotes are from the New International Version (NIV).

repopulating their lands with wild animals, displaying wisdom and might in creation, and bringing new life to nature and to his people.

3 The Spirit and Prophets

As in many prophetic books, the book of Isaiah has no claim of the Spirit upon the prophet, despite the generous amount of biographical material. However, a close search may yield several passages. Possibly coming from the same context of the Assyrian crisis as in ch. 31, the beginning passage of ch. 30 rebukes the foreign policy of the day:

> Woe … to those who carry out plans that are not mine, forming an alliance, but not by my Spirit …; who go down to Egypt without consulting me; who look for help to Pharaoh's protection, to Egypt's shade for refuge.
> 30:1–2

Verse 1 identifies their "sin upon sin" with carrying out the plans that are not God's. The parallelism elaborates that the plans to form an alliance with Egypt but are "not mine" means that the plans were not by God's Spirit. The latter is yet further explained as the nation's failure to consult with God for the plans. Most commentators, therefore, agree that this refers to the prophetic "inquiry" of God's will over any political decision, such as war. This indirectly establishes a long-held notion that the Spirit is the source of prophetic proclamation, even allowing this claim to be extended to Isaiah's oracles against Kings Ahaz (7:13–17) and Hezekiah (39:5–7).

In the coming age, the Spirit continues inspiring the prophets in two ways. One is God's promise of the perpetual office of the prophets. Isa 59:21 reads like a fragment, not closely attached to the preceding (both judgment and salvation) oracles. God seals his "covenant" with the unknown addressees ("them"):

> My Spirit, who is on you, will not depart from you, and my words that I have put in your mouths will always be on your lips, on the lips of your children and on the lips of their descendants.

The Spirit is at the core of the prophetic vocation and ministry. The pairing of the Spirit and the word helps us to identify the verse referring to a group of prophets. God promises that the prophetic office continues with the gift of the Spirit and Spirit-inspired messages ("my words … put in your mouth"). The emphasis on continuity is unusually strong with "always," "your lips," "your children," "their descendants," and "this time on and forever." By implication, the Spirit also calls the prophets to be his servants. Although their role is not specified, the positioning of the verse at the end of the series of judgment and salvation oracles suggests the prophetic role in the process. The other way the prophetic Spirit has manifested itself in the new age is in the increasing integration of the prophetic features into the Spirit-inspired future leaders, as seen below.

The oft-quoted 61:1–3 is the most significant passage on the prophetic Spirit tradition in Isaiah. The Spirit is directly linked to the prophetic vocation: "The Spirit of the Sovereign Lord is on me, because the Lord has anointed me to proclaim good news to the poor." Recalling the ancient tradition of anointing (here, more figuratively) and the coming of the Spirit (for example, David in 1Sam 16:13), the Spirit both commissions and inspires. Although some commentators see a royal function in freeing the captives and releasing prisoners, the commission is to "proclaim," suggesting the prophetic ministry. The prophetic call is to bring justice and restoration to the community's marginalized, the "poor," "brokenhearted," "captives," and "prisoners" (v. 1). The turn of fortune for God's people ("Zion") is expressed in the "year of the Lord's favor" (or Jubilee), a "crown of beauty," the "oil of joy," and a "garment of praise" (vs. 2–3). The other side of God's restoration is his "vengeance" to Zion's enemy (v. 2). The exact nature of suffering, however, is not certain. As the following passage (4–7) brings the devastation of the nation (with the destruction of Jerusalem and the temple, and the exile) into the picture, it is possible that the suffering refers to circumstances beyond individuals' control and a literal interpretation.

The Spirit-anointed prophet's focus is no longer on challenging powers but renewing and restoring the oppressed and suffering. This reflects two social realities: the absence of the social establishment, especially the king, who frequently violated the rule of justice, and the hardship that God's people are experiencing. In this setting, through the empowering work of the Spirit, the prophet serves as a catalyst between God and the suffering people to bring God's full restoration. The call to vocation, the Spirit's anointing, and the Spirit-inspired message are the characteristics of the charismatic work of the Spirit.

The prophets play a pivotal role in the nation's affairs. In the pre-exilic setting, the prophetic activities were predominantly to challenge political leadership to be obedient to God following his covenant stipulations. The Spirit gave them legitimacy and authority as they declared the Spirit-inspired messages. In the exilic and postexilic era, under the Spirit, their role and message are of restoration. In both settings, the prophets stand between God and the king or the people, making them "charismatic" figures as the Spirit empowers them.

4   The Spirit and Leadership

Throughout the book, surprisingly, no reference to the Spirit is found upon the kings. Even for Hezekiah, the most praiseworthy king of Judah, no accomplishment of his is attributed to God's Spirit. However, suddenly the Spirit becomes prominent upon the future leader. It is plausible that the leadership Spirit tradition is prominent in a sociopolitical environment where there is no stable leadership succession system, as in the period of judges and the northern kingdom. On the other hand, the dynastic system of Judah gradually eliminates the charismatic role of the Spirit. Three passages showcase the Spirit's presence upon the future leader.

Isaiah 11:1–5 contains the expectation of an ideal king in Jesse's lineage. Whether the "stump" assumes the destruction of Zion or denotes the Davidic descent is not clear. Most commentators agree with the pre-exilic date, and some argue for a priestly prayer for the coronation of a prince as the likely setting. This future king is characterized by the presence of God's Spirit: "The Spirit of the Lord will rest on him—the Spirit of wisdom and of understanding, the Spirit of counsel and of might, the Spirit of the knowledge and fear of the Lord" (11:2). Unlike in other "introductions" with their many epithets (such as Isa 42:1 below), the "resting of the Spirit" is the single characteristic of this ideal king. This special endowment is manifested in three pairs of qualities that equip him to rule in justice and righteousness (3b, 4a), and to judge the wicked and evildoers with his "rod" and "breath" (4b). The passage places a heavy emphasis on the king's inner quality: his faithfulness to God (or "the fear of the Lord," appearing twice in vs. 2 and 3) and his righteous rule over his people. Conversely, downplayed or absent is a reference to military might or political acumen. The literary arrangement suggests that his righteous and just rule restores not only the community but also the whole creation or "a return to Eden" (6–9).[5] By implication of the Spirit, the king is chosen and called by God. The Spirit's empowering presence with the king has to do with the well-being of God's people, the nation, and the whole creation, by remaining loyal to God, administering justice and righteousness, and eliminating evil to the nation.

Isaiah 42:1–4 introduces the first of the so-called "Servant Songs." To the unknown audience, God introduces his "servant," upheld, chosen, and delighted by God. The highlight is the presence of the Spirit: "I will put my Spirit on him," and the task requiring the Spirit's commissioning and empowerment

---

5   Robin Routledge, "The Spirit and the Future in the Old Testament: Restoration and Renewal," in Firth and Wegner, *Presence, Power and Promise*, 364.

is to "bring justice to the nations" (v. 1). Although the connection between the Spirit and justice is known, the exact nature of "bring justice to the nations" is unclear. The next three verses describe the challenge of adverse forces and his modest behavior and precarious state:

> He will not shout or cry out, or raise his voice in the streets. A bruised reed he will not break, and a smoldering wick he will not snuff out ... he will not falter or be discouraged.
>
> vs. 2–4

The true focus, however, is not his suffering: his empowered resilience to fulfill his God-given mission: "In faithfulness, he will bring forth justice" (v. 3) and "he establishes justice on earth" (v. 4). Thus, the empowerment of the Spirit enables him to endure hardship and to persevere, show tender care to the suffering, and fulfill his God-given mission. The downplay of the royal or military feature of the king/leader is already detected in ch. 11. Here, the servant displays a hybrid characteristic between the king and the prophet, whom the former often persecuted. The precarious nature of the servant reaches its climax in Isa 53. Whether "justice" (or "judgment") refers to the servant's role as a prosecutor is less likely, as the task is also identified as his "teaching" (*torah*), which the islands await (v. 4).

Isaiah 44:1–5, briefly mentioned above, contributes uniquely to the present discussion. God addresses his people ("Jacob, my servant, Israel," v. 1), who have been chosen by God. After his assurance as Israel's creator ("he who made you, who formed you in the womb," v. 2), God pronounces his plan to restore his people: the pouring out of his Spirit on their offspring, which is explained to be his blessing upon their descendants (v. 3). As a result, Israel will experience flourishing and multiplication: "They will spring up like grass in a meadow, like poplar trees by flowing streams" (v. 4). Their restored life will draw the nations to Israel's Lord: "Some will say, 'I belong to the Lord'; others will call themselves by the name of Jacob; still others will write on their hand, 'The Lord's,' and will take the name Israel" (v. 5). Besides the strong creative link with the Spirit, there are three points to highlight. The first is that Israel is the chosen servant of God. Throughout the second half of the book of Isaiah, the servant's identity is sometimes fluid between individual and collective entities. However, in this passage, the servant is clearly God's people, and God pours his Spirit upon them. The second is the role of the recipient of God's Spirit: no role whatsoever. It is God's one-sided act of redemption and restoration through his Spirit with no conditions. The assumption is Israel's grateful recognition of his favor. The third is the effect of the process: the nations voluntarily submitting to the lordship of Israel's God, echoing the servant's task to the nations. This is the fulfillment of God's covenant with Israel: to be God's special possession and his priestly nation (to the nations, Ex 19:6a). In this passage, the renewed Israel stands between God and the nations, and the Spirit "empowers" God's people to "bring" the nations to God.

5   Conclusion

The book of Isaiah presents the nature and work of God's Spirit in two large areas. First, the Spirit denotes God's unrivaled power in creation, his supremacy over the nations, and his lordship over Israel. The latter two are expressed in God's power of judgment and salvation without human agents (except for the nations that God uses to punish his people). When human agents are present, the Spirit, as the "extension of God's personality" graciously extended to them, equips and empowers God's chosen agent to exercise the prophetic and leadership tasks. They stand between God and Israel or the nations to bring about God's grace to the recipients. The agents could be both individuals and the people of God. This is where the Spirit's two traditions, creation and charismatic, merge together in the of flourishing God's people, the nations, and the whole of creation.[6]

---

6   Wonsuk Ma, "Isaiah," in *A Biblical Theology of the Holy Spirit*, eds. Trevor J. Burke and Keith Warrington (London: SPCK, 2014), 34–45.

The Spirit in Ezekiel: The Presence of Yahweh with His People

Alicia R. Jackson

1   Introduction

It was July 31, 593 BC. He sat by the river, among his fellow refugees, dejected in despair (Ezek 1:1). This was it: his thirtieth birthday—the day he had so long awaited as the inauguration of his priestly ministry at the Jerusalem temple—when the Judean community should have laid their hands upon him in consecration to sacred Levitical service (Num 4:30; 8:10).[1] Yet, here he sat—not at the Jerusalem temple, and not amid songs of jubilant worship—but alongside the River Chebar and among the mourners raising their voices in lament, "If I forget you, O Jerusalem, let my right hand wither! Let my tongue cling to the roof of my mouth, if I do not remember you, if I do not set Jerusalem above my highest joy" (Ps 137:5–6).[2] Was there any hope of encountering the presence and glory of Yahweh in this desolate place?

Yet at precisely that unlikely and unexpected moment, Ezekiel felt a hand laid upon him—not the hand of a fellow refugee, but that of Yahweh himself—commissioning Ezekiel into his prophetic priestly ministry. Representing the power and authority of Yahweh, this anthropomorphic description of Yahweh's hand upon the prophet occurs throughout the book of Ezekiel (Ezek 3:14, 22; 8:1; 37:1; 40:1).[3] A. Rebecca Basdeo Hill explains that in the book of Ezekiel, the hand of Yahweh "is homologous with the activity of the Spirit in relation to divine revelation and the prophetic word."[4] Ezekiel's Spirit-led visionary expe-

---

1 Victor Harold Matthews, Mark W. Chavalas, and John H. Walton, *The IVP Bible Background Commentary: Old Testament*, electronic ed., (Downers Grove, IL: InterVarsity Press, 2000), Ezek 1:1–2.
2 *The Holy Bible: New Revised Standard Version* (Nashville: Thomas Nelson Publishers, 1989). All subsequent biblical quotations in English come from the NRSV unless otherwise noted.
3 Biblical Studies Press, *The NET Bible First Edition Notes* (Richardson, TX: Biblical Studies Press, 2006), Ezek 1:2–3; and Daniel Isaac Block, *The Book of Ezekiel, Chapters 1–24*, The New International Commentary on the Old Testament (Grand Rapids, MI: Eerdmans, 1997), 79–89.
4 A. Rebecca Basdeo Hill, *Visions of God in Ezekiel: Pentecostal Explorations of the Glory and Holiness of Yahweh* (Cleveland, TN: CPT Press, 2019), 72; Andreas Schuele, "The Spirit of YHWH and the Aura of Divine Presence," *Interpretation* 66, no. 1 (January 2012): 27; and Pieter de Vries,

rience of the glory of Yahweh launched him into a Spirit-empowered journey from lament and judgment to hope and restoration, revealing the Spirit as the purifying, personal, and permanent presence of Yahweh among his people.[5]

2 The Spirit as the Purifying Presence of Yahweh

The first mention of רוּחַ (wind, breath, spirit) occurs in Ezekiel's description of the movement of the living creatures and their wheels: "wherever the spirit would go, they went" (Ezek 1:12, 20). Recognizing the intentional literary wordplay with רוּחַ throughout the book, sometimes swiftly shifting from breath to wind to spirit (for example, Ezek 37:1–14), a strong possibility remains that the use of רוּחַ in chapter 1 refers to the Spirit of Yahweh.[6] The pattern of connection between the glory (כָּבוֹד) of Yahweh and the Spirit is repeated throughout the book (Ezek 1:28–2:1, 3:23–24, 8:3–4, 10:18–11:5, 11:23–24, 43:4–5).[7] With good reason, scholars identify Ezekiel as both the prophet of the glory of Yahweh and the prophet of the Spirit of Yahweh, and the first to connect the "efficacy of the Spirit" to the "task of prophecy."[8] Yahweh's כָּבוֹד in chapter 1 should be associated with what rabbinic literature later identified as his שְׁכִינָה (dwelling): the theophanic presence of Yahweh throughout the Old Testament.[9] Often Yahweh's כָּבוֹד appeared as a fire or cloud, revealing his holiness in all of its terrifying potency, transcendent mystery, and transformative power (Exod 3:2, 19:16, 19; 20:18, 21; Deut 4:12, 15, 33, 36; 5:4, 22–26; 10:4).[10]

"The Relationship between the Glory of YHWH and the Spirit of YHWH in the Book of Ezekiel Part One," *Journal of Biblical and Pneumatological Research* 5 (Fall 2013): 114–116.

5   See Werner E. Lemke, "Life in the Present and Hope for the Future," *Interpretation* 38, no. 2 (April 1984): 165–180.

6   David L. Thompson, "Ezekiel," in *Cornerstone Biblical Commentary: Ezekiel & Daniel*, ed. Philip W. Comfort, vol. 9 (Carol Stream, IL: Tyndale House Publishers, 2010), 46.

7   de Vries, "The Relationship between the Glory of YHWH and the Spirit of YHWH," 109–127; and Basdeo Hill, *Visions of God in Ezekiel*, 72–74, 115.

8   Walther Zimmerli, *The Fiery Throne: The Prophets and Old Testament Theology* (Minneapolis: Augsburg Fortress, 2003), 107–117; Schuele, "The Spirit of YHWH and the Aura of Divine Presence," 21–22; de Vries, "The Relationship between the Glory of YHWH and the Spirit of YHWH," 112; and Daniel I. Block, "The Prophet of the Spirit: The Use of Rwh in the Book of Ezekiel," *Journal of the Evangelical Theological Society* 32, no. 1 (March 1989): 27–49.

9   For more on שְׁכִינָה, see Ludwig Blau and Kaufmann Kohler, "Shekinah," in the *JewishEncyclopedia.com: The Unedited Text of the 1906 Jewish Encyclopedia*, https://jewishencyclopedia.com/articles/6713-glory-of-god; and Cheryl Bridges Johns, "Grieving, Brooding, and Transforming: The Spirit, the Bible, and Gender," *Journal of Pentecostal Theology* 23, no. 2 (2014): 141–153.

10 Basdeo Hill, *Visions of God in Ezekiel*, 94.

The Spirit who directs the movement of the living creatures in Ezekiel's inaugural vision does so in part to reveal Yahweh's purifying presence to Ezekiel and to the exilic community. Later identified as cherubim (Ezek 10:22–24), these living creatures follow the Spirit's leading both in guarding sacred space (Gen 3:24; Exod 25:18–22, 26:1; 1 Kings 6:23–29; Ezek 41:15) and in separating the holiness of Yahweh's presence from sinful humanity, particularly when Ezekiel watches the Spirit-led cherubim escort Yahweh's כְּבוֹד from the Jerusalem temple and the city (Ezek 10:18–19, 11:22–23).[11] Yet despite the imminent judgment that would ensue, Yahweh's desire was to be a sanctuary for his people even in exile (Ezek 11:16), and to purify them by the power of his Spirit so that a remnant might remain in his presence.[12] Yahweh's purifying presence is a crucial aspect of his personal pursuit of his covenant people, even in the face of their adulterous idolatry with foreign nations and their gods.

3   The Spirit as the Personal Presence of Yahweh

The Spirit in Ezekiel as the purifying presence of Yahweh is also revealed as the personal presence of Yahweh, demonstrated by the Spirit's involvement in divine actions and divine anthropomorphisms. The Spirit acts by coming into Ezekiel and raising him to his feet (Ezek 2:2, 3:24); lifting him up and taking him to various places in visionary experiences, including to Jerusalem, to the eastern gate of the temple, to the exiles, to the middle of a valley, and to the inner court of the temple (Ezek 3:12, 14; 8:3; 11:1, 24; 37:1; 43:5); and finally, participating in divine speech (Ezek 3:24; 11:5).[13]

In addition to actions of the Spirit, Hebrew parallelisms emphasize poetically the Spirit's connection to divine anthropomorphisms. First, let us consider this series of consecutive, parallel actions in Ezek 8:1 and Ezek 8:3:

---

11   See Brian Neil Peterson, *Ezekiel in Context: Ezekiel's Message Understood in Its Historical Setting of Covenant Curses and Ancient Near Eastern Mythological Motifs*, Princeton Theological Monograph Series (Eugene, OR: Pickwick Publications, 2012), 115–140; Matthews, Chavalas, and Walton, *The IVP Bible Background Commentary: Old Testament*, Ezek 10:1; and Stacy Knuth and Douglas Mangum, "Cherubim," in *The Lexham Bible Dictionary*, ed. John D. Barry et al. (Bellingham, WA: Lexham Press, 2016).

12   Peterson, *Ezekiel in Context*, 114.

13   While וַיְדַבֵּר (Ezek 3:24) and וַיֹּאמֶר (Ezek 11:4) as masculine verbs point to Yahweh as the speaker, the Spirit is directly involved in divine speech. Ezekiel 11:4 refers to the רוּחַ יְהוָה (Spirit of Yahweh), a construct phrase used only two times in the book of Ezekiel (Ezek 11:4, 37:1). See de Vries, "The Relationship between the Glory of YHWH and the Spirit of YHWH," 124; and Stanley Monroe Horton, "Old Testament Foundations of the Pentecostal Faith," *Pneuma* 1, no. 1 (Spring 1979): 26.

Ezek 8:1

שָׁם	עָלַי	וַתִּפֹּל [יַד אֲדֹנָי יְהוִה]
(there)	(upon me)	(and [the hand of the Lord Yahweh] fell)

Ezek 8:3

יָד	תַּבְנִית	וַיִּשְׁלַח
(a hand)	(the shape of)	(and he stretched out)
רֹאשִׁי	בְּצִיצִת	וַיִּקָּחֵנִי
(my head)	(by the hair of)	(and he took me)
אֹתִי		וַתִּשָּׂא [רוּחַ]
(me)		(and [the Spirit] lifted up)

The antecedent to the first "he" in Ezek 8:3 is דְּמוּת כְּמַרְאֵה־אֵשׁ (a figure like the appearance of fire, or of a man [LXX]), who has the anthropomorphic quality of a waist (Ezek 8:2). The image of the fiery figure clearly conveys the presence of Yahweh's כָּבוֹד upon the prophet. The text progresses from the hand of Yahweh falling, to the fiery figure stretching out the shape of a hand, to the fiery figure's hand taking Ezekiel by the hair of his head, to the Spirit lifting Ezekiel up. While equating Yahweh with the fiery figure and with the Spirit may lack the nuance warranted by the text's progressive parallel structure, there seems to be an intentional correlation of the divine actions in Ezekiel's visionary and yet surprisingly tactile experience. The text indicates a strong connection between the hand of Yahweh, the hand of the fiery figure, and the action of the Spirit in lifting Ezekiel up, emphasizing the personal involvement of the Spirit in divine prophetic and visionary activity. As Block writes regarding the relation of the Spirit to Yahweh in the book of Ezekiel, "When the divine רוּחַ acts, God acts."[14]

Another parallelism highlighting the Spirit's involvement in a divine anthropomorphism occurs in Ezek 39:29:

---

14   Block, "The Prophet of the Spirit," 49.

Ezek 39:29

וְלֹא־אַסְתִּיר עוֹד	פָּנַי	מֵהֶם
(And I will not hide again)	(my face)	(from them)

אֲשֶׁר שָׁפַכְתִּי	אֶת־רוּחִי	עַל־בֵּית יִשְׂרָאֵל	נְאֻם אֲדֹנָי יְהוִה
(when I pour out)	(my Spirit)	(upon the house of Israel)	(declaration of the Lord Yahweh)

The contrast between Yahweh hiding his face and pouring out his Spirit also suggests a parallelism between the face of Yahweh and the Spirit of Yahweh. Thus, the Spirit is revealed as the personal presence of Yahweh in restorative relational pursuit of his people. Verena Schafroth explains, "The reference to God hiding His face is usually connected to His wrath in Ezekiel (cf. 7:8; 9:8; 20:8; 30:15; 36:18)." Therefore, "what was a stereotypical threat of judgement" transforms into "God's restorative activity."[15] Yahweh's personal pursuit of Ezekiel mirrors his personal pursuit of his errant bride (Ezek 16; 23), vividly portraying Yahweh's divine movement *toward* his people, even in their unfaithfulness. The promised outpouring of the Spirit in Ezek 39:29 reveals not only the personal presence of Yahweh, but also the promise of permanent presence among his people.

4   The Spirit as the Permanent Presence of Yahweh

From Ezekiel's initial vision of the כָּבוֹד of Yahweh in chapter 1 to his final vision of the new temple in chapters 40–48, the unified theme tying the book together is clear: Yahweh's presence with his people. Repeated sixty-five times in the book of Ezekiel, the recognition formula וְיָדְעוּ כִּי אֲנִי יְהוָה אֱלֹהֵיהֶם (then they will know that I am Yahweh their God) expresses Yahweh's desire to dwell in intimate covenant relationship with his people, so that all the nations of the world would also know that he is Yahweh. Yet, this promise of permanent presence could only be enacted by the Spirit of Yahweh in the internal transformation of his people by giving them a new heart and a new spirit and enabling them to

---

15   Verena Schafroth, "An Exegetical Exploration of 'Spirit' References in Ezekiel 36 and 37," *Journal of the European Pentecostal Theological Association* 29, no. 2 (2009): 73.

walk faithfully with their God in the covenant of peace (Ezek 11:19–20; 16:60–63; 34:25; 36:26–27; 37:26–28).[16] Known as "Ezekiel's gospel," this promise of a new heart and a new spirit occurs first in Ezek 11:19–20 and then again in Ezek 36:26.[17] Ezekiel 36:27 explains how Yahweh will perform this heart transplant from stone to flesh: וְאֶת־רוּחִי אֶתֵּן בְּקִרְבְּכֶם (and I will place my Spirit into your inner parts). In fact, the new spirit promised (Ezek 11:19–20, 36:26) is the Spirit of Yahweh, who will take up permanent residence internally in his people.[18]

Following the Spirit's visionary transportation of Ezekiel to the valley of dry bones, where Ezekiel prophesies to the רוּחַ (wind) and the רוּחַ (breath) enters the dry bones and brings them to life, this promise of permanent indwelling is repeated in Ezek 37:14: וְנָתַתִּי רוּחִי בָכֶם (and I will place my Spirit in you). The Spirit resurrects, reunifies, and restores the nations of Israel and Judah, acting, as Jacqueline Grey writes, "to achieve the re-creation of the despairing community through the words of the prophet, inspiring hope and life."[19] The permanence of Yahweh's dwelling is emphasized again in Ezek 37:27, when he promises that his sanctuary will be among them forever, followed by the recognition formula and the covenant formula: וְהָיִיתִי לָהֶם לֵאלֹהִים וְהֵמָּה יִהְיוּ־לִי לְעָם (and I will be their God, and they will be my people). Block describes the promised outpouring of the Spirit (Ezek 39:29) as "the permanent witness and seal of the בְּרִית שָׁלוֹם [covenant of peace] and the בְּרִית עוֹלָם [eternal covenant]."[20] This promised outpouring anticipates both the inaugural outpouring of the Spirit on the day of Pentecost (Joel 2:28–29; Acts 2:1–21) and the permanent indwelling of the Spirit in the hearts of Yahweh's people—the salvation of Israel by faith in Jesus their Messiah (Rom 9–11).[21]

---

16   Horton, "Old Testament Foundations of the Pentecostal Faith," 27.
17   Block explains how Jesus built upon Ezek 36:25–29 in his conversation with Nicodemus (John 3:5–8). See Daniel I. Block, *The Book of Ezekiel, Chapters 25–48*, The New International Commentary on the Old Testament (Grand Rapids, MI: Eerdmans, 1997), 360–361.
18   Allen writes, "their lives were to be governed by a new impulse that was to be an expression of Yahweh's own spirit." Leslie C. Allen, *Ezekiel 20–48*, Word Biblical Commentary (Dallas, TX: Word Books, 1990), 179.
19   Jacqueline Grey, "Acts of the Spirit: Ezekiel 37 in the Light of Contemporary Speech-Act Theory," *Journal of Biblical and Pneumatological Research* 1 (Fall 2009): 70.
20   Daniel I. Block, "Gog and the Pouring Out of the Spirit: Reflections on Ezekiel 39:21–29," *Vetus Testamentum* 37, no. 3 (July 1987): 270.
21   Horton, "Old Testament Foundations of the Pentecostal Faith," 23.

5 Conclusion

Finally, after encountering the Spirit as the purifying, personal, and permanent presence of Yahweh, Ezekiel returns again to a river—not to the River Chebar, but to the River of Life flowing from the glorious new temple (Ezek 47:1–12). Ezekiel's journey from mourning along the banks of lament to wading into the waters of life-giving source pictures the trajectory of the entire book from judgment and desolation to hope and restoration. As Ezekiel gradually ventures deeper into the waters of life, he invites his readers to dare to hope that an invitation to Spirit-empowered encounters with Yahweh remains available—perhaps not *in spite of*, but *especially because of* places of loss, devastation, and trauma, places awaiting that glorious transformation where heart-wrenching pain gives way to life-giving hope, accessible only in the very presence of the Spirit of the Living God.

The Spirit in Daniel and The Twelve: When Divine Winds Blow

Rick Wadholm

1 Introduction

The collection of the scrolls of the OT examined for this essay includes the final thirteen books in the Protestant Old Testament—Daniel and The Twelve (Minor Prophets). A study of the "Spirit"[1] (Hebrew and Aramaic רוח) in these texts provides a number of challenges, such as how to engage usage, whether canonically book-by-book, attempting categories of use (semantic ranges formatted much like theological lexicons that include synonyms), or reconstructing historical-chronological settings and developments (akin to the *Religionsgeschichtliche Schule* and its offspring).[2] Each of these may provide a help to the topic as well as a challenge by failing to offer other avenues of critical reflection. However, this study follows an approach that seeks to hear these texts in a literary-theological fashion within a canonical framework.[3]

Some texts have been eliminated from the study due to their seeming nonconnection to being what later Christian reflection confesses as "Holy Spirit." Other texts have been retained, some despite the fact that many readers reject connections to the divine Spirit, others because of the way they function within the book in relation to other clearer divine uses and their interplay with

---

[1] All translations are the author's unless otherwise indicated. All versification follows the Masoretic Text (MT) versification, with differing English translation (ET) versification indicated in footnotes.

[2] Concerning this last category a number of monographs have been published along this trajectory with only a representation here: R. Koch, *Der Geist Gottes im Alten Testament* (Bern: P. Lang, 1991); Daniel Lys, *Rûach: le souffle dans l'ancien testament: enquête anthropologique à travers l'histoire théologique d'Israël*, Etudes d'histoire et de philosophie religieuses 56 (Paris: Presses Universitaires de France, 1962); Lloyd R. Neve, *The Spirit of God in the Old Testament*, Centre for Pentecostal Theology Classics Series (Cleveland, TN: CPT Press, 2011), Johannes H. Scheepers, *Die Gees van God en die Gees van die mens in die Oud Testamentische Studien* (Kampen: J.H. Kok, 1960). Along a similar aim of tracing a recreated historical development, but of a decidedly more theological bent for categorizations, is George T. Montague, *The Holy Spirit: Growth of a Biblical Tradition* (New York: Paulist Press, 1976).

[3] It follows a somewhat similar approach to works such as Stanley M. Horton, *What the Bible Says about the Holy Spirit* (Springfield, MO: Gospel Publishing House, 2005) in moving canonically through the biblical texts in summative fashion.

such.⁴ There are ambiguities in relation to the disposition, wind, spirit, and Spirit in a number of these texts, and here we will attempt to discuss those pertinent to a hearing of the Spirit in these texts (where possible multiplicity of sense may be present). The narrow focus upon the lexeme רוח and its various nominal forms within these texts will be traced through each respective book, followed by an attempt toward a brief constructive theology of the Spirit in Daniel and The Twelve. According to Daniel Block, the Hebrew⁵ root רוח occurs forty-eight times in the books of Daniel and the Minor Prophets (Daniel fifteen times, Hosea seven times, Joel twice, Amos once, Jonah twice, Micah three times, Habakkuk twice, Haggai four times, Zechariah nine times, Malachi three times),⁶ though not all of these seem to have the divine Spirit directly in their human purview.

2 The Spirit in Daniel

The "spirit" of Nebuchadnezzar is disturbed by a dream in the night (2:1, 3) by the one who gave it and will provide the interpretation of it through his Spirit-enabled interpreter, Daniel. In fact, seven statements concerning Daniel as one known to be endowed with "the spirit of the holy gods" or "extraordinary spirit" are found in this book (4:5–6, 15; 5:11–12, 14; 6:4).⁷ This functions in the book as a testimony in the mouth of the nations concerning the presence of the divine benevolence among the exiles.⁸ This is contrasted with the arrogant "spirit" of Nebuchadnezzar, who would have his glory and authority stripped (5:20). In a

---

4   As examples of the latter, see Amos 4:13 "wind"; Habakkuk 1:11 "wind," 2:19 "breath." It is certain that there is considerable debate among scholars regarding texts (even whether there are *any* texts) that speak properly of the Holy Spirit in the OT. This article is not intended to address such debates but presupposes in the course of God's self-revelation that many things that are obscure in the OT become clearer in the NT and find faithful expression in the confession of the church concerning God's progressive self-revelation in Scripture. The only criterion for inclusion in this article was some sense of possibility (however ambiguous or problematic) of pointing to the person and work of the Spirit in relation to the lexical use of רוח.
5   Including the Aramaic in Daniel 2:35; 4:5–6, 15 (4:8–9, 18 ET); 5:11–12, 14, 20; 6:4 (6:3 ET); 7:2, 15.
6   See Daniel I. Block, "The View from the Top: The Holy Spirit in the Prophets," in David G. Firth and Paul D. Wegner, eds., *Presence, Power, and the Promise: The Role of the Spirit of God in the Old Testament* (Downers Grove, IL: IVP Academic, 2011), 177n10. The Amos (4:13) citation is not discussed here, as it speaks of the creation of the "mountains" and the "wind."
7   4:8–9, 18; 5:11–12, 14; 6:3 ET.
8   Amos Yong, *Mission after Pentecost: The Witness of the Spirit from Genesis to Revelation* (Grand Rapids, MI: Baker Academic, 2019), 139, 141.

"spirit-disturbing" night vision (7:14)[9] Daniel sees "four winds of heaven" (7:2) that stir the waters representing the earth until four creaturely empires have emerged that would at last be overcome by the one "like a son of man" and would have dominion over every kingdom. In other visions of coming kings and kingdoms there are two mentions of the "four winds of heaven" that are the aims of the blaspheming ruler (8:8) who finds his kingdom scattered to the "four winds of heaven" in judgment (11:4). The voice of the Spirit may be heard in the scattering "wind" of judgment (2:35), who has not abandoned plans of final redemption.

3   The Spirit in Hosea

There is a wordplay on רוח throughout the book where the enveloping "wind" of judgment (4:12) will blow against Israel (in the form of the encroaching Assyrian invasion) because of their "spirit of whoredom" (4:19; 5:4).[10] This was the "wind" they had sown and the whirlwind they would reap (8:7). In this "spirit of whoredom" and under this "wind" of judgment, Israel would claim that "a man of the Spirit is a fool" (9:7). This "wind" that Ephraim (Israel) chases after is their very judgment (12:2)[11] all the while they reject the Spirit-ed prophets. Finally, Hosea 13:15 speaks of the east "wind" (likely the *sirocco*) as metaphor of the rising power in the East to bring judgment. These mixing of the metaphoric functions of רוח may themselves not utterly exclude the personal coming of Spirit of Yahweh that will come bearing this judgment.[12]

4   The Spirit in Joel

The prophetic Spirit would be poured out in the Day of Yahweh (3:1–2 MT),[13] bringing about the salvation of all who are called and all who call on the name

---

9   7:15 ET.
10 William C. Williams, "Hosea," in John Christopher Thomas, ed., *The Book of the Twelve* (Pentecostal Commentary Series; Leiden: Brill, 2020), 64–65.
11 12:1 ET.
12 Wilf Hildebrandt, "Spirit of Yahweh," in Mark J. Boda and J. Gordon McConville, eds., *Dictionary of the Old Testament: Prophets* (Downers Grove, IL: IVP Academic, 2012), 751.
13 The verses indicated here are MT chapters/verses that are represented in English translations by Joel 2:28–29, respectively. The most extended treatment of the Spirit in Joel to date is Larry R. McQueen, *Joel and the Spirit: The Cry of a Prophetic Hermeneutic*, JPTSup 8 (Sheffield: Sheffield Academic Press, 1995).

of Yahweh. This inundation and democratization of the experience of the Spirit is a sign of "judgment and salvation" and also includes ethical elements as borne by the Spirit.[14] The reign of Yahweh would be declared and commenced in the midst of this Spirit-filled community whose very nature would be prepared (and preparing) for the fullness of that reign that is testified to on the Day of Pentecost as testimony of its cosmic implications and intent (Acts 2:17–21).[15]

5 The Spirit in Jonah

While Yahweh sends "wind" upon the sea in Jonah 1:4 as a tempest of judgment, it canonically and contrastively calls to mind the creation narrative of the "Spirit" that hovered over the waters of the deep in Genesis 1:2, thereby bringing life.[16] By the end of the Jonah tale, the scorching east "wind" (4:8) is divinely blowing upon Jonah, provoking his longing for the goodness of death and (in his estimation) of the goodness of the death of the Ninevites. Might it be that the divine winds that bear judgment in their scorching heat also bear echoes of the compassion of Yahweh to accomplish the divine will of redemption?

6 The Spirit in Micah

The "Spirit of Yahweh" in Micah 2:7 will not forever tolerate the injustice of the people.[17] Micah testifies to being himself "filled" with both "power" and "with the Spirit of the LORD" (3:8). This seems to function for him as paralleled with "justice" and "might" and signifies his empowerment to set things to rights and bear the message in word and deed of Yahweh's purposes for Yahweh's people.[18]

---

14 Montague, *The Holy Spirit*, 86.
15 Hildebrandt, "Spirit of Yahweh," 754–755, and Yong, *Mission after Pentecost*, 142–44.
16 Lee Roy Martin, "Jonah," in John Christopher Thomas, ed., *The Book of the Twelve*, Pentecostal Commentary Series (Leiden: Brill, 2020), 273–74.
17 Numerous translations seem to utterly obscure the use of רוח in Micah 2:7 (ESV, LEB, NAB, NIV84, NIV2011, NET, NJB, NRSV) and 2:11 (NIV84, NIV2011, NLT, NRSV).
18 For a detailed discussion of this passage see W.J. Wessels, "Empowered by the Spirit of Yahweh: A Study of Micah 3:8," *Journal of Biblical and Pneumatological Research* 1 (2009): 33–47.

7 The Spirit in Haggai

In Haggai, the Spirit is paralleled with the presence of Yahweh in the midst of the community (1:13–14) and is fulfillment of the promise given at the Exodus (2:5). This is how Yahweh will dwell among this people as they seek to rebuild his house. This is the Spirit of Yahweh (2:5) as encouragement and enablement.

8 The Spirit in Zechariah

In Haggai's contemporary, Zechariah, the Spirit is specifically upon the leaders of this returned community (Zech.4:6). John Rea interprets these two leaders as indicative of the Spirit's intent to be poured out upon the wider community.[19] This may be hearing the winds that drive one to see prophetically the Spirit-baptized Spirit-baptizer, High Priest, and Son of David. Though the people have been scattered to the "four winds" (Zech. 2:10 MT),[20] they are not irredeemable (as one would expect of such a phrase), but are specifically to be regathered as Zechariah himself is among such ingathering. It is the "wind" (better translated "Spirit")[21] in the wings of two women bearing away wickedness from the land that brings the cleansing for holiness (Zech.5:9). The four chariots with their horses as "four winds of heaven" (6:5) announce the resting of the "Spirit"[22] in the north (6:8) upon the vindication of judgment and redemption of God's people. It was "in the Spirit of Yahweh" that the prophets of old called hard-hearted and deaf Israel to repentance (7:12). If Yahweh is the one who made the "human spirit" (12:1), Yahweh would be the one to bring to repentance through the outpoured "Spirit of grace and supplication" on the house of David and Jerusalem (12:10). Yahweh would at last remove even the memory of the "unclean spirit" from the land (13:2) through repentance by the outpoured Spirit.[23]

---

19 John Rea, *The Holy Spirit in the Bible: All the Major Passages about the Spirit: A Commentary* (Orlando, FL: Creation House, 1990), 110.
20 Following MT versification. In ET it is Zechariah 2:6.
21 As argued by Hannah Harrington, "Zechariah," in John Christopher Thomas, ed., *The Book of the Twelve*, Pentecostal Commentary Series (Leiden: Brill, 2020), 626.
22 For reading "Spirit" see Harrington, "Zechariah," 630–31, who also notes others who read רוח here as "anger," 631n159, citing specifically Meyers and Meyers in the Anchor Bible commentary series.
23 Montague, *The Holy Spirit*, 88; Harrington, "Zechariah," 584–85.

9 The Spirit in Malachi

The three uses in Malachi 2:15–16 have been read as referring only to a disposition or "the creative, spiritual life given to humans."[24] Such human orientation seems to miss the fluidity of the language of רוח that still seems to draw upon the divine Spirit for whatever elements of faithfulness in covenantal relations may be present, however negligible. The *spirit* is guarded by the *Spirit* (2:16), as the *Spirit* compels to faithfulness and righteousness (2:15).

10 A Constructive Theology of the Spirit in Daniel and The Twelve

There are four potentially constructive theological reflections that seem to emerge from this brief reading of the Spirit in Daniel and The Twelve (though certainly numerous others might also be offered). The first two speak to what the Spirit *does*; the last two speak to who the Spirit *is*. Spirit and wind flow intermingled across these writings, where one reference may speak of the other even if only in hinted whispers or in driving gales. The presence of רוח is felt and witnessed as ever moving but unable to be contained or barely defined except in passing.

First, the Spirit testifies. The witness of the Spirit is always to the God of Israel: who this God *is* and what this God *does* (has done and will do). The Spirit drives, motivates, compels, sends, guards, empowers, sanctifies, and fills. All of these actions speak to the work of the Spirit of Yahweh to bear witness to life in Yahweh *in* and *for* the world. The Spirit is poured out in the direction of the Spirit-baptized, Spirit-baptizer of all people. The in-Spirited Daniel, Joel, Micah, and Zechariah bear witness to the nations (via Israel) concerning Yahweh.

Second, the Spirit judges. Through Daniel the Spirit troubles dreams and interprets them with regard to the nations and Yahweh's sovereignty over all things. In Hosea the whoring spirit of the people and the meaningless winds they chase after are judged by the blowing winds of Yahweh. The Spirit carries away sin and cleanses peoples in Hosea and Zechariah. The Spirit of Yahweh judges between the spirit of holiness and an unclean or troubling spirit (Daniel and Zechariah). This same Spirit also carries, reveals, and confronts with the righteousness, compassion, and loving-kindness of Yahweh as judge in Jonah.

---

24 Larry R. McQueen, "Malachi," in John Christopher Thomas, ed., *The Book of the Twelve*, Pentecostal Commentary Series (Leiden: Brill, 2020), 707.

Third, the Spirit is life. The Spirit of Yahweh is the life of Yahweh in the world. According to Haggai, the community of God's people both exists as at the first covenant at Sinai until the end, as the community made, sustained, and enlivened in every way by the Spirit. The Spirit promised to Israel is the Spirit promised for the redemption of the nations as entering into the life of the God of Israel in Joel and Micah. It is this guarded breath of the God of Israel via Malachi that is in and for and through Israel toward faithfulness and righteousness as the very flourishing of life.

Fourth, the Spirit is gift. In Joel the Spirit is always the freely given gift of the God of Israel as salvation. There is no possessing of the Spirit or taking the Spirit for granted (Malachi), but only reception of the inundating Spirit as ever free flowing gift of God to all who call on Yahweh (Joel). In Daniel, this Spirit is given in ever overflowing, unrestrained abundance to make known the life of the God of Israel for the sake of the world through the redeemed community of the Spirit-filled.

The Spirit in Matthew: Righteousness and Obedience

Blaine Charette

Matthew contains fewer references to the Holy Spirit than is the case with Luke and John, and for that reason the pneumatology of Matthew, along with that of Mark, has received far less discussion.[1] Yet, when attention is directed to those places in the Gospel narrative in which Matthew mentions the Spirit, it is clear that the Spirit of God plays a very important role in Matthew's account. It is also important to note that Matthew refers to the Spirit in ways that are distinctive. For example, among the evangelists only Matthew speaks of the Spirit of God (3:16; 12:28), and Matthew is unique in the NT in referring to the Spirit of the Father (10:20; cf. 12:18). This manner of nuancing the Spirit is analogous to the varied ways in which Matthew describes the kingdom, a concept qualified by such terms as "heaven," "God," "Father," and "Son of Man." This similarity is appropriate, since a further unique feature of the gospel is that Matthew is careful to associate the Spirit of God with the presence of the kingdom of God (cf. 12:28). This discussion will focus on Jesus's own experience of the Spirit, the work of the Spirit in the redemptive (or kingdom) activity of Jesus, and how this activity in continued through the community of the disciples as a result of their own experience of the Spirit. Moreover, since redemption in Matthew

---

[1] In Matthew the term πνεῦμα refers to the Holy Spirit or divine Spirit thirteen times; elsewhere in the Gospel the term is used with reference to the human spirit (twice), and to demonic or unclean spirits (four times). A detailed analysis of Matthew's pneumatology can be found in B. Charette, *Restoring Presence: The Spirit in Matthew's Gospel* (Sheffield: Sheffield Academic, 2000). The following discussion does not seek to summarize that study (apart from taking over the threefold structure of the Spirit and the messianic identify of Jesus, the Spirit and the redemptive work centered in Jesus, and the Spirit in the life of the community of disciples who continue the redemptive work of Jesus), but rather to look at Matthew's theology of the Spirit with fresh eyes. The brief overview provided by G.T. Montague (*Holy Spirit: Growth of a Biblical Tradition* [Peabody, MA: Hendrickson, 1976], 302–10) is still quite instructive as well as, more recently, the chapter on Mark and Matthew in J.T. Carroll, *The Holy Spirit in the New Testament* (Nashville: Abingdon, 2018), 43–55. Certain otherwise helpful studies obscure many of the distinctive features of the individual evangelists by discussing the three Synoptic Gospels together; cf. K. Warrington, "The Synoptic Gospels," in T.J. Burke and K. Warrington, eds., *A Biblical Theology of the Holy Spirit* (Eugene, OR: Cascade, 2014), 84–103; and L.C.S. Holmes, "The Holy Spirit in the Synoptic Gospels," in D. Castelo and K.M. Loyer, eds., *T&T Clark Handbook of Pneumatology* (London: T&T Clark, 2020), 7–15.

is so closely tied to righteousness, the discussion will examine how the work of the Spirit relates to righteousness and to the obedience to God's will that is essential to righteousness.

1   The Spirit and the Identity of Jesus

The first mention of the Holy Spirit in Matthew is at 1:18 with reference to the birth of Jesus. Especially noteworthy is that his birth is described as a γένεσις, literally a "genesis" or "beginning", brought about by the Holy Spirit. This echoes the earlier and only other use of the term in the title of the Gospel (1:1), wherein the narrative is presented as a "book of genesis" centering on Jesus himself. Matthew intends his readers to understand his Gospel as an account of a new beginning through which God accomplishes his purposes for creation. Moreover, this new beginning is realized through the birth of Jesus which is the consequence of Mary being with child from the Holy Spirit. This language is, of course, evocative of OT descriptions of the Spirit's role in creation. Passages such as Gen 1:2; 2:7; Job 26:13; and Ps 33:6 speak of God's רוּחַ ("spirit" or "breath") as the agent bringing life to creation. What Matthew is emphasizing by twice noting that the child born of Mary is from the Holy Spirit (1:18, 20) is that through this child the creative, or re-creative, activity of God is now at work to bring about the renewal of God's creation (cf. 19:28). The birth of Jesus marks a new beginning, inasmuch as God is now active in the present age, through his Spirit and his Son, to bring about restoration and transformation, the essential message of the kingdom, that will result in the full realization of his intentions for creation.

Following the infancy narrative, Matthew next mentions the Holy Spirit in the context of the preaching of John the Baptist. John announces the coming of a person more powerful than himself who "will baptize you in the Holy Spirit and fire" (3:11).[2] The meaning of this baptism is explained in part through reference to the metaphor of winnowing: this coming one will clear his threshing floor, gathering the wheat into the storehouse but burning the chaff with

---

2   Whereas in Mark the coming one will baptize in the Holy Spirit, in Matthew and Luke he will baptize in the Holy Spirit and fire. It is clear from the context that fire signifies judgment. D.W. McManigal (*A Baptism of Judgment in the Fire of the Holy Spirit: John's Eschatological Proclamation in Matthew 3* [New York: Bloomsbury/T&T Clark, 2019], 159), provides a thorough analysis of John's words at 3:11 and argues that Jesus's commitment to obey and experience the judgment of God on the cross fulfills the righteous requirements of the divine will; cf. F.D. Macchia, *Jesus the Spirit Baptizer: Christology in the Light of Pentecost* (Grand Rapids: Eerdmans, 2018), 252–56.

unquenchable fire (3:12). This suggests that an essential aspect of the baptizing activity of this coming one is to effect a separation. The negative image of the chaff's destruction by fire closely aligns to the words of judgment John had spoken against the unrepentant who do not bear good fruit (3:7–10). Conversely, the gathering of the wheat is descriptive of the redemption experienced by those who do repent, are fruitful, and thus are prepared for the coming of the kingdom. To a certain extent, the baptism in the Holy Spirit and fire is descriptive of the entire ministry of Jesus. Those who accept the redemption he offers will experience the creative redemptive activity of the Spirit, whereas those who reject it will experience judgment.

The closest parallel in Matthew to the positive aspect of baptism in the Holy Spirit is found in Jesus's commissioning of his disciples at the conclusion of the Gospel (28:18–20). The risen Jesus charges his disciples to make disciples of all nations by baptizing them into the name of the Father, and of the Son, and of the Holy Spirit and teaching them to obey all that Jesus had commanded. The activity of baptizing into the name of the triune God might appear to express something different from what is suggested by the language of "baptism in the Holy Spirit," due to the additional references to the Father and the Son. However, it is very probable that the same reality is in view. With respect to the Father, it is significant that in the mission discourse of Matthew 10 the disciples are given the assurance that when they are brought before hostile audiences they are not to be concerned about how or what they are to speak because the Spirit of their Father will be speaking through them (10:19–20). Similarly, although Jesus will not be physically present with his disciples beyond this final appearance, he assures them he will be with them until the end of the age (28:20). It is clearly the Spirit who mediates his presence to the disciples.[3] For Matthew, the Spirit unites disciples with both the Father and the Son during the time period between Jesus's resurrection and his return to judge the nations, the very time when his followers are engaged in discipling the nations. In this sense, being baptized in the Holy Spirit is essentially equivalent to being baptized into the name of the Father, Son, and Spirit.[4] The baptism described in the great commission signifies entrance into covenant relationship with the

---

3 Note also the promise of 18:20, which states that where two or three disciples are gathered in the name of Jesus he is among them.

4 Jesus' commissioning of his disciples assumes that they have been baptized in the Holy Spirit. Matthew does not explicitly describe the fulfillment of John's promise within the narrative of Jesus's ministry. The judgment aspect of this baptism (in fire) awaits the eschatological judgment, mentioned frequently in Matthew, but also finds fulfillment in part at the crucifixion of Jesus. Presumably, the positive redemptive aspect of this baptism (in the Holy Spirit) occurs as a consequence of the death and resurrection of Jesus. More on this will be noted later.

triune God, but in functional terms the disciples are now able to carry out this commission in the present because of their own baptism in the Holy Spirit.

Jesus is himself the first to experience this baptism in the Holy Spirit. When John seeks to deter him from submitting to his baptism, Jesus is determined, observing that this action is necessary in order "to fulfill all righteousness" (3:15). This is the first appearance of "righteousness" (δικαιοσύνη) in Matthew, and its association with the baptism of Jesus indicates that this event holds importance for understanding the nature of righteousness in the Gospel.[5] When Jesus submits to John's baptism as an act of obedience, the Spirit of God descends upon him.[6] At that moment a voice from heaven declares, "This is my beloved Son, with whom I am well pleased." This announcement is echoed by the voice of God at the transfiguration (17:5), but even more relevant to understanding the meaning of Jesus's baptism is the similar language found in the Isaiah 42 (vv. 1–4) quotation at 12:18–21. In that passage Jesus is described as fulfilling the role of the servant who is described as the "beloved" (ἀγαπητός) in whom the soul of the Lord is "well pleased" (εὐδοκέω).[7] God promises to put his Spirit upon this servant, who in turn will proclaim justice (κρίσις) to the nations. Ultimately, the servant will bring justice to victory and in his name the nations will hope. The coming of the Spirit upon Jesus at his baptism not only constitutes his messianic anointing but also prepares him to fulfill his mission of taking God's justice or righteousness to the nations. Jesus, of course, does not himself go to the nations. This part of the servant's task is fulfilled by his disciples once they are commissioned by Jesus to baptize and teach obedience to the nations. The disciples are able to undertake that mission because, like Jesus, they also will have been baptized in the Spirit.

Following his baptism, Jesus is led by the Spirit into the wilderness to be tempted by the devil (4:1–11). There he is tested at the level of his faithful obedience as the Son of God. It is noteworthy that the baptism ends with the declaration of the Father that Jesus is the "beloved Son," and the temptation proper begins with the tempter's taunt that he should use to his advantage this filial status. Through each temptation Jesus expresses his commitment to God through trust, obedience, and devoted worship. That Jesus responds to all three

---

[5] Righteousness, a very important concept in Matthew's thought, essentially means acting in accordance with the will of the Father. Note that at 21:32 Jesus describes John as coming in the way of righteousness since he called the people to repentance and obedience.

[6] Matthew is alone among the gospels in using the designation "Spirit of God" (3:16; 12:28). In Mark and John it is "the Spirit" who descends; in Luke it is "the Holy Spirit."

[7] These two terms appear in Matthew only in the contexts of the baptism, the Isaiah quotation, and the transfiguration.

temptations with statements drawn from Deuteronomy 6–8 reveals he is committed to a way of righteousness that Israel (also described as God's son in that section of Deuteronomy) had not adhered to in the past. The close association in Matthew of the baptism and temptation accounts indicates that as a result of the Spirit coming upon Jesus, he is now supported and strengthened in his obedience to the Father.[8] This commitment of Jesus to righteousness and obedience, displayed in these scenes that are preparatory to his ministry, sets the tone for his own activity and the content of his teaching throughout the rest of the Gospel.

2 The Spirit and the Redemptive Activity of Jesus

Although Jesus was born to be king, it is his baptism that constitutes his messianic anointing.[9] Following his baptism he begins to function as the messianic ruler. At the start of his ministry he announces the presence of the kingdom of heaven (4:17) and appropriately carries himself with power and authority. Matthew presents Jesus's kingly authority primarily through teaching, healing, and exorcisms (see the summary statements of 4:23–24 and 9:35–36). Notably, when at 11:2–6 John asks from prison if Jesus is truly the coming one, Jesus answers by directing John's emissaries to the things they hear and see, namely, his teaching and healing activity. Throughout his teaching Jesus emphasizes and summarizes what it is that God wills for his people (cf. 7:12; 22:40; 23:23) and defends the integrity of God's commandments against those religious teachers who, although making a show of righteousness, in fact do harm to the commandments through their teaching and actions (cf. 15:1–9). Matthew presents Jesus as one who, having received his messianic anointing when the Spirit came upon him at his baptism, executes his Spirit anointing by living out and teaching others to follow in the righteousness and obedience that is characteristic of covenant faithfulness. Given this emphasis, it is not surprising that when reference is made to baptism in the Spirit later in the Gospel, in the context of the Great Commission, it is associated with obedience to Jesus's commandments.

---

8 Mark also links the temptation to the baptism but does not include the series of exchanges between Satan and Jesus. Luke does include the three temptations, with their Deuteronomic references, but separates the temptation from the baptism by inserting the genealogy of Jesus and thus weakens the connection between the two narratives.

9 In the infancy account, Jesus is brought into the Davidic line (1:20–23), identified as the king of the Jews (2:2), and born in Bethlehem with its royal associations (2:4–6).

Jesus's commitment to covenant faithfulness identifies him with the OT prophets. Matthew is careful to note that virtually every aspect of Jesus's life and work corresponds to what had been written in the prophets. A continual refrain of the Gospel is that significant events "fulfill what had been spoken" through various prophets (cf. 1:22; 2:5, 15, 17, 23; 4:14; 8:17; 12:17; 13:35; 21:4; 26:56). This linking of prophetic expectation and messianic fulfillment, along with Jesus's commitment to upholding righteousness, is key to the way in which Jesus fulfills both the Torah and the Prophets (5:17). Yet Jesus not only fulfills prophecy; as a person of the Spirit he comes to be regarded as a prophet (16:14; 21:11, 46), and along with that recognition he faces the typical antagonism that all too often was the circumstance of the prophet in Israel (13:57). An important theme in Matthew is that of the persecution and killing of the prophets, which previews the fate of Jesus himself.

It is in the context of preparing his disciples for such persecution, disciples whom he also identifies as prophets (5:12; 23:34), that Jesus makes a remarkable observation concerning the activity of the Spirit on such occasions.[10] They will be handed over to councils, scourged in synagogues, and brought before governors and kings (10:17–18).[11] At such times they are not to worry about how they are to speak or what they are to say, since what they are to say will be given to them in that hour. It will not be they who speak, but "the Spirit of your Father" will speak through them (10:19–20).[12] Although perhaps not recognized as prophets by those who oppose them, the disciples will function as prophets speaking the words directed by the Spirit of the Father.[13] They are to discern what the Spirit wishes to speak through them and in this way bear witness to

---

10   Characteristic of Matthew, the prophet and the righteous person are presented as associated figures (10:41; 13:17; 23:29). For Matthew the prophet serves as a representative and advocate of covenantal righteousness. C. Keener (*Gift & Giver: The Holy Spirit for Today* [Grand Rapids: Baker, 2001], 153) notes that during the Second Temple period the two most frequent emphases among Jewish groups concerning the Spirit were the Spirit of purification and the Spirit of prophecy. In Jesus's teaching in Matthew (cf. 15:1–20; 23:25–28), purification, properly understood, is subsumed under the broader category of righteousness.

11   The description of persecution in 10:16–23 anticipates what is stated in 23:34 and also matches the account of Jesus's own passion.

12   There are parallels to this statement at Mark 13:11, in the context of the eschatological discourse, and at Luke 12:11–12, where it is linked to the saying about blasphemy against the Holy Spirit (12:10). In those gospels it is the "Holy Spirit" who speaks (Mark) or who teaches them what to say (Luke). Matthew is unique in this reference to "the Spirit of the Father."

13   The role of the Spirit in prophetic speech is also evident at 22:42–45 when Jesus bases his interpretation of Psalm 110:1 (that the Christ, as David's Lord, is clearly greater than what is denoted by the description "son of David") on what David had said "in the Spirit."

the nations.[14] It was noted earlier that Jesus, as the anointed servant of the Lord, will bring justice and hope to the nations. In a comparable manner the disciples, inspired by the Spirit, witness to the nations. This prophetic role of the disciples is seen clearly at the close of Matthew's Gospel when they, having now been baptized in the name of the Father, Son, and Spirit, make disciples of all nations and thus extend righteousness and obedience to all peoples.

The temptation episode following Jesus's baptism describes his encounter with the devil, yet he most forcefully confronts the power of evil through his exorcisms. The public ministry of Jesus is characterized by several occasions of Jesus casting out spirits or demons (for example, 8:16; 8:28–34; 15:22–28; 17:14–18). Of special interest are two scenes, when Jesus first casts a demon out of a man who was mute (9:32–34) and then out of a man who was both blind and mute (12:22–24). Both times the Pharisees attribute Jesus's power to cast out demons to Beelzebul, the ruler of demons. In the latter episode this accusation leads Jesus to question their argument, since it suggests that Satan is divided against himself; yet, more importantly, he makes the extraordinary claim that since he casts out demons by "the Spirit of God," then the kingdom of God has come to them (12:28). Only Matthew so closely associates the activity of the Spirit with the presence of the kingdom. The power of God's Spirit at work through Jesus in redeeming people from the demonic is for Matthew the clearest and strongest evidence for the presence of the kingdom.

As forceful demonstrations of God's redemptive activity, Jesus challenges his opponents to accept his exorcisms as originating from the Spirit of God and as effective signs that God is now at work establishing his redemptive rule. To reject what God is doing in their midst and, even worse, to continue to attribute this work of the Spirit of God to Satan is to speak against or to blaspheme the Holy Spirit (12:31–32). The consequence of holding this position is to place oneself outside of the context of forgiveness, since what they are rejecting is nothing other than the forgiving work of God. Their rejection and denunciation of God's redemption identifies them as bad trees producing evil fruit (12:33–37) and thus clearly those who have no place in the kingdom.

3 The Transfer of the Spirit to Disciples in Matthew

Jesus's words at 10:19–20 and 28:19–20 anticipate a time in the future when the disciples have been baptized in the Holy Spirit. Matthew does not explicitly

---

14 Note the emphasis in Matthew's eschatological discourse, that even though the followers of Jesus will be handed over and put to death, nonetheless the good news of the kingdom will be proclaimed as a witness to the nations (24:9–14).

describe when this baptism occurs, but there is evidence within the Gospel narrative to suggest that it occurs as a consequence of Jesus's death. The death of Jesus, of course, holds great redemptive significance for Matthew. The question to be considered here is whether the Spirit, who plays such a major role in the redemptive work of Jesus, features in the account of Jesus's death. Of particular interest is the unique manner in which Matthew describes the moment of Jesus's death (27:50–53). When describing Jesus's last breath, Matthew uses the unique expression "he let go the S/spirit" (ἀφῆκεν τὸ πνεῦμα).[15] This reference to τὸ πνεῦμα is commonly understood to refer to the life spirit within Jesus that he gives up at death, yet presumably Matthew intends more by this language and wishes to suggest the Spirit of God.[16] Matthew indicates more than simply that Jesus had died. He wants to affirm, albeit in an understated and indirect way, that at the death of Jesus the same Spirit that had defined and empowered his life and ministry is now "released" by him at the very moment that marks the culmination of his messianic work.

This interpretation is supported by the remarkable sequence of events that Matthew associates with the death of Jesus. The curtain of the temple is torn in two, an earthquake occurs, and tombs are opened from which will appear raised saints following Jesus's resurrection. One implication of this series of astonishing scenes, each of which holds significant theological meaning, is that an extraordinary power breaks forth at the moment of Jesus's death. The eschatological Spirit that had come upon him at his baptism is now discharged to both complete and continue the redemptive purpose of his death. Implicit in this movement of the Spirit is that the creative and redemptive power of the Spirit is now available to the followers of Jesus so they can continue every aspect of his messianic work under his authority to the end of the age. The community of disciples, now baptized into the name of the Father, and of the Son, and of the Holy Spirit, becomes the means by which the righteousness of God and obedience to the commands of Jesus are testified among the nations.

---

15   Matthew's wording is not dissimilar to that of John 19:30, which states, "he handed over the S/spirit" (παρέδωκεν τὸ πνεῦμα), which is often interpreted in terms of Jesus handing over the Spirit at the moment of his death.

16   When referring to the Spirit, Matthew at times uses anarthrous constructions; at other times he uses the article with some qualifier; yet at 4:1 (as at 27:50) he uses the articular form without any qualification, which clearly refers to the Spirit of God who comes upon Jesus at his baptism. For a fuller account of the Spirit and the death of Jesus, see Charette, *Restoring Presence*, 92–96.

The Spirit in Mark: Power and Suffering

Blaine Charette

There are fewer direct references to the Holy Spirit in Mark's Gospel than in the other Gospels.[1] For this reason, there has been much less discussion of the significance of the Spirit to Mark's theology in comparison with other gospels, particularly Luke and John.[2] Yet in the case of Mark it is not helpful or appropriate to assess the importance of this subject based merely on the frequency of use of certain key terms. Of greater importance is the placement of references to the Spirit within the narrative structure of the Gospel and the manner in which the Spirit is brought into relation to other themes and topics that are central to the interests of the Gospel. For example, there are three references to the Spirit in the opening section of Mark (1:8, 10, 12), in which Jesus is introduced to the reader, indicating the importance of the Spirit for understanding the identity of Jesus and the nature of his mission. Of particular interest to this discussion is Mark's linking of the Spirit with power and authority, which is demonstrated in various ways, but ultimately the Spirit's association with the suffering of both Jesus and his disciples.

1   The Spirit in the Introduction to Jesus

The Gospel of Mark begins with the declaration that it addresses the beginning of the good news centered in Jesus, who is both Christ and Son of God. (1:1) The term "good news" (εὐαγγέλιον) forms a bracket around the prologue to Mark (1:2–13), as can be seen in the transitional statement at 1:14–15 that expands on the meaning of the good news: it is the good news of God and it signifies the coming of the kingdom of God. Jesus, as Christ, is the anointed one (who will also anoint others) and also the Son of God, who as a representative figure becomes the primary agent of the redemptive activity that defines the kingdom of God.

---

1   In Mark the term πνεῦμα refers to the Holy Spirit or divine Spirit six times; elsewhere in the Gospel the term is used with reference to "unclean" spirits (fourteen times), Jesus's own spirit (twice), or the human spirit (once).

2   The fullest study of the Spirit in Mark's Gospel is M.R. Mansfield, *"Spirit and Gospel" in Mark* (Peabody, MA: Hendrickson, 1987), which interprets the teaching in Mark on the Spirit as serving the purpose of bringing balance and correction to problematic charismatic activity that had neglected elements central to the gospel message, particularly suffering.

Before Mark describes the anointing of Jesus, which occurs at his baptism, John "the baptizer" makes an important promise, in fact the very first promise about Jesus in the Gospel. Someone more powerful is coming after John who will effect a more profound baptism. John himself has baptized the people in water, but of this coming one he asserts that "he will baptize you in the Holy Spirit" (1:8). By giving this promise a position of priority within the narrative, Mark underscores its importance. As the defining statement of what Jesus as this powerful eschatological figure will do for others, this promise creates expectation within the Gospel as to what this baptism in the Holy Spirit means and how and when it is fulfilled. Since the narrative does not provide straightforward answers to these questions, the reader of Mark must attend closely to the narrative clues within Mark to fully understand the meaning of the promise. It should also be noted that this promise that others will be baptized by Jesus, presumably to continue the anointed work he begins, adds a further dimension to the opening word of the Gospel, namely that it concerns the "beginning" (ἀρχή) of the good news. Jesus's activity, reported throughout Mark's account, signifies only the beginning of God's redemptive work, which will continue through the activity of those whom he baptizes. It is not only Jesus who comes after John, but also a powerful movement proclaiming the kingdom of God.

The baptism of Jesus is described in a brief and extraordinary manner. As he comes up out of the water, the heavens are "split apart" (1:10: σχίζω), and the Spirit descends on him. The splitting of the heavens allows for the descent of the Spirit, yet the forceful image is also suggestive of the Spirit of God bursting forth into the present age. Jesus now becomes the powerful figure of John's description. This splitting apart of the heavens holds further significance in view of the fact that the only other time Mark uses the verb σχίζω is in the context of the splitting in two of the temple curtain at the moment of Jesus's death.[3] It would appear that through the repetition of this striking term Mark is seeking to link the baptism and death of Jesus. The two events do, of course, bracket the ministry of Jesus, but more to the point, they are probably intended to shed light on each other with respect to Mark's theology of the Spirit. More will be said on this matter when the topic of Jesus's death is discussed. At this point it is sufficient to note that the baptism of Jesus is described in a manner that intimates, albeit subtly, the event of his death.

---

3 Both Matthew and Luke use σχίζω when describing the tearing of the temple curtain, but in their descriptions of the baptism they use the verb ἀνοίγω, the heavens were "opened."

In their descriptions of the descent of the Spirit, Matthew (3:16) and Luke (3:22) refer to the Spirit coming "upon" Jesus (ἐπ' αὐτόν). Mark, in keeping with the more dramatic manner in which he describes the baptism, portrays the Spirit as coming "into" Jesus (1:10: εἰς αὐτόν). The use of the preposition εἰς gives further emphasis to the overpowering nature of the experience.[4] Mark uses εἰς in the previous verse to describe the immersive character of Jesus's baptism in the Jordan. That now finds its complement in the corresponding immersive character of Jesus's experience of the Spirit. The Spirit breaks forth from heaven to earth or, to give the event a fuller eschatological meaning, from the future into the present, and profoundly enters into Jesus. The preposition denotes the interior dimension of the work of the Spirit in transforming and endowing Jesus so he can effectively carry out his messianic task. Through the power of the Spirit Jesus is now prepared to act as the powerful eschatological agent who will accomplish God's purpose. As expressed by the voice of God, which concludes the scene of the baptism, Jesus is the beloved Son who now enjoys the good pleasure of the Father.

The baptism of Jesus is closely connected to Mark's account of Jesus's temptation in the wilderness.[5] The Spirit, which had just entered into Jesus, now drives him out into the wilderness, where he is tempted by Satan for a period of forty days. In representing the Spirit as "casting out" (ἐκβάλλω) Jesus, Mark once again draws on language that is quite striking and evocative. Elsewhere in the Gospel the verb ἐκβάλλω is used in contexts of casting out demons or unclean spirits and essentially functions as a technical term for exorcisms.[6] It would seem that Mark, through the use of this term, seeks to establish a connection between the temptation narrative and the later reports of Jesus exercising authority over unclean spirits. This finds support in the exchange between Jesus and the scribes from Jerusalem at 3:22–30. When the scribes charge Jesus with casting out demons by the authority of Beelzebul, the ruler of demons, he counters by arguing the absurdity of Satan casting out Satan, since it would undermine his effectiveness, and telling the parable of the binding of the strong man. If someone is to take what the strong man holds, that

---

4 In view of Mark's penchant for dynamic expression, it seems best to read the phrase more forcefully, notwithstanding the argument of J. Marcus (*Mark 1–8*, AB [Doubleday: New York, 2000], 60), that in Koine Greek εἰς with the accusative can be equivalent to ἐπι with the accusative.

5 The simple and terse transition "and immediately" (καὶ εὐθὺς) marks the shift from the baptism to the temptation.

6 The verb ἐκβάλλω appears sixteen times in Mark, ten times with reference to exorcisms. In other places the term can be used, as here, with dramatic and even ironic import as when at 11:15 Jesus "casts out" those who were selling and buying in the temple.

person must first bind the strong man. It is probable that this illustration of the binding of the strong man represents what happened when Jesus, in the power of the Spirit, confronted Satan in the wilderness. It is noteworthy that Satan in the parable is characterized as a "strong man" (ἰσχυρός); the only other time the term is used in Mark is at 1:7, where the comparative form "stronger" (ἰσχυρότερός) describes Jesus as the one coming after John who is more powerful. Jesus is more powerful than Satan, because of the Spirit within him, and is therefore able to cast out Satan. The temptation event best describes the occasion when Jesus demonstrates his power over Satan, thus binding him and making possible the exorcisms by which Jesus releases those whom Satan had seized.

2   The Spirit and the Work of Redemption

Following the baptism of Jesus, the Gospel of Mark provides numerous examples of the power and authority at work through Jesus as a consequence of his experience of the Spirit. In addition to frequent references to Jesus's authority over unclean spirits and demons (1:23–27; 1:32–34; 1:39; 3:11; 5:2–13; 7:26–30; 9:25–27), he also teaches with authority (1:22) and even has authority to forgive sins (2:10). Jesus repeatedly demonstrates his power to heal (1:30–34; 1:40–42; 2:3–12; 3:1–5; 3:10; 5:25–34; 6:2, 5; 7:32–35; 8:22–26; 10:46–52) and even to raise the dead (5:38–43). The connection between these demonstrations of authority and power and Jesus's experience of the Spirit is corroborated by the scene at 6:1–6, which recounts the response of the people of his hometown to his teaching in the synagogue. They are astonished and provoked to ask: "Whence did this man get these things?"; "What is this wisdom given to him?"; "How is it that such powers are done through his hands?" They know Jesus merely as the carpenter who had once lived among them. It is significant they should ask about the source of his wisdom and power. The Jesus they now see is surprisingly different from the Jesus they had known earlier before his baptism. The difference, of course, is that the Spirit is now operating through him in a manner they had not witnessed before.

An additional passage that links Jesus's authority with the experience of his baptism is the dialogue in the temple between Jesus and the chief priests, scribes, and elders at 11:27–33. Like the people of Nazareth, they ask about the source of Jesus's authority: "By what authority do you do these things?" and "Who gave you this authority to do these things?" Jesus responds with the question: "Was the baptism of John of divine or human authority?" They refuse to answer, wishing neither to acknowledge John as a prophet authorized by God nor to deny him that authority for fear of the crowd. Jesus, therefore, refuses to answer their question about the source of his authority. This exchange implies the divine source of the authority of both John and Jesus, yet more to the point it identifies John's baptism as the occasion of Jesus receiving his own remarkable authority. The Holy Spirit that had entered him at the time of his baptism by John is the source of his authority and what distinguishes his activity.

As noted earlier, central to the redemptive activity of Jesus in Mark's account are his exorcisms. He confronts Satan immediately following his baptism, and his messianic authority is often shown through these acts of deliverance. Mark describes the spiritual entities that negatively affect humans as "demons" (δαιμόνιον), or more characteristically as "unclean spirits" (πνεῦμα modified by ἀκάθαρτος).[7] Those possessed by such spirits can be described as "demonized" (δαιμονίζομαι; 1:32; 5:15, 16, 18) or as "having" (ἔχω) an unclean spirit (7:25; cf. 3:30; 9:17). Of special interest, and unique to Mark, is the description of a person being "in an unclean spirit" (ἐν πνεύματι ἀκαθάρτῳ). This language is used both for the man at the synagogue in Capernaum (1:23) and for the Gerasene demoniac (5:2). The description is quite evocative and reveals an important feature of Mark's understanding not only of demonic possession but also of the experience of the Holy Spirit.

The prepositional phrase "in an unclean spirit" indicates that the unclean spirit is the sphere or reality in which the person exists and that now influences and directs them.[8] They are not only possessed by the spirit but function within the structures of the unclean spirit. This explains why the speech of the demon possessed often alternates between the plural "us" and the singular "I" and why the demonized often show remarkable insight regarding the identity of Jesus (cf. 1:21–28; 5:1–20).[9] It is noteworthy that this description of demonized people closely parallels two references to the Holy Spirit in Mark. John the Baptist at

---

[7] The two terms each occur eleven times in Mark and should be seen as synonymous, since at times they are used interchangeably. Both terms are also used by Matthew and Luke, yet Mark is distinctive in his frequent use of "unclean spirits." On the role of the Spirit in Jesus's conflict with opposition, both demonic and human, see G.M. Barnhill, "Jesus as Spirit-Filled Warrior and Mark's Functional Pneumatology," *CBQ* 82 (2020): 605–27.

[8] M.E. Boring (*Mark: A Commentary*, NTL [Louisville: Westminster/John Knox, 2006], 62) observes that to Mark's Hellenistic audience the phrase "would suggest that the man is actually engulfed in the demonic power of evil."

[9] For a discussion of insight and perception as a property of "spirit" in Mark, see B. Charette, "Insight as a Characteristic of S/spirit in the Gospel of Mark," in R. Herms, J.R. Levison, and A.T. Wright, eds., *The Spirit Says: Inspiration and Interpretation in Israelite, Jewish, and Early Christian Texts* (Berlin: De Gruyter, 2021), 21–38.

1:8 refers to the coming one who will baptize "in the Holy Spirit" (ἐν πνεύματι ἁγίῳ); later at 12:36 Jesus describes David as being "in the Holy Spirit" (ἐν τῷ πνεύματι τῷ ἁγίῳ) when he speaks the words of Psalm 110:1. In these contexts, the one who is baptized in the Spirit and the one who makes a critical declaration by means of the Spirit operate within the sphere of the Spirit. The one who is baptized in the Spirit functions to a significant degree under the direction of the Spirit just as David's words are not merely his own but are given to him by the Spirit. Likewise, in the case of those who are demon possessed, although they are the ones who speak, it is evident that the insights they declare are due to the influence of the unclean spirits. The perception they show is a result of their possession by the demonic in whose sphere they exist.

Mark's detailed description of the influence of both unclean spirits and the Holy Spirit imparts great significance to Jesus's warning about blasphemy against the Holy Spirit at 3:28–30, which marks the culmination of his exchange with the scribes from Jerusalem who attribute his exorcisms to Satan and who also denounce him as one possessed by an unclean spirit. To blaspheme against the Spirit in this context is to refuse to acknowledge that the redemptive activity of Jesus, evident in his exorcisms, is done through the power of the Holy Spirit within the sphere of divine authority. To perversely characterize such holy activity as the work of Beelzebul and of an unclean spirit makes one guilty of an eternal sin that places one beyond the forgiveness that is also key to the work of God's Spirit.

This adverse speech act of uttering blasphemies against the Holy Spirit stands in marked contrast to the constructive speech inspired by the Holy Spirit, which finds expression in the final two references to the Spirit in Mark. As noted earlier, David at 12:36 is depicted as speaking "in the Holy Spirit" when, in the words of Psalm 110:1, he declares that his Lord is invited to sit at the right hand of the Lord, indicating that the Christ, whom David refers to as his Lord, is much greater than David, thus qualifying the meaning of the term "son of David."[10] Inspired speech is also in view in Jesus's instruction to his disciples at 13:11. Looking to the future, when the disciples will persecuted on account of his name, and presumably anticipating a time when they will have been baptized in the Spirit, he counsels them that when brought to trial they are not to worry about what to say since it will be given to them in that hour. They will not be speaking but rather the Holy Spirit will speak through them. They will speak as

---

10   A thorough analysis of this passage, which focuses on Jesus as the Spirit-empowered interpreter of Scripture, can be found in E.B. Powery, "The Spirit, the Scripture(s), and the Gospel of Mark: Pneumatology and Hermeneutics in Narrative Perspective," *JPT* 11 (2003): 184–98.

those influenced and informed by the Holy Spirit. It is clear that as the disciples continue the redemptive activity begun by Jesus, they will do so as people operating, as he had done, within the sphere of the Spirit.

3   The Transfer of the Spirit in Mark

It was noted that the first promise made about Jesus in Mark is that he will baptize others in the Holy Spirit. Jesus is best understood as the paradigm of what baptism in the Holy Spirit means since it is following his own baptism that the Spirit begins to motivate and distinguish his ministry. Yet the Gospel does not plainly indicate how or when Jesus fulfills this promise of extending his experience of the Spirit to others. Jesus's directive to his disciples at 13:11 assumes a future in which they have undergone such a baptism, but the circumstances of the event are not stated. Even so, there are clues within the narrative suggesting that disciples receive the Spirit as a consequence of Jesus's death and, more specifically, as a result of their own personal immersion in the meaning of his death. It is often noted that the disciples in Mark are slow to understand Jesus's messianic identity and unwilling to accept his inevitable suffering and death. This resistance must be overcome before they can truly know Jesus and follow him in an appropriate and consistent manner.

It is significant that following the third and final passion prediction, when James and John request positions of authority, Jesus asks them if they are able to drink the cup that he drinks and to be baptized with the baptism with which he is baptized (10:36–40). It is probable that the metaphors of "cup" and "baptism" refer to the sufferings that await Jesus in Jerusalem.[11] The metaphor of baptism is especially suggestive, since the term is used elsewhere in Mark only with reference to the baptism of John or to the Spirit-baptizing activity of the one who comes after John. It is also significant that Jesus would use the language of baptism with reference to his death since it draws attention to the immersive nature of the experience.[12] When Jesus further states that James and John will indeed drink his cup and be baptized with his baptism, his words suggest that

---

11   With respect to the cup metaphor, two subsequent passages in Mark link the cup to Jesus's death. In the context of Jesus's final Passover meal with his disciples, he identifies the cup with his blood poured out for many (14:23–25); at Gethsemane, following the meal, Jesus asks the Father to remove "this cup" from him (14:36), which in the context of the distress he is experiencing undoubtedly refers to his imminent death.
12   The closest parallel to this use of the baptism metaphor is Jesus's statement at Luke 12:50, "I have a baptism with which to be baptized and how pressed upon I am until it is completed," which almost certainly alludes to his death.

they must fully participate in and actualize for themselves the meaning of his death. They are not only to be beneficiaries of the consequences of his death but are to join with him in suffering and death.

The actual description of Jesus's death in Mark, specifically that he "expired" (15:37, 39: ἐξέπνευσεν), is also relevant to the transfer of the Spirit from Jesus to others and may reflect an additional link to Jesus's baptism. Mark states twice that Jesus "expired," employing the verb ἐκπνέω as a framing device enveloping the description of the splitting of the temple veil. Mark's creative use of this literary device, along with the double use of the verb σχίζω, suggests that the baptism and death of Jesus interpret each other. As such, the description of Jesus's death signifies more than Jesus simply "breathing his last," but rather is suggestive of the Spirit going out from him.[13] The connection Mark seeks to draw between the baptism and death of Jesus supports this interpretation inasmuch as at his baptism the Spirit comes "into" Jesus (1:10: εἰς αὐτόν), whereas now at his death the Spirit goes out from him. The use of the compound verb ἐκπνέω, which denotes breath or spirit going out from Jesus, serves to balance and complement the Spirit's entrance into Jesus at his baptism. As a consequence of his death, the Spirit goes from him in order that his followers may now be baptized in the same Spirit. The motivating power of the Spirit in Jesus is unmistakable throughout his ministry, but now that the most crucial aspect of the messianic mission is accomplished through his death, the Spirit is able to proceed from him to others. As a result of Jesus's death, his followers receive the experience of baptism in the Holy Spirit, which now empowers them to participate fully in the continuation of the messianic mission, yet in a manner made more meaningful through their own identification with and immersion into his death.

---

13   For a similar argument that ἐξέπνευσεν contains an allusion to the gift of the Spirit, see J.E. Aguilar Chiu, "A Theological Reading of ἐξέπνευσεν in Mark 15:37, 39," CBQ 78 (2016): 682–705.

The Spirit in Luke-Acts: Empowering Prophetic Witness

Robert P. Menzies

The name "pentecostal" flows from the book of Acts, and for good reason. The pentecostal movement was inspired by a fresh appraisal of Luke-Acts. It is precisely here, in Luke-Acts, where we find the distinctive message of this dynamic movement. From the earliest days of the modern pentecostal revival, Pentecostals have proclaimed that all Christians may, and indeed should, experience a baptism in the Holy Spirit "distinct from and subsequent to the experience of new birth."[1] This understanding of Spirit baptism is rooted in the conviction that the Spirit came upon the disciples at Pentecost (Acts 2), not as the source of new covenant existence, but rather as the source of power for effective ministry. This understanding of Spirit baptism has given the modern pentecostal movement its identity, its unifying experience, and its missiological focus.

Despite its uniqueness, the pentecostal movement did not emerge in a vacuum. The pentecostal movement is rooted in a foundational theological insight, admittedly not always consciously acknowledged or clearly expressed, that had just begun to find articulation toward the end of the nineteenth century. That insight, which we shall defend in this short essay, is this: a thorough study of Luke-Acts and the rest of the New Testament reveals that there was development in the early church's understanding of the Spirit's work.[2] The key point for our study is the recognition that Luke's theology of the Spirit is *different* from that of Paul. Unlike Paul, who frequently speaks of the soteriological dimension of the Spirit's work, Luke consistently portrays the Spirit as a charismatic or, more precisely, a prophetic gift, the source of power for service. This thesis was forcefully advanced by Hermann Gunkel in 1888 and asserted in different ways in the years that followed by R.A. Torrey, Eduard Schweizer, Gonzalo Haya-Prats, and Roger Stronstad, among others.[3] So, with this thesis in mind, let us examine Luke's two-volume work.

---

1 *Minutes of the 44th Session of the General Council of the Assemblies of God* (Portland, OR: August 6–11, 1991), 129.
2 Robert P. Menzies, *The Development of Early Christian Pneumatology with Special Reference to Luke-Acts* (Sheffield: JSPT, 1991). Here I argue that Paul was the first Christian to attribute soteriological functions to the Spirit and that his distinctive insights did not impact the non-Pauline sectors of the early church until after the writing of Luke-Acts.
3 Hermann Gunkel, *The Influence of the Holy Spirit: The Popular View of the Apostolic Age and*

Before we proceed, however, a word regarding definitions will be helpful. In the pages that follow I will argue that Luke consistently presents the gift of the Spirit as a prophetic enabling that empowers its recipient for participation in the mission of God. In Luke's view, the Spirit is "the Spirit of [God's] redeeming love, active in [believers] toward others."[4] The primary manifestations of this prophetic enabling that may be traced throughout Luke-Acts are charismatic wisdom and inspired speech.[5] Since my purpose is, at least in part, to compare Luke with Paul so that Luke's distinctive theological insights might be fully appreciated and ultimately integrated into a holistic biblical theology of the Spirit, my definition of "soteriological" must be understood in relation to Paul's theology and language. Paul presents the Spirit as: mediating the blessings of Christ (1 Cor 6:11), the necessary and defining element of Christian life (Rom 8:9), the source of our filial relationship with God (Rom 8:15–16), new covenant existence (2 Cor 3), and ultimately, the resurrection of our bodies (1 Cor 15:42–49). All of these theological affirmations are lacking in Luke-Acts and conflict with Luke's narrative at various points (Luke 11:13; Acts 8:16, 19:2). I firmly believe that the insights of Luke and Paul are theologically compatible and, indeed, complementary, but only when we let Luke be Luke and read him on his own terms. Legitimate diversity within the New Testament canon must be acknowledged if we are to hear the full richness of the New Testament witness.[6]

1   Jesus and the Spirit

Throughout his two-volume work, Luke consistently portrays the gift of the Spirit as a prophetic enabling.[7] Whether it is John in his mother's womb, Jesus

---

  the Teaching of the Apostle Paul, trans. R.A. Harrisville and P.A. Quanbeck II (Philadelphia: Fortress Press, 1979; German orig., 1888); R.A. Torrey, The Baptism with the Holy Spirit (Minneapolis: Bethany Fellowship, 1972; orig. 1895); Eduard Schweizer, "πνεῦμα," TDNT VI, 389–455; Gonzalo Haya-Prats, Empowered Believers: The Holy Spirit in the Book of Acts, trans. Scott Ellington; ed. Paul Elbert (Eugene, OR: Cascade, 2011; Spanish orig., 1967); Roger Stronstad, The Charismatic Theology of St. Luke (Peabody, MA: Hendrickson, 1984).

4 Roland Allen, "The Revelation of the Holy Spirit in the Acts of the Apostles," IRM 7, no. 2 (1918): 167.

5 As we shall see, Luke also *cautiously* relates miracles of healing, exorcism, and marvelous deeds to the Spirit. Cf. W. and R. Menzies, Spirit and Power: Foundations of Pentecostal Experience (Grand Rapids: Zondervan, 2000), 145–158.

6 Youngmo Cho, Spirit and Kingdom in the Writings of Luke and Paul: An Attempt to Reconcile These Concepts (Milton Keynes: Paternoster, 2005).

7 Craig Keener offers a similar assessment, though he suggests that Luke 3:16 might be the sole exception (The Spirit in the Gospels and Acts: Divine Purity and Power [Peabody, MA: Hendrickson, 1997], 190).

at the Jordan, or the disciples at Pentecost, the Spirit comes upon them all as the source of prophetic inspiration, granting special insight and inspiring speech. This should not surprise us since the literature of intertestamental Judaism also closely identifies the Spirit with prophetic inspiration.[8]

From the very outset of his two-volume work, Luke emphasizes the prophetic dimension of the Spirit's activity. The profusion of Spirit-inspired pronouncements in the infancy narratives herald the arrival of the era of fulfillment (Luke 1:41–45, 67–79; 2:25–32). A host of pious figures declare the wonders of God in language that anticipates Pentecost (Luke 1:46–47; Acts 2:11, 26): Elizabeth, Zechariah, Mary, Simeon, and Anna all declare that the fulfillment of God's glorious promises is at hand. Each of these figures speaks under the inspiration of the Spirit, with the sole exception of the prophetess Anna, whose specific words are not recorded.[9] Filled with the Spirit from his mother's womb (Luke 1:15, 17), John, too, anticipates the inauguration of Jesus's ministry.

1.1   *John the Baptist's Prophecy (Luke 3:16–17)*

John the Baptist's prophecy concerning the one who will baptize in Spirit and fire, recorded in Luke 3:16–17, is particularly important for our study:

> John answered them all, "I baptize you with water. But one more powerful than I will come, the thongs of whose sandals I am not worthy to untie. He will baptize you with the Holy Spirit and fire. His winnowing fork is in his hand to clear his threshing floor and to gather the wheat into his barn, but he will burn up the chaff with unquenchable fire."[10]
>
> Luke 3:16–17

The interpretation of this prophecy—specifically, the functions it attributes to the Spirit—is crucial, for Luke clearly sees this prophecy at least partially fulfilled at Pentecost in the disciples' baptism in the Spirit (Acts 1:4–5). James Dunn speaks for many when he states that the prophecy presents that Spirit as "purgative and refining for those who had repented, destructive … for those who remained impenitent."[11] However, I believe this interpretation must be

---

8   This is the dominant perspective. The only exceptions are found in sapiential writings and are rare (Menzies, *Development*, 52–112).

9   Mary's Magnificat (Luke 1:46–55) is not explicitly attributed to the inspiration of the Spirit because the reader has already been informed of the Spirit's presence in her life (Luke 1:35).

10   All English Scripture citations are taken from the NIV unless otherwise noted.

11   James Dunn, *Baptism in the Holy Spirit* (London: SCM Press, 1970), 13. So also J. Kienzler, *The*

rejected in light of the Jewish background, the immediate context with its winnowing metaphor, and the larger context of Luke-Acts.

The Jewish background is particularly instructive. There are no pre-Christian references to a messianic bestowal of the Spirit that purifies and transforms *the individual*. However, there is a wealth of passages that describe the Messiah as charismatically endowed with the Spirit of God so that he may rule and judge (for example, *1 En* 49:3; 62:2). Isaiah 4:4 refers to the Spirit of God as the means by which the nation of Israel (not individuals) shall be sifted, with the righteous being separated from the wicked and the nation thus cleansed. Several texts tie these two concepts together. Perhaps most striking is *Psalms of Solomon* 17:26–37, a passage that describes how the Messiah, "powerful in the Holy Spirit" (17:37), shall purify Israel by ejecting all aliens and sinners from the nation. Isaiah 11:2–4 declares that the Spirit-empowered Messiah will slay the wicked "with the breath [*ruach*] of his lips."[12] Against this background it is not difficult to envision the Spirit of God as an instrument employed by the Messiah to sift and cleanse the nation. Indeed, these texts suggest that when John referred in metaphorical language to the messianic deluge of the Spirit, he had in mind Spirit-inspired oracles of judgment uttered by the Messiah (cf. Isa 11:4), blasts of the Spirit that would separate the wheat from the chaff.

Luke, writing in light of Pentecost, sees the fuller picture and applies the prophecy to the Spirit-inspired witness of the early church (Acts 1:4–5).[13] Through their witness, the wheat is separated from the chaff (Luke 3:17). This interpretation is reinforced by the winnowing metaphor, which portrays the wind as the source of sifting. Since the term translated "wind" in Greek (*pneuma*) and Hebrew (*ruach*) is also used to refer to "the Spirit," the symbolism is particularly striking. This Spirit-inspired witness and its impact are foreshadowed by Simeon's prophecy. Simeon, referring to Jesus, declares: "This child is destined to cause the falling and rising of many in Israel" (Luke 2:34).

In short, John described the Spirit's work, not as cleansing repentant individuals, but rather as a blast of the "breath" of God that would sift the nation. Luke sees this prophecy, at least with reference to the sifting work of the Spirit, fulfilled in the Spirit-inspired mission of the church. The essential point for our

---

Fiery Holy Spirit: The Spirit's Relationship with Judgment in Luke-Acts (Blandford Forum, UK: Deo, 2015), 61–72, 208–216.

12   This passage is echoed in *1 Enoch* 62:2 and 1QSb 5:24–25.

13   Note the omission of "fire" in Acts 1:5, evidence that Luke links the final judgment prophesied by John to Jesus's second coming rather than to Pentecost. The "tongues of fire" (Acts 2:3) signify that the disciples will be "a light to the nations" (Isa 49:6; Luke 2:32; Acts 1:8; 13:47; cf. Kienzler, *Fiery Holy Spirit*, 69).

purpose is that Luke presents the Spirit here, not as the source of cleansing for the individual, but rather in prophetic terms as animating the church's witness.

1.2   Jesus at the Jordan (Luke 3:21–22; 4:16–30)

Luke declares that the Spirit-baptizer himself was anointed with the Spirit (Luke 3:22; 4:18; Acts 10:38). This leads us to another question of central importance: What significance does Luke attach to Jesus's pneumatic anointing?

The description of Jesus's pneumatic anointing accounts for only two sentences in Luke's gospel (Luke 3:21–22). Fortunately, Luke has provided an extended commentary on the significance of this event. This commentary is found in Luke's account of Jesus's sermon at Nazareth. This account is recorded in Luke 4:16–30, but I shall only quote the portion critical for our task, vv. 17–19:

> The scroll of the prophet Isaiah was handed to him. Unrolling it, he found the place where it is written:
> "The Spirit of the Lord is on me,
> because he has anointed me to preach good news to the poor.
> He has sent me to proclaim freedom for the prisoners
> and recovery of sight for the blind,
> to release the oppressed,
> to proclaim the year of the Lord's favor."
>   Luke 4:17–19

The significance of this passage is underscored by a comparison with Mark's gospel. Luke normally follows Mark's chronology of Jesus's ministry very closely. But here, Luke takes an event—Jesus's ministry in Nazareth, which occurs in the middle of Mark's gospel (Mark 6:1–6)—and places it at the forefront of his description of Jesus's ministry. Luke's account of the Nazareth event is much fuller than Mark's and includes details important for Luke's purposes. That these purposes include helping the reader understand the significance of Jesus's reception of the Spirit is confirmed, not only by the content of the quotation from Isaiah 61:1–2 that we have just read (Luke 4:17–19), but also by the references to the Spirit in Luke's narrative that link the accounts of Jesus anointing (Luke 3:21–22) with his sermon at Nazareth (Luke 4:16–30). Luke reminds us in Luke 4:1 that Jesus was "full of the Holy Spirit" as he entered into the desert of temptation. And he also affirms that Jesus departed this desert experience "in the power of the Spirit" (Luke 4:14).[14] With this "redactional bridge," Luke

---

14   The Scriptures rather than the Spirit are presented as the means by which Jesus with-

highlights the connection between Jesus's pneumatic anointing and his sermon at Nazareth. So, the sermon at Nazareth is important because it calls us *to look back*—to look back and understand more fully the significance of Jesus's reception of the Spirit.

However, this passage also calls us *to look forward*. Luke crafts his narrative so that the parallels between Jesus's experience of the Spirit (Luke 3–4) and that of the disciples on the day of Pentecost (Acts 1–2) cannot be missed. Both accounts:

- are placed at the outset of Luke's gospel on the one hand, and the book of Acts on the other;
- associate the reception of the Spirit with prayer;
- record visible and audible manifestations;
- offer explanations of the event in the form of a sermon that alludes to the fulfillment of OT prophecy.

In this way, Luke presents Jesus's reception of the Spirit as a model for that of the disciples in Acts and future generations of believers, including his own (cf. Luke 11:13; Acts 2:17).

It is evident, then, that this passage is crucial for understanding the significance of Jesus's reception of the Spirit and that of the disciples in Acts. It thus also provides important definition for Luke's understanding of the gift of the Spirit. With this mind, let us address the question at hand: What significance does Luke attach to Jesus's pneumatic anointing? Luke's answer is unequivocal. The quotation from Isaiah, which plays such a prominent role in the narrative, answers our question with precision: Jesus's reception of the Spirit at the Jordan was the means by which he was equipped to carry out his messianic mission. Furthermore, the verbs in the text—"he has anointed me *to preach* good news to the poor ... He has sent me *to proclaim* freedom for the prisoners ... *to proclaim* the year of the Lord's favor"—highlight *proclamation*, inspired speech, as the primary product of Jesus's anointing.[15] Luke thus presents Jesus's reception

---

stands the temptations of the devil (Luke 4:4, 8, 12). With his references to the Spirit in Luke 4:1, 14, Luke declares that *because* Jesus is faithful and upright, he is the bearer of the Spirit—unlike Israel in the wilderness, who grieved the Spirit (Isa 63:10). As Haya-Prats notes (*Empowered Believers*, 167–177), there is also no indication that Luke considered the diverse aspects of community life mentioned in Acts 2:42–47; 4:31–36; or 5:11–16 to be the direct result of the Spirit's activity.

15 Since Luke never uses καλέω (to summon or announce) with reference to preaching, his use of κηρύσσω (to proclaim) rather than the LXX's καλέω in the phrase "to proclaim the year of the Lord's favor" (Luke 4:19=Isa 61:2), reflects his emphasis on preaching as the preeminent activity inspired by the Spirit. Martin Rese, *Alttestamentliche Motive in der Christologie des Lukas* (Gütersloh: Gütersloher Verlagshaus, 1969), 146.

of the Spirit at the Jordan as a prophetic anointing, the means by which he was equipped to carry out his divinely appointed task.

1.3 The Sending of the Seventy (Luke 10:1–16)

All three Synoptic Gospels record Jesus's words of instruction to the Twelve as he sends them out on their mission. However, only Luke records a second, larger sending of disciples (Luke 10:1–16). In Luke 10:1 we read, "After this the Lord appointed seventy-two [some mss. read 'seventy'] others and sent them two by two ahead of him to every town and place where he was about to go." A series of detailed instructions follow. Finally, Jesus reminds them of their authority: "He who listens to you listens to me; he who rejects you rejects me; but he who rejects me rejects him who sent me" (10:16).

A central question centers on the number of disciples that Jesus sent out and its significance. The manuscript evidence is, at this point, divided. Some manuscripts read "seventy," while others list the number as "seventy-two." Bruce Metzger, in his article on this question, notes that the external manuscript evidence is evenly divided and that internal considerations are also inconclusive. Metzger thus concludes that the number "cannot be determined with confidence."[16] More recent scholarship has largely agreed with Metzger, with a majority opting cautiously for the authenticity of "seventy-two" as the more difficult reading.[17] Although we cannot determine the number with confidence, it will be important to keep the divided nature of the manuscript evidence in mind as we wrestle with the significance of this text.

Most scholars agree that the number (for convenience, we will call it "seventy") has symbolic significance. Certainly, Jesus's selection of twelve disciples was no accident. The number twelve clearly symbolizes the reconstitution of Israel (Gen 35:23–26), the people of God. This suggests that the number seventy is rooted in the Old Testament narrative and has symbolic significance as well. A number of proposals have been put forward,[18] but I would argue that the background for the reference to the "seventy" is to be found in Numbers 11:24–30. This passage describes how the Lord "took of the Spirit that was on [Moses] and put the Spirit on the seventy elders" (Num 11:25). This resulted in the seventy elders, who had gathered around the Tent, prophesying for a short duration. However, two other elders, Eldad and Medad, did not go to the Tent; rather, they remained in the camp. But the Spirit also fell on them and

---

16   Bruce Metzger, "Seventy or Seventy-Two Disciples?," *NTS* 5 (1959): 306.
17   One exception is John Nolland, who favors the "seventy" reading (*Luke 9.21–18.34* [Dallas, TX: Word, 1993], 546).
18   For the various options see Metzger, "Seventy or Seventy-Two Disciples?," 303–304.

they, too, began to prophesy and continued to do so. Joshua, hearing this news, rushed to Moses and urged him to stop them. Moses replied, "Are you jealous for my sake? I wish that all the Lord's people were prophets and that the Lord would put his Spirit on them!" (Num 11:29).

The Numbers 11 proposal has a number of significant advantages over other explanations: it accounts for the two textual traditions underlying Luke 10:1 (how many actually prophesied in Numbers 11?); it finds explicit fulfillment in the narrative of Acts; it ties into one of the great themes of Luke-Acts, the work of the Holy Spirit; and numerous allusions to Moses and his actions in Luke's travel narrative support this reading.[19]

With this background in mind, the significance of the symbolism is found in the expansion of the number of disciples "sent out" into mission from the Twelve to the Seventy. The reference to the Seventy evokes memories of Moses' wish that "all the Lord's people were prophets," and, in this way, points ahead to Pentecost (Acts 2), where this wish is initially and dramatically fulfilled. This wish continues to be fulfilled throughout Acts as Luke describes the coming of the empowering Spirit of prophecy to other new centers of missionary activity, such as those gathered together in Samaria (Acts 8:14–17), Cornelius's house (Acts 10:44–48), and Ephesus (Acts 19:1–7). The reference to the Seventy, then, does not simply anticipate the mission of the church to the Gentiles; rather, it foreshadows the outpouring of the Spirit on all the servants of the Lord and their universal participation in the mission of God (Acts 2:17–18; cf. 4:31).[20]

In Luke's view, every member of the church is called (Luke 24:45–49; Acts 1:4–8/Isa 49:6) and empowered (Acts 2:17–21; cf. 4:31) to be a prophet.[21] Far from being unique and unrepeatable, Luke emphasizes that the prophetic enabling experienced by the disciples at Pentecost is available to all of God's people. At Pentecost, Moses' wish now begins to be realized. Luke 10:1 anticipates the fulfillment of this reality.

It is important to note that the ecstatic speech of the elders in Numbers 11 constitutes the backdrop against which Luke interprets the pentecostal and subsequent outpourings of the Spirit.[22] It would appear that Luke views every

---

19 For more discussion, see Robert P. Menzies, *The Language of the Spirit: Interpreting and Translating Charismatic Terms* (Cleveland, TN: CPT, 2010), 73–82.

20 Keith F. Nickle, *Preaching the Gospel of Luke: Proclaiming God's Royal Rule* (Louisville: Westminster John Knox, 2000), 117.

21 Craig S. Keener, *Acts: An Exegetical Commentary*, Vol. 1 (Grand Rapids: Baker Academic, 2012), 881.

22 Gordon Wenham describes the prophesying narrated in Numbers 11:24–30 as an instance of "unintelligible ecstatic utterance, what the New Testament terms speaking in tongues" (*Numbers* [Downers Grove, IL: InterVarsity, 1981], 109).

believer as (at least potentially) an end-time prophet, and that he anticipates that they too will issue forth in Spirit-inspired ecstatic speech.[23] This is the clear implication of his narrative, which includes repetitive fulfillments of Moses' wish that refer to glossolalia. The motif is transparent: the pentecostal gift, as a fulfillment of Moses' wish (Num 11:29) and Joel's prophecy (Joel 2:28–32), is a prophetic anointing that enables its recipient to bear bold witness for Jesus *and, this being the case, it is marked by the ecstatic speech characteristic of prophets* (that is, glossolalia). This explains why, as we shall see, Luke considered tongues to be a sign of the reception of the pentecostal gift.

It is interesting to note that Luke does not share the angst of many modern Christians concerning the possibility of false tongues. Luke does not offer guidelines for discerning whether tongues are genuine or fake, from God or from some other source. Rather, Luke assumes that the Christian community will know and experience that which is needed and good. This observation leads us to our next text.

1.4   *Prayer for the Spirit (Luke 11:9–13)*

Another text that reflects Luke's desire to encourage his church to experience the prophetic inspiration of the Spirit and all that entails (such as joyful praise, glossolalia, and bold witness) is found in Luke 11:13. This verse, which forms the climax to Jesus's teaching on prayer, again testifies to the fact that Luke views the work of the Holy Spirit described in Acts as relevant for the life of his church. Luke is not writing wistfully about an era of charismatic activity in the distant past.[24] Luke 11:13 reads, "If you then, though you are evil, know how to give good gifts to your children, how much more will your Father in heaven give the Holy Spirit to those who ask Him!" It is instructive to note that the parallel passage in Matthew's gospel contains slightly different phrasing: "how much more will your Father in heaven give *good gifts* to those who ask Him!" (Matt 7:11). It is virtually certain that Luke has interpreted the "good gifts" in his source material with a reference to the "Holy Spirit."[25] Luke, then, provides us with a Spirit-inspired, authoritative commentary on this saying of Jesus. Three important implications follow:

---

23   With the term, "ecstatic," I mean "flowing from an experience of intense joy" rather than a loss of control.

24   Contra Hans Conzelmann, *Acts of the Apostles* (Philadelphia: Fortress, 1987; German orig., 1963), 15, 159–160.

25   Reasons for this conclusion include: the reference to the Holy Spirit breaks the parallelism of the "good gifts" given by earthly fathers and "the good gifts" given by our heavenly Father; Luke often inserts references to the Holy Spirit into his source material; and Matthew never omits or adds references to the Holy Spirit in his sources.

First, Luke's alteration of the Matthean (or Q) form of the saying anticipates the post-resurrection experience of the church.[26] This is evident from the fact that the promise that the Father will give the Holy Spirit to those who ask begins to be realized only at Pentecost. By contemporizing the text in this way, Luke stresses the relevance of the saying for the post-pentecostal community to which he writes. It would seem that for Luke there is no neat line of separation dividing the apostolic church from his church or ours. Quite the contrary, Luke calls his readers to follow in their footsteps.

Second, the context indicates that the promise is made to disciples (Luke 11:1). Thus, Luke's contemporized version of the saying is clearly directed to the members of the Christian community.[27] Since it is addressed to Christians, the promise cannot refer to an initiatory or soteriological gift.[28] This judgment finds confirmation in the repetitive character of the exhortations to pray in Luke 11:9:[29] prayer for the Spirit (and, in light of the promise, we may presume this includes the reception of the Spirit) is to be an ongoing practice. The gift of the Holy Spirit to which Luke refers neither initiates one into the new age, nor is it to be received only once;[30] rather, this pneumatic gift is given to disciples, and it is to be experienced on an ongoing basis.

Third, Luke's usage elsewhere indicates that he viewed the gift of the Holy Spirit in 11:13 as a prophetic enabling.[31] On two occasions in Luke-Acts the Spirit is given to those praying;[32] in both the Spirit is portrayed as the source of prophetic activity. Luke's account of Jesus's baptism indicates that Jesus received the Spirit after his baptism while praying (Luke 3:21). As we have noted,

---

26   J. Fitzmyer, *The Gospel According to Luke*, Vol. 2 (New York: Doubleday, 1985), 916; E.E. Ellis, *The Gospel of Luke* (London: Oliphants, Marshall, Morgan, & Scott, 1974), 164; Stronstad, *The Charismatic Theology of St. Luke*, 46.
27   The scholarly consensus affirms that Luke-Acts was addressed primarily to Christians.
28   G.T. Montague, *The Holy Spirit: Growth of a Biblical Tradition* (New York: Paulist, 1976), 259–260.
29   Note the repetitive or continuous action implicit in the verbs in 11:9: αἰτεῖτε (ask), ζητεῖτε (seek), κρούετε (knock).
30   F. Büchsel notes the repetitive character of the exhortation (*Der Geist Gottes im Neuen Testament* [Gütersloh: C. Bertelsmann, 1926], 189–190). So also Montague, *Spirit*, 259–260.
31   Contra Jack Levison, who suggests that the call to pray for the Spirit is not about receiving a supernatural gift or dramatic experience; it is, rather, about becoming a holy person through a process of discipline and growing intimacy (*An Unconventional God: The Spirit according to Jesus* [Grand Rapids: Baker, 2020], 93–95).
32   The gift of the Spirit is also related to prayer in Acts 8:15, 17 and 9:17, though the prayers here are not offered by the recipients but by others. Prayer is also implicit in the Pentecost account (Acts 1:14; 2:4). In all of these texts, the gift of the Spirit is presented as a prophetic endowment.

this gift of the Spirit, portrayed principally as the source of prophetic power (Luke 4:18–19), equipped Jesus for his messianic task. Later, in Acts 4:31, the disciples, after having prayed, "were all filled with the Holy Spirit and spoke the word of God boldly." Again, the Spirit given in response to prayer is the impetus for prophetic activity.

What sort of prophetic activity did Luke anticipate would accompany this bestowal of the Spirit? Luke's narrative suggests a wide range of possibilities: joyful praise, glossolalia, visions, bold witness in the face of persecution, to name a few. However, several aspects of Luke's narrative suggest that glossolalia was one of the expected outcomes in Luke's mind and in the minds of his readers.

First, Luke's narrative suggests that glossolalia typically accompanies the initial reception of the Spirit. Furthermore, Luke highlights the fact that glossolalia serves as an external sign of the prophetic gift. These elements of Luke's account, which we shall examine shortly, would undoubtedly encourage readers in Luke's church, as they have with contemporary readers, to seek the prophetic gift, *complete with its accompanying external sign.*

Second, in view of the emphasis in this passage on asking (v. 9) and the Father's willingness to respond (v. 13), it would seem natural for Luke's readers to ask a question that again is often asked by contemporary Christians: How will we know when we have received this gift? Here we hear echoes of Paul's question in Acts 19:2. Of course, Luke provides a clear answer. The arrival of prophetic power has a visible, external sign: glossolalia. This is not to say that there are not other ways in which the Spirit's power and presence are made known to us. This is simply to affirm that Luke's narrative indicates that a visible, external sign does exist and that he and his readers would naturally expect to manifest this sign.

Finally, the question should be asked, why would Luke need to encourage his readers not to be afraid of receiving a bad or harmful gift (note the snake and scorpion of vv. 11–12)?[33] Why would he need to encourage his church to pursue this gift of the Spirit? If the gift is quiet, internal, and ethereal, why would there be any concern? However, if the gift includes glossolalia, which is noisy, unintelligible, and has many pagan counterparts,[34] then the concerns make sense.[35]

---

33 Luke's comparisons feature dangerous objects ("snake" and "scorpion," Luke 11:11–12), whereas Matthew's comparisons include one that is simply useless ("stone" and "snake," Matt 7:9–10). The "snakes and scorpions" of Luke 10:19 suggest that Luke here seeks to help his readers overcome their fear.

34 For Jewish and pagan examples of ecstasy and inspired utterances, see Keener, *Acts*, 807–812.

35 Note that the Beelzebub controversy immediately follows (Luke 11:14–28).

Luke's response is designed to quell any fears. The Father gives good gifts. We need not fret or fear.

Through his skillful editing of this saying of Jesus (Luke 11:13), Luke encourages post-pentecostal disciples to pray for a prophetic anointing, an experience of spiritual rapture that will produce power and praise in their lives, an experience similar to those modeled by Jesus (Luke 3:21–22; 10:21)[36] and the early church (Acts 2:4; 10:46; 19:6). The reader would naturally assume glossolalia to be a normal, frequent, and expected part of this experience. The fact that Luke viewed glossolalia as a significant component of this bestowal of the Spirit is suggested by the larger context of Luke-Acts, which portrays tongues as an external sign of the Spirit's coming, and also by the more immediate context, which indicates that Luke's encouragement to pray for the Holy Spirit is a response to the fears of some within his community. This text, then, not only reveals the prophetic character of Luke's pneumatology, it also indicates that Luke viewed tongues as positive and available to every disciple of Jesus.

1.5 *Blasphemy against the Spirit (Luke 12:10)*

Jesus's saying concerning blasphemy against the Holy Spirit is preserved in two distinct forms by Mark and Q (Mark 3:28–29=Matt 12:31; Matt 12:32=Luke 12:10). Careful examination of these texts reveals that Luke has taken the blasphemy saying from its original context in Mark and Q (the Beelzebub controversy) and placed it into another block of Q material (Luke 12:2–9, 11–12). The result is that the meaning of the saying is transformed. In the context of the Beelzebub controversy (Mark and Q), blasphemy against the Spirit involves attributing to the agency of Satan the exorcisms that Jesus performs by the Holy Spirit. In Luke's gospel "blasphemy against the Spirit" refers to Christians who resist the leading of the Spirit and, in the face of persecution, renounce Christ (Christian apostasy). The immediate context, with its warnings against denying Christ (Luke 12:9), with its distinction between "a word against the Son of Man" and "blasphemy against the Spirit" (the former committed by non-Christians, the latter by Christians), and with its promise of pneumatic aid in the face of persecution (Luke 12: 11–12), all point in this direction.[37] This interpretation also

---

36   Luke's description of Jesus's exultation and inspired speech in Luke 10:21, a text unique to Luke's gospel, anticipates the reference to "my tongue rejoices" (καὶ ἠγαλλιάσατο ἡ γλῶσσά μου) in the psalm cited by Peter in his Pentecost sermon (Acts 2:26=Psalm 16:9 [15:9 LXX]), which the early church read prophetically of Jesus, and demonstrates that the prophecy it contains was fulfilled by Jesus. Cf. Robert P. Menzies, *Speaking in Tongues: Jesus and the Apostolic Church as Models for the Church Today* (Cleveland, TN: CPT, 2016), 47–65.

37   Robert P. Menzies, *Empowered for Witness: The Spirit in Luke-Acts* (Sheffield, UK: Sheffield

finds significant support from Acts 26:11, where Paul confesses, "I went from one synagogue to another to have them punished, and I tried to force them to blaspheme [βλασφημεῖν]." Luke's "governing motive for such bold editing is his overriding interest in pneumatology and witness."[38] Once again, the prophetic character of Luke's pneumatology is revealed. Through his careful redaction of this saying, Luke presents the Spirit as the source of bold witness in the face of persecution rather than the power behind Jesus's exorcisms.[39]

This text highlights an important aspect of Luke's theological perspective. Luke presents inspired speech (along with its corollary, charismatic wisdom) rather than miracle-working power as the *primary* product of the Spirit's inspiration. Although Luke frequently presents the Spirit as the exclusive source (without reference to "power" or other qualifying terms) of prophetic activity, he *never* does so with reference to miracles of healing, exorcism, or marvelous deeds. This is the case although it means that Luke has had to alter his sources on several occasions (Luke 4:18; 11:20; 12:10). Luke's penchant for introducing miracle stories with references to Jesus's teaching is also striking.[40] All of this indicates that, for Luke, Jesus is more than a miracle worker, he is the long-anticipated prophet-teacher (Acts 3:22; 7:37). And his disciples, as a band of end-time prophets (Acts 2.17–21), follow in his footsteps with their inspired witness.[41]

1.6   *The Promise of the Father (Luke 24:49; Acts 1:4; 2:33, 39)*

As we arrive at the end of Luke's gospel, we encounter a striking feature of Luke's carefully crafted two-volume work. The end of volume one and the beginning of volume two describe the same scenes. There is an amazing amount of overlap: Jesus commands the disciples to wait in Jerusalem, for they will receive the promise of the Father (Luke 24:49; Acts 1:4), which is associated with power to proclaim the gospel to all people (Luke 24:47–49; Acts 1:8); Jesus then ascends into heaven (Luke 24:50–51; Acts 1:9); and the disciples remain in Jerusalem in a state of expectant prayer and joyful praise (Luke 24:52–53; Acts

---

Academic, 1994), 193. For an alternative view, see M. Mittelstadt, who argues that here "blasphemy against the Spirit" should be understood as the "persistent rejection of the gospel witness" by nonbelievers (*The Spirit and Suffering in Luke-Acts: Implications for a Pentecostal Pneumatology* [London: T & T Clark International, 2004], 79).

38   J. Shelton, *Mighty in Word and Deed* (Peabody, MA: Hendrickson, 1991), 107.
39   Not a single text in the OT or in the Jewish intertestamental literature attributes the exorcism of demons to the agency of the Spirit (Menzies, *Development*, 195–196).
40   Luke 5:1; 6:6; 13:10; cf. 5:15; 6:17–19; 9:1–2.
41   Paul S. Minear, *To Heal and to Reveal: The Prophetic Vocation According to Luke* (New York: Seabury, 1976), 148–149.

1:14), reminiscent of the pious figures described in the infancy narratives. The repetition seeks to drive the point home. Luke's message may be summarized with one phrase, "the promise of the Father."

Luke refers to "the promise" of the Spirit four times in close proximity (Luke 24:49; Acts 1:4; 2:33, 39). "The promise" is identified with the pentecostal gift of the Spirit (2:33) and explicitly defined: reception of "the promise" will result in the disciples being "clothed with power from on high" and enable them to be effective "witnesses" (Luke 24:48–49; Acts 1:8). Furthermore, for Luke "the promise" with reference to the Spirit refers to the gift of the Spirit of prophecy promised in Joel 2:28–32. This is made clear through Luke's citation of Joel 2:28–32 in Acts 2:17–21 and further emphasized in his redactional introduction of the citation.

This introduction includes the phrase "God says" (Acts 2:17) and thus identifies the prophecy of Joel as "the promise of the Father"—the full description of "the promise" in three of the four Lukan references (Luke 24:49; Acts 1:4; 2:33). In Joel's prophecy the Spirit comes as the source of prophetic inspiration, a point that Luke highlights by inserting the phrase "and they will prophesy" (Acts 2:18) into the Greek text of Joel. Another alteration, Luke's transformation of Joel's "slaves" into "servants of God"—accomplished by his double insertion of "my" into Acts 2:18—highlights what is implicit in the Joel text: the gift of the Spirit is given only to those who are members of the community of salvation.[42] Thus, Luke's explicit definitions (Luke 24:49; Acts 1:4–8) and his use of the Joel citation indicate that the "promise" of the Spirit, initially fulfilled at Pentecost (Acts 2:4), enables the disciples to take up their prophetic vocation to the world.

Although the Lukan "promise" of the Spirit must be interpreted in light of Joel's promise concerning the restoration of the Spirit of prophecy, Acts 2:39 does include an additional element. The passage reads:

> Peter replied, "Repent and be baptized, every one of you, in the name of Jesus Christ so that your sins may be forgiven. And you will receive the gift of the Holy Spirit. The promise is for you and your children and for all who are far off—for all whom the Lord our God will call."
>
> Acts 2:38–39

In Acts 2:39 Luke extends the range of the promise envisioned to include the promise of salvation offered in Joel 2:32 (as well as the promise of the Spirit

---

[42] Contra Amos Yong, *Beyond the Impasse: Toward a Pneumatological Theology of Religions* (Grand Rapids: Baker Academic, 2003), 131. Cf. Robert P. Menzies, *Christ-Centered: The Evangelical Nature of Pentecostal Theology* (Eugene, OR: Cascade, 2020), 134–136.

of prophecy in Joel 2:28). Acts 2:39 echoes the language of Joel 2:32/Acts 2:21: "everyone who calls on the name of the Lord will be saved." In Acts 2:39 Luke extends the range of "the promise" to include this salvific dimension because the audience addressed now includes nonbelievers.

The "promise" of Acts 2:39, then, embraces more than the experience of conversion. Consistent with the other references to "the promise" (Luke 24:49, Acts 1:4, and 2:33), the promised gift of the Spirit in Acts 2:39 refers to the promise of Joel 2:28, and thus it is a promise of prophetic enabling granted to the repentant. The promise of Acts 2:39, like the promise of Jesus in Acts 1:8, points beyond the restoration of the faithful of Israel: salvation is offered (Joel 2:32), but the promise includes the renewal of Israel's prophetic vocation to be a light to the nations (Joel 2:28; cf. Isaiah 49:6 and Acts 1:8).[43]

Some have criticized this approach, suggesting that we should read Luke's earlier references to the promise of the Spirit in light of the promise of salvation offered in Acts 2:39.[44] However, as we have seen, Acts 2:39 does not indicate that the Spirit comes as the source of new covenant existence.[45] Rather, it simply reminds us that the prophecy of Joel 2:28–32 includes two elements: the gift of the Spirit of prophecy (v. 28) and the offer of salvation to those who call upon the name of the Lord (v. 32). Acts 2:39 refers to both but does not suggest that the two are identical. Indeed, this sort of equation runs counter to Luke's explicit statements in Luke 24:49 and Acts 1:4–8, his use and redaction of the Joel citation in Acts 2:17–18, and the broader context of his two-volume work. In particular, Luke's description of baptized believers (Acts 8:16) and "disciples" (Acts 19:1), all without the Spirit, raises insurmountable problems for this position.

---

43   In "The Spirit and Salvation in Luke-Acts" (in Graham Stanton, Bruce Longenecker, and Stephen Barton, eds., *The Holy Spirit and Christian Origins: Essays in Honor of James D.G. Dunn* [Grand Rapids: Eerdmans, 2004], 103–116), Max Turner places great weight on veiled references to Isaiah 32:15 in Luke 24:49 and Luke 1:35, much more weight, it would appear, than on Luke's direct statements (Luke 11:13; 24:47–49; Acts 1:8, 2:17–18). These allusions encourage Turner to suggest that in Luke's view the Spirit is the agent of the Christian community's "righteousness, peace, and life" (110). I find Isaiah 49:6, which has a missiological focus, to be a much more convincing backdrop for Luke 24:49 and Acts 1:4–8. In any event, none of this should obscure the force of Luke's explicit statements. These allusions also lead Turner to see Jesus's miraculous birth by the Spirit (Luke 1:35) as a parallel to the believer's experience of the Spirit at Pentecost (113, n. 31). Yet Luke has crafted his narrative so as to present Jesus's experience of the Spirit at the Jordan—which Turner himself acknowledges to be an empowering for mission—as the true parallel to the disciples' experience on Pentecost.

44   James Dunn, "Baptism in the Spirit: A Response to Pentecostal Scholarship," *JPT* 3 (1993): 12, 21.

45   Contra Luke Timothy Johnson, *Prophetic Jesus, Prophetic Church: The Challenge of Luke-Acts to Contemporary Christians* (Grand Rapids: Eerdmans, 2011), 53–54.

It is possible to argue that Luke's understanding of the promise of the Spirit—clearly shaped by Joel 2:28–32—was also informed by a number of other Old Testament prophecies regarding the Spirit's eschatological role, especially Isaiah 44:3–5 and Ezekiel 36:26–27. Yet this approach fails to examine how these Old Testament texts were interpreted in the Judaism that gave rise to the Christianity Luke knew. Rather than simply reading our own agenda and exegesis into the first-century setting, surely it is better to ask how those Jews closest in time to the early Christians understood the relevant texts and what significance they attached to them.

This is particularly important at this point, for the eschatological outpouring of the Spirit was generally interpreted in light of Joel 2:28–29 as a restoration of the Spirit of prophecy (*MHG* Gen. 140; *Num. R.* 15.25). By way of contrast, Ezekiel 36:26–27 was usually interpreted as a prophecy concerning the end-time removal of the evil "impulse," and most frequently without reference to the activity of the Spirit (*Exod. R.* 15.6; *Num. R.* 14.4). Indeed, the eradication of the evil "impulse" was presented as a prerequisite for the end-time bestowal of the Spirit of prophecy (*Deut. R.* 6.14; *Midr. Ps.* 14.6).[46] This means that calls for us to interpret the promise of the Spirit in light of a plethora of Old Testament texts conflict with the evidence from early Jewish sources and Luke's own hand. Luke, unlike Paul and John, cites none of these other Old Testament texts. There simply is no evidence to support the notion that by referring to Joel 2:28–32, Luke intended his readers to think of some commonly expected, all-embracing soteriological bestowal of the Spirit.

Should the collocation of repentance, baptism, and reception of the Spirit in Acts 2:38 cause us to reconsider these conclusions? I think not, for it tells us little about the nature of the gift of the Spirit. While the collocation may indicate that for Luke the rite of water baptism is normally accompanied by the bestowal of the Spirit, Luke's usage elsewhere suggests that even this conclusion may be overstating the case. There is nothing in the text that would suggest that the Spirit is presented here as the source of new covenant existence. If it could be established that the text presupposes an inextricable bond between water baptism and forgiveness of sins on the one hand and reception of the Spirit on the other, then we would need to reconsider our position. However, this conclusion is unwarranted. Since Luke fails to develop a strong link between water baptism and the bestowal of the Spirit elsewhere, and regularly separates the rite from the gift (Luke 3:21–22; Acts 8:12–17; 9:17–18; 10:44;

---

46   For further discussion of these points and the relevant Jewish texts, see Menzies, *Development*, 104–111.

18:24–25), the phrase "and you will receive the gift of the Holy Spirit" in Acts 2:38 should be interpreted as a promise that the Spirit shall be "imparted to those who are already converted and baptized."[47] In any case, the most that can be gleaned from the text is that repentance and water baptism are the normal prerequisites for reception of the Spirit, which is promised to every believer.

I believe it is prudent to interpret Acts 2:38–39 in the light of Luke's explicit testimony concerning the promise of the Spirit recorded in Luke 24:49; Acts 1:4; and 2:17–18—all of which describe the pneumatic gift as a prophetic enabling for engagement in God's great mission. This reading also fits nicely with Luke's usage elsewhere (Acts 8:4–17; 18:24–19:7). Additionally, calls for us to interpret the promise of the Spirit against the backdrop of a plethora of Old Testament texts, none of which is mentioned by Luke or linked in the suggested manner with the Joel text by contemporary Jewish thinkers, must be rejected. Again, wisdom dictates that we understand the promise of the Spirit against the backdrop of the text that Luke does cite, Joel 2:28–32, and contemporary Jewish expectations.

We are now in a position to summarize our findings to this point. We have discovered that the pentecostal outpouring of the Spirit represents the initial fulfillment of:

- *John the Baptist's prophecy* (Luke 3:16–17): just as the wind separates the wheat from the chaff, so also will the Spirit-inspired witness of Jesus's disciples "cause the falling and rising of many in Israel" (Luke 2:34) and beyond.
- *the prophetic anointing anticipated by Jesus at the Jordan* (Luke 3:21–22; 4:16–30) and "promised" to his disciples through the literary parallels with Pentecost that Luke creates.
- *Moses' wish* that all the Lord's people might be prophets (Luke 10:1–16; cf. Num 11:29).
- *Jesus's promise concerning prayer for the Spirit* (Luke 11:9–13).
- *Jesus's promise concerning the Spirit's aid when facing persecution* (Luke 12:11–12).
- *the promise of the Father* (Luke 24:49; Acts 1:4; 2:33, 39).

These findings validate our claim that Luke writes in order to present his readers with models for their life, experience, and ministry. Additionally, they resonate well with R.A. Torrey's declaration, "The baptism with the Holy Spirit

---

47 Schweizer, "πνεῦμα," 412. So also S. Brown, "'Water-Baptism' and 'Spirit-Baptism' in Luke-Acts," *ATR* 59 (1977): 144, and Paul Elbert, "Acts 2:38 in Light of the Syntax of Imperative-Future Passive and Imperative-Present Participle Combinations," *CBQ* 75, no. 1 (2013): 94–107.

is always connected with testimony and service."[48] We have seen that Luke's narrative reflects a prophetic (or charismatic) rather than soteriological understanding of the gift of the Spirit. Luke not only fails to speak of the Spirit as a soteriological agent in a manner similar to Paul or John; his narrative stands decidedly against it (Luke 11:9–13; cf. Acts 8:4–17; 18:24–19:7). We simply need to read Luke on his own terms in order to see that his theological perspective complements that of Paul and John.[49]

With this rich theological and literary background in mind, let us now examine Luke's Pentecost account.

2   The Disciples and the Spirit

In Acts 2:4 we read that those present were all filled with the Holy Spirit and began to "speak in other tongues (λαλεῖν ἑτέραις γλώσσαις) as the Spirit enabled them." This phenomenon creates confusion among the Jews of the crowd who, we are told, represent "every nation under heaven" (Acts 2:5). The crowd gathered in astonishment because "each one heard them speaking in his own language" (διαλέκτῳ; Acts 2:6). These details are repeated as Luke narrates the response of the astonished group: "Are not all these men who are speaking Galileans? Then how is it that each of us hears them in his own native language?" (διαλέκτῳ; Acts 2:7–8). After the crowd lists in amazement the various nations represented by those present, they exclaim, "we hear them declaring the wonders of God in our own tongues" (γλώσσαις; Acts 2:11)! Since Acts 2:11 clearly relates γλώσσαις to the various human languages of those present in the crowd, most scholars understand the "tongues" (γλώσσαις) of Acts 2:4 and 2:11 as referring to intelligible speech. The disciples are enabled by the Spirit to declare "the wonders of God" in human languages they had not previously learned.

This language miracle at Pentecost is not a literal reversal of Babel. The disciples of Jesus who were "filled with the Holy Spirit and began to speak in other

---

48   Torrey, *Baptism*, 17. For an alternative view, see Matthias Wenk, *Community-Forming Power: The Socio-Ethical Role of the Spirit in Luke-Acts* (Sheffield, UK: Sheffield Academic, 2000), passim. Wenk is unhappy with those who ask questions about the Spirit's role in conversion-initiation in Luke-Acts (315–316). Yet, these questions are demanded by the language and theology of Paul and John. Indeed, we must pose them of Luke's writings if we are to produce a fully orbed biblical theology of the Spirit.

49   See Robert P. Menzies, "Subsequence in the Pauline Epistles," *Pneuma* 39 (2017): 339–360, and "John's Place in the Development of Early Christian Pneumatology," in Wonsuk Ma and R. Menzies, eds., *The Spirit and Spirituality: Essays in Honor of Russell P. Spittler* (London: T & T Clark International, 2004), 41–52.

tongues" (Acts 2:4) did not speak a single tongue that all understood. Rather, they spoke in *the multiple mother-tongues* of each individual present. The cultural distinctives were not obliterated. On the contrary, the Holy Spirit enabled Jesus's disciples to embrace them and to minister through them. There were many languages, but only one message: Jesus is the resurrected and exalted Lord (Acts 2:33–36).

Luke's account of Pentecost calls every disciple of Jesus to see that we, too, have a clear mandate to take the gospel of Jesus Christ to the ends of the earth. The fact that the Spirit inspires the disciples at Pentecost to speak in multiple and diverse tongues—tongues unknown to them—this fact should encourage us to recognize that we, too. are called to identify with and embed ourselves within the cultures of the diverse people groups that populate this planet. Like Jesus, we, too, must become incarnate. This is the nature of our mission, and Luke's description of Pentecost clarifies and reinforces this fact.

2.1   *Acts 2:4 and Luke's Narrative*

Luke describes the initial coming of the Spirit on four occasions in the book of Acts: Acts 2:4; 8:17; 10:46; and 19:6. Many scholars include Paul's reception of the Spirit (Acts 9:17–19) in this list; thus they argue that Luke only refers to tongues in three out of five instances. They then conclude that 60 percent is good as a batting average in baseball, but not sufficient to prove that Luke intended to establish a normative pattern. However, if we are to understand Luke's purposes, I believe deeper probing into Luke's narrative is required.

First, it should be noted that Luke nowhere actually describes the Spirit coming upon Paul. This is simply implied in the narrative (Acts 9:17–19). So, we really have only four episodes that actually describe the initial reception of the Spirit in the book of Acts. Of the four instances in the book of Acts where Luke actually describes the initial coming of the Spirit, three explicitly cite glossolalia as the immediate result (Acts 2:4; 10:46; 19:6) and the other one (Acts 8:14–19) strongly implies it. Even the most inept reader can hardly miss that in Acts 8:14–19 something striking took place when the Samaritans received the Spirit. In light of the larger context of Luke-Acts, the striking sign that encouraged the magician Simon to seek to purchase the ability to dispense the gift of the Spirit can only be glossolalia.

So, let us examine these three, central texts. What is immediately eye-catching is the consistent manner in which Luke describes the Spirit-inspired speech that accompanies the coming of the Spirit in these three passages. In each of these passages, Acts 2:4, 10:46, 19:6, Luke uses the words λαλέω and γλώσσαις to refer to Spirit-inspired utterances. How should we understand these words? The usage of the phrase λαλέω γλώσσαις in the New Testament is instructive.

In 1 Corinthians 12–14 Paul refers to the gift of tongues (γλώσσαις)[50] and uses the phrase λαλέω γλώσσαις to designate unintelligible utterances inspired by the Spirit.[51] The fact that this gift of tongues refers to unintelligible utterances rather than to known human languages is confirmed by the fact that Paul explicitly states that these tongues must be interpreted by one spiritually gifted if they are to be understood (1 Cor 14:6–19, 28; cf. 12:10, 30). Paul does not even consider the possibility that one who knows the language could be present as we might expect if a human language was in view.

In Acts 10:46 and 19:6 Luke also uses the phrase λαλέω γλώσσαις to designate utterances inspired by the Spirit. In Acts 10:46 Peter and his colleagues hear Cornelius and his household "speaking in tongues and praising God." Acts 19:6 states that the Ephesian disciples "spoke in tongues and prophesied." The literary parallels between the descriptions of speaking in tongues in these passages and 1 Corinthians 12–14 are impressive. All of these texts associate speaking in tongues with the inspiration of the Holy Spirit; utilize similar vocabulary (λαλέω γλώσσαις); and describe inspired speech associated with worship and prophetic pronouncements. Additionally, since 1 Corinthians 12–14 clearly speaks of unintelligible utterances and there is no indication in either of the Acts passages that known languages are being spoken—indeed, there is no apparent need for a miracle of xenolalia in either instance (what foreign language would they have spoken?)—most English translations translate the occurrences of λαλέω γλώσσαις in these texts with reference to speaking in tongues.

The references to γλώσσαις in Acts 2:4–11, however, raise interesting questions. In Acts 2:4 we read that those present were all filled with the Holy Spirit and began to "speak in other tongues (λαλεῖν ἑτέραις γλώσσαις) as the Spirit enabled them." As we have noted, this phenomenon creates an uproar among the Jews of the crowd who represented diverse nations and languages. The astonished group cries out, "we hear them declaring the wonders of God in our own tongues" (γλώσσαις; Acts 2:11)! It seems evident that the "tongues" (γλώσσαις) of Acts 2:4 and 2:11 refer to intelligible speech. The disciples are enabled by the Spirit to declare "the wonders of God" in the various mother tongues of those present. This reading of the text has encouraged some translators, including those who produced the NRSV, to translate the γλώσσαις of Acts 2:4 and 2:11 with the term "languages" rather than "tongues."

While we can understand why translators are tempted to translate the same words in these passages differently—they actually refer to different activities

---

50 1 Cor 12:10; 12:28; 13:8; 14:22, 26.
51 1 Cor 12:30; 13:1; 14:2, 4, 6, 13, 18, 23, 27, 39.

(xenolalia in Acts 2:4 and glossolalia in Acts 10:46 and 19:6)—this sort of translation creates a real problem. It obscures the fact that Luke uses the same Greek terms to describe what takes place when the Spirit is received in Acts 2:4, Acts 10:46, and Acts 19:6. Why, we may ask, does Luke use the same language to describe each of these events even though they actually refer to different activities? This striking literary connection suggests that Luke has intentionally shaped his narrative in order to highlight this linkage. In other words, the pattern is important to him. Luke *desired* to make the connection. He *desired* to establish Acts 2 as a model.

The significance of the verbal connections between the γλώσσαις (tongues) of these three passages becomes apparent when we examine Luke's understanding of the role of tongues in the life of the church. A close reading of Luke's narrative reveals that he views speaking in tongues as a special type of prophetic speech and, as such, an important sign. Speaking in tongues is associated with prophecy and presented as a significant sign in each of the three passages that describe this phenomenon in Acts. The stage is set, the model unveiled, in Acts 2.

In Acts 2:17–18 (cf. Acts 2:4) speaking in tongues is specifically described as a fulfillment of Joel's prophecy that in the last days all of God's people will prophesy. The strange sounds of the disciples' tongues-speech, Peter declares, are in fact not the ramblings of drunkards; rather, they represent prophetic utterances issued by God's end-time messengers (Acts 2:13, 15–17). The meaning of the symbolism of the speaking "in other tongues," which enables "Jews from every nation under heaven" to hear the message in their "own language" (Acts 2:5–6), is clearly explained. It marks this group as members of Joel's end-time prophetic band and indicates that the "last days" and the salvation associated with it have arrived. Thus, Luke narrates Peter's powerful declaration concerning Jesus, "Exalted to the right hand of God ... he [Jesus] has poured out *what you now see and hear*" (Acts 2:33). "Therefore," Peter declares, "let all Israel be assured of this: God has made this Jesus, whom you crucified, both Lord and Christ" (Acts 2:36). The logic of the narrative is transparent: Since the Spirit of prophecy is only given to the "servants" of God (Acts 2:18)—that is, the true people of God, the heirs of the promise God made to Israel (Joel 2:28–32)—and since the disciples of Jesus are those who are now receiving this gift, it follows that Jesus is Lord (Acts 2:33) and that his disciples constitute the true people of God. In Acts 2 tongues-speech, then, serves as a sign that both validates the disciples' claim that Jesus is Lord and confirms their status as members of Joel's end-time prophetic band.

The association with prophecy is made again in Acts 10:42–48. In the midst of Peter's sermon to Cornelius and his household, the Holy Spirit "came on all those who heard the message" (Acts 10:44). Peter's colleagues "were astonished that the gift of the Holy Spirit had been poured out even on the Gentiles, for they heard them speaking in tongues and praising God" (Acts 10:45–46). It is instructive to note that the Holy Spirit interrupts Peter just as he declares, "[Jesus] commanded us to preach to the people and to testify that he is the one whom God appointed as judge of the living and the dead. *All the prophets testify about him* that everyone who believes in him receives forgiveness of sins through his name" (Acts 10:42–43).

In view of Luke's emphasis on prophetic inspiration throughout his two-volume work and, more specifically, his description of speaking in tongues as prophetic speech in Acts 2:17–18, it can hardly be coincidental that the Holy Spirit breaks in and inspires glossolalia precisely at this point in Peter's sermon. Indeed, as the context makes clear, Peter's colleagues are astonished at what transpires because it testifies to the fact that God has accepted uncircumcised Gentiles. Again, the connection between speaking in tongues and prophecy is crucial for Luke's narrative. In Acts 2:17–18 we are informed that reception of the Spirit of prophecy (the pentecostal gift) is the exclusive privilege of "the servants" of God and that it typically results in miraculous and audible speech.[52] Speaking in tongues is presented as one manifestation of this miraculous, Spirit-inspired speech (Acts 2:4, 17–18). So, when Cornelius and his household burst forth in tongues, this act provides demonstrative proof that they are, in fact, part of the end-time prophetic band of which Joel prophesied. They too are connected to the prophets that "testify" about Jesus (Acts 10:43). This astonishes Peter's colleagues, because they recognize the clear implications that flow from this dramatic event. Since Cornelius and his household are prophets, they must also be "servants" of the Lord (that is, members of the people of God). How, then, can Peter and the others withhold baptism from them? (Acts 10:47–48).

The importance of this connection in the narrative is highlighted further in Acts 11:15–18. Here, as Peter recounts the events associated with the conversion of Cornelius and his household, he emphasizes that "the Holy Spirit came on them as he had come on us at the beginning" (Acts 11:15) and then declares, "God gave them the same gift as he gave us" (Acts 11:17). The fact that Jewish disciples at Pentecost and Gentile believers at Caesarea all speak in tongues is not incidental to Luke's purposes; rather, it represents a significant theme in his story of the movement of the gospel from Jews in Jerusalem to Gentiles in Rome and beyond.

---

52   Luke 1:41; 1:67; Acts 2:4; 4:8, 31; 10:46; 13:9–10; 19:6; cf. Acts 8:15, 18 (implied). In Luke 3:22 and Acts 9:17 inspired speech follows shortly after reception of the Spirit (Luke 4:14, 18–19; Acts 9:20).

Finally, in Acts 19:6 the connection between prophecy and speaking in tongues is again explicitly stated. When Paul laid hands on the Ephesian disciples, the Holy Spirit "came on them, and they spoke in tongues and prophesied." Here, again, tongues serves as a significant sign. Paul's prior question posed to the Ephesian disciples, "Did you receive the Holy Spirit when you believed?" (Acts 19:2), implies another question, "How would we know?" Of course, the pattern and literary connections that Luke has created enable us to answer this question and anticipate the outcome that follows.

All of this demonstrates that Luke has carefully crafted his narrative in order to highlight the connections between Acts 2:4, 10:46, and 19:6. Luke creates this literary linkage by presenting, in each instance, "speaking in tongues" as the definitive and expected sign for reception of the Spirit of prophecy promised by Joel. This sign confirms that the disciples are the true people of God and also validates their proclamation that Jesus is Lord. I would add that this sort of apologetic suggests that Luke's readers routinely experienced this sign themselves. If "speaking in tongues" was relatively unknown to Luke's readers, this message—that tongues validates their proclamation and standing before God—would carry little encouragement. However, if they too experienced glossolalia, then the dialogue in Luke's narrative takes on fresh meaning. Peter's declaration that "[t]hey have received the Holy Spirit just as we have" (Acts 10:47) speaks directly to them and reminds them of the apostolic calling and power that is also theirs. Paul's question "Did you receive the Holy Spirit when you believed?" encourages Luke's readers to reflect on their experiences of Spirit-inspired rapture and recognize that their own expressions of tongues-speech mark them as end-time prophets, people called and empowered to bear witness for Jesus.

These literary connections, which hinge on the phrase "to speak in tongues," challenge us to take a fresh look at Luke's narrative. As I have noted, Luke's record of Jesus's exhortation on prayer (Luke 11:9–13) constitutes a dominical saying that encourages every believer to pray earnestly and expectantly for a prophetic anointing, the pentecostal gift. The full New Testament experience includes speaking in tongues, the external sign of this prophetic gift. Should we settle for anything less?

2.2 *Pentecost as a Paradigm (Acts 2:17–21)*

Every New Testament scholar worth his salt will tell you that Luke 4:16–30, Jesus's dramatic sermon at Nazareth, is paradigmatic for Luke's gospel. All of the major themes that will appear in the gospel are foreshadowed here: the work of the Spirit; the universality of the gospel; the grace of God; and the rejection of Jesus. And, as we have noted, this is the one significant point where the chronology of the Gospel of Luke differs from the Gospel of Mark. Here Luke takes an event from the middle of Jesus's ministry and brings it right up front to inaugurate the ministry of Jesus. Luke does this because he understands that this event, particularly Jesus's recitation of Isaiah 61:1–2 and his declaration that this prophecy is now being fulfilled in his ministry, provides important insights into the nature of Jesus and his mission. This passage, then, provides us with a model for Jesus's subsequent ministry.

Luke provides a similar sort of paradigmatic introduction for his second volume, the book of Acts. After the coming of the Spirit at Pentecost, Peter delivers a sermon (Acts 2:14–41) that parallels that of Jesus in Luke 4. In his sermon, Peter also refers to an Old Testament prophecy concerning the coming of the Spirit, this time Joel 2:28–32, and declares that this prophecy too is now being fulfilled (Acts 2:17–21). The message is clear: Just as Jesus was anointed by the Spirit to fulfill his prophetic vocation, so also Jesus's disciples have been anointed as end-time prophets to proclaim the word of God. The text of Joel 2:28–32 that is cited here, like the paradigmatic passage in Luke 4, also shows signs of careful editing on the part of Luke.

The text of Acts 2:17–21 reads:

> [v. 17] *In the last days*, God says,   [Joel: "after these things"]
> I will pour out my Spirit on all people.
> Your sons and daughters will prophesy
> *Your young men will see visions,*   [Joel: these lines are inverted]
> *Your old men will dream dreams.*
> [v. 18] *Even* on *my* servants, both men and women,   [additions to Joel]
> I will pour out my Spirit in those days,
> *And they will prophesy.*
> [v. 19] I will show wonders in the heaven *above*
> And *signs* on the earth *below*,
> Blood and fire and billows of smoke.
> [v. 20] The sun will be turned to darkness and the moon to blood
> Before the coming of the great and glorious day of the Lord.
> [v. 21] And everyone who calls on the name of the Lord will be saved.
>
>   Acts 2:17–21; modification of Joel 2:28–32 italicized

Luke carefully shapes this quotation from the LXX in order to highlight important theological themes. Three modifications are particularly striking.

2.2.1 Vision and Divine Direction

First, in v. 17 Luke alters the order of the two lines that refer to young men having visions and old men dreaming dreams. In Joel, the old men dreaming dreams comes first. But Luke reverses the order: "Your young men will see visions, your old men will dream dreams" (Acts 2:17). A study of Acts reveals that this alteration is not simply an insignificant stylistic change. Luke gives the reference to "visions" pride of place in order to emphasize its importance. With this modification of the LXX, Luke highlights a theme that he sees as vitally important and that recurs throughout his narrative.

A survey of the key terms is instructive. First, we find that the terms associated with dreams and dreaming occur only here in the book of Acts. The term translated "shall dream" is a future passive of ἐνυπνιάζω. This verb occurs only here and in Jude 8. The noun, ἐνύπνιον ("dream"), is found nowhere else in the New Testament. Clearly, Luke is not big on dreaming.[53]

Luke, however, loves to recount stories that refer to guidance through "visions." At first glance this may not appear to be the case. The noun translated "visions" in v. 17, ὅρασις, occurs four times in the New Testament and only here in Acts. But appearances are often misleading, and this is the case here. Luke uses another term, a close cousin to ὅρασις, the neuter noun, ὅραμα, often and at decisive points in his narrative to refer to "visions." The noun ὅραμα occurs twelve times in the New Testament, and eleven of these occurrences are found in the book of Acts.[54] Luke is, indeed, fond of visions. Although in Acts 2:17 Luke retains the language of the LXX, elsewhere in his narrative he employs his preferred, very similar term to speak of "visions."

References to visions are not only plentiful in Luke's narrative; they also come at strategic moments.[55] Thus, Luke's alteration at this point appears to be theologically motivated. Visions are not the only way that God guides the church in the book of Acts. Yet Luke's point is hard to miss: by linking the "visions" of Joel's prophecy (Acts 2:17) with the visions of the early church, Luke is in effect saying that in "these last days"—that period inaugurated with Jesus's birth and leading up to the Day of the Lord—the mission of the church must be directed by God, who will lead his end-time prophets in special and personal ways, including visions, angelic visitations, and the prompting of the Spirit, so that we might fulfill our calling to take the gospel to "the ends of the earth."[56]

---

53 Note how Luke describes revelatory experiences at night as "visions" and not "dreams" (for example, Acts 16:9–10).

54 Acts 7:31; 9:10, 12; 10: 3, 17, 19; 11:5; 12:9; 16:9, 10; 18:9; and then also in Matt 17:9.

55 For the strategic role of visions in the narrative of Acts see: Acts 9:10–12; 10:3, 17, 19; 11:5; 16:9–10; 18:9–10.

56 While the Spirit is loosely associated with visions in Acts 2:17, elsewhere the Spirit is not

For Luke, the experience of the early church, a church that is supernaturally led by God, serves as a model for his church (and ours).

2.2.2 Signs and Wonders

Second, with the addition of a few words in v. 19, Luke transforms Joel's text to read: "I will show wonders in the heaven *above*, and *signs* on the earth *below*." In this way, Luke consciously links the miracles associated with Jesus (notice the very first verse that follows the quotation from Joel: "Jesus ... was a man accredited by God to you by miracles, wonders and signs," Acts 2:22) and the early church (for example, 2:43) together with the cosmic portents listed by Joel (Acts 2:19–20). All are "signs and wonders" that mark the end of the age. For Luke, "these last days"—remember, Luke's church and ours are firmly rooted in this period—represents an epoch marked by "signs and wonders." Luke, then, is not only conscious of the significant role that miracles have played in the growth of the early church, but he also anticipates that these "signs and wonders" will continue to characterize the ministry of the church to whom he writes.

This text also demonstrates that for Luke, the salvation history presented in his narrative cannot be rigidly segmented into discrete periods. The kingdom of God (or the new age when God's covenant promises begin to find fulfillment) is inaugurated with the miraculous birth of Jesus (or, at the very latest, with Jesus's public ministry, which was marked by miracles) and continues to be progressively realized until his second coming and the consummation of God's redemptive plan. Acts 2:17–22 thus offers an important insight into Luke's view of salvation history. Pentecost is indeed a significant eschatological event, but it does not represent the disciples' entrance into the new age; rather, Pentecost is the fulfillment of Moses' wish that "all the Lord's people were prophets" (Num 11:29; cf. Joel 2:28–29/Acts 2:17–18) and, as such, represents an equipping of the church for its divinely appointed mission.[57] In this crucial passage Luke stresses

---

explicitly described as their source. Although the Lord directs the church through the Spirit (such as in Acts 16:6–7), in Acts the Lord also frequently communicates with and guides his church through other closely related (Acts 8:26–29) but apparently nonpneumatic means (angels, for example, cf. 5:19; 7:31; 8:26; 10:3, 7, 22; 11:13; 12:7–23; 27:23).

57 How are the Spirit and the kingdom of God related in Luke-Acts? The former is the means by which the latter is proclaimed (miracle and word are inextricably related) and thus made available to the world. E. Franklin correctly notes that in Luke-Acts the "Spirit ... is neither a substitute for, nor an embodiment of the Kingdom" ("The Ascension and the Eschatology of Luke-Acts," *SJT* 23 [1970]: 198). According to Luke, the kingdom is present, above all, in Jesus. One can only enter into the kingdom, the realm of God's redemptive blessing, by responding in faith to the proclamation of Jesus. For more on this topic, see Menzies, *The Language of the Spirit*, 59–72 and Cho, *Spirit and Kingdom*, 110–195.

the continuity that unites the story of Jesus and the story of the early church. Luke's two-volume work represents the "one history of Jesus Christ,"[58] a fact that is implied by the opening words of Acts: "In my former book, Theophilus, I wrote about all that Jesus began to do and to teach ..." (Acts 1:1).

One significant implication that flows from this insight is that the birthday of the church cannot be dated to Pentecost. Graham Twelftree argues, correctly I believe, that for Luke, the beginning of the church must be traced back to Jesus's selection of the Twelve.[59] Furthermore, Twelftree asserts that "the ministry of the Church is not seen as distinct from but continues the ministry of Jesus."[60] These conclusions, drawn largely from Luke's portrait of the apostles, are supported by Luke's citation of Joel's prophecy. They have a significant impact on how we view Pentecost and Luke's pneumatology.

2.2.3 Prophecy and Bold Witness

Third, Luke inserts the phrase "And they will prophesy" into the quotation in v. 18. This insertion simply emphasizes what is already present in the text of Joel. Acts 2:17 quotes Joel 2:28 verbatim: "I will pour out my Spirit on all people. Your sons and daughters will prophesy." Now, in v. 18, Luke echoes this refrain. Luke highlights the fact that the Spirit comes as the source of prophetic inspiration because this theme will dominate his narrative. It is a message that Luke does not want his readers to miss. The church in "these last days," Luke declares, is to be a community of prophets—prophets who are called to bring the message of "salvation to the ends of the earth" (Isa 49:6; Acts 1:8). And now Luke reminds his readers that they also have been promised power to fulfill this calling. The Spirit will come and enable his church (and ours) to bear bold witness for Jesus in the face of opposition and persecution.

This theme of bold, prophetic witness is anticipated in Luke's gospel. Jesus is anointed with the Spirit so that he might "preach good news to the poor," so that he might "proclaim freedom for the prisoners" and "proclaim the year of the Lord's favor" (Luke 4:18–19). The parallels between Jesus's experience at the Jordan and that of the disciples at Pentecost are striking and intentional. Through his careful shaping of the narrative, Luke presents Jesus, the ultimate prophet, as a model for all of his followers, from Pentecost onward. Luke's church has a mission to carry out, a message to proclaim.

---

58 Martin Hengel, *Acts and the History of Earliest Christianity*, trans. J. Bowden (London: SCM Press, 1979), 59.
59 Graham H. Twelftree, *People of the Spirit: Exploring Luke's View of the Church* (Grand Rapids: Baker, 2009), 28.
60 Twelftree, *People of the Spirit*, 28.

This motif of bold, Spirit-inspired witness is also highlighted in the teaching of Jesus. Luke foreshadows events that will follow in his second volume by relating the important promise of Jesus recorded in Luke 12:11–12: "When you are brought before synagogues, rulers and authorities, do not worry about how you will defend yourselves or what you will say, for the Holy Spirit will teach you at that time what you should say."

Immediately after Pentecost, in the first story Luke recounts, we begin to see how relevant and important this promise is for the mission of the church. Luke describes the dramatic story of Peter and John's encounter with a crippled beggar and the beggar's miraculous healing. A large crowd gathers, gaping at this marvelous event. The story builds to a climax as the Jewish leaders arrest Peter and John for preaching about the resurrection of Jesus. "You killed the author of life," Peter declares, "but God raised him from the dead. We are witnesses of this" (Acts 3:15). The Jewish leaders, upset with this turn of events, move in and apprehend Peter and John. After spending the night in prison, Peter and John are called before the leaders and questioned. Peter, filled with the Holy Spirit, declares, "Salvation is found in no one else, for there is no other name under heaven given to men by which we must be saved" (Acts 4:12). Peter and John's courage is so striking that it leaves the Jewish leaders astonished and amazed. Finally, after deliberations, the leaders command the apostles to stop preaching about Jesus. But Peter and John reply with incredible boldness. They declare, "Judge for yourselves whether it is right in God's sight to obey you rather than God. For we cannot help speaking about what we have seen and heard" (Acts 4:19–20).

This is merely the beginning of the persecution the end-time prophets must face. Very soon the apostles are again arrested. The Jewish leaders interrogate the apostles and angrily declare, "We gave you strict orders not to teach in this name ... Yet you have filled Jerusalem with your teaching" (Acts 5:28). Peter and the apostles incur the wrath of their opponents when they declare, "We must obey God rather than men! The God of our fathers raised Jesus from the dead ... We are witnesses of these things, and so is the Holy Spirit" (Acts 5:29–32). The apostles are flogged and warned not to speak about Jesus. But the beatings do not have their desired effect. The apostles rejoice that they have been "counted worthy of suffering" for Jesus and continue to proclaim "the good news that Jesus is the Messiah" (Acts 5:41–42).

The persecution intensifies. What began with warnings in Acts 4 and led to beatings in Acts 5 now extends to Stephen's martyrdom in Acts 7. Just as the apostles were strengthened by the Spirit to bear bold witness for Jesus, so also Stephen's witness unto death is inspired by the Spirit (Acts 6:10). In the midst of his sermon to his persecutors recorded in Acts 7, Stephen declares, "You always resist the Holy Spirit! Was there ever a prophet your fathers did not persecute?" (Acts 7:51–52). The powerful irony should not be missed, for this same crowd moves to kill Stephen, a man "full of the Holy Spirit" (Acts 7:55). The witness of another prophet is rejected.

This pattern of bold, Spirit-inspired witness in the face of opposition continues with Paul, the dominant character in the latter portion of Acts. Paul is chosen by the Lord to take the gospel to the Gentiles. We are told that his journey will not be easy. The Lord, speaking to Ananias, declares, "I will show him how much he must suffer for my name" (Acts 9:16). And suffer he does. Yet, in the face of mind-numbing opposition, Paul is guided and strengthened by the Holy Spirit. A trail of churches filled with believers who worship Jesus is left in his wake. The narrative of Acts ends with Paul in prison in Rome, where he "boldly and without hindrance" preaches about Jesus (Acts 28:31).

2.3 Luke's Purpose

Luke's motive in presenting these models of Spirit-inspired ministry—Peter, John, Stephen, and Paul, to name a few—should not be missed.[61] Nevertheless, some dismiss the notion that Luke intended his narrative to serve as a model for the mission of his church. They insist that Luke wrote to provide his contemporaries with a record of the beginnings of the church so that they would know that the message about Jesus is reliable and that the origins of the church were indeed a part of God's divine plan. With these purposes in mind, they insist that Pentecost is a unique event that can never be repeated. The Holy Spirit inspired the apostles for their special function as eyewitnesses to the ministry and resurrection of Jesus (Acts 1:21–22). So also, the Lord validated this apostolic preaching with signs and wonders unique to the early church. Although we are called to faithfully pass on the apostolic message, the missionary methods of the apostolic church, we are told, are unique and not paradigmatic for later generations.[62]

---

61 I agree with Karris, who posits that Luke wrote shortly after the destruction of Jerusalem and its temple (around 75 CE) to "communities whose missionary work and daily existence are prone to danger and suffering—both from Jew and Gentile, but primarily from the Jewish synagogal authorities" (Karris, "Missionary Communities: A New Paradigm for the Study of Luke-Acts," *CBQ* 41 [1979]: 96).

62 For example, Keith J. Hacking, *Signs and Wonders, Then and Now: Miracle-working, Commissioning and Discipleship* (Nottingham: Apollos/IVP, 2006), passim. Hacking argues that the miracles of Jesus and the apostles were not intended to serve as models for the post-apostolic church and that the commissioning accounts are relevant only to a select few. See my review of Hacking's book in *EQ* 79 (2007): 261–265.

Yet two aspects of Luke's narrative call us to challenge this reductionistic perspective. First, it should be noted that Joel's promise, amplified in Acts 2:18, "and they shall prophesy," characterizes potentially every member of the church—young and old, men and women—in the period described as "the last days." According to Luke, this epoch begins with the miraculous birth of Jesus and extends until his second coming, the climax of God's redemptive plan. This promise of prophetic power is thus applicable to Luke's church and ours, not simply to the apostles.

Additionally, this conclusion is supported by the fact that Luke's description of Spirit-inspired prophetic witnesses is not limited solely to those who are apostles in the Acts 1 sense of the word (that is, those who were with Jesus during his ministry and witnessed his resurrection and ascension, Acts 1:21–22). Luke repeatedly describes how the Spirit comes upon the entire community of believers and not just the apostles, first at Pentecost and then in response to prayer in the face of persecution. The latter account explicitly states, "they were all filled with the Holy Spirit and spoke the word of God boldly" (Acts 4:31). Although Peter, John, and the rest of the Twelve bear witness for Jesus, so also do others who are not a part of the apostolic band. Stephen, Philip, and Paul—none of whom qualifies as an apostle according to Acts 1:21–22—are all anointed and directed by the Spirit to bear bold witness for Jesus. Indeed, this is precisely the message that Luke prepares his readers to receive with his account of the Sending of the Seventy (Luke 10:1–16), and it is the message that he dramatically highlights through his summary of Peter's sermon: "In the last days, God says, I will pour out my Spirit on all people ... and they will prophesy" (Acts 2:17–18).[63]

3   Conclusion

Luke has a unique and significant contribution to make to a holistic biblical theology of the Spirit. His pneumatology, I have argued, is different from that of Paul. It is missiological rather than soteriological in nature. The Spirit of Pentecost is, in reality, the Spirit for others—the Spirit that compels and empowers the church to bring the "good news" of Jesus to a lost and dying world. It is this

---

63   Roger Stronstad, *The Prophethood of All Believers: A Study in Luke's Charismatic Theology* (Sheffield, UK: Sheffield Academic, 1999), 85–124. Max Turner, on the other hand, argues that only a select group is empowered for prophetic witness ("Does Luke Believe Reception of the 'Spirit of Prophecy' Makes All 'Prophets'? Inviting Dialogue with Roger Stronstad," *JEPTA* 20 [2000]: 3–24).

Lukan, missiological perspective that gives rich texture to a pentecostal understanding of the Holy Spirit and his work. Pentecostals do recognize that we must do justice to Paul's soteriological contribution by emphasizing the Spirit's role in conversion, regeneration, and sanctification. Yet Pentecostals feel justified in speaking of a baptism in the Spirit that is distinct from conversion, an anointing for service, for we see this as an accurate reflection of Luke's terminology and theology.

Pentecostals, then, recognize that the New Testament speaks of two baptisms in the Spirit—one that is soteriological and initiates the believer into the body of Christ (1 Cor 12:13) and one that is missiological and empowers the believer for service (Acts 1:8). However, Pentecostals believe that it is particularly appropriate to adopt Luke's language and speak of the pentecostal gift as a "baptism in the Holy Spirit." After all, this baptism in the Holy Spirit is promised to every believer, to all of the servants of God (Acts 2:18). And Luke uses the phrase on three occasions, Paul only once. Pentecostals also fear that if Paul's language is employed and the gift of the Spirit received at conversion is designated "the baptism in the Holy Spirit," then a proper understanding of the pentecostal gift will be lost.

The tendency in Protestant churches has been to read Luke in the light of Paul.[64] Paul addresses pastoral concerns in the church; Luke writes a missionary manifesto. Perhaps this explains why Protestant discussions of the Spirit have centered more on his work in the Word and sacraments, the "inner witness" of the Spirit, and less on his mission to the world. Protestant theologians tend to associate the pentecostal gift with conversion and regeneration, which effectively blunts the sharpness of Luke's message. When the pentecostal gift of the Spirit is understood in soteriological terms, Luke's missiological focus and our expectation of it is lost. For it is always possible to argue, as many do, that while all experience the soteriological dimension of the pentecostal gift at conversion, only a select few receive gifts of missiological power. Yet Luke calls us to remember that the church, by virtue of its reception of the pentecostal gift, is a prophetic community empowered for a missionary task.

---

64 NT scholars often share presuppositions that give Paul pride of place. This fact is illustrated by Anthony Thiselton's *The Holy Spirit—In Biblical Teaching, through the Centuries, and Today* (Grand Rapids: Eerdmans, 2013). Thiselton repeatedly questions the wisdom of those who "wish to drive a wedge between Luke and Paul" (490) and flatly states, "Luke and Paul do not stand on equal footing" (496). Nevertheless, the pentecostal reading of the NT described above has gained considerable traction among NT scholars. This judgment finds support in the *Festschrift* published in 2004 to honor James Dunn. See R. Menzies, "A Fitting Tribute: A Review Essay of *The Holy Spirit and Christian Origins: Essays in Honor of James D.G. Dunn*," Pneuma 28, no. 1 (2006): 131–140.

The Spirit in the Gospel according to John, 1John, and 2John: "Rivers of Living Water"

John Christopher Thomas

Though it is often claimed that when it comes to the subject of pneumatology Pentecostals work with a canon within the canon consisting of Luke-Acts, this judgment does not quite fit the evidence of the tradition's written record. As a recent examination of the reception of John 4 and 7 in early pentecostal periodical literature has shown, Pentecostals have drawn often, and extensively, from the Johannine literature in the construction of its pneumatology.[1] While a certain pride of place is given to Luke-Acts owing to the explicit passages that describe the Spirit baptism of various individuals within the narrative, it may not be insignificant to note that there are actually more words of Jesus about the Spirit contained in the Fourth Gospel (FG) than in the other three canonical gospels combined. As the reception of the Johannine literature within early Pentecostalism continues to be tracked, the scope of its significance will likely be seen to be even more extensive than currently appears.

This study seeks to trace the role and significance of pneumatology within the Gospel according to John and 1–2John using a narrative, literary approach that has emerged with an amazing amount of consistency among a variety of biblical scholars who have sought to discern an approach to the interpretation of Scripture worthy of the Pentecostal tradition. This exploration draws heavily from and builds upon my previous studies on this theme within the broader Johannine literature.[2]

---

[1] Cf. Matthew A. Paugh, "Receiving the Living Water: John 4 and John 7 in Early Pentecostal Literature," in D.D. Isgrigg, M.W. Mittelstadt, and R. Wadholm, Jr., eds., *Receiving Scripture in the Pentecostal Tradition: A Reception History* (Cleveland, TN: CPT Press, 2020), 194–224.

[2] Cf. J.C. Thomas, "The Spirit in the Fourth Gospel: Narrative Explorations," in J.C. Thomas, *The Spirit of the New Testament* (Blandford Forum: Deo, 2005), 157–174; "The Johannine Epistles," in K. Warrington and T. Burke, eds., *A Biblical Theology of the Spirit* (London: SPCK, 2014), 250–256; "Revelation," in K. Warrington and T. Burke, eds., *A Biblical Theology of the Spirit* (London: SPCK, 2014), 257–266; "The Spirit in the Book of Revelation: A Narrative Hearing," in Riku P. Tuppurainen, ed., *Reading St Luke's Text and Theology: Pentecostal Voices—Essays in Honour of Roger Stronstad on his 75th Birthday* (Eugene, OR: Wipf & Stock, 2019), 254–264; and "The Spirit in the Book of Revelation," in Craig R. Koester, ed., *Oxford Handbook of the Book of Revelation* (Oxford: Oxford University Press, 2020), 241–255.

1 The Spirit in the Gospel According to John

As most students of the Gospel according to John are aware, the FG falls rather naturally into two major parts, the Book of Signs (1:19–12:50) and the Book of Glory (13:1–20: 31), enveloped by a Prologue (1:1–18) and an Epilogue (21:1–25). A survey of the gospel reveals that explicit references to the Spirit are almost equally divided between the two major books, with no explicit references in either the Prologue or Epilogue, though some interpreters see an implicit reference in the Prologue's occurrences of "grace" in 1:14 and 16 (twice).

2 John 1:32–33

The first explicit reference to the Spirit occurs in the testimony of John (1:19–34) in the context of his prophetic words identifying Jesus as "the Lamb of God who takes away the sin of the world" (1:29) and as the one who was before him, of whom he had spoken earlier (1:15, 27). The meaning of John's baptism is connected to the manifestation of Jesus to Israel (1:31). The reader encounters the following words in vv. 32–33:

> And John testified saying, "I beheld the Spirit coming down as a dove out of heaven and he was remaining upon him." Even I did not know him, but the one who sent me to baptize in water, that one said to me, "The one upon whom you see the Spirit coming down and remaining on him, this is the one who will baptize in the Holy Spirit."

Significantly, John's words are enveloped by explicit reference to his testimony (1:19, 34).[3] While it is rightly observed that the FG nowhere describes the baptism of Jesus by John, the implied connection between the purpose of John's baptism and John's understanding of the significance of the Spirit's descending and remaining upon Jesus may well indicate that the words of John in v. 32 are somehow connected to his ministry of water baptism. The Spirit is described as coming down and remaining upon Jesus, perhaps causing the reader to wonder why the Logos Incarnate, whose role in the creation of all things has been recounted (1:3) and who has been described as God (1:1), even the only begotten God (1:18), would have need of the Spirit coming and residing upon him continually, as the imperfect tense of the verb (ἔμεινεν) implies. The narrative

---

3 J. Ramsey Michaels, *The Gospel of John*, NICNT (Grand Rapids: Eerdmans, 2010), 113.

here reveals that despite the dominant Logos Christology with which the FG begins, a Spirit Christology stands alongside it, creating for the reader a dialectic between the Spirit coming and remaining upon Jesus, on the one hand, and Jesus's activity as the one who will baptize in the Holy Spirit, on the other hand (1:33).[4] Significantly, in the FG, unlike the Synoptics, it is only after the Spirit has come down out of heaven and remained upon Jesus that he is identified as the one who will baptize with the Holy Spirit. Thus, Jesus is not only the one upon whom the Spirit descends, but he is also the one who will baptize with this very Spirit.

3   John 3

The next occurrence of Spirit language in the FG is found in Jesus's well-known encounter with Nicodemus.

3.1   Verse 3

When Jesus enters into the dialogue, he does not respond to Nicodemus's initial words of praise. Rather, demonstrating that he knows what is in "man" (τῷ ἀνθρώπῳ—John 2:25), Jesus speaks past the praise to the real issue facing Nicodemus, "Amen, amen, I say to you, unless anyone is born again (ἄνωθεν), it is not possible to see the kingdom of God." The phrase "unless one is born from above" could not help but remind the reader of the Prologue's words that "those who believe in his name are given authority to become children of God" for they are born of God.[5] On the surface of it, the words speak of being "born again." But with this term (ἄνωθεν), the reader are introduced to a phenomenon that will occur at numerous places as the FG unfolds, where Jesus will employ a word that has a double meaning, which his dialogue partners misunderstand, taking the meaning of the word at its most literal level, while Jesus speaks at another level. Here, the Greek word (ἄνωθεν) is taken to mean "again." But what the reader understands is that the term also means "from above," an understanding that fits perfectly with the words of the Prologue—"unless one is born from

---

4 Tricia Gates Brown, *Spirit in the Writings of John: Johannine Pneumatology in Social-Scientific Perspective*, JSNTSup 253 (London and New York: T & T Clark International, 2003), 89–90; Andrew T. Lincoln, *The Gospel according to Saint John*, BNTC 4 (London: Continuum, 2005), 114; and Marianne Meye Thompson, *John: A Commentary*, NTL (Louisville: Westminster John Knox, 2015), 47.

5 D.A. Carson, *The Gospel according to John* (Grand Rapids: Eerdmans, 1991), 651–655; Lincoln, *The Gospel according to Saint John*, 150; Michaels, *The Gospel of John*, 180; and Thompson, *John: A Commentary*, 80.

above—born of God—one is not able to see the kingdom of God." The nearest the readers have come to the idea of the "kingdom of God" is in Nathaniel's declaration that Jesus is "the king of Israel" (1:49),[6] perhaps suggesting some kind of connection between this king and this kingdom.

3.2 Verse 4

Nicodemus's response indicates that he misunderstands Jesus's words, taking Jesus's words to mean a second physical birth—and he is obviously right about this, but he quite misunderstands "again" (ἄνωθεν) to mean a "second" (δεύτερον) birth rather than a birth "from above."

3.3 Verse 5

Jesus continues this dialogue with the words, "Amen, amen I say to you, unless one is born of water and blood, one is not able (δύναται) to enter into the kingdom of God." The phrase "unless one is born of water and Spirit" is filled with interpretive challenges and not a little ambiguity. Owing to their narrative location, where "birth from above" seems very much to be the point of Jesus's initial statement, it would appear likely that the reader might well understand water and Spirit as having reference to things that come "from above."[7] In other words, it seems that "water and Spirit" would serve to clarify "from above" in ways not unlike the fashion in which the words "from above" clarify "born of God." The Spirit has already been described as "coming down … out of heaven" (1:32), suggesting that the place of the Spirit's origin is "from above."[8] Such an understanding would seem straightforward enough. However, the reference to water is a bit more difficult to discern. While it might be reasonably thought that water, in the form of rain, for example, is to be associated with coming "from above," water has other associations within the narrative, where it exhibits a theologically significant function (1:31; 2:1–11). But in addition to the way water and Spirit might clarify birth "from above," such an understanding would not exhaust the meaning of water in 3:5, as water may have a secondary reference to the baptism of John, by means of which the Lamb of God is manifested to Israel. For though the reader does not yet know it, both Jesus (3:22; 4:1) and his disciples (4:2) will be described in the FG as baptizing, indicating an appreciation for this practice and its meaning. Another interpretive option is that the hearers would see in water and Spirit reference to the amniotic fluids that accompany childbirth, while Spirit is understood as having reference to birth from above and

---

6 Michaels, *The Gospel of John*, 180.
7 On this question cf. Thompson, *John: A Commentary*. 80.
8 Lincoln, *The Gospel according to Saint John*, 150.

a heavenly one.[9] Unfortunately for this interpretation, the external evidence to which appeal is often made is later than the time of Jesus—and even later than the composition of the FG. Other views are less likely to be in the minds of the reader, for example that water here refers to full-blown Christian baptism. Fourth, once again reference is made to the kingdom of God, likely bringing further clarity to their understanding of birth "from above."

3.4   Verse 6

Jesus continues, "That which is born of flesh is flesh, and that which is born of Spirit is Spirit." Despite any ambiguity in the text, the reader would likely see here a reference to the Prologue where those who believe in his name are not "born out of blood, nor the desire of the flesh, nor the desire of a man, but are born of God" (1:13). While it is just possible that this verse continues a distinction between birth by water and birth by the Spirit, the contrast between the births spoken of in v. 6 point back to Nicodemus's misunderstanding of Jesus's words as having reference to a second physical birth. Birth "from above" is birth by the Spirit and that born of the Spirit is Spirit. Thus, the reader's understanding of what it means to be born of God has increased exponentially.

3.5   Verse 7

Jesus continues the dialogue with the words, "Do not be amazed that I said to you, it is necessary for you to be born from above." Such words suggest that Nicodemus is a bit lost by this point, perhaps even exasperated. Jesus's admonition for Nicodemus not to be amazed reveals a certain inability on Nicodemus's part to understand the significance of Jesus's words about birth from above, and though the reader does not yet know it, in the FG the word "amazed" (θαυμάσῃς) will become a term that expresses this inability on the part of others to understand and, consequently, their inability to respond by believing Jesus and his claims (4:17; 5:20, 28; 7:15, 21).

3.6   Verse 8

If Nicodemus is amazed to the point of incomprehension, it doesn't get easier for him to understand as Jesus delves deeper still with regard to the work of the Spirit. "The Spirit blows where he desires and you hear his voice, but you do not know from whence he comes and where he goes; so it is with each one who has been born of the Spirit." Such language moves in and out of double meaning, for while the subject of the verse appears to be the Spirit, in the Greek language the

---

9 Brown, *Spirit in the Writings of John*, 120–121.

word for "wind" (πνεῦμα) is the same as the word for "Spirit." Jesus begins with a description of the fact that the wind blows where it desires to blow and the human being, though not necessarily seeing where the wind blows, can hear its sound—literally its "voice" (φωνὴν). But no one is able to control in which direction the wind blows, where it comes from and when it goes. The mysterious nature of the wind's (πνεῦμα) movements is completely beyond the control and comprehension of humankind. At best, one can see its effects and hear its sound. It is this image that Jesus likens to the one who is born of the Spirit. The activity of the Spirit comes from another world. One cannot control or domesticate it any more than one can domesticate the wind. So, it would seem that the one born of the Spirit can feel and hear the power and voice of the Spirit.

3.7   Verse 9

Such an analogy leaves Nicodemus completely exasperated, evidenced in his answer, "How are these things able (δύναται) to be?" Nicodemus's earlier statement with regard to no one being able to perform the signs that Jesus does unless God is with him gives way to his lack of understanding of how one can be born of God and, now, the way in which the Spirit of God works. Thus, despite Jesus's admonition to the contrary, Nicodemus is amazed, even bewildered, by all that he has heard. And with these words Nicodemus seems to disappear from the stage—for a while.

3.8   Verse 10

Nicodemus's exasperation and lack of understanding are met by a stern rebuke from Jesus: "You are the teacher of Israel and these things you do not know?" The emphatic personal pronoun "you" (σὺ) appears here, making clear Jesus's rebuke. It is also apparent that Jesus expects the teacher of Israel to know the things about which Jesus has spoken, a knowledge that seems tied to the emerging meaning of Israel in the FG. From outside the land of Israel proper John comes baptizing in water that the Lamb of God might be manifested to "Israel." Nathaniel, identified by Jesus as a "true, or authentic Israelite," offers testimony to Jesus that he is "the king of Israel." Nicodemus as "the teacher of Israel" should know at least as much as the "true Israelite," who—without the extended dialogue that Nicodemus enjoys with Jesus—goes so far as to declare Jesus to be the Son of God. Such a contrast makes Nicodemus's lack of understanding all the more significant.

3.9   Verse 11

Jesus continues with the words, "Amen, amen I say to you, that which we know we are speaking and that which we have seen we are testifying, and our testimony you do not receive." The fact that Jesus uses this solemn authoritative formula, "Amen, amen I say to you," to address Nicodemus for a third time underscores the importance of this dialogue. For what has been revealed in this dialogue conveys more about what being "born of God" means than had been revealed to this point; it underscores the importance of being born "from above," and the way in which the Spirit works in those who are so born of the Spirit.

3.10　*Verse 12*

Jesus sharpens the point further in v. 12: "If the earthly things I said to you and you do not believe, how if I speak to you the heavenly things will you believe?" Despite the fact that Jesus has at least ostensibly spoken of some heavenly things—being born "from above," for example—here he characterizes the things about which he has spoken with Nicodemus as "earthly things." Such language suggests that, all evidence to the contrary, he has not yet begun to speak of "heavenly things"! Here, Nicodemus's lack of belief is so pronounced that instead of a promise of hearing of "heavenly things," he is rebuked for not being able to understand "earthly things."

4　John 4

The next passage in which the Spirit figures prominently is in the story of the Samaritan woman.

4.1　*Verse 10*

Jesus's response to the woman's push-back to his request for a drink is reminiscent of his words to Nicodemus[10] in that they bypass her words of surprise and speak to her spiritual need. Just as Nicodemus misunderstood Jesus to be a teacher, the Samaritan woman mistakes him to be simply a weary traveler. "Jesus answered and said to her, 'If you knew the gift of God and who is the one who says to you, "Give me a drink," you would ask him and he would give to you living water.'" Once again attention is given to what is and is not known, when Jesus says, "if you knew," implying that the woman does not know who Jesus is at this point. While the phrase "gift of God"[11] might theoretically mean any number of things, for the reader it is clear that Jesus is the unrivaled gift of

---

10　Michaels, *The Gospel of John*, 240.
11　A phrase that appears only here in the four canonical gospels.

God, who loved the world so much that he gave his unique Son, who would take away the sin of the world. Jesus's words suggest that this Samaritan woman is part of the world for whom Jesus was given. By now it is becoming clear that the phrase "Give me a drink" is of specific spiritual significance and is an invitation to that of which Jesus speaks. If she asks him for such a drink, he would give her what could literally be translated "running water" (ὕδωρ ζῶν).[12] Given their experience with the term "again/from above" in the Nicodemus dialogue, the reader may well suspect that with this term, too, there may be more depth than its surface meaning.

4.2   Verse 11

Just as Jesus's words were misunderstood in the temple and by Nicodemus, so the woman misunderstands him: "She says to him, 'Sir (κύριε), you have no bucket and the well is deep; therefore, from where do you have the running water?'" The woman clearly understands Jesus as referring to the "running water" into which the well has tapped, understanding "running water" as the water of a stream or river rather than the flat-tasting water from a cistern. For a second time a form of the word "bucket" (ἄντλημα) appears in this passage; earlier (v. 7) the Greek verb translated "to draw" (ἀντλῆσαι) comes from the same root word. The term both underscores the literal nature of the woman's understanding of Jesus's words and prepares the reader for the deeper significance that will be attached to this term later in the narrative.

4.3   Verse 12

She continues in v. 12, "You are not greater than our father Jacob are you, who gave to us the well and he drank of it and his sons [drank of it] and his livestock [drank of it]?" With these words the readers are introduced to Johannine irony, where the speaker intends his or her words in one way, but ironically speaks the truth through them. In this somewhat sarcastic question, she is actually stating the truth, as the reader knows that Jesus is indeed greater than "our father Jacob"; in point of fact he is much greater.[13]

4.4   Verses 13–14

"Jesus answered and said to her, 'Each one who drinks of this water will thirst again. But whoever drinks of the water which I will give to him, will never, ever

---

12   As the phrase appears to mean in the Didache 7.1, 2, where the reader is instructed to be baptized in "running water" rather than in a pool of water.

13   Lincoln, *The Gospel according to Saint John*, 174.

thirst forever, but the water which I give will be in him a well of water springing up into eternal life.'" Jesus contrasts the water of which he speaks with the water in the well. His words in v. 13 appear to make a rather mundane point, the one who drinks of this well water will have to drink again. The verb tenses found in this verse underscore the ongoing nature of such drinking, with "each one who drinks" (πᾶς ὁ πίνων) occurring in the present tense—indicating habitual drinking—with the verb translated "will be thirsty" (διψήσει) occurring in the future tense—indicating the need for continual drinking.

Jesus's words in v. 14 about the water that he will give contrast in almost every way with what has been said about the water from the well. First, the reader would likely notice the appearance of the emphatic first-person personal pronoun "I" (ἐγώ), which would at the least be taken as a point of contrast between the water Jacob gave, mentioned by the woman, and the water that Jesus will give—a partial response to her ironic question, "you are not greater than our father Jacob are you?" Second, they would also likely be struck by the fact that whoever drinks of the water Jesus will give will never, ever thirst again. Such a statement would push the reader to contemplate the fact that this water is as different from the well water as birth from above is different from natural birth. Third, in the phrase "will never, ever thirst again forever," the reader are introduced to a formula that will reappear in the FG with some degree of regularity. The grammatical construction consists of the following combination in the Greek text: the double negative (οὐ μὴ), a future active or aorist subjunctive verb (here the future, διψήσει), and the phrase "into the age" (εἰς τὸν αἰῶνα). This construction is the strongest form of negation in the Greek language, and with one notable exception (13:8), this construction will be used in the FG with reference to Jesus's offer of eternal life (8:51, 52; 10:28; 11:26). Fourth, the water that Jesus promises will not simply slake their thirst forever, it will be "a well of water springing up into eternal life." Rather than having to come to a well for this water, the well will be located within the one who drinks of it. If Jacob's well taps into an underground stream of "running water," the one who drinks of the water Jesus gives will have in him- or herself a well that taps into this "living water," the other meaning of the phrase translated "running water" (ὕδωρ ζῶν), which the reader by this point may have figured out. Fifth, though the water is not technically described as "living water" here, its chief characteristic—"leaping up" (ἁλλομένου)—makes this point clear, as this term is normally used to describe "the quick movements of living beings, like jumping," with this apparently being the only instance in antiquity of it describing the actions of water.[14]

---

14 R.E. Brown, *The Gospel according to John I–XII*, AB 29 (Garden City, NY: Doubleday, 1966), 171.

Sixth, again eternal life language appears. Such an appearance would not take the reader by surprise, for this phrase has previously occurred three times in the narrative, where the reader has learned that it designates "life of the coming age," "unending life," "life that comes from one who is himself Life," "divinely endowed life," "life from another world." It is ultimately equated with being born from above, with the lifting up of the Son of Man (3:14–15), and with believing in the Son (3:16, 36). Here, it comes from drinking the "living water" that Jesus gives.

4.5   Verse 15

"The woman says to him, 'Sir, give to me this water in order that I might not thirst nor come here to draw.'" In contrast to Nicodemus, who never asks to be born from above, the woman does indeed ask Jesus to give her this water, a request he had encouraged earlier in the dialogue (v. 10). But she has not yet left her literal understanding that the purpose clause, "in order that" (ἵνα), makes clear, as she understands that if he gives her this water, she will not thirst any longer and will not have to come back to Jacob's well to provide for her daily physical needs. Once again, a term from the "bucket" word family appears here in the verb translated "draw" (ἀντλεῖν).

4.6   Verse 22

Jesus continues the dialogue with words that have often been misunderstood. "You worship what you do not know; we worship what we know, because salvation is of the Jews." The reader would likely notice the occurrence of the emphatic personal pronouns, "you" (ὑμεῖς) and "we" (ἡμεῖς), which serve to distinguish between the Samaritans and the Jews, language that appears to pick up on the woman's own use of "our fathers" and "you" in v. 20. Second, following on the heels of Jesus's somewhat inclusive words in v. 21 about "you will worship," his words, "you worship what you do not know" might initially strike the reader as being overly harsh. But these words are not some expression of ethnic or even theological rivalry; rather, they seem based on the fact that the Samaritans have cut themselves off from a large portion of redemptive history by holding only to the Torah. Although they are indeed looking for "the prophet," which is in accordance with the teaching of the Torah, they have cut themselves off from the revelation about the Messiah found in the prophets and the writings, especially the Psalms.[15] If the Samaritan woman desires to drink of the "living

---

15   Craig S. Keener, *The Gospel of John: A Commentary 1* (Peabody, MA: Hendrickson, 2016), 610–611.

water" that Jesus offers, she must modify her view of redemptive history and the sacred texts, for salvation is of the Jews. As it turns out, through the Jews God has prepared for and made his fullest revelation in the incarnation of his unique Son. Third, the reader might well be struck by the statement, "salvation is of the Jews." Though this is the first appearance of the word "salvation" (σωτηρία) in the FG, the reader would be well aware that the unique Son was sent "in order that the world might be saved (σωθῇ) through him" (3:17). Thus, the offer of salvation is not the exclusive domain of any particular group, but rather has the whole world in its purview.

4.7 Verse 23

"But an hour comes and now is, when the true worshippers will worship the Father in Spirit and Truth; for the Father seeks such ones as these to worship him." Here, the contrast, "but" (ἀλλά), isn't drawn between current Samaritan and Jewish worship practices, as the reader might expect. Rather, the contrast is between places of worship—Mt Gerizim and Jerusalem, on the one hand, and true worship, on the other hand. Earlier Jesus had informed the woman that an hour comes when neither of these sites will be the place in which "you" worship (v. 21). In this verse Jesus reveals that the hour has already arrived—"and now is"—recalling the way in which eschatological realities are already in play in the FG (3:18–21). Attention turns from the proper place of worship to "true worshippers." The emphasis observed in the repetition, "true worshippers will worship," underscores the activity of worship itself. The focus of authentic worshipers' worship is the Father (cf. v. 21). It takes place "in Spirit and in Truth." While this statement might be taken as a hendiadys being translated "the Spirit of Truth," here the readers learn that the Spirit is not only the means by which one is "born from above," but the Spirit also makes true worship possible. True worship of the Father is possible only for those who are children of God, those "born from above" by means of the Spirit. It would hardly be surprising to the reader that true worshipers worship the Father "in Truth." The reader is likely to see a reference to Jesus with this mention of Truth, for he is full of grace and Truth (1:14), out of whose fullness we all have received one grace after another (1:16). It naturally follows that "the one who does the truth comes to the Light" (3:21). If this is the reader's suspicions, they will be confirmed as the FG unfolds, for Jesus will say of himself, "I am the Way, the Truth, and the Life" (14:6). Neither would it be going too far to suggest that in this sense the reader would be encountering the idea that true worship is trinitarian in nature, involving Father, Son, and Holy Spirit.[16]

---

16   I am indebted to my late colleague R. Hollis Gause for first bringing this interpretive pos-

The import of Jesus's words is that he is essential for true worship, perhaps causing the reader to wonder if "the temple of his body" mentioned in 2:21 does not suggest that his body is a vehicle for true worshipers.

4.8   Verse 24

"God is Spirit, and it is necessary for those who worship him to worship in Spirit and in Truth." From the beginning of the FG the reader has known of the unique relationship that exists between the Father and Jesus. Now the reader learns of the special identity that is shared by God and the Spirit when Jesus says, "God is Spirit." Such a statement reveals that not only is the Spirit essential for true worship, owing to the Spirit's role in the believer's birth from above, but that the Spirit is also essential to true worship, owing to the Spirit's shared identity with God.

4.9   Verse 25

Unlike Nicodemus, the Samaritan woman does not disappear from the stage;[17] rather, she utters an incredible statement: "I know that messiah comes, the one called the Christ; when that one comes, he will proclaim to us everything." Although it does not appear that the Samaritans held to a belief in the Messiah,[18] the Samaritan woman makes this claim employing "knowledge" language, "I know" (οἶδα). In contrast to Jesus's words about the Samaritans worshiping what they do not know, her knowledge and belief are almost startling. At the least, it shows her continual drawing near to Jesus and growing belief in him. Her statement about what the Messiah will do dovetails nicely with the Samaritan belief about the prophet like Moses, the Taheb: "when he comes, he will tell us everything."[19]

4.10   Verse 26

The dialogue culminates in the words of Jesus, "I Am, the one who speaks with you." This is the first of many occasions when Jesus will use the words "I Am" (ἐγώ εἰμι) as a means of self-identification. Here, the reader would likely be struck by the way in which this formula so parallels Yahweh's self-identification in the words he speaks to Moses to tell Israel, "I Am has sent you" (Exod 3:14). For the reader, this identification dovetails nicely with all that they know about

---

sibility to my attention. Cf. also the comments of Lincoln, *The Gospel according to Saint John*, 177–178.
17   Brown, *Spirit in the Writings of John*, 138.
18   The evidence from Justin Martyr (*Apology* I 53.6) notwithstanding.
19   Cf. Michaels, *The Gospel of John*, 255–257, and Thompson, *John: A Commentary*, 106.

Jesus, who was with God, who is God, who is the only begotten God, who is the creator of the world, and who speaks on the basis of his own authority.

4.11 Verses 28–30

The effect of this dialogue on the Samaritan woman is described in the next verses: "Therefore, the woman left her water pot and departed into the city and says to the men, 'Come see a man who said to me everything I ever did, is this not the Christ?' They went out of the city and were coming to him." In v. 28, the leaving of the pot (ὑδρίαν) seems to be a sign that the woman has believed in Jesus and drunk from the "living water,"[20] while her testimony ultimately leads to the belief of the Samaritans and their confession of Jesus as "the savior of the world."[21] Jesus's acknowledgement of the validity of their belief is indicated by his remaining with them two more days (vv. 39–42).

5 John 6:63

The next reference to the Spirit in the FG is found in 6:63 just after the bread of life discourse. Here the reader learns of the very tight interplay that exists between eating the flesh and drinking the blood of Jesus, on the one hand, and the work of the Spirit, on the other. Just as drinking of the living water brings eternal life, so eating his flesh and drinking his blood is tied to eternal life. Jesus's statement that his words are Spirit and life is consistent with the fact that from the beginning of the FG, Jesus (the Word) is closely identified with life (1:3–4), and in 14:6 he will make this identification explicit. Neither is it surprising that the one upon whom the Spirit descends and remains (1:32), the one who will baptize with the Holy Spirit (1:33), and the one who has been given the Spirit without measure (3:34) should speak words that bring life.[22] This statement reinforces the close relationship that exists between the Spirit and the Truth suggested earlier in 4:23.

---

20 Cf. J. Thomaskutty, "Johannine Women as Paradigms in the Indian Context," *Acta Theologica* Supplementum 27 (2019), 87.
21 Brown, *Spirit in the Writings of John*, 138.
22 F. Porsch (*Pneuma und Wort: Ein exegetischer Beitrag zur Pneumatologie des Johannesevangeliums* [Frankfurt: J. Knecht, 1974], 210–212) argues that Jesus conveys the Spirit through his words.

6 John 7:37–39

Another clear reference to the Holy Spirit found in the Book of Signs (John 1–12) occurs in 7:39, a text filled with interpretive challenges. The narrative context of the verse is the last great day of the feast (of Tabernacles). Jesus stands and cries out inviting all who are thirsty to come and drink. But at this point a host of questions arises, each of which has some bearing upon the meaning of the text.[23]

The words of v. 39 are most germane for this study.

"He said this concerning the Spirit which those who believed in him were about to receive. For the Spirit was not yet, because Jesus had not yet been glorified."

What do the words "the Spirit was not yet" (οὔπω γὰρ ἦν πνεῦμα) mean in this verse? Clearly, they cannot be taken in an overly literal way to mean that the Spirit was not yet in existence.[24] Nor does the reader understand them to mean that the Spirit can only work apart from Jesus—after his glorification—for the FG has gone to great lengths to indicate that the Spirit is extraordinarily active in Jesus and his ministry.[25] Nor does it appear that the reader would be inclined to take this statement to mean that the Spirit was not yet active in the lives of those who already believe in Jesus. As has been made clear, those who believe in Jesus are given authority to become children of God (1:12), a birth that takes place only by means of the Spirit (3:5); those who drink of the living water that Jesus gives will have "a well of water leaping up into eternal life" (4:14); and those who so experience the Spirit are true worshipers who worship the Father in Spirit and Truth (4:23–24). The unequivocal belief of the Samaritans and the disciples in Jesus strongly suggests that the Spirit is already active to some extent in their lives, a reality that will be reaffirmed later (14:17).

Failing to appreciate this narrative context of 7:39 can result in a one-dimensional understanding of the Spirit's activity in John, an interpretation that the narrative itself tends to subvert. What, then, does the phrase "the Spirit was not yet" mean? If Jesus is the source of the rivers of living water, this imagery fits rather well with the imagery found in Jesus's dialogue with the Samaritan woman. There the reader learns that those who drink of the liv-

---

23 On these questions cf. Thomas, "The Spirit in the Fourth Gospel," 163–165.
24 However, cf. the attempt to take the phrase literally by H. Boer, *Pentecost and Missions* (Grand Rapids: Eerdmans, 1975), 77–87.
25 Despite his acknowledgement of this fact, D. Holwerda (*Holy Spirit and Eschatology in the Gospel of John* [Kampen: Kok, 1959], 1–2) still regards the Holy Spirit as "primarily a post-ascension figure in the Gospel of John."

ing water will have in themselves "a well of water leaping up to eternal life." As such, it is clear that a well is not a source of water but rather a channel by which one gains access to a source of water. Just as Jacob's well tapped into a stream or river of subterranean running water, so the one who drinks of the living water that Jesus provides has within him/herself a well that taps into the living water that has its origin in Jesus. It comes as little surprise, then, when the reader learns in 7:38–39 that rivers of living water come from Jesus. Thus, this passage is in continuity with that which has come before it in the narrative.

There is also some degree of discontinuity with what precedes, for the reader would not expect from the imagery of "a well of water leaping up into eternal life" to find "rivers of living water" as the source, but rather a river of living water. Therefore, the imagery found in 7:38–39 is pregnant with meaning. While the "rivers of living water" certainly includes the idea of salvation (and in abundance: cf. 3:34), it suggests that there is more in store for those who believe in him than they have previously understood, as a dimension of the Spirit's work will only be experienced after Jesus's glorification. With this, the reader detects a rather subtle shift in emphasis on the Spirit's work in the FG. The tension created by the statement in v. 39 that "the Spirit was not yet," despite the Spirit's activity earlier in the narrative, prepares the reader for the extensive teaching about the future role of the Paraclete that awaits in John 14–16 and may remind them that Jesus is the one who will baptize in the Holy Spirit (1:33).

7   John 14:15–31

The story of the Spirit in the FG continues in the Farewell Materials.[26] In fact, the bulk of the FG's teaching about the Spirit is found in chapters 14–16. The first Paraclete passage appears in 14:15–31,[27] where the work of the Paraclete is linked both to Jesus's departure and the keeping of his words. Several aspects of the Spirit's nature and identity are revealed in this section.

First, the Paraclete comes from the Father as a result of Jesus's own request. Jesus, who had earlier encouraged the disciples to ask the Father for anything

---

26 While the Greek term πνεῦμα occurs in John 11:33 and 13:21, in both texts reference is being made to Jesus's (human) spirit. With both uses one is not far from a description of the inward emotions of Jesus.

27 The origin of the term παράκλητος has been much debated. For an intriguing proposal regarding the word's etymology cf. G.E. Ladd, *A Theology of the New Testament* (Grand Rapids: Eerdmans, 1974), 293.

in his name (14:13–14), states in v. 16 that "Even I (κἀγὼ) will ask …," a statement that serves to encourage the disciples to ask. It might at first glance be surprising that the one who is anointed by the Spirit, who has been given the Spirit without measure, and who will baptize with the Spirit would have to ask that the Father send the Paraclete. However, it should be remembered that in the FG Jesus does nothing on his own, but only those things which the Father desires that he do.

Second, the Paraclete is called "another Paraclete" in v. 16, implying that Jesus himself functions as a Paraclete,[28] pointing to the intimate relationship of Jesus and the Paraclete, while also serving to underscore the fact that the Spirit is to function in a way analogous to Jesus in the lives of the disciples. While Jesus is soon to depart, the Paraclete will be with them forever.

Third, it comes as no surprise that the Paraclete is called the Spirit of Truth, for earlier in the FG Jesus is said to be "full of Truth" (1:14) and identifies himself as "the Truth" in 14:6. This title and/or name underscores the intimate connection between Jesus and the Spirit, indicates the trustworthiness of the Spirit, and reminds the reader of the relationship between Spirit and Truth found in 4:23.

Fourth, like Jesus (cf. 1:10–11), the Paraclete is not received by the world, for he is not seen or known by it (v. 17). In contrast, the believers know the Spirit for he remains among them and *is* in them (v. 17).[29] This statement at once affirms the basic continuity between the Spirit's work with the disciples to this point in the narrative while pointing to the discontinuity of his future work. Not only has the Paraclete been present among the disciples through the ministry of the Spirit-anointed Jesus, but he is also in those (mainly the disciples, but others as well) who, believing in his name, have become children of God through birth by the Spirit, who have drunk of the living water, and have *in* them "a well of living water leaping up into eternal life."[30]

---

28   Michaels, *The Gospel of John*, 783; Brown, *Spirit in the Writings of John*, 191; and Thompson, *John: A Commentary*, 312–313.

29   Following the textual tradition that supports the present-tense verb ἐστιν rather than the future tense ἔσται. The manuscript support for ἐστιν [p66* B D* W] is slightly better than that for ἔσται [p66c p75vid a A Db L], given the combination of B and D* with the original reading of p66, and in this context ἐστιν would not only be the more difficult reading, but also the reading that best explains the origin of the other reading, since a scribe would be more likely to change the present to the future to conform to the future context of the promise of the coming Paraclete.

30   For an interpretation that builds on the future tense ἔσται and sees the presence of the Spirit among the disciples as confined to the ministry of Jesus, cf. I. de la Potterie, "Parole et esprit dans S. Jean," in M. de Jonge, ed., *L'Évangile de Jean: Sources, Rédaction, Théologie* (Leuven: Leuven University Press, 1987), 192–193.

Fifth, in v. 26 the Spirit is called the Paraclete, the Holy Spirit, and is identified as coming from the Father. The Spirit will do two things. 1) He will teach the disciples all things. The reader of the FG knows that one of Jesus's primary roles is that of teacher (1:38; 3:2; 6:59; 7:14, 28, 35; 8:20; 11:28; 13:13, 14; cf. also 18:20; 20:16). Thus, the Paraclete, the Spirit of Truth, the one who is sent by the Father, will do precisely what Jesus has done—teach, a function necessitated by Jesus's departure. 2) The Paraclete will remind the disciples of the things that Jesus said to them. Although the disciples believe throughout the FG, they do not always fully understand what Jesus has done or said. The first time the reader learns this is after Jesus has cleansed the temple (2:22). This also occurs in 12:16 and is implied in 13:7. In 14:26 Jesus promises that the Paraclete will play an active role in the disciples' memory and understanding. It is significant that both in 2:22 and 12:16 the disciples remember after the resurrection/glorification of Jesus. It is the Paraclete who is responsible for the disciples remembering the things that Jesus said and did.

8 John 15:26

In Jesus's words about the world's hatred of him and the disciples, the Paraclete is mentioned again. While the Paraclete comes from the Father, Jesus himself has a role in his sending. Identified again as the Spirit of Truth, it is now revealed that the Paraclete will be active in his witness to Jesus. Although the text does not explicitly state that the Spirit will inspire the witness of the disciples, 15:27–16:4a strongly suggests that the disciples will not experience the persecution of a hating world passively but will offer witness to Jesus that is anointed by the Spirit.[31]

9 John 16:4 B-15

The next Paraclete passage (16:4b-15), reveals for the first time that Jesus must depart in order for the Paraclete to come (v. 7). This unexpected revelation coincides with the fact that the Paraclete will in many ways be to the disciples what Jesus has been. While the promise of the Paraclete in the first passage focused primarily upon his work within the circle of believers, this passage focuses primarily upon his role in relation to the world, a theme introduced in 15:26.

---

31   For this idea cf. Holwerda, *Holy Spirit and Eschatology in the Gospel of John*, 51–52.

The FG consistently presents the story of Jesus as a trial, with terms like testimony, interrogation, belief, and judgment appearing frequently.[32] Continuing this motif, v. 8 reveals that the Paraclete will serve as a legal representative. However, instead of being an "advocate," he will serve as a prosecuting attorney, convicting the world on three counts: sin, righteousness, and judgment. In the FG, Jesus's Jewish opponents confront him about the matter of sin, even accusing him of being a sinner (cf. esp. 9:24). The Paraclete will convict the world of sin because they did not believe in Jesus. Not only will the world be proven wrong about its accusations, it will also discover that its refusal to believe Jesus is itself sin (16:9)!

Righteousness (δικαιοσύνη) in 16:10 is connected to the validity of Jesus's claims that he is going to the Father: "And concerning righteousness because I am going to the Father and you will see me no longer." The reader has been prepared for this idea as early as 5:30, where Jesus, in speaking of his authority, says, "I am not able to do anything of myself; just as I hear I judge, and my judgment is righteous (δικαία), because I do not seek my will but the will of the one who sent me." This language, no doubt, includes the vindication of Jesus's frequent claims that he is going to the one who sent him and the Jews will be able to see him no longer (7:33; 8:14, 21; 13:3, 33; 14:4, 28; 16:5).

The world will also be convicted of judgment because the ruler of this world stands judged already, a judgment already signaled in 12:31, where in connection with the lifting up of the Son of Man the time has come for the world's judgment and its leader to be driven out.[33]

This section then returns to the idea of the Paraclete's work among the disciples. Owing to the sorrow in the disciples' hearts, Jesus is unable to tell them all that he desires. Thus, much of the additional teaching they need must be conveyed by the Paraclete, who may be trusted, for he is again identified as the Spirit of Truth (v. 13). Specifically, the Paraclete will guide into all truth. While such teaching will not be at variance with what Jesus has earlier taught, it does not appear that Jesus anticipates this additional teaching by the Paraclete to be identical to what precedes it. The Paraclete's teaching will also glorify Jesus, underscoring the essential unity of the Father, Son, and Spirit.

---

32 Cf. A.T. Lincoln, *Truth on Trial: The Lawsuit Motif in the Fourth Gospel* (Peabody, MA: Hendrickson, 2000).

33 Michaels, *The Gospel according to John*, 833–835, and Thompson, *John: A Commentary*, 338.

10   John 19:30

Another reference to Spirit (πνεῦμα) occurs in a text devoted to the death of Jesus. Immediately following Jesus's final words on the cross ("It is completed!"), bowing his head "he gave [up] the Spirit" (παρέδωκεν τὸ πνεῦμα). At one level, the reader would likely take these words as describing Jesus's expiration, an idea that goes back to 10:17–18 where Jesus speaks of laying down his life voluntarily. However, this phrase (παρέδωκεν τὸ πνεῦμα) apparently is never used in antiquity in a strict sense for "to die."[34] Given that παραδίωμι rather properly means "to hand over, give, or deliver,"[35] it is possible to take the phrase as having reference to the bestowal of the Spirit by Jesus at the moment of his exaltation/glorification on the cross. Attempts to see here, in the light of 19:26–27, a bestowal of the Spirit that constitutes the foundation of the community of believers appear to go beyond the evidence of the text.[36] Based on the distinctive formula used to describe Jesus's death, the connections between water and Spirit in 7:37–39 and (apparently) in 19:34, as well as the numerous promises of the coming of the Paraclete, it may very well be that this phrase points to the future bestowal of the Spirit in a proleptic way.[37]

11   John 20:22

The FG's pneumatological story concludes in 20:22,[38] the meaning of which has been widely debated. The broader context (20:19–23) describes an encounter between the risen Jesus and his disciples, who are behind locked doors on

---

34   P. Létourneau, "Le double don de l'Esprit et la Christologie du quatrième évangile," *Science et Esprit* 44 (1992): 283. Cf also Porsch, *Pneuma und Wort*, 328.

35   W. Bauer, W. Arndt, F.W. Gingrich, and F.W. Danker, *A Greek-English Lexicon of the New Testament and Other Early Christian Literature*, 2nd ed. (Chicago: University of Chicago Press, 1958), 619.

36   For this position cf. esp. M.-A. Chevallier, *Souffle de Dieu: Le Saint-Esprit dans le Nouveau Testament*, II (Paris: Beauchesne, 1990), 409–564; J.P. Heil, *Blood and Water: The Death and Resurrection of Jesus in John 18–21*, CBQMS 27 (Washington, DC: Catholic Biblical Quarterly, 1995), 102–109; and Létourneau, "Le double don de l'Esprit et la Christologie du quatrième évangile," 281–306.

37   For this general idea cf. R.E. Brown, *The Gospel according to John XIII–XXI*, AB 29A (Garden City, NY: Doubleday, 1970), 951, and G.M. Burge, *The Anointed Community*: The Holy Spirit in the Johannine Tradition (Grand Rapids: Eerdmans, 1987), 134–135. Contra Porsch, *Pneuma und Wort*, 332–339.

38   Keener, *The Gospel of John: A Commentary I*, 461, notes that 1.33 along with 20.22 frames the FG.

account of the "fear of the Jews." Mention of the "fear of the Jews" might suggest that the disciples are in danger of not remaining in Jesus and his word (cf. 8:31). After speaking "peace" to the disciples, Jesus shows them his side and hands, prompting great rejoicing, before again speaking peace to them. Jesus then commissions the disciples to be sent, just as the Father had send him. At this point, "he breathed" (on them?) and says to them, "Receive the Holy Spirit" (λάβετε πνεῦμα ἅγιον) and authorizes them to forgive and retain sins.

How would the reader understand the phrase "Receive the Holy Spirit"? If the aorist imperative (λάβετε) is taken to signify an "immediate and forthright reception of the Holy Spirit,"[39] the phrase "Receive the Holy Spirit" might be interpreted in one of several ways. On this interpretation, the phrase could be taken as having reference to (1) the disciples' regeneration or birth by the Spirit,[40] (2) the equipping of the disciples for ministry, especially with regard to the forgiving of sins,[41] (3) a special measure of the Spirit given to the disciples before Pentecost owing to their unique situation in salvation history,[42] (4) a gift of the Spirit that enables them to have Easter faith,[43] (5) a gift of the Spirit that later assumes the functions of the Paraclete,[44] or (6) the Johannine Pentecost.[45]

---

39   So F.L. Arrington, "The Indwelling, Baptism, and Infilling with the Holy Spirit: A Differentiation of Terms," *Pneuma* 3 (1981): 5.
40   H.M. Ervin, *Spirit Baptism: A Biblical Investigation* (Peabody, MA: Hendrickson, 1987), 14–21, and B. Aker, "'Breathed': A Study on the Biblical Distinction Between Regeneration and Spirit-Baptism," *Paraclete* 17 (Summer 1983): 13–16. This suggestion is also made by J.D.G. Dunn, *Baptism in the Holy Spirit* (Philadelphia: Westminster, 1970), 180, which appears to be followed by H.D. Hunter, *Spirit-Baptism: A Pentecostal Alternative* (Lanham, MD: University Press of America, 1983), 110. Cf. also a modified version of this view in M. Turner, *The Holy Spirit and Spiritual Gifts: Then and Now* (Carlisle: Paternoster, 1996), 97–102.
41   H. Windisch, *The Spirit-Paraclete in the Fourth Gospel*, trans. J.W. Cox (Philadelphia: Fortress, 1968), 33–34. Cf. also Chevallier, *Souffle de Dieu*, 430–438; Létourneau, "Le double don de l'Esprit et la Christologie du quatrième évangile," 281–306; and apparently B. Aker, "Gospel of John," S.M. Burgess and G.B. McGee, eds., *Dictionary of the Pentecostal and Charismatic Movements* (Grand Rapids: Zondervan, 1988), 510. Holwerda (*Holy Spirit and Eschatology in the Gospel of John*, 24) views 20:22 as describing the ordination of the apostles for their future ministry.
42   S.M. Horton, *What the Bible Says about the Holy Spirit* (Springfield, MO: Gospel Publishing House, 1976), 130–133.
43   de la Potterie, "Parole et esprit dans S. Jean," 196–201.
44   Porsch, *Pneuma und Wort*, 375–376.
45   Cf. among others Brown, *John XIII–XXI*, 1038–1039; Dunn, *Baptism in the Holy Spirit*, 173–182; Burge, *The Anointed Community*, 123–131; and R. Schnackenburg, *The Gospel according to St. John*, III, trans. D. Smith and G.A. Kon (New York: Crossroad, 1987), 324–325.

However, most of these views fail to convince owing to textual indicators in the narrative that are at odds with taking λάβετε to demand an immediate and forthright reception of the Spirit. Significantly, earlier in the FG Jesus reveals that the Paraclete cannot come unless he departs. It is only after Jesus's departure that he will send the Paraclete (16:7), which may suggest that Jesus's glorification of which the FG speaks in 7:37–39 includes more than his exaltation on the cross, as John 17:5 seems to indicate.[46] Thus, there are indications in the narrative that the Paraclete will not come until Jesus's departure.

Despite the fact that Jesus commands the disciples to "Receive the Holy Spirit," their later conduct and behavior do not reveal any perceptible change. Instead of bearing Paraclete-inspired witness to Jesus, something implicitly anticipated in 15:26–16:4, the disciples are still hiding behind locked doors (20:26) after they had earlier received the command to receive the Spirit, indicating that their "fear of the Jews" had not diminished. Thus, despite Jesus's commissioning of the disciples to be sent as he was sent by the Father and to forgive sins (20:21–23), the disciples remain inactive in this regard. Furthermore, there are no other anticipated activities of the Paraclete described after and as a result of Jesus's command in 20:22.[47]

The way in which 20:22 resembles 7:39 and 14:17 should also be noted. In contrast to the texts that speak of drinking from the living water (Spirit) or being born of the Spirit, these texts use receiving terminology to describe this Spirit experience. The fact that "receiving" vocabulary is reserved for a post-resurrection experience of the Spirit suggests that the reader would discern a difference in the work of the Spirit here described and the Spirit's work described earlier in the narrative. Thus, it appears that the FG makes room for distinct works of the Spirit.

If the narrative of the FG itself subverts an interpretation of 20:22 that calls for an immediate and forthright reception of the Spirit, what does the phrase "Receive the Holy Spirit" mean? Given the fact that the Paraclete will come only after Jesus's departure, that there are no expected signs of the Paraclete's activity after the command to receive the Spirit in 20:22, and that the FG not only allows for but also appears to expect distinct works of the Spirit, it appears that Jesus's action of breathing and utterance of the phrase "Receive the Holy Spirit" should be taken as a parabolic and/or proleptic action that points beyond itself to a reception of the Spirit that is not described in the narrative.[48] Such a read-

---

46 On this cf. Turner, *The Holy Spirit and Spiritual Gifts*, 95.
47 Cf. Turner, *The Holy Spirit and Spiritual Gifts*, 96–97.
48 An interpretive position that goes back at least as far as Theodore of Mopsuestia. Cf. Ladd, *A Theology of the New Testament*, 297; D. Guthrie, *New Testament Theology* (Down-

ing coincides with Jesus's anticipated work as Spirit Baptizer (1:33), the coming of the Paraclete after Jesus's departure (16:7), and the anticipated activities of the disciples after the Paraclete arrives (14–16; 20:21–23).[49] From the standpoint of the narrative, such an understanding of John 20:22 is less problematic than views that see an immediate and forthright reception of the Spirit in this verse.[50]

As can be seen, the FG touches on a number of different aspects of the Spirit's role, function, and identity/person. First, it describes an intimate and somewhat unexpectedly complex relationship between Jesus and the Spirit. Although he is the Word Incarnate, Jesus is anointed by the Spirit and only then is identified as the Holy Spirit Baptizer (1:32–33), indicating that he will be one through whom the Spirit comes. He has been given the Spirit without measure (3:34). Jesus's words are Spirit and Life (6:63). From his side flow rivers of living water (7:37–39). The Spirit comes to the disciples from the Father at Jesus's request (14:16), and Jesus plays a role in sending the Spirit from the Father (15:26). The Spirit is identified as another Paraclete, implying that his activity continues that of Jesus (14:16). The intimacy of their relationship is indicated in part by the fact that the Paraclete is called the "Spirit of Truth" (14:17; 15:26). It is the Spirit who will teach the disciples and remind them of all the things Jesus said and did (14:26). Though the Paraclete is active throughout Jesus's ministry, Jesus must depart for the Paraclete to come (16:6). Jesus is able to offer the Spirit to the disciples at various points in the FG both in actuality and proleptically. Second, the Spirit's relationship with believers is robust. The Spirit makes possible birth from above (3:1–16), is synonymous with the living waters that Jesus gives (4:1–30), enables true worship (4:23–24), and the FG also envisions other distinct works of the Spirit (7:37–39)—including inspired witness (15:27)—many of which appear to be left unfulfilled by narrative's end. Third, in addition to the Father's role in the giving of the Spirit (14:26; 15:26), the nature of the relationship between God and the Spirit is revealed in part by the fact that in the FG God is identified as Spirit (4:24), an identification pregnant with meaning as to God's essential nature. Fourth, the Spirit's relationship

---

ers Grove: IVP, 1981), 534; Carson, *The Gospel according to John*, 651–655; D. Petts, *The Holy Spirit: An Introduction* (Mattersey: Mattersey Hall, 1998), 47–48; and apparently R.H. Gause, *Living in the Spirit: The Way of Salvation* (Cleveland, TN: Pathway Press, 1980), 66.

49 In this, the FG is not unlike the Synoptics, which also leave the promise that Jesus will baptize with the Holy Spirit unfulfilled within their respective narratives.

50 However, cf. Turner (*The Holy Spirit and Spiritual Gifts*, 97–102), who understands the Spirit's work in John 20:22 as an eschatological new creation, which later will include the work attributed by Jesus to the Paraclete.

to the world is threefold in the FG: 1) Though the world is unable to receive the Spirit (14:17), 2) the Spirit offers its witness to Jesus (15:26)—and apparently inspires the disciples' faithful witness to the world (15:27), and 3) proves the world wrong concerning sin, righteousness, and judgment regarding its assessment of Jesus (16:8–11) as revealed in the broader narrative of the FG.

12 The Spirit in 1 John and 2 John

The pneumatology of 1 and 2 John is influenced by that found in the FG or reacts in some way to a misinterpretation of the FG's teaching on the Spirit. There are, however, significant differences between the Spirit vocabulary of the FG and that found in 1 and 2 John, with certain key terms used to describe the Spirit's work in the FG (such as Paraclete) missing from the discussion of the Spirit in 1 and 2 John.

The first hint as to the pneumatology of 1 and 2 John may come from 2 John 9, perhaps the second of these documents to have been written (immediately) after 3 John,[51] in the words, "Each one who goes beyond and does not remain in the teaching of Christ does not have God." These words suggest that the opponents that John and his churches faced were not content to stay within the teaching of Jesus, as revealed in the testimony of the FG, but were claiming to go beyond this teaching to other truths made known by the Paraclete, who is said to lead and guide into all truth (John 16:12–15). If the opponents were indeed appealing to the activity of the Paraclete as the basis of their teaching, it might explain why the term "Paraclete" is completely absent from 1–3 John as a designation for the Spirit.

Several allusions and explicit references to the Spirit occur in 1 John.[52] The first appears in a section devoted to the false teaching of the antichrists and the true knowledge of the Johannine believers. In contrast to the antichrists, the Johannine believers are defined by the fact that they have an "anointing" from the Holy One (2:20). The Greek term translated "anointing" (χρῖσμα) occurs only three times in the whole of the NT with all of its appearances in this section of 1 John. The term appears to be part of a play on words, for its stem lies behind the word "Christ" (Χριστός) as well as "antichrist" (ἀντίχριστος). Given that the word "Christ" literally means "anointed one" and that reference is made to the

---

[51] Cf. J.C. Thomas, "The Order of the Composition of the Johannine Epistles," *Novum Testamentum* 37 (1995): 68–75.

[52] For more extensive treatments of these texts cf. J.C. Thomas, *1 John, 2 John, 3 John* (PCS: London: T & T Clark, 2004).

Spirit's descent upon Jesus in John 1:32–33, it would seem likely that reference to the believer's "anointing" in 1John 2:20 is closely associated with the activity of the Holy Spirit, as a comparison of the function of the "anointing" in 1John and the function of the Paraclete in the FG bears out. Both are spoken of as being received by (John 14:17; 1John 2:27), abiding in (John 14:17; 1John 2:27), and teaching all things to (John 14:26, 1John 2:20, 27) the believers.[53] As followers of "the anointed one," the believers are reminded that they themselves have an "anointing." The purpose of this anointing is related to knowledge. If the words "and you know all things" is the original reading (some manuscripts read "and you all know"), they are perhaps a response to claims the antichrists may have been making about possessing a unique, superior knowledge. Emphasis is here placed upon the believers' "complete" knowledge, resulting from the anointing they have from the Holy One, making additional teaching (from the antichrists) unnecessary. Thus, the "anointing" functions just as Jesus says the Paraclete will function, "That One will teach you all things (πάντα)" (John 14:26).

This thought is followed up in 1John 2:27, where, in contrast to those who seek to deceive you (the "antichrists" and "liars" are now called "those who deceive"), the Johannine believers are told that they have "received" (ἐλάβετε) the "anointing." Such language not only suggests that a specific reception is in mind, but also reminds the reader of the command Jesus gave to his disciples to "receive the Holy Spirit" (John 20:22).[54] The appearance of the term "received" would likely remind the reader of their own Spirit baptism. While v. 20 states that the reader "has" an anointing, in v. 27 the reader is told that the anointing "remains" in them. Here, two of the dominant themes found in vv. 20 and 24 are combined, underscoring the close connection that exists between the "anointing" and "that which you have heard from the beginning." The more general statement of v. 20 gives way to a more detailed discussion of the teaching role of the anointing in v. 27. Not only do the believers know all things as a result of the anointing, but they also do not need anyone to teach them. This bold statement both continues the polemic against the antichrists and deceivers and continues to underscore that the role of the Spirit as teacher within the Johannine community is unrivalled.[55]

---

[53] Cf. esp. R.E. Brown, *The Epistles of John*, AB 30 (Garden City, NY: Doubleday, 1982), 345–346.
[54] On this interpretation cf. J.C. Thomas, "The Spirit in the Fourth Gospel: Narrative Explorations," 157–174.
[55] The title "teacher" is reserved positively for Jesus (1:38, 49; 3:2; 4:31; 6:25, 59; 7:14, 28, 35; 8:20; 9:2; 11:8, 28; 13:13–14; 18:20; 20:16; 2John 9), the Father (8:28), and the Paraclete (14:26), but is used negatively for Nicodemus (3:10), Balaam (Rev 2:14), the Nicolatians (2:15), and Jezebel (2:20; 24). The only exceptions to this trend are John the Baptist, who is once called Rabbi

The Spirit is mentioned explicitly for the first time in 1John 3:24. He is here identified as the means by which the believer can know that God remains in him or her. The primary evidence of the Spirit's activity to this point concerns the anointing that the believers have received: an anointing that knows all things (2:20) and teaches the believer all things, so much so that the believer has no need of human teachers (2:27). Such teaching would no doubt be made manifest in a variety of concrete ways, including the spoken testimony of various members of the community, the confirmation of one's status by means of one's walk witnessed by the brothers and sisters, Spirit-inspired confession, and prophetically spoken words. Thus, this aspect of the Spirit's activity is assuring believers that he abides in them.

In 1John 4:1–6, the Spirit receives explicit and extensive treatment. Bounded on either side by references to the Spirit and spirits, this passage is devoted to testing the spirits to determine their origin and distinguishing between "the Spirit of Truth" and "the Spirit of Deception." The warning with which this passage begins comes in the form of a command meaning something like "do not keep believing every spirit."

These words make clear that appeals to (inspiration by) the Spirit are being made both by those in the community and those who have left it. Not only would Johannine believers understand the Spirit as operative in their lives, but it also appears that the deceivers, too, have appealed to the Spirit as the basis of their own teaching and interpretive positions.

The reader of 1John is instructed to "test the spirits if they are of God." Such testing is to involve all the believers—note the second-person plural "you," which testifies to the egalitarian nature of the community. It is also to be an ongoing activity in the community, an idea conveyed by the present-tense verb translated "test."[56] The goal of such testing is to determine whether or not a given "spirit" finds its origin in God or some other source. The language, "false prophets," reveals that the testing of the spirits refers to individuals who function in a "prophetic" capacity.[57] Thus, testing the spirits is testing the S/spirit that inspires the words and actions of a given individual who claims Spirit inspiration as the basis of his or her activity.

(John 3:26), and the man born blind (9:34), who is asked with derision by the Pharisees if he, being born wholly in sin, would teach them.

56 This approach contrasts with the emerging practice reflected in the epistles of Ignatius to place most responsibility for distinguishing between true and false teaching in the hands of the bishop.

57 The need for discernment with regard to the Spirit's activity is evidenced more widely in the writings of Paul (1 Cor 12:1–3; 14:29; 1 Thess 5:20–21); the *Didache* (11:1; 12:1); Hermas (*Mandate* 11:7); and 1 Clement (42:4.)

The specific criterion of testing the spirits involves one's confession. Positively, "each spirit who confesses Jesus Christ in the flesh having come is of God." This confession is not simply a doctrinal confession, but is the confession of a person, his salvific work, and the ongoing significance of his incarnational life. The Spirit of God generates this confession in the believer as a result of and growing out of one's experiential relationship to Jesus in the various dimensions of his person. Thus, the Spirit not only inspires one's speech and actions, but the Spirit also validates them. It should not be a surprise that the Spirit-inspired utterances, which claim their origin in (the Spirit of) God, must speak the truth about Jesus. This confession appears to be shorthand for a whole matrix of beliefs about and experiences with Jesus, including: that fellowship with the Father includes fellowship with the Son (1:3); that cleansing from sin is accomplished through Jesus's blood (1:7); that the righteous Jesus acts as an Advocate for the believer (2:1) based on his atoning sacrifice (2:2); that Jesus is a model for the believer's walk (2:6); that forgiveness of sin comes through his name (2:12); that Jesus remains in the believer (2:14); that this righteous one will be manifest at his appearing (2:28–29); that his mode of existence and purity are the model for the believer (3:2–3); that Jesus came to take away sin and is himself without sin (3:5–6); that he came to destroy the works of the devil (3:7); that he laid aside his life on behalf of the believers; and that all these things were accomplished because he came in the flesh. These are not simply doctrinal points to be affirmed but are experiences in which the believers become participants in various ways. Conversely, whereas the "prophetic" figures in v. 2 "confess Jesus Christ coming in the flesh," the "prophetic" figures in v. 3 "do not confess" Jesus. If confession of Jesus entails belief in all he is and all he accomplishes, lack of such confession is synonymous with unbelief and denial of him and the significance of his life (cf. esp. 1 John 2:22–23). If the Spirit-inspired confession of "Jesus Christ having come in the flesh" reveals that this "spirit" finds its origin in God, so any "spirit"-inspired utterance that does not confess Jesus reveals that its origin is not from God or his Spirit. Just as the confession "Jesus Christ coming in the flesh" is a kind of shorthand, so not confessing Jesus may be a kind of shorthand that stands for utterances, beliefs, and practices that advocate and embrace a false Christology. It would appear that the situation envisioned in 1 John 4:1–3 is one where "S/spirit"-inspired individuals, speaking prophetically to the community, espoused teachings and practices at variance with the teachings and practices of the Johannine community as revealed in the FG. Their teaching appears to claim fellowship with the Father without the Son, to have no place for Jesus's role in the forgiveness of sins, to ignore his role as a model of behavior for their lives, and to deny his messianic status. The origin of such deception and false teaching is literally "that of the antichrist."

Standing in diametric opposition to "the Spirit of Truth" is "the spirit of deception," a title that occurs only here in the NT. Just as "the deceiver" is synonymous with "the antichrist" in 2 John 7, so "that of the antichrist" is synonymous with "the spirit of deception" in 1 John 4:6, making it very clear that "the spirit of deception" is responsible for the many "deceivers" who have gone out into the world to "deceive" as many as possible. However, the community has nothing to fear, for it knows the difference between "the Spirit of Truth" (God) and "the spirit of deception" (the evil one) and is capable of testing the "spirits," for they have received the Spirit (3:24).

The final explicit references to the Spirit in 1 John come in 5:6, 8, a passage devoted to the identity and function of witnesses to Jesus. The first of the two witnesses is the cleansing and atoning blood of Jesus, for which the opponents appear to have no place in their theology. The second witness is the water, which appears to include a reference to water baptism and is informed by the many soteriological associations water comes to have in the FG, the preponderance of which makes clear the close relationship between water and the Spirit. These witnesses together point to Jesus as the one who came through the water (of baptism and the Spirit) and through the blood of his passion, John 19:34 offering a supreme Johannine summary of their grounding and meaning.

In 1 John 5:6c, the Spirit is identified as the one who certifies, by his witness, that Jesus Christ came through the water and the blood, bringing to mind the teaching of Jesus found in John 15:26. The witness of the Spirit may be trusted because the Spirit is Truth. Since Jesus is himself identified as "the Truth," the authentic nature of the Spirit's witness should be all the more apparent. The present-tense verb in 5:6 indicates that the witness of the Spirit is an ongoing reality in the community. As in 4:2, the Spirit's activity as witness may well include prophetic speech.

In 1 John 5:7–8 the Spirit is identified as one of three witnesses, alongside the water and the blood. The change in gender from the masculine, "those who bear witness" (v. 6c), to the neuters, "the Spirit and the water and the blood" (v. 8) may point to the fact that certain events of Jesus's life and death serve as witnesses that have enduring effects (John 19:34). In addition to foot washing—a sign of continual cleansing from sin, it would appear that other signs were also practiced by the community, including water baptism and the Eucharist. Therefore, v. 8 likely refers to Jesus's life, filled with salvific significance, his continuing presence among the community members by means of the Spirit whom he sent, and by means of the signs of water and blood that continue among them. The statement in v. 8 "and these three are one" suggests that these witnesses stand or fall together and cannot be separated, converging on the same truth: Jesus Christ, the one who came through the water and the blood, is the Son of God, the atoning sacrifice for sins, the Savior of the world.

Thus, there appear to be four primary dimensions of the Spirit's role in 1–2 John, all of which are related, to a certain extent, to knowledge or knowing. These include: an anointing by which believers can know all things; the means by which believers have assurance of their mutual indwelling in and with God; the ability to distinguish between the Spirit of Truth and the spirit of deception; and the way in which the Spirit continues to serve as a witness to Jesus.

The Spirit in Romans: God's Community and Life in the Spirit

Finny Philip

God's Spirit and life in the Spirit are crucial themes addressed by Paul in his letter to the faithful in Rome. Although conspicuous by the absence of references to the Spirit in the first part of the letter, the rich resource on the Spirit appears exhaustively throughout the letter.[1] Key to our exploration is to engage in Paul's conversation on God's Spirit[2] with the Romans as he relates to various theological discourses and experiences of the Spirit of God.

The believers in Rome had been gathering as house churches[3] for many years by the time[4] Paul composed the letter (15:22–23), and he had not yet visited them (1:10, 13; 15:14, 22–23; 16:5). Paul wrote when he was occupied with a wide range of mission destinations, namely, his anxious desire to visit Rome (15:23–24); his desire to evangelize in Spain (15:24, 28);[5] and his plans to return shortly

---

1 See 1:4, 9; 2:29; 5:5; 7:6; 8:2, 4, 5, 6, 9, 10, 11, 13, 14, 15, 16, 23, 26, 27; 9:1; 12:11; 14:17; 15:13, 16, 19, 30. See for discussion J.D.G. Dunn, *The Theology of Paul the Apostle* (Grand Rapids: Eerdmans, 1998), 438; C.G. Kruse, *Paul's Letter to the Romans* (Grand Rapids: Eerdmans, 2012), 26.
2 A growing number of scholars acknowledges that Paul's use of the Spirit is important for the interpretative framework since Paul maintains an interplay of pneumatology with other theological themes in the letter. See J.R.D. Kirk, *Unlocking Romans. Resurrection and the Justification of God* (Grand Rapids: Eerdmans, 2008), 43; D. Moo, *The Epistles of Romans* (Grand Rapids: Eerdmans, 1996), 47–50; G.D. Fee, *God's Empowering Presence. The Holy Spirit in the Letters of Paul* (Peabody, MA: Hendrickson, 1994), 474.
3 The decentralized nature of Christianity in Rome during most of the first two centuries has been documented by Peter Lampe, *From Paul to Valentinus, Christians at Rome in the First Two Centuries*, ed. M.D. Johnson (Minneapolis: Fortress Press, 2003). Interestingly, Paul seldom uses the term *ekklesia* (Rom 16:1, 4, 5, 16 & 23) in Romans, compared to fifty-seven times in his other letters. He designates the term for the assembly of believers from different strata of Roman society who affirm Jesus as Lord and the crucified and resurrected Messiah and constitute the renewed Israel of God. They met as smaller groups including households in houses. For Paul, it is a countercultural usage to the *ekklesia* of the Greco-Roman city, city council with a group of male elders who met to deliberate about local issues and ensured that the *polis* was faithful to its heritage and values, particularly loyalty to Rome and its lord, the emperor. See Robert J. Banks, *Paul's Idea of Community: The Early House Churches in Their Cultural Settings* (Grand Rapids: Baker Academic, 1994); Young-Ho Park, *Paul's Ekklesia as a Civic Assembly. Understanding the People of God in their Politico-Social World* (Tübingen: Mohr Siebeck, 2015).
4 Joseph A. Fitzmyer, *Romans* (New Haven and London: Yale University Press, 1993), 62.
5 See Robert Jewett, *Romans: A Commentary* (Hermeneia; Minneapolis: Fortress, 2007), 88–91.

to Jerusalem (15:26–28, 31). Whether he composed Romans while sitting on the dock in Corinth awaiting the ship that would take him to a port near Jerusalem[6] or at his residence in Corinth (Rom 16:23; cf. Acts 18:7; 1 Cor 1:14),[7] Paul was engaging with mature reflections on the Spirit in his address. His major reasons for writing the letter were probably these:[8] 1) his anticipation of rejection by the church in Jerusalem suspicious of the collections and the persecution by unbelieving Jews because of his pro-Gentile vision; 2) to gain the church's support for a Gentile mission to Spain; 3) to set out a most detailed defense of his gospel[9] in order to unify the Christian community (10:14–21; 11:13–36)[10] after Claudius's edict expired[11] The role of God's Spirit is crucial as he navigates through these challenges.

With all probability, the letter was written to multiple house churches in Rome composed ethnicically of believers who were Jewish, including his migrant friends, and a majority of Gentile Christians among the Greek-speaking minority in a majority Latin-speaking city.[12] Two contextual features are important for us to observe. On the one hand, the exiled Jewish Christians who would have returned to Rome and found themselves no longer welcome in the synagogues joined Gentile believers in mixed assemblies. During their exile, the Roman house churches may have added Gentile converts and returning Jewish Christians, who were formerly a majority in the churches but now found themselves in the minority (Rom 14:1–15:6; 16:3). And on the other hand, Paul,

---

6   See Johannes Munck, *Christ and Israel: An Interpretation of Romans 9–11* (Philadelphia: Fortress Press, 1967), 8–13.
7   See discussions in Jewett, *Romans*, 21–22; Fitzmyer, *Romans*, 127.
8   Jewett (*Romans*, 83–88) lists six possible reasons for the writing of the letter to the Romans.
9   Dunn, *Theology of Paul*, 25.
10 Most scholars agree with the context of tensions between Jewish and Gentile groups within the Roman house churches—that the majority of "strong" or Gentile-oriented groups was discriminating against the minority of "weak" or Jewish-oriented groups. See Paul S. Minear, *The Obedience of Faith: The Purposes of Paul in the Epistle to the Romans* (London: SCM, 1971), 8–20; N.T. Wright, *The Climax of the Covenant: Christ and the Law in Pauline Theology* (Minneapolis: Fortress Press, 1991), 235; Philip F. Esler, *Conflict and Identity in Romans* (Minneapolis: Fortress Press, 2003), 339–352.
11 A.J.M. Wedderburn, *The Reasons for Romans* (Edinburgh: T & T. Clark, 1988), 14–15, 64–65, 83; W. Wiefel, "The Jewish Community in Ancient Rome and the Origins of Roman Christianity," in *The Romans Debate*, ed. K.R. Donfried (Peabody, MA: Hendrickson, 1991), 85–101.
12 A few scholars contend that Paul was writing to an almost exclusively Gentile audience. See, e.g., Stanley K. Stowers, *Rereading of Romans: Justice, Jews, and Gentiles* (New Haven: Yale University Press, 1994); A. Andrew Das, *Solving the Romans Debate* (Minneapolis: Fortress Press, 2007), 53; For an alternative position see Mark D. Nanos, *The Mystery of Romans: The Jewish Context of Paul's Letter* (Minneapolis: Fortress, 1996).

a formidable missionary, urges the audience to greet his friends and migrant representatives (Rom 16:1–15)[13] who are engaged in the mission to the Gentiles, among them Priscilla and Aquila, who were Jewish coworkers in their missionary work among the Gentiles (16:3; cf. Acts 18:2), and possibly Phoebe as well, who worked for the conciliation of the house churches so that they would be able to support Paul's desired mission to Spain.[14]

Further, anyone interested in Pauline pneumatology[15] encounters Paul's deep-rooted conviction that he is called to be the apostle to the Gentiles.[16] Such a clear self-perception is consistently seen as he addresses the believers in Rome whom he considers within the sphere of his apostolic labors (1:5–6, 13; 11:13; 15:15–16).[17] Again, what is much more important for our discussion is Paul's recognition that Gentiles have received the Spirit and that the Spirit is freely given to them—an equally ingrained conviction that is found in almost all his writings (1Thess 1:5; Gal 3:1, 5, 14; 1Cor 1:4–9; 6:9–11; 12:13; 2Cor 1:21; 3:3, 17) but particularly in Romans (5:5; 6:1; 7:6; 8:2, 9, 14, 15; 15:15–16). These two compounding factors are essential to understanding Paul's presentation of God's Spirit in his letter to the Romans.

1   God's Spirit: Power, Holiness, and Resurrection

Paul begins (1:3–4) by defining the gospel that he and the faithful in Rome share as "the gospel concerning his Son, who was descended from David according to the flesh" (1:3). For him, Jesus's earthly life fulfilled Jewish messianic hopes (15:12; cf. 2Sam 7:14–16; Pss 2:6–7; 89:26–33). His present appointed sta-

---

13   Other likely migrants mentioned in chapter 16 are Epainetos, Miriam, Andronikos and Junia, Ampliatus, Urbanus, Stachys, Apelles, Herodion, Tryphena, Tryphosa, Persis, and Rufus and his mother. See Miriam T. Griffin, *Nero: The End of a Dynasty* (New Haven: Yale University Press, 1984), 50–82.

14   Jewett, *Romans*, 89–91.

15   For further reading Finny Philip, *The Origins of Pauline Pneumatology: The Eschatological Bestowal of the Spirit upon Gentiles in Judaism and the Early Development of Paul's Theology* (Tübingen: Mohr Siebeck, 2005), and L.A Jervis, "The Spirit Brings Christ's Life to Life," in *Reading Paul's Letter to the Romans*, ed. J.L. Sumney (Atlanta: Scholars Press, 2021), 139–156 (139), suggests the pneumatological reasons for Paul writing to Romans.

16   See Gal 1:15–16; cf. Rom 11:13; cf. 1:5, 13; 15:16–19 cf. 1Cor 1:17, 1Cor 9:17 cf.; 1Thess 2:4; Col 1:25; cf. Acts 9:15; 22:6, 11, 14; 26:13. T.L. Donaldson, *Paul and the Gentiles, Remapping the Apostle's Convictional World* (Minneapolis: Fortress Press, 1997), 249ff.

17   Here the language should not be pressed to exclude the Jews, but it implies that most of the readers were Gentiles (6:14–15; 7:1, 4).

tus[18] as "Son of God (2 Sam 7:14; Pss 2:7; 89:26–27; 1QSa 2:11–12; 4QFlor 1:10 ff.) in power" is according to the "spirit of holiness" by his resurrection from the dead.

Paul contends that Jesus was appointed through God's power (cf. 1 Cor 6:14; Phil 3:10, 20 cf. Acts 10:42; 17:31)[19] before the resurrection. The reference to "power" is more than christological because the gospel about Christ is "the power of God for salvation" (1:16) and thus soteriological. The subsequent association of Holy Spirit with power (15:13, 19), indicates how the "righteousness of God" is now restored to all. Paul was doubtlessly setting the course for the Romans to engage in a broader mission (15:13; cf. 15:19).

Paul's use of the phrase "according to the spirit of holiness"[20] refers to the sphere of Spirit life (cf. 5:5). It refers not so much to qualitative or descriptive terms[21] as to a dynamic form that corroborates the enthronement of Jesus as Son of God in power, the inaugurated age of the Spirit,[22] and the outpouring and ministry of the Spirit. The Spirit supplies holiness ("sanctified by the Holy Spirit," 15:16).[23] To describe it further, he intends that the Son's divine nature will encompass the moral obligations (chaps. 5–8) as the one who effects the "righteousness of God" in the lives of believers in Rome.

Paul stresses Jesus's resurrection as a prominent feature of his gospel (4:24–25; 6:4–5, 9; 7:4; 8:11, 34; 10:9). The passage does not hint at the Spirit as an agent whereby God raised Christ from the dead,[24] nor is it to be understood as Christ having now assumed Spirit existence. Perhaps the best way is to understand

---

18   See Cranfield, *Romans* 1:61.
19   Ernst Käsemann (*Commentary on Romans* [Grand Rapids: Eerdmans 1980]) comments on "power" as "declared to be the powerful Son of God." See Cranfield (*Romans*, 1:62), who sees "in power" as Son 'invested with power'—as a power source, Son enthroned in the heavenly sphere of power. Oscar Cullmann (*The Christology of the New Testament* [Westminster: John Knox Press, 1959], 292) infers from the phrase "in power" that "Jesus is the 'Son of God' from the beginning." Perhaps we need to see the phrase as God's power, whereby God effects Jesus's resurrection and endows him with a source of life to enliven human beings who turn to him as the risen Lord.
20   The phrase "spirit of holiness" appears in *Test. Lev.* 18:11; QS 4:21; 8:16; 9:3: 1QH 7:6,7; 9:32. Craig S. Keener suggests (*Romans. A New Covenant Commentary* [Cambridge: Lutterworth Press, 2009], 8–10) that in Paul, "the Spirit of holiness" may associate the Spirit with setting us apart for God (1 Thess 4:7–8).
21   See discussion in Fee, *God's Empowering Presence*, 483.
22   See Martin Hengel, *The Son of God: The Origin of Christology and the History of Jewish-Hellenistic Religion* (London: SCM. Press, 1976).
23   Fee, *God's Empowering Presence*, 483.
24   T.J. Burke, "Romans," in *A Biblical Theology of the Holy Spirit*, ed. Trevor J. Burke and Keith Warrington (London: SPCK, 2014), 284–285. James M. Scott, *Adoption as Sons of God* (Tübingen: J.C.B. Mohr [Paul Siebeck], 1992), 240.

the phrase "according to" as relational, which means that the Spirit in the passage refers to the heavenly "eschatological sphere of life" to which Christ has entered by his resurrection,[25] thus indicating the precise relationship of the Spirit of God and the Son of God.

By describing three interrelated themes—power, Spirit, and resurrection—in 1:3–4, Paul lays the foundation for his conversation on the Spirit.[26] Characteristically, the Spirit mediates the newness of life in a relational existence in Christ that takes transformative effect in the lives of all those who believe, particularly those in Rome.[27]

2 God's Spirit Empowers Inward Transformation (2:29)

Paul contends that this gospel is God's power unto salvation, is by faith and intended for all people, regardless of ethnicity (1:16–17). All must live by faith because all are equally wounded through sin (1:18–3:29). In discussing the old and the new covenants, Paul challenges the Jews' dependence on circumcision[28] as the identity marker for salvation (Rom 2:26). He insists that it is the Spirit of God who transforms a person who comes to Christ (2:29).[29] Paul affirms that what identifies a person as a member of the people of God is no longer adherence to the outward boundary markers of Jewish ritual but, rather, their relation with Christ and the Spirit alone (2:29), that of an inward circumcision of the heart.[30] For Paul, this is what the prophets expressed in terms of new covenant—the Spirit who brings obedience of the heart (Deut 10:16; 30:6; Jer 31:31–34; Ezek 11:19; 36:26; cf. 1QS 5:5; 1QpHab 11:13; 4Q 177, 184). The literal circumcision ("the letter" cf. 7:5–6) would serve only for human praise and probably refers to those seeking affirmation and praise from fellow believers,

---

25 Fee, *God's Empowering Presence*, 484.
26 John Barclay (*John. Paul and the Gift* [Grand Rapids: Eerdmans, 2015], 460–461) refers to the related themes of power (1:16, 20; 4:17, 21; 11:23), the Spirit (2:29; 5:5; 7:6; 8:1–39; 15:13, 19), and the resurrection of Jesus (4:24–25; 6:1–12; 8:9–11), as the leitmotif of the letter.
27 Fee, *God's Empowering Presence*, 484.
28 See W.S. Campbell, "Romans III as a Key to the Structure and Thought of the Letter," in *Romans Debate*, ed. L Donfried (Peabody, MA: Hendrickson, 1995), 251–264 (259–260).
29 A.J. Hultgren, *Paul's Letter to the Romans. A Commentary* (Eerdmans: Grand Rapids, 2011), 130. The OT usage "circumcision of the heart" was well understood to apply to Jews alone and only within the Israelite community (Lev 26:41; Deut 10:16; Jer 4:4). Paul, while addressing Jews and Gentiles (1:16; 2:9; 2:29; 3:29; 9:24; 10:12), extends the covenant to include both Gentile and Jew.
30 See the detailed discussion in Volker Rabens, *The Holy Spirit and Ethics in Paul. Transformation and Empowering for Religious-Ethical Life* (Tübingen: Mohr Siebeck, 2010).

and this is probably the root of the relational conflict in the house gatherings in Rome, while those who circumcised their heart by the Spirit rely on God's praise alone. Thus, God's Spirit brings in an internal transformation that constitutes the new identity of the people of God that will enable them to live in the promised new covenant.

3   God's Spirit Infuses Love and Enables a New Sphere of Living (5:5)

Paul asserts that the believers are in a new realm—a place of peace with God (5:1)—countering any boasting, because they have access to grace (5:2) and are reconciled to God by the death of his Son (5:10). This new eschatologically oriented environment in which believers live is in the realm of Christ Jesus and of the Spirit. This was possible because the love of God was poured out into their hearts[31] through the Holy Spirit (cf. 2 Cor 1:22; 4:6).[32] The Spirit infuses the love of God into all believers and creates a new center of existence (Phil 4:23; 1 Cor 5:4–5; 14:14; 2 Cor 2:13; 7:3) that overcomes any hatred between Jewish and Gentile believers. Paul's interest is to direct the attention of the believers in Rome to their shared experience of the unconditional love of God. This love is conveyed as the Spirit's internal presence, which enables them to overcome any inner wounds of division and hostility. Such a love envelops any shame that puts Gentiles into imperilment with God by not observing the obligations of Torah observance or boasting about the superior value of Torah that might qualify Jews to be instructors of Gentiles (Rom 2:17–20). The Spirit enables a new living by drawing believers into the loving and empowering presence of God.

4   God's Spirit Enables New Obedience and Fruitfulness (7:6)

Paul informs his readers about the newness of life, enacted in baptism, that simultaneously constitutes death (6:6) and life (6:4) and was made possible through the resurrection of Christ and the presence of the Spirit (6:1–8:39). He addresses their freedom from the law (7:1–6) through a metaphor from the Jewish legal tradition of marriage wherein a wife is bound to her husband

---

31   The idea of the "heart" as the location for encountering God is seen in 1 Thess 3:11–13; 2 Thess 2:16–17; 3:5.
32   See a similar usage in 2 Cor 13:14. Paul also speaks of the "love of Christ" (2 Cor 5:14).

only during his lifetime.³³ Paul shifts the metaphor to accommodate believers' union with Christ,³⁴ but instead it is not a believer's husband who has died but believers themselves (Rom 6:2–11). The purpose of the new relationship is to bear fruit for God (7:4) as opposed to bearing fruit for death (7:5; cf. 6:21–22). Paul places the purpose of their marriage with Christ in two distinct directions.³⁵ The current experience of believers as bearers of the fruit of God are "still servants," but servants of God (cf. 6:22; 7:6). The "newness of the Spirit" experience is the positive definition of slavery that provides a new framework of obedience that replaces the legal constraints of the "obsolete letter."³⁶ The "newness," a new sphere of existence in the Spirit, is seen as their allegiances, dispositions, emotions, and actions are marked by love, joy, peace, patience, kindness, goodness, faithfulness, gentleness, and self-control (Gal 5:22–23, cf. Rom 12–15) as opposed to hatred and competition—a bearing of fruit unto death (7:5). Believers serve Christ "as slaves" enabled by the Spirit who directs them to serve others rather than to be served. Thus, God's Spirit brings new fruitfulness and a new frame of reference of obedience in a believer's life.

5 God's Spirit Creates a Familial Relationship for a Life of Righteousness (Chap. 8)

The believers in Rome are free from condemnation because Christ frees them to fulfill the law through the Spirit (8:2–4). For Paul, a fundamental argument to the controversy with the law (8:3) was that, although it teaches right from wrong, it does not transform a person to be righteous. What flesh could not accomplish, God did in Christ,³⁷ which opened the way for the Spirit, who enables believers to live righteously (8:4; Jer 31:32–33; Ezek 36:27).

Paul then distinguishes life according to the Spirit from life according to the flesh. In contrast to the mindset of flesh (cf. 7:22–23)—a basic human moral condition and nature corrupted, directed, and controlled by sin—Paul speaks here of a "mind" guided by the Spirit (8:5–7). He speaks of a new prospect by God's Spirit in which one's life does not depend on a death-dealing (8:6) obsession with one's ways (8:5) but on a new norm on what the Spirit desires that

---

33 See the detailed discussion in Dunn, *Romans* 1:360.
34 J.M.D. Derrett, "Romans vii.1–4: The Relationship with the Resurrected Christ," in *Law in the New Testament*, ed. J.M.D. Derrett (London: Darton, Longman & Todd, 1970), 463–470.
35 Jewett, *Romans*, 510.
36 Cranfield, *Romans* 1:339–340; Dunn, *Romans* 1:373.
37 Thomas R. Schreiner, *Romans* (Grand Rapids: Baker Books, 1998), 399.

yields life and peace (8:6; 5:1, 21; 6:23). The fleshly mind is at hostility with God (8:7) and cannot submit to God's law (8:7), nor can it please God (8:8), but rather it seeks glory and honor for itself (contra 8:30). But all who belong to Christ have the Spirit dwelling in them and hence are in the realm of the Spirit (8:9). Such a transfer from the realm of the flesh into the realm of the Spirit has established a new filial and personified relationship (8:12–17). The Spirit enables the Romans to honor God in a way that befits the members of God's household, like that of the first-century Mediterranean world.[38]

For Paul, those (8:9–11) belonging to Christ have the residency of the Spirit or the personal presence of God. The effect of the indwelling Spirit is that, contrary to the condition of the body, which is dead through sin (cf. 7:24), the Spirit produces life through righteousness (8:2, 6). Although Paul forges a close link between the risen Christ and the Spirit, for him, God the Father as the one raising Jesus would also raise the bodies of the faithful. The Spirit is the presence of both God and Christ in the present, giving life to the believer and assuring life for the future (8:11).[39]

After setting the tone of a new relationship with God by the Spirit, Paul addresses those who are "in Spirit," having an obligation that is not to be determined by life according to bodily practices[40] that leads to death, but to the Spirit that leads to life (8:14; 8:4–6, 13; cf. Gal 5:18 with 5:16–23). Paul clarifies the new obligation in familial terms, that is, the Spirit is not that of fearful slavery but one of sonship, as exhibited in the "Abba" cry.[41] Paul then amplifies the relationship as the Spirit bears witness to the new status as "children of God" (8:16),[42] thus the Spirit-created household of God,[43] a fellowship of the Spirit. The adoption[44] of the believers into God's family (Eph 2:19; 1 Tim 3:15 cf. 2 Cor 6:18) and the loving relationship initiated by the Spirit implies their inheritance

---

38 The house members will not do anything that tarnishes the name of the father or household. See T.J. Burke, *Adopted into God's Family: Exploring a Pauline Metaphor* (Downers Grove: InterVarsity Press, 2006), 143–148.
39 See Fee, *God's Empowering Presence*, 545–546.
40 John W. Yates III, *The Spirit and Creation in Paul* (Tübingen: Mohr Siebeck, 2008), 152.
41 Timothy Wiarda, "What God Knows When the Spirit Intercedes," BTB 17 (2007): 297–311; Richard J. Dillon, "The Spirit as Taskmaster and Troublemaker in Romans 8," CBQ 60 (1998): 682–702.
42 K.S. Kim, "Another Look at Adoption in Romans 8:15 in Light of Roman Social Practices and Legal Rules," BTB 44 (2014), 133–143.
43 Note how the concentration of filial terms in chapter 8—sons, (8:14) slaves, (8:15a); adopted son, (15b); children, and heirs (16)—fits well in an honor–shame society of the first-century Mediterranean world of Paul's day.
44 See the discussion in Erik Konsmo, *The Pauline Metaphors of the Holy Spirit. The Intangible Spirit's Tangible Presence in the Life of Christians* (New York: Peter Lang, 2010), 89 ff.

from God and identity as joint heirs with Christ, a status that involves sharing in his sufferings and a guarantee in his resurrected glory (8:17).[45] Therefore, Paul wants the Romans to be aware that the Spirit creates a familial relation with God that empowers them to deal with the challenges of their socioreligious lives.

Paul makes a decided shift, placing the role of the Spirit in the present life of suffering into the broadest possible creational context (8:18–25). All creation stands on the edge awaiting final redemption. Because the Spirit serves as the "first fruits,"[46] God guarantees the final harvest (8:23),[47] so the believer can live in hope despite the groaning.

Paul directs the discussion to the role of the Spirit in groaning creatures: the Spirit assists in human weakness since humans do not know how to pray; the Spirit intercedes with inarticulate prayers since God knows and understands the "mind of the Spirit" who intercedes on their behalf before God (8:26–27). As God's overarching design, the Spirit works in us for good. That is to say, the Spirit restores the glory of the good that is to be achieved by believers as those who love God. "For those whom he foreknew he also predestined to be conformed to the image of his Son.... And those whom he predestined he also called; and those whom he called he also justified; and those whom he justified he also glorified (8:28–30)" The Spirit is the experiential key to the whole of life.

6   God's Spirit as a Guide to Our Conscience (9:1)

In 9:1 Paul calls on God as his witness and brings about the Spirit as he shares the tragic riddle of Israel's unbelief (9:1–5). He affirms his sorrow in three ways: the witness of Christ to the truth of Paul's sorrow, his oath of honesty, and the independent witness of Paul's conscience about the presence of his sorrow.[48] His conscience (2:15) bears witness with him as he speaks.[49] A unique feature

---

45   Peter Orr, *Christ Absent and Present* (Tübingen: Mohr Siebeck, 2014), 201–212; Fee, *God's Empowering Presence*, 548, 554.

46   For a detailed discussion see Dunn, *Romans*, 1:473–474. See also Konsmo, *Pauline Metaphors*, 180 ff.

47   The "first fruits" are not to be taken as partially available by the work of the Spirit but as "a genitive of apposition ... which identifies the present experience of the spirit as constituting the first fruits." See Jewett, *Romans*, 518.

48   J.L. North, "Paul's Protest That He Does Not Lie in the Light of His Cilician Origin," *JTS* 47 (1996): 441.

49   Philip Bosman, *Conscience in Philo and Paul: A Conceptual History of the Synoida Word Group* (Tübingen: Mohr Siebeck, 2003), 253–254.

of this reference to conscience is the link with the Holy Spirit (Rom 14:17; 1 Cor 12:3; 2 Cor 6:6; 1 Thess 1:5), indicating that just as Christ attests to his speaking of truth, so, too, the Spirit attests to the trustworthiness of his conscience as it bears its independent witness.[50] His conscience acts on behalf of God's Spirit or is directly controlled[51] or guided by the Spirit,[52] an emphasis that carries ethical implications for the people of God. Hence, the presence of the Spirit within, guiding his conscience and enabling him to speak, think and perform as a believer.

7   God's Spirit and Gifts of God (12:3–8)

Though there are no direct references to "Spirit" in 12:3–6, Paul assumes that the house churches in Rome are fundamentally charismatic and involve the Spirit's operation in one's own relationship with God and to others. Operating on the premise that every Christian has charismatic gifts (12:6),[53] Paul begins with an elaboration of sober self-assessment on the exercise of charismatic gifts.[54] While dismissing superior-mindedness, Paul suggests that the standard for sober-mindedness is a measure consisting of faith that God deals out to "each" (12:3), and each Christian is "a member of others." Here Paul describes how charismatic people function within the community of faith, both as a gathered community for worship (prophesying, serving, teaching, encouraging, 12:6–7), and in various ways of caring for the needs of others (giving, caring for, showing mercy, 12:8). For Paul, as with all the early church, the reference to prophecy was indeed a clear manifestation of the Spirit in their midst (1 Cor 12, 14).[55] This indeed established their understanding of the Spirit as a primarily eschatological reality now present in the house churches.

---

50   Robert Jewett, *Paul's Anthropological Terms: A Study of Their Use in Conflict Situations* (Leiden: Brill, 1971), 446.
51   Schreiner, *Romans*, 479.
52   Käsemann, *Romans*, 257.
53   See John Koenig, *Charismata: God's Gifts for God's People* (Philadelphia: Westminster, 1978), 93–127; Siegfried S. Schatzmann, *Pauline Theology of Charismata* (Peabody, MA: Hendrickson, 1987), 70–80.
54   Cranfield, *Romans*, 2:619.
55   Dunn *Romans*, 2:726.

8 God's Spirit Instills Kingdom Character (14:17)

Given that the time of Torah has come to an end, how then do the weak—Torah-observant Christian Jews—and the strong—nonobservant Gentiles—get along together as one people of God? This is the issue addressed in Rom 14:1–15:13. In 14:17, Paul admonishes both the weak and the strong[56] that either abstention or partaking cannot become matters of law but are matters of relationships within the community. For Paul, the essential character of the kingdom of God[57] has nothing to do with kosher food and drink but true righteousness along with peace and joy (Ps 84:4), which is a life in the Holy Spirit.[58] This is effected through Christ's death and resurrection, seen in the lives of God's people as they walk by the Spirit. Joy, one of the nine fruits of the Spirit (Gal 5:22; cf. Isa 11:6–9; 25:6–8) is evidence that one is in the Spirit.[59] The peace of God (Gal 5:22) among the people of God is an effect of the Spirit in an environment of social superiority, discrimination, and numerous barriers preventing them from welcoming one another as equals.

9 God's Spirit Sanctifies (15:13, 16)

In 15:7–13, Paul repeats to his readers, Jews and Gentiles, an inclusive ethic whereby they accept one another just as Christ did. He became a servant to the circumcised (Jews), and he confirmed the promise to the patriarchs (Gentiles) (15:8). The purpose is that the nations might glorify God in response to the mercy received. The promise is that the Gentiles will share in the promises and praise God.[60] The God of hope is the source of the future conversion of the Gentiles (15:13).[61] As Paul shares a benediction, it is in the empowerment by the Holy Spirit that God fills the believers with joy and peace—a constitutive factor in the kingdom of God (14:17; cf. 1:7; 2:10; 3:17; 5:1; 8:6) as they trust in Christ. The

---

56 Dunn, *Romans*, 2:817.
57 George Johnston, "'Kingdom of God' Sayings in Paul's Letters," in *From Jesus to Paul: Studies in Honour of Francis Wright Beare*, ed. P. Richardson and J.C. Hurd, Jr. (Waterloo: Wilfrid Laurier University, 1984), 153. See also Dunn, *Romans*, 2:822.
58 Murray, *Romans*, 2:194,
59 Cranfield, *Romans*, 2:719.
60 Paul uses OT citations Ps 17:50 and 2 Sam 22:50 concerning glorifying God among the nations; Deut 32:43 concerning the nations rejoicing with Israel; Ps 117:1 concerning all peoples praising God; and Isa 11:10 concerning the nations hoping for Christ.
61 Gordon P. Wiles, *Paul's Intercessory Prayers: The Significance of the Intercessory Prayer Passages in the Letters of St. Paul* (Cambridge: Cambridge University Press, 1974), 90.

purpose of the "filling" is that the believers will abound in hope (15:13) for transformation of the nations. The existence of hope among the faithful for mission is created by the Spirit of God because the gospel embodies the power of God (1:16). Paul is communicating a broader and collective vision for mission to the house churches in Rome.

In continuation, Paul reiterates with authority "as minister of Jesus to the Gentiles" his missionary calling and strategies to the Roman believers (15:16).[62] He reinforces his mission as a priestly duty and the purpose is to bring the nations as an "offering to God"[63] and to sanctify the nations in the Spirit. Paul's ministry results in a transformation of the Gentiles into "an acceptable offering" in the fulfillment of the future announced in 11:11–12, 25—a reversal derived from Isa 66:20.[64] The offering turns out to be the Gentiles themselves, because they have been sanctified by the Holy Spirit (15:16; 1:4). The Gentile believers in Romans are being separated unto God at the time when they first believed in the good news (1 Cor 1:2; 6:11). It also implies that they have been set apart for God's own holy purposes (Exod 19:14; Lev 11:44; 20:8; 22:32; Deut 33:3; Ezek 20:41; 28:25; 37:28; 39:27).[65] Thus the Spirit has brought them into the sphere of the Messiah, which effectively consecrates them to their moral and mission obligations.

10   God's Spirit Empowers Mission (15:18–19)

Finally, Paul encapsulates the winning of the "obedience" (cf. 1:5) of the Gentiles as the accomplishment of Christ "through me" since Christ uses Paul's "word and deed" (2 Thess 2:17, Col 3:17). The goal of Christ's activity is the obedience of the nations. The presence of Christ is seen through the work of the Spirit,[66] signs and wonders, in the power of the Holy Spirit (15:19; 1:16).[67] The miracles are not his doing but are of Christ and the Spirit to authenticate Paul's

---

62 He reinforces themes that he sets at the beginning: his ministry to the Gentiles (1:13; cf. 15:15–21), the frequent hindrances to his visit to Rome (1:13; cf. 15:22)—which he hopes will be mutually beneficial (1:11–12; cf. 15:23–24, 28–29)—and his prayer for them (1:9–10), as well as his request for prayer from them (15:30–32).
63 D.W.B. Robinson, "The Priesthood of Paul in the Gospel of Hope," in *Reconciliation and Hope*, ed. R.J. Banks (Grand Rapids: Eerdmans, 1974), 231–245.
64 The prophet (Isa 66:20) expects that the Gentiles will bring the Jews back from exile as an offering to God; Paul is bringing the converted Gentiles themselves as the offering.
65 Dunn, *Romans* 2:861.
66 Fitzmyer, *Romans*, 713; Fee, *God's Empowering Presence*, 629.
67 Cranfield, *Romans*, 2:759; Jewett, *Romans*, 910.

divinely appointed status (Deut 13:1–2; Isa 20:3), and to prove God's presence in the miraculous experience of the early church (Acts 4:30; 5:12; 6:8; 14:3; 15:12).[68] By referring to his ministry of signs and wonders in the "power" of the Spirit,[69] he is integrating what he indicated in 1:3–4, the presence of the exalted Lord and the presence of the power of the Spirit among the believers. For Paul, therefore, the gospel involves words and deeds empowered by the Spirit.[70] And the result of his ministry is "that from Jerusalem and as far around as Illyricum I have fulfilled the gospel of Christ" (Rom 15:19b).

11   Conclusion

Paul's pneumatology in the letter emerges as he interacts with the multiple house churches in Rome. As their apostle, Paul brings to attention the foundational basis and the goal of spreading the gospel. But his perspectives are sharpened by his concerns, which include the upcoming visit to Jerusalem with the collections from Gentile churches for the poor in Jerusalem, his awareness of tensions among the house churches over Torah stipulations, and the opportunity for a broader mission.

For Paul, the Roman believers need to see the larger picture. The Jewish-Gentile salvation emanates from the Christ-event as God's answer to human sin (Rom 1–4). The obedience of faith that defines the Roman believers operates through the Spirit without any ethnic or moral considerations (5–8). The foundational calling of Israel is based on the promises (9–11) and Spirit-shaped communities have been formed (12–15).

What is foundational for his gospel is the understanding that the new era of the Spirit, which Christ inaugurated by his resurrection, has arrived and exemplifies a new identity. The Spirit embodies and empowers this new sphere of existence, a domain in which both Jewish and Gentile believers in Rome are to live and conduct themselves.

Paul elaborates on multiple dimensions of the role of the Spirit in a comprehensive way throughout the letter. First, the sanctifying role of the Spirit: an inward "circumcision of the heart," characteristic of the new covenant ushered in by the Spirit (2:29). Here, the Spirit makes the believer aware of the

---

68   Petrus J. Gräbe, *The Power of God in Paul's Letters* (Tübingen: Mohr Siebeck, 2000), 209–210.
69   Paul's letters in Rom 1:4; 15:13, 19 (twice); 1 Cor 2:5; 4:20; 15:43; 2 Cor 6:7; 1 Thess 1:5; cf. Col 1:29; 2 Thess 1:11.
70   Fee, *God's Empowering Presence*, 629.

overwhelming love of God and an assurance that this love was poured out as the manifestation of the Spirit's internal presence in a believer (5:5). The result is the Spirit-formed obedience wherein the sanctification is manifested in various forms—thoughts, habits, and attitudes—that nurture righteousness, peace, and joy, reflecting the character of the kingdom of God (7:6). Further, the Spirit-directed obligation in their new status as children of God calls the believers to serve others rather than to be served. And as adopted children, Paul believed that the Spirit intercedes on their behalf and leads them. However, the Spirit also brings both the reality of suffering and more profound experiences of God's love to the Romans (8:27–28).

The second is the charismatic dimension. For Paul, sober-mindedness is a measure consisting of faith that God grants to "each" and "each believer belongs to all the others"—a facet of being sanctified by Spirit. Thus, the gift of the Spirit equips them to function within the community of faith as they gather for worship and engage in caring for the needs of others (12:3–8).

Third, the missional dimension, where Paul reminds the Romans of what Christ has accomplished through him in his previous missions, particularly the setting apart of the Gentiles as an offering to God. His Spirit-empowered missions were ministered "by the power of signs, and wonders, through the power of the Spirit of God" (15:19). The "overflow of hope by the power of the Holy Spirit" strengthens Paul's desire to see more worshipers praise and glorify God, so that he might rely on them to assist him in his mission to Spain.

Thus, we see that in the letter to the Romans Paul's mature and realistic conversation with the house churches in Rome provides us with a rich, profound theology of the Spirit.

The Spirit in 1 Corinthians: Spiritual Formation and Giftedness

J. Ayodeji Adewuya

The Holy Spirit plays a significant role in 1 Corinthians. Paul discusses the role of the Spirit in personal lives, community formation, and worship, among other aspects of Christian living. Paul's teaching about the Holy Spirit in 1 Corinthians cannot be understood apart from the situation of the congregation in Corinth. Many of the problems in this letter are rooted in the background and surroundings of the Corinthian believers. A major one of those problems is autonomous absolutism. The thinking of the Corinthians is much colored and dominated by individualism. As such, it is important to note that Paul's discussion about the Holy Spirit in 1 Corinthians is about the community of which the individual is a constituent member. This is the thread that links several passages in which Paul explicitly deals with the Holy Spirit in 1 Corinthians, as we shall see below.

1 Corinthians is unique in its content, for beyond any other letter of Paul, one might say, it deals with an array and complexity of problems that might well find their parallel in today's world and churches. It was beset with various problems such as divisions over leadership and ethical and doctrinal issues, most of which are related to understanding true spirituality. As such, the congregation needed to be established and grounded in God's Word and, consequently, to live as befitted their calling as God's people. It is not possible to address every issue related to the Holy Spirit in an essay of this length.[1] However, Paul highlights and sometimes elaborates on different aspects of the ministry and function of the Holy Spirit among believers in several passages. Therefore, the approach in this essay is to look at some of the passages and see how much they foster the understanding of the Holy Spirit's work in 1 Corinthians.

1   1 Corinthians 1

The importance Paul attaches to the Holy Spirit is evident from the opening verses of the letter. Immediately after Paul gives thanks to God for the grace

---

[1] Admittedly, some questions will remain unaddressed or unanswered about the Holy Spirit in 1 Corinthians in this essay due to the limitation of space. The importance of the essay does not lie in its comprehensiveness but in its heuristic value.

given to his readers, he mentions the enrichment of the Corinthians with spiritual gifts, explicitly speaking and knowledge, which is part of a broader range of *charismata* bestowed on them (1 Cor 1:5–7). Although the Spirit is not expressly mentioned at this point, there is no doubt that these gifts, here said to be given "in Christ," are the gifts imparted by the Spirit, who enters into a living relationship with individual believers and bestows different gifts upon them.[2] As Fee notes, these gifts were selected because of their prominence and high value in the community, which comes into focus in chapters 1–4, 8–10, and 12–14.[3]

2   1 Corinthians 2

In 1 Corinthians 2, Paul articulates a soteriological pneumatology.[4] He does so by showing the role of the Spirit in proclamation of the gospel, especially as it relates to wisdom, illumination by the Spirit, and the Spirit's relationship to Christ.

2.1   *The Holy Spirit and Proclamation/Preaching: 1 Cor 2:1–5*

In 1 Cor 2, Paul addresses the problem of "wisdom" preaching in Corinth, where some people were placing undue emphasis on the wisdom of the Greeks. When Paul came to Corinth, there was nothing of oratory or rhetoric, no "enticing words of human wisdom, but … demonstration of the Spirit and of power" (1 Cor 2:4). Weakness, fear, and trembling marked the vessel, but the message came with the demonstration of the Holy Spirit and the power of God. The conversion of the Corinthians was a testimony to the power of God, by implication the Holy Spirit, and not to the persuasion of logic.

---

[2] I. Howard Marshall, *New Testament Theology: Many Witnesses, One Gospel* (Downers Grove, IL: InterVarsity Press, 2004), 272–274. See also Ben Witherington III, *Conflict and Community in Corinth: A Socio-Rhetorical commentary on 1 and 2 Corinthians* (Grand Rapids: Eerdmans, 1995), 88–89; *contra* Preben Vang, *1 Corinthians*, Teaching the Text Commentary Series (Grand Rapids: Baker Books, 2014), 17.

[3] Gordon Fee, *God's Empowering Presence: The Holy Spirit in the Letters of Paul* (Peabody, MA.: Hendrickson, 1994), 87.

[4] There are differences of opinion among scholars concerning the origin of Paul's soteriological pneumatology: for example, between R.P. Menzies, *The Development of Early Christian Pneumatology with Special Reference to Luke-Acts* (Sheffield, UK: Sheffield Academic Press, 1991), chap. 13, who argues that Paul was the first to articulate a soteriological pneumatology, and Max Turner, *The Holy Spirit and Spiritual Gifts* (Peabody, MA: Hendrickson Publishers, 1996), 107–111, who critiques this approach.

2.2 The Holy Spirit and Illumination: 1 Cor 2:6–16[5]

In 1 Cor 2:6–16, Paul says that he does have wisdom that he speaks among the "perfect" (1 Cor 2:6), but this is not wisdom by the standards of this age nor from the leaders of this age, who are passing away. The Corinthians fancied themselves as fully wise and thus "perfect." The wisdom that he imparts is not recognized by those considered wise, powerful, and well-born in this age, the pre-eschatological and disobedient period of human history (see 1 Cor 1:20, 26). He calls his wisdom "a wisdom in mystery," meaning a hidden or inaccessible wisdom not understood by the "rulers of this age" (2:7–8). What God has prepared soteriologically for those who love him is known only through the illumination of the Spirit (2:9). He says that this hidden wisdom comes to human beings only by a revelation through the Spirit of God (2:10). Paul adds, "The Spirit searches all things, even the depths of God" (2:10).

In this context, the "depths of God" appears to refer to God's ultimate salvation-historical purposes, in particular the death and resurrection of Christ (see Rom 11:33); these depths the Spirit reveals to believers. This explains how believers come to accept the gospel, which is foolishness by human standards: the Spirit reveals to them the truth of the gospel, and without the Spirit, there would be no such understanding.

Paul explains by analogy that just as the human Spirit knows the things about humans, so, too, does the Spirit of God know the things of God; thus, because they have the Spirit of God, believers have access to an understanding of God's salvation-historical purposes that others do not have. Paul's statement that believers have not received "the spirit of the world" but the Spirit of God is probably intended to stress that the Spirit of God does not originate in the world or this age (2:12). If so, then Paul is not identifying two "spirits" operative among human beings. Instead, Paul's point is that what a believer knows about "the things freely given to us by God," by which he means salvation in the present and the future, is because of the indwelling Spirit, who originates from God. As Thiselton rightly notes, "Paul disengages the activity of the Holy Spirit from mere innate human 'spirituality.' Spiritual is what pertains to the Holy Spirit … . It does not denote deploying some *'higher' human capacity*."[6]

---

[5] In recent years, scholars, especially Pentecostals, have highlighted the important role of the Holy Spirit in Scripture interpretation. Several essays, journal articles, and publications that utilize pentecostal hermeneutics have been written. Two major works among others in this regard are Kenneth J. Archer, *A Pentecostal Hermeneutic: Spirit, Scripture and Community* (Cleveland, TN.: CPT Press, 2009), and Craig S. Keener, *Spirit Hermeneutics: Reading Scripture in Light of Pentecost* (Grand Rapids: Eerdmans, 2017).

[6] Anthony C. Thiselton, *1 Corinthians: A Shorter Exegetical and Pastoral Commentary* (Grand Rapids: Eerdmans, 2006), 57.

Paul differentiates between the "unspiritual, soulish person" (*ho psuchikos anthrôpos*) and the "spiritual" person (*ho pneumatikos anthrôpos*).[7] The former is what a person is because one has not "received" the Spirit; as such, one does not accept revelation that comes from the Spirit. Finally, Paul concludes with another quotation from Isaiah (Isa 40:13), making the point that no one can instruct the Lord (Yahweh). Paul adds, however, that Christians have at least partial access to a knowledge of God's salvation-historical purposes because they have the mind of Christ. Given the context, it seems to mean that to have the mind of Christ is to have the Spirit. Without the Spirit, no one can comprehend the things of God.[8]

3 The Holy Spirit and Spiritual Formation

In 1 Cor 3:1–5; 16–17; 6:11–20; 12:13, Paul discusses the role of the Spirit both in personal and community formation. The Spirit brings transformation.[9]

3.1 *1 Cor 3:1–4*

Paul regarded some members of the congregation in Corinth as lacking in the Spirit and, therefore, unable to receive and understand his message (1 Cor 3:1). This lack of the Spirit was evidenced by the failure to develop in Christian character; they were still dominated by their non-Christian character and were like mere infants who had not grown as Christians. Therefore, Paul conceived of a

---

7   Paul uses *pneumatikos* in three places in 1 Cor 2:12, 15 and 3:1. In 1 Cor 2:12 and 15 it probably refers to the spiritual in terms of status as God's people in antithesis to those of "this age." See, for example, James D.G. Dunn, *Jesus and* Spirit (London: SCM, 1975), 207–208, who argues that "Pneumatikos ... expresses so clearly the sense of belonging to Spirit, embodying Spirit, manifesting Spirit, of the essence or nature of Spirit." In 1 Cor 3:1, Paul uses it to refer to the immature character of those whose attitudes do not reflect their status as God's people. There, Paul redefines the readers' understanding of *pneumatikos*. See Anthony Thiselton, "The Holy Spirit in 1 Corinthians," in *The Holy Spirit and Christian Origins: Essays in Honor of James D.G. Dunn* (Grand Rapids: Eerdmans, 2004), 209.
8   Michael Green, *I Believe in the Holy Spirit*, rev. ed. (Grand Rapids: Eerdmans, 2004), 115.
9   David J. Lull, *1 Corinthians*, Chalice Commentaries for Today (Danvers, MA.: Chalice Press, 2007), 21. For a more detailed discussion on spiritual formation in the undisputed letters of Paul, see James G. Samra, *Being Conformed to Christ in Community: A Study of Maturity, Maturation and the Local Church in the Undisputed Pauline Epistles*, LNTS 320 (London: T & T Clark). For a specific link between the role of the Spirit and community formation see Max Turner, "Spiritual Gifts and Spiritual Formation in 1 Corinthians and Ephesians," *Journal of Pentecostal Theology* 22 (2013): 187–205; Volker Rabens, *The Holy Spirit and Ethics in Paul*, 2nd rev. ed. (Minneapolis: Fortress Press, 2014).

process of developing fuller insight—thanks to the working of the Spirit. Paul believed that there was such a thing as spiritual development and progress. The Spirit enabled people to appreciate and understand the mind of God, but this development could be arrested by sub-Christian forms of behavior, specifically envy and quarreling. He also believed that people could return to making spiritual progress through repentance and turning away from these sins.

3.2   1 Cor 3:16–17

In 1 Cor 3:16–17, Paul warns the Corinthians against destroying God's temple. Here, the term is used in a collective sense, a reference to the body of believers. The idea of the metaphor is clear. The temple, the Corinthian church, belongs to God and is indwelt by the Holy Spirit. It is significant to note that Paul asserts that the community, not individuals or subgroups, is the locus of the indwelling Spirit. The temple image firmly locates the indwelling of the Spirit within the community as a whole. When he states that the Spirit "dwells in you," the plural pronoun underscores that the Spirit dwells within the community rather than just within the individual. Although it is apparent that Paul recognizes the work of the Spirit within individuals, Paul insists that personal inspiration be understood within the context of community edification. Therefore, Paul could say that if anyone destroys the temple of God, God will destroy that person. He is making a strong point. The division of the Corinthian church into numerous cliques contradicts the unity of the one temple in which God has chosen to dwell through the one Spirit. As God's eschatological temple, the Corinthian community must maintain its unity. To be divided into various factions was, within the believing community, equivalent to the destruction of Solomon's temple at the hands of the Babylonians.

3.3   1 Cor 6:19–20

Here, Paul applies the temple metaphor to the individual believer. To be a Christian is to be a member of the body of Christ, not an isolated, saved individual. At the same time, Paul holds individuals responsible for their behavior, expecting the community to discipline them. Thus, the Corinthians should "flee sexual immorality" (6:18), Paul says, because each believer's body, within the community, functions as the temple of God, the residence of the Holy Spirit, and therefore should be used to glorify God (6:19–20). Paul is telling the Corinthians that they are, as individuals within the believing community, the eschatological locus of God's presence, the residence of his Spirit. As such, they must live in a way that is consistent with the presence of God within them. Thus, the focus remains on the community. In 1 Cor 3:16, Paul makes a solemn statement that the assembly is the temple of God and is indwelt by the Spirit of God. He makes a similar argument concerning the believer's body in chapter 6. The agency of the Spirit in the life of believers is attested in 1 Cor 6:11, where the changes wrought in their lives take place "in the name of the Lord Jesus Christ and by the Spirit of our God." It is probable that all three changes, washing, sanctifying, and justifying, are to be seen as aspects of becoming a Christian. The process of conversion thus takes place in virtue of what Christ has done, but at the same time, the Spirit is the agent in applying what Christ has done to the individual. The Holy Spirit is not an outside agent. The Spirit is said to be "in" believers. So, what is true of the believing community as a corporate body is true of individuals as constituent members of the Body.

3.4 Baptized into One Body by One Spirit

In 1 Cor 12:12–13, Paul employs the analogy of the human body to stress the assertions he has been making about ministry in the church (vv. 4–11), emphasizing the significance of unity. Specifically, in v. 13, he makes an emphatic statement that the Holy Spirit is the source of unity: "For by one Spirit *are we* all baptized into one body, whether we be Jews or Gentiles, whether slave or free." The baptism of the Spirit is a corporate formation; the baptism in the Spirit of the Corinthians initiated them into one body. They are now formed into one community that transcends ethnic barriers, social status, and gender distinctions. All, too, drink the water, which is the Spirit, probably an allusion to the cup that all believers shared.[10] As Barnett aptly states, "At their initiation, all believers were immersed in the one Spirit and drank of the one Spirit and so became members of 'the Christ,' his assembly. Here the Spirit is not the divine agent who does the baptizing but is the figurative fluid into which believers are plunged and from which each drinks."[11] Although Schnelle's conclusion that this verse points to a transformation is correct, his suggestion that "drinking" may be pointing to absorption of water as in plants (cf. 1 Cor 3:7, 8), rather than the simple reference to drinking, is forced and unconvincing.[12]

4 1 Corinthians 12–14

Perhaps one of the greatest contributions of 1 Corinthians to the conversation about the Holy Spirit is Paul's discussion on the "gifts of the Spirit" in 1 Cor

---

10 Craig Keener, *1–2 Corinthians*, The New Cambridge Bible Commentary (Cambridge, UK: Cambridge University Press, 2005), 103.
11 Paul Barnett, *1 Corinthians*. (Ross-Shire, UK: Christian Focus Publications, 2000), 232.
12 Udo Schnelle, *Apostle Paul: His Life and Theology* (Grand Rapids: Baker, 2012), 488–489.

12–14.[13] Paul's arguments in 1 Cor 12–14, written in response to questions about worship in the Corinthian congregation, are sometimes polemical, suggesting that his purpose is primarily corrective, not instructive. This is especially clear in chapters 13 and 14, where tongues appear to be the culprit. The Corinthians and Paul were at odds (1 Cor 14:36–37) as they seemed to have elevated tongues above the other gifts and probably saw it as a mark of greater spirituality. Such misunderstanding by the Corinthians resulted in both excessive zeal for tongues and consequent disorder in their assembly. Hence, in his effort to curb their misguided enthusiasm, Paul first argues for the necessity of diversity—if the community is indeed to be "of the Spirit" (1 Cor 12:4–30). He then contends that love must be the motivation for the exercise of the gifts (1 Cor 13:1–13). He concludes that in terms of Spirit manifestations, love demands that they seek after intelligible utterances (1 Cor 14:1–25) and order (1 Cor 14:26–40) if the community is to be built up (1 Cor 14:1–19, 26–33) and outsiders converted (1 Cor 14:20–25). In the process, Paul lists various charismata, ministries, and forms of service at seven different points in his argument (1 Cor 12:8–10, 28, 29–30; 13:1–3, 8; 14:6, 26). There are no two alike (not even 1 Cor 12:28 and 29–30). Also, they appear in ways that make systematizing nearly impossible.

For Paul, the Holy Spirit equips every believer with what the Bible calls "gifts." A spiritual gift is a supernatural ability sovereignly bestowed upon every Christian by the Holy Spirit, enabling him or her to carry out their divinely assigned function as a member of Christ's body, the church (1 Cor 12:4–7). These gifts are perfectly suited to each believer's situation in life and, when exercised in the context of community, will contribute to the nurture and edification of the

---

13   For an exhaustive study about the gifts, see A. Bittlinger, *Gifts and Graces* (Grand Rapids: Eerdmans, 1967); K. Berger, "χάρισμα" *EDNT* 3.458; Trevor J. Burke and Keith Warrington, *A Biblical Theology of the Holy Spirit* (Eugene, OR: Cascade Books, 2014); J.D.G. Dunn, *Jesus and the Spirit* (Philadelphia: Westminster, 1975); G.D. Fee, *The First Epistle to the Corinthians*, NICNT (Grand Rapids: Eerdmans, 1987); Fee, *God's Empowering Presence: The Holy Spirit in the Letters of Paul* (Peabody: Hendrickson, 1993); Fee, "Gifts of the Spirit," in *Dictionary of Paul and His Letters* (Downers Grove, IL: InterVarsity Press, 1993), 339–347; R.Y.K. Fung, "Ministry, Community and Spiritual Gifts," *EvQ* 56 (1984): 3–14; D. Gee, *Concerning Spiritual Gifts* (Springfield: Gospel Publishing, 1947); Gee, *Spiritual Gifts in the Work of the Ministry Today* (Springfield: Gospel Publishing, 1963); Michael Green, *I Believe in the Holy Spirit*, rev. ed. (Grand Rapids: Eerdmans, 2004); E. Käsemann, "Ministry and Community in the New Testament," in *Essays on New Testament Themes* (London: SCM, 1964), 63–94; Craig S. Keener, *Gift & Giver: The Holy Spirit for Today* (Grand Rapids: Baker Academic, 2001; 2020); David Lim, *Spiritual Gifts: A Fresh Look* (Springfield: Gospel Publishing House, 1996); Anthony C. Thiselton, *The Holy Spirit* (London: SPCK, 2013); Max Turner, *The Holy Spirit and Spiritual Gifts* (Peabody: Hendrickson, 1996); J. Rodman Williams, *The Holy Spirit in the Bible* (Florida: Creation House, 1990).

body. Thus, the gifts are a vital part of spiritual formation. Due to Paul's letters' ad hoc nature and the ambiguity in the "vocabulary" that he uses for the spiritual gifts, it is difficult to classify the gifts into neat categories. One should instead look at the discussions of the gifts in their contexts rather than superimpose an outside grid on what Paul was saying.

4.1 *1 Cor 12:8–10*

After speaking in general terms, Paul mentions different manifestations of the Spirit in verses 8–10. He begins by mentioning the word of wisdom. This is the unique ability to speak forth the wisdom of God, especially in an important or difficult situation, as shown in Solomon (1 Kings 3:16–18), Jesus (Luke 20:20–26), Stephen (Acts 7), and Paul (Acts 23). This is followed by the word of knowledge. Harold Horton, a pentecostal preacher, once defined it as "a divinely granted flash of revelation concerning things which were hopelessly hidden from the senses,"[14] citing the example of God's judgment for Eli, given as a voice in the night to Samuel (1 Sam 3:13), and God's word to Peter regarding the arrival of messengers from Cornelius (Acts 10:19). Next on the list is the gift of faith. Faith is an essential part of every Christian's life. Paul is not referring to the initial faith that is necessary for salvation. The gift of faith is the unique ability to trust God in all circumstances, as Peter did when he walked out of the boat onto the water (Matt 14:22–33). Next are the "gifts of healing." The plural form "gifts" may suggest that the manifestation of these gifts takes different forms at different times, depending on the particular needs.

Moreover, it is to be observed that these gifts are for the benefit of the community. Next is the "working of miracles," which seems to be a general term encompassing supernatural activity, including healing. In most cases, the Holy Spirit overrides the power of nature. The gift of prophecy refers both to the foretelling of the future and the forthtelling of God's mind for a particular situation. Some have defined prophecy as preaching, but there are different words for preaching and prophecy. Whereas preaching deals with proclamation, prophecy involves a supernatural revelation and words spoken under direct inspiration from God. "Distinguishing between spirits" or "discerning of spirits" (KJV) describes the God-given ability to determine whether or not a supernatural manifestation has its source in God.

An example is that of Paul in Acts (16:16–18). The list continues with "speaking in different kinds of tongues." This refers to a supernatural utterance in a

---

14 As cited by Robert Willoughby, *First Corinthians: Fostering Christian Spirituality* (Ithaca, NY: Christian Publications, 1996), 162.

language that the speaker did not learn, and it may or may not be a language known to others. Lastly, Paul mentions the "interpretation of tongues." Essentially, it refers to an intelligible presentation of the content of what was spoken in an unknown tongue.

4.2 1 Cor 12:27–30

Paul ends chapter 12 with a list of some of the gifts that God gives to the community. The emphasis remains the same: the need for diversity. Paul's juxtaposition of the special gifts and the various ministry functions in the church in 1 Cor 12 (8–10 and v. 28) shows the close relationship between the two. There are three observations. First, God distributes gifts and callings according to his pleasure. In the same manner that the church does not bestow the gifts of healings, tongues, and interpretation of tongues, and so forth, upon individuals, the church does not create apostles, prophets, teachers, and other ministry gifts.

The second observation is that the list does not precisely match the earlier one in 12:8–10, suggesting that both lists are not exhaustive. Paul discusses the ministry functions in dialogue with the existing situation at Corinth and in the light of the forms of leadership that suited his cultural context. Paul does not suggest that these offices are either the only exact forms of leadership that are both timeless and universally normative.

Third, in context, these verses press home Paul's argument in the entire chapter by way of summary. If these gifts are given generously as God wills (vv. 4–6), and if they are for the common good of the whole church (v. 4), it is right that the gifts do not serve the purpose of comparison and competition among ministers for the sake of enhancing one's status. The members of Christ's body ought not to compete with one another to gain prestige, position, or power. Instead, they should work together for the well-being of the whole assembly. Paul does not suggest that there is any particular individual who functions in all these capacities. The gifts transcend the ability of any individual to possess them. Significantly, these gifts are complementary. They function together within the community—the church. In v. 28, Paul lists several gifts, starting with the apostle. The list itself has several interesting features: (1) He begins with a list of persons whom he seems to rank in the order of first, second, third. (2) With the fourth and fifth items (miracles and gifts of healings), he reverts to charismata, taking two from the list in 1 Cor 12:8–10. These are both prefaced with the word "then," as though he intended the ranking scheme to continue. (3) The sixth and seventh items (helpful deeds and acts of guidance), which are deeds of service, are noteworthy in three ways: (a) they are the only two not mentioned again in the rhetoric of 1 Cor 12:29–30; (b) nor are they mentioned again in the NT; (c) they do not appear to be of the same kind—

that is, supernatural endowments—as those on either side (miracles, healings, tongues). Paul probably chose. This list represents a whole range of "ministries" in the Church, probably for that reason. Paul neither grades the gifts nor creates a hierarchical structure. Instead, what he does is simply to enumerate the gifts. Apostles included not only the Twelve but also those like Paul and others. The climax of Paul's argument comes in vv. 29–30. He does not think that everyone will have every gift. The diversity of the gifts within the body of Christ is not only acceptable or expected; it is God's plan for how the body of Christ would function. Thus, Paul's argument comes full circle.

5 Conclusion

This essay has offered a broad overview of the Holy Spirit in 1 Corinthians. As suggested at the beginning, the significance of the Holy Spirit in 1 Corinthians cannot be overstated. There is to be no facet of the believer's life excluded from the reach of the Holy Spirit. Regarding the spiritual gifts, as significant as they are, the attention on them almost to the neglect of the other aspects of the Holy Spirit in 1 Corinthians does vital injustice to Paul's overall discussion of the role of the Spirit in the Christian life. For Paul, character, and charismata are never a matter of either/or but both/and. It is not one without the other. The "fruit of the Spirit" must never be separated from the "gifts of the Spirit."

The Spirit in 2 Corinthians: A Glorious Covenant and Consummation

Jacob Cherian and Joe Thomas

The Holy Spirit plays an indispensable role in Paul's configuration of the Christian life.[1] The apostle declares that God's new creation in Christ is ordered under the aegis of the Spirit. 2 Corinthians will both reinforce this foundational theological reality and point in a few distinctive directions.

This article briefly examines the significance of the Spirit in Paul's overall argument in 2 Corinthians.[2] There is general consensus that eleven out of the seventeen occurrences of *pneuma* in this letter explicitly refer to the Spirit.[3] As with most of the letter, it is necessary to read the Spirit passages against the backdrop of Paul's opponents at Corinth and the resulting malaise in the church that he deals with.[4] These rivals are clearly Jewish, whether from Judea or elsewhere, who appeal to Moses (cf. 3:7–13; 11:22) and employ criteria different from Paul's to judge "rhetorical or possibly charismatic superiority."[5] It is in this context that Paul appeals to the Spirit to regain the trust of the congregation, to defend his gospel and apostolic fidelity, and to appeal for unity in the Spirit.

The Spirit texts will be explored under three main themes: (1) the Spirit as a seal and deposit (2 Cor 1:21–22; 5:5); (2) the Spirit and the New Covenant (2 Cor 3); and (3) the Holy Spirit and the Trinity (2 Cor 13:14).

---

1 Gordon D. Fee's magisterial treatment, *God's Empowering Presence: The Holy Spirit in the Letters of Paul* (Peabody, MA: Hendrickson, 1994), remains the most comprehensive treatment of the Spirit in the Pauline corpus.
2 Apart from Fee's detailed study (*God's Empowering Presence*, 282–266), two significant contributions are: R.P. Martin, "The Spirit in 2 Corinthians in Light of the 'Fellowship of the Holy Spirit' in 2 Corinthians 13:14," in *Eschatology and the New Testament*. ed. W.H. Gloer (Peabody, MA: Hendrickson, 1988), 113–128, and Linda. L Belleville, "Paul's Polemic and Theology of the Spirit in Second Corinthians," *CBQ* 58, no. 2 (1996): 281–304.
3 The uncontested texts are: 2 Cor 1:22; 3:3; 3:6 (2); 3:8; 3:17 (2); 3:18; 5:5; 6:6; 13:14.
4 For a brief account of the situation in Corinth and the identification of Paul's opponents, see Craig S. Keener, *1–2 Corinthians*, NCBC (New York: Cambridge University Press, 2005), 143–146.
5 Keener, *1–2 Corinthians*, 145.

1 The Spirit as a Seal and Deposit (1:21–22; 5:5)

To understand Paul's argument in 1:12–2:4, it is necessary to grasp the backdrop of Paul's changed itinerary,[6] which leads some Corinthians to accuse him of being unstable and functioning *kata sarka* (from a worldly standpoint; 1:17).[7] Paul vehemently maintains that in this new order inaugurated by God in Christ, his apostolic functioning is deliberately *kata pneuma*.[8]

In vibrant trinitarian terms, Paul explains that God establishes *both* the apostles *and* the Corinthians in Christ, by the Spirit. He appeals to their shared and ongoing experience of the Spirit in order to dismiss the Corinthians' flimsy charges. The robust metaphors in 1:22 and 5:5—where the Holy Spirit is portrayed as sealing[9] God's people, who receive the Spirit as a deposit—assist him admirably in his apologetic task.

A seal denoted ownership or certified something.[10] The Holy Spirit among them was the evidence of God's ownership, securing their identity in Christ. Further, using a Semitic loan word (*arrabōn*; used thrice in the NT; in 1:22, 5:5, and Eph 1:14), Paul assures them that the Holy Spirit was God's first installment of a full and glorious future payment.[11] Harris suggests that it may be best not to press all the commercial nuances of this metaphor, especially since God's gracious gift of the Spirit is "an unsolicited gift."[12]

In 5:5, Paul proclaims that the Spirit is God's pledge, which anticipates "the complete transformation of a perishable, mortal mode of existence into an imperishable, immortal mode of existence."[13] This emphasis on the Spirit—as a foretaste of the age to come but presently manifested in weakness (a major theme in 2 Corinthians)—is something his triumphalist opponents at Corinth are unable to see.

---

6   For a concise explanation, see Jacob Cherian, "2 Corinthians," 1587–1589 in *South Asia Bible Commentary*, ed. Brian Wintle (Grand Rapids, MI: Zondervan/Open Door Publications, 2015).
7   This phrase also occurs in 5:16 (2); 10:2, 3; 11:18.
8   This dichotomy is clearly stated in such passages as Rom 8:4 and Gal 4:29.
9   The verb *sphragizō* is found in three other texts in Paul (Rom 15:28; Eph 1:13; 4:30).
10 For Paul, the Corinthians themselves were a seal attesting to his apostleship (1 Cor 9:2). The two other Pauline texts in which the noun *sphragis* occurs are Rom 4:11 and 2 Tim 2:19.
11 Belleville, "Spirit in 2 Corinthians," 283–286.
12 Murray J. Harris, *The Second Epistle to the Corinthians: A Commentary on the Greek Text*, NIGTC (Grand Rapids, MI: Eerdmans/Paternoster, 2005), 208.
13 Belleville, "Spirit in 2 Corinthians," 287. Another metaphor that serves a similar purpose for Paul is first-fruits (*aparchē*); see Rom 8:23; 1 Cor 15:20; 2 Thess 2:13.

2 The Spirit and the New Covenant (3:1–18)

The defensive tone of this passage again reveals the nature of the challenge facing Paul. It is in this intense context that "the largest single block of Spirit material occurs in the letter (3:3–18)."[14] Paul is being pushed to the wall by rivals who seek to destroy the very foundations of his gospel and apostleship. So, he reminds the Corinthians that they are a letter written on the hearts of the apostles. They also count as his commendation letter, written not with ink but rather with "the Spirit of the living God" (a unique phrase in the NT). Later, in a catalogue of credentials, he mentions the phrase "and in the Holy Spirit" (6:6), a probable reference to his Spirit-led character attesting to his genuineness.[15]

Thomas Blanton argues that while Paul's rivals at Corinth saw themselves as "agents of righteousness," using the standard concept of covenant renewal, the Pauline team claimed that they were authentic ministers of a far more glorious new covenant initiated by the Spirit.[16] Paul's argument is infused with the prophetic hopes found in texts such as Jer 31:31–34, Ezek 11:19; 36:26–27, and Joel 2:2–9.

Paul's point is singular: The glorious day that the prophets longed for has arrived. In this new era, unlike during the old covenant, Christ writes on human hearts through the agency of the Holy Spirit. God has made the Pauline team competent as ministers of the long-awaited new covenant[17] which is "not of the letter" but instead is "of the Spirit" (3:6). He makes similar claims elsewhere (Rom 2:27–29; 7:6; Phil 3:3).

In a lengthy appeal, Paul contrasts "the letter" (which kills and condemns) and "the Spirit" (who gives life). While the old covenant mediated by Moses came with its attendant glory, it was transitory; whereas the new covenant mediated by the Spirit has surpassing glory and is everlasting. While this would be bitter medicine for many in Corinth, Paul demonstrates that "the Spirit, as an eschatological reality, and as fulfilment of the promised new covenant, renders the old covenant obsolete."[18]

A brief comment on the statement in 3:17, "The Lord *is* the Spirit," is necessary. While these words can be (and have been) misunderstood, there is schol-

---

14   Fee, *God's Empowering Presence*, 284.
15   So, Belleville, "Spirit in 2 Corinthians," 291–293.
16   Thomas R. Blanton, "Spirit and Covenant Renewal: A Theologoumenon of Paul's Opponents in 2 Corinthians," *JBL* 129, No. 1 (2010): 150–151.
17   The term "new covenant" is found in three other places in the NT: Luke 22:20; 1 Cor 11:25; and Heb 9:15.
18   Fee, *God's Empowering Presence*, 365.

arly consensus that Paul's point here is not that the Spirit is absolutely identical with "the Lord" (whether Yahweh or Christ), but, rather, here we have an exegetical "is."[19] The Lord and the Spirit are equal in function and experience. People can and do resist the Lord; similarly, they can also resist and grieve the Spirit (as in Isa 63:10; Acts 7:51).[20]

3 The Holy Spirit and the Trinity (2 Cor 13:14)

The widely used benediction in 2 Corinthians 13:14 is recognized as "the most developed *trinitarian affirmation* in the NT."[21] With these closing words, Paul has scaled a stunning pinnacle. Gordon Fee's assessment is not an overstatement: "In many ways this benediction is *the most profound theological moment in the Pauline corpus* ... [I]t also serves as our entrée into Paul's theology proper."[22]

Two related matters could be considered: Is there any significance to the stated order (Jesus–God–Holy Spirit)? And should the third genitive construction ("of the Holy Spirit") be read as an objective or a subjective genitive?

Harris suggests that the unusual order "points to the chronological order of believers' experience of the Godhead."[23] This explanation is unconvincing if we examine other passages in which Paul presents a different sequence. For example, 1:21–22 provides the traditional order (God–Christ–Spirit). However, notice a Spirit–Lord–God arrangement in 1 Cor 12:4–6 and a God–Holy Spirit–Christ sequence in Tit 3:4–7. This flexible order in Paul's thinking points to an intrinsic equality within the Godhead and a perfect unity of function and salvific purpose.

Many have argued that the three genitive constructions in 13:14 (including "of the Holy Spirit") be taken as subjective, that is, the Holy Spirit authors or inspires the *koinōnia*. However, Martin, at the end of his study, suggests that an objective sense should be preferred—the believers are to participate in the Spirit.[24] This surely is in line with much of Pauline thought of "being full of the Spirit" (Eph 5:18) and of "sharing in the Spirit," which leads to the unity of fellow-

---

19 Anthony C. Thiselton, *The Living Paul* (Downers Grove, IL: IVP, 2009), 65–66.
20 Cherian, "2 Corinthians," 1591–1592.
21 Harris, *The Second Epistle to the Corinthians*, 116; author's emphasis.
22 Fee, *God's Empowering Presence*, 363; emphasis added.
23 Harris, *The Second Epistle to the Corinthians*, 117.
24 Martin, "The Spirit in 2 Corinthians," 114, 127. Similarly, the footnote in the NRSV ("the sharing in").

ship (Phil 2:1). While Paul is definitely desiring the unity of the Spirit at Corinth, he also knows that this beautiful reality is created when believers themselves share in the life-giving Spirit.

4 Conclusion

Having encountered the crucified and resurrected Lord, and being sealed by the eschatological Spirit, Paul thoroughly reworked his Jewish monotheism within a magnificent trinitarian framework. Fundamental to his theology was the intricate interweaving of the work of Christ and the Spirit. For Paul, God has inaugurated the new age in Christ (5:17–19) in which "the dialectic of present and future ... finds its focal point in [the] concept of the Spirit."[25] In this new covenant, believers must live out their calling *kata pneuma*. United in the Spirit, being transformed into Christlikeness, they now wait confidently for the glorious consummation of the new age.

---

25 Victor P. Furnish, *Theology and Ethics in Paul* (Nashville: Abingdon, 1968), 132.

The Spirit in Galatians: The Holy Spirit in Paul's Soteriological Arguments

Roji Thomas George

This article explores how Paul relates the Spirit in his soteriological argument in the letter against the Galatian agitators, the cultural imperialists.[1] Paul relies on the Galatian believers' Spirit experience at conversion to resist Gentile Christians from being coerced into submission to the requirements of the Jewish law. For him, the reception of the Spirit by faith at conversion proves the Galatians' justification apart from "the works of the law." In the ensuing discussion, the three vital aspects of his theological argument help us make concrete observations on his soteriological arguments centered on the Spirit within the specific Galatian context.[2] They are about a believer's filial bonding with God, the actual fulfillment of God's promise to Abraham, and a believer's ethical formation. These three aspects of Paul's arguments shall be discussed in the light of Paul's rhetoric in the letter. We shall reserve a deeper and exhaustive discussion on the Spirit in the contemporary Galatians studies for another occasion due to the limitation of permitted space and scope of the present article.

---

1 The identity of the Galatian agitators/opponents of Paul has been widely discussed and debated. Their identity has been construed differently by the students of Paul in Galatian studies. For a broad discussion on the topic see my book, Roji T. George, *Paul's Identity in Galatians: A Postcolonial Appraisal* (New Delhi: CWI, 2016), 126–136. I contend that the Jewish Christian opponents of Paul from Jerusalem (the native colonizers) were on a cultural imperialistic mission as agent of Jewish cultural nationalists among the Gentiles in Galatia. They extended the Jewish cultural imperialistic agenda among the Gentiles even outside of Palestine under fear of violent backlash from the Jewish cultural nationalists in Palestine. The opponents' mission in Galatia was prompted by the strongly emerging Jewish nationalism in Palestine apart from the complex native circumstances in Galatia under Roman rule. The Jewish Christians in Jerusalem stood under threat from the Jewish nationalists in Palestine for extending Abrahamic blessings to Gentiles by faith in Christ without requiring the Gentiles to submit to the Jewish identity markers. Similarly, the local Galatian Jews threatened exposing the uncircumcised Gentile Christian churches in Galatia to Roman imperial sanctions for availing the special privileges (such as exemption from participating in the Roman imperial cult) given solely to Jews without culturally identifying with the Jewish ethnic community. This seems to subvert the Roman law and to invite the empire to take coercive measures against Jews in Galatia and Galatian Gentile Christians who behave like Jews in public without being quite Jewish in essence.
2 For a brief discussion on issues related to the general background of Galatians see George, *Paul's Identity in Galatians*, 113–126.

1 The Spirit, the Indwelling Spirit's Testimony to the Filial Bond

Paul appeals to the native Galatian believers' initial conversion experience and their reception of the Holy Spirit in Galatians 3:1–5 while arguing against the cultural imperialistic mission of the troublemakers in Galatia. For him, God gives them the Spirit, who indwells in their hearts (4:6). They received it by their faith in the gospel of Christ Jesus (3:3, 5). At first, for Paul, their experience of receiving the Spirit by believing in the gospel of Christ at their conversion is a nonnegotiable reality. Paul speaks about his own indwelling Spirit experience by saying, "Christ lives in me" (2:20; cf. Eph 3:16–17)[3] because he identifies the two very closely in their function (cf. 4:6). Hence, in 4:6, he calls the Spirit "the Spirit of his Son" because the Spirit "carries on the work of Christ following his resurrection and subsequent assumption of the place of authority at God's right hand."[4]

For Paul, the indwelling Spirit given by God enables the Galatian believers to experience the powerful works of the Spirit in them by believing in the gospel (3:1 and 5). While in 3:1 the emphasis of Paul's words—"before your very eyes Jesus Christ was clearly portrayed as crucified"—falls on the graphic oral description of Christ's death before them, it also underlines the truth that the gospel came convincingly to them in their personal experience. The latter would imply the function of the Holy Spirit in the justification of a sinner by the preaching and hearing of the word (cf. 1 Thess 1:5). The powerful continuing function of the indwelling Spirit in a person since their reception of the gospel is pointed out in the miracles happening among the Galatians (3:5). Hansen rightly states that "[t]he reference to miracles in verse 5 is evidence that they also experienced outward manifestations of the Spirit's presence."[5] Interestingly, writing at the same time to the believers in Thessalonica, Paul repeats the twin function of the Spirit—the charismatic role of the Spirit and the deep conviction—in the conversion experience of a believer (1 Thess 1:5). Paul seemingly viewed the two as coinciding in the event of the justification of the Galatians.[6] Hence, for him, the Spirit, ushering justification through faith, excludes the role of the works of the law.

3　Gordon D. Fee, *Paul, the Spirit, and the People of God* (Peabody, MA: Hendrickson, 1996), 33. Fee correctly maintains that "although Paul does not identify the Spirit and Christ, he does assume the same kind of close relationship between the two as exists between the Spirit and God." Such a close relationship in Paul's thought is observable in the use of the language of indwelling.

4　Fee, *Paul, the Spirit, and the People of God*, 31.

5　G. Walter Hansen, *Galatians*, IVP New Testament Commentary Series (Downers Grove, IL: InterVarsity Press, 1994), 79.

6　Hansen, *Galatians*, 79.

Further, in 4:5–7, for Paul, the changed status of a Galatian believer from a "slave" of the principalities of the world to a God's child in Christ is evidenced by the indwelling Spirit. The Spirit not only enables a believer to verbalize the spiritual mystery of one's adoption into the family of God through the work of Christ, but the Spirit also gives a new identity[7] to a believer as one born according to the Spirit (4:29). The indwelling Spirit calls out to God from within our hearts, "*Abba*, Father" (4:6; Rom 8:15–16). Such a cry from within a human heart not only proves one's membership in the family of God as a result of one's incorporation by faith in Christ (3:26), but it is also a testimony borne by the divine Spirit in unison with the human spirit (Rom 8:15–16).[8] According to Longenecker, the primary function of the Spirit in a believer's life is "to witness to the filial relation of the believer with God that has been established by the work of Christ."[9]

Within the New Testament, the term "*Abba*" is strictly limited to the lips of Jesus addressing his heavenly Father (Mark 14:36), apart from its use in the Spirit-inspired utterances of a believer (Gal 4:6). In Jewish prayers, Jews at times addressed God as "my Father" (*Abi* in Hebrew, 4Q372).[10] The ancient literary pieces of evidence prove that the term was used to affirm intimacy to God without diluting the sense of reverence, adopted sonship, and demand of obedience from children.[11] However, now Gentle Christians in Galatia can address God as "Abba" by the enabling of the Spirit, "the Spirit of his Son" (4:6). The Spirit-inspired prayer of a believer expresses one's special standing before God in Christ.

---

7   Fee, *God's Empowering Presence*, 383. See Stephen Kerry, "An Exegetical Analysis of Galatians 3:1–5, with Particular Reference to Pneumatological Themes that Relate to the Onset and Continuation of Christian Identity, with Respect to Law and Gospel," *JBPR* 2 (2010): 57–86.
8   David A. Gundersen, "Adoption, Assurance, and the Internal Testimony of the Holy Spirit," *JFM* 2, no. 1 (2011): 19.
9   Richard N. Longenecker, *Galatians*, Word Biblical Commentary 41 (Dallas, TX: Word Books, 1990), 174.
10 Following Joachim Jeremias's reseach, the term "Abba" is mistakenly credited as unique to Jesus based on its morphology. Joachim Jeremias, *The Prayers of Jesus* (Philadephia: Fortress Press, 1978); Joachim Jeremias, *The Central Message of the New Testament* (London: SCM, 1965). Thus, it came to be considered as a term never used by a Jew to address God. See Craig S. Keener, *Galatians: A Commentary* (Grand Rapids, MI: Baker Academic, 2019), 346.
11 James A. Rimbach, "God-Talk or Baby-Talk: More on 'Abba,'" *Currents in Theology and Mission* 13, no. 4 (1986): 232–235; Mary Collins, "Naming God in Public Prayer," *Worship* 59, no. 4 (1985): 295–300.

2 The Spirit, the Fulfillment of God's Promise to Abraham

We appreciate the central role of the Spirit in the argument of Paul in Galatians 3–4 as we recognize the trajectory of his thoughts behind his constant appeal to the fulfillment of God's promise of blessing to Abraham in the lives of the believers in Christ. Undoubtedly, the Galatians' reception of the Spirit is present in his mind directly or indirectly on most occasions as he speaks about the fulfillment of God's promises to Abraham. For him, their salvation accomplished by the work of Christ appropriated by faith at conversion and the reception of God's gracious gift of the Spirit coincide indistinguishably in a believer's salvation experience.

In Galatians 3:14, Paul equates "the blessing of Abraham" coming to Gentiles with the reception of "the promised Spirit." It is a remarkable twist in his argument against the requirement for Gentiles to submit to the demands of the law by being circumcised. While God's promise of seed to Abraham in Genesis 15:4–5 is fulfilled through David in Christ Jesus (Gal 3:16), the promise of land (15:18–21), for Paul, is to be fulfilled eschatologically in the coming of Jerusalem from above (cf. 4:24–31). God's promise to Abraham to bless all the nations through him (Gen 12:3) is wrought by Jesus upon the cross, but the Spirit actualizes the foretaste of the future blessing here and now for all in Christ (Gal 5:21). In Isaiah 44:3, God promised to pour out his Spirit upon the offspring of Israel and his blessings upon the descendants who thereby will claim to belong to the LORD (Isa 44:3, 5; Joel 2:28). Hence, in 3:18, Paul places the law and the promise of God antithetically while speaking about the gracious promise to Abraham. The fulfillment of the promise for Galatians saved by faith appears to be the gift of the Spirit.[12] It is coherent with the argument he makes in 3:14.

An idea closely associated with the fulfillment of God's promise to Abraham by sending the Spirit to the Galatian believers is their inheritance in Christ as the heirs of God's promise. The logical consequence of the Spirit's undeniable testimony from within their hearts is that the Galatian believers become the heirs of the blessings that God promised to Abraham (4:7; 3:29). Paul's insistence that the promise of God is available to the Gentile Christians in Christ is a radical claim in the context of a Judaizing mission to Galatia that demands their submission to the requirements of the Mosaic law in order to inherit the covenantal promises. The eschatological hope of righteousness inherited by the Galatian believers is the promise of God to Abraham. In 5:5, Paul says that

---

12   R.A. Cole, *The Epistle of Paul to the Galatians: An Introduction and Commentary* (Grand Rapids, MI: Eerdmans, 1965), 103.

the Gentile believers "eagerly await by faith" the hope of righteousness through the Spirit (Gal 5:5). By "hope," Paul implies the eschatological expectations, including the resurrection of the righteous ones that he mentions (1 Thess 4:13) and, later in Romans, the restoration of the entire creation at the end (Rom 8:20, 24).[13] However, the Spirit that God graciously imparts to the Galatian believers partially actualizes the promised inheritance to the children of God as the heirs of the future hope (cf. 1:4). In short, the Spirit is the harbinger of the eschatological hope of righteousness residing in Galatian believers here and now.

3 The Spirit, the Agent of Christian Ethical Formation

Having established his argument based on Scripture, in 5:1–6:10 Paul cautions the believers from using their freedom in Christ to indulge in the desires of flesh. The antidote to the desires of the flesh is to be guided by the Spirit. In 5:16–6:10, Paul exhorts the Galatians to lead an ethical life. He differentiates the two spheres of life: a life gratifying the desires of the flesh and a life lived in submission to the Spirit. The two are antithetical to each other. The "flesh desires what is contrary to the Spirit, and the Spirit what is contrary to the flesh" (5:17). The consequence of sowing to the former is "corruption," while the latter produces "eternal life" (6:8). So, Paul lays two choices before them but strongly urges them to choose the Spirit.

Paul employs a present active imperative verb "walk," which is probably explained by two other verbs, "led" (passive verb) and "live" (active verb), in 5:18 and 25, respectively. The role of the Holy Spirit in a Christian walk of life, signifying the way Paul repeatedly uses the term "walk" in his letters (Rom 8:4; 13:13; 2 Cor 4:2; 5:7; Phil 3:17–18), is suggested by the dative use of the Spirit (*pneuma*) in Greek. It implies "both origin and instrumentality ('by the Spirit')"[14] of the Spirit in the ethical walk of life. Paul encourages the Galatians to continue in their ethical walk of life aided by the Spirit.[15] Though the Spirit is instrumental in a believer's ethical living, human responsibility in conducting oneself while constantly experiencing the Holy Spirit is further reinforced by Paul in 5:25. Here, Paul assumes that a believer's continuous living experience of the indwelling Spirit is an undeniable reality. He says, "since (*ei*) we live by

---

13   Keener, *Galatians*, 457.
14   Longenecker, *Galatians*, 245. See J.D.G. Dunn, *The Theology of Paul's Letter to the Galatians*, New Testament Theology (Cambridge, UK: Cambridge University Press, 1993), 295.
15   H. Seesemann, "Pateo," *TDNT*, ed. Gerhad Kittel and Gerhard Friedrich, vol. 5 (Grand Rapids, MI: Eerdmans, 1967), 944. See George, *Paul's Identity*, 220.

the Spirit." But he hastily completes the sentence by reminding them of their responsibility to live a life suitable to their existence in Christ by exhorting them: "Let us keep in step with the Spirit." The exhortation implies conscious self-alignment involving "active concentration and discipline of the whole person"[16] to follow the pattern of the Spirit mentioned as the fruit of the Spirit and the ethical exhortations listed in 5:22–23 and 6:1–10, respectively. He directs his ethical appeals (6:1–10) to those who are saved, led, and preserved in Christ by the Spirit (cf. 6:1 lit. "the ones who are spiritual").[17]

If so, how does the Spirit function in a person who yield to the moral pattern of the Spirit? For Paul, while a believer is held responsible for intentionally aligning oneself to the moral pattern of behavior of the Spirit, it is the Spirit that leads a believer (5:18). If grammatically "*ei*" is translated as "since" and not "if," then in 5:18 Paul affirms as reality that they are "led by the Spirit" indwelling in them, since they believed in the gospel. In other words, the Spirit functions as their guide who enables them not to do whatever they wish to do (5:17–18). One who submits to the Spirit's prompting walking in the moral pattern of the Spirit enjoys the guidance of the Spirit to bear the fruit of the Spirit and to fulfill the law of Christ in love (6:1–10).

In short, Paul's attempt to persuade the Gentile believers in Galatia to refrain from submitting to the requirements of the Jewish law in order to be saved hangs on his understanding of the Spirit's ongoing function in a believer's life since conversion. Paul maintains that the Galatians' reception of the Spirit by faith at conversion initiates his activity in them. This experience of the Spirit's activity in the Galatian believer continues in life both as fulfilling God's promise to Abraham in the past and as the ethical formation of a believer in the present. The Spirit bears testimony within the Galatian believers concerning their new filial relationship with God in Christ. The Spirit gives a partial foretaste and guarantee of the eschatological blessing at present. Meanwhile, the Spirit guides a believer who submits to the Spirit's prompts in leading a life patterned after the Spirit's guidance.

16   Hansen, *Galatians*, 181.
17   Longenecker, *Galatians*, 273.

The Spirit in Ephesians and Philippians: Together by Divine Enabling

Daniel K. Darko

The differing use of πνεῦμα and its cognates in Ephesians stands out in the Pauline corpus, relative to size. Conversely, there are only five occurrences of πνεῦμα lexemes in Philippians with a narrow scope, even with no mention of "Holy Spirit" as full ascription to the Third Person of the triune God. As I have argued elsewhere,[1] an isolated study of pneumatology, Christology, or theology proper along the lines of systematic theology has its own limitations. An alternative would locate such inquiry in the framework of the spirit cosmology of Paul. For example, his portrait of God the Father, Jesus Christ, and the Holy Spirit as spiritual agents working in concert on behalf of the church vis-à-vis evil spiritual powers serving as opposing forces in the world without Christ may be misconstrued by such isolated treatment. A quest to untangle the role of the Spirit from God and Jesus Christ would be a near impossible task. However, this does not negate the merits of lexical analyses, as we have here, since it enables readers to observe the way language is employed to convey important concepts. This study aims to shed light on the richness, essence, and range of πνεῦμα lexemes in Paul's correspondence to Christ followers in Western Asia Minor and Roman Philippi. I will endeavor to show the import of each occurrence of πνεῦμα or its cognate in these letters and provide a synthesis of the findings at the conclusion. It will become apparent that Paul does not have one consistent referent for πνεῦμα, either to the Holy Spirit or to other spiritual activities. The study will also show that Paul's use of πνεῦμα lexemes is predicated upon the occasion and provenance of the letter in question. The analysis begins with Ephesians due to its higher frequency (sixteen times and in every chapter)[2] and range of πνεῦμα usage compared to Philippians.

1   Πνεῦμα in Ephesians

The frequency of "spirit language" in Ephesians may be accounted for partly by its provenance in Western Asia Minor, a region known for religious activi-

---

1 D.K. Darko, *Against Principalities and Powers: Spiritual Beings in Relation to Communal Identity and the Moral Discourse of Ephesians* (Carlisle: Langham Publishing, 2020).

2 Ephesians 1:3,13, 17; 2:2, 18, 22; 3:5, 16; 4:3, 4, 23, 30; 5:18; 6:12, 17, 18.

ties and pilgrimage. The temple of Artemis of Ephesus was one of the seven wonders of the ancient world; it was also here that the popular magical words of the time known as *Ephesia grammata* originated.[3] The attendant challenges to Christ followers and ensuing spiritual realities are reflected in both the cosmological framework and actual content of Ephesians. Πνεῦμα is only one of several terminologies employed in its framework. Ephesians is conceptually broad in its use of πνεῦμα lexemes, referring (1) adjectivally to "spiritual blessings/forces," (2) the Holy Spirit, (3) human spirit, and (4) evil spirit/s.

1.1 Adjectival Use of Πνεῦμα in 1:3

The letter begins with a benediction in which Paul praises God for conferring πάσῃ εὐλογίᾳ πνευματικῇ in the heavenly realms in Christ (1:3). Structurally, the letter closes also with a call to combat readiness against τὰ πνευματικὰ τῆς πονηρίας (6:10–20). Reference to spiritual blessings in 1:3 is a debated matter as to the *nature* of blessings or the *source* thereof. Paul depicts the substance or aspects of the blessings to include selection, adoption, redemption, and being sealed by the Spirit as a people of God with an eschatological inheritance (1:3–14). To render "spiritual blessings" as spirit empowerment in the inner person,[4] gifts of the Spirit,[5] or blessings pertaining to the work of the Spirit[6] is not necessarily warranted. It is also misleading to read it as noncorporeal benefits being "mediated by the Holy Spirit"[7] or to translate it as "every kind of Spirit 'blessing' in Christ."[8] In ancient cosmology, spiritual beings were believed to be active in human affairs—blessing, empowering, punishing wrongdoing and so forth. It would not be inconceivable for unbelievers to characterize benevolence from a deity as spiritual blessing. Here, God is the divine benefactor. These are not blessings presumed to be reserved for the afterlife but that which has immediate existential effects. The adjective qualifies the nature of or manner in which God bestowed the blessings. Πνευματικός in itself ought not to be equated with the Holy Spirit, but this does not negate the potential instrumentality of the Spirit. Fee argues that the adjective refers to that which "pertains to the Holy Spirit" elsewhere, but he does not provide any text of reference to that effect.[9]

---

[3] C.E. Arnold, *Power and Magic: The Concept of Power in Ephesians* (Grand Rapids: Baker Academic, 1989), 5–40.

[4] T.K. Abbot, *Epistles to the Ephesians and to the Colossians* (Edinburgh: T&T Clark, 1897), 4.

[5] F. Thielman, *Ephesians* (Grand Rapids: Baker Academic, 2010), 46–47.

[6] L.H. Cohick, *The Letter to the Ephesians* (Grand Rapids: Eerdmans, 2020), 90.

[7] R. Schnackenburg, *The Epistle to the Ephesians* (London: T&T Clark, 1991), 50.

[8] G.D. Fee, *God's Empowering Presence: The Holy Spirit in the Letters of Paul* (Peabody, MA: Hendrickson, 1994), 32 and 666.

[9] Fee, *God's Empowering Presence*, 666.

His assertion that "the Spirit is the present means whereby God appropriates to the believing community the 'blessings' that flow from the redemptive work of Christ"[10] is a sound theological construct that may be deduced by inference (cf. 1:13–14). God is the actor and benefactor of the stated blessings. The mere use of the adjective "spiritual" qualifying God's blessings is not in itself a reference to the Holy Spirit.[11] One may reasonably assume the possibility that the Holy Spirit was instrumental in bringing about the blessings.

1.2 *The Holy Spirit of Promise in 1:13*

If we took the benediction to be one long sentence in Greek (1:3–14), then the articulation of spiritual blessings culminates in a crucial role of the Spirit—that the Ephesians are sealed "by the Holy Spirit of promise." God has sealed those who *heard* the gospel and *believed* by the promised Holy Spirit: ἐσφραγίσθητε τῷ πνεύματι τῆς ἐπαγγελίας τῷ ἁγίῳ (1:13). The seal is a mark of ownership, authentication (Matt 27:66), or certification in quality assurance. As a seal, the Spirit serves as an identity marker (God's own people) with eschatological ramifications. Ἀρραβών is a commercial parlance for a transaction in which partial payment is made to guarantee full custody and ownership of the commodity upon full payment (cf. 2 Cor. 1:21–22; 5:5). The presence of the Holy Spirit is the seal and deposit guaranteeing all rights and privileges pertaining to their inheritance with God.

1.3 *Spirit of Wisdom and Revelation in 1:17*

Paul shares his prayers for the church to become fully aware of her standing with God. Paul petitions God to grant the "S/spirit" of/for illumination (1:17). The phrase πνεῦμα σοφίας καὶ ἀποκαλύψεως may be rendered (1) "spirit of wisdom and revelation" along the lines of the Semitic idiom for "wise spirit" or (2) reference to the Holy Spirit as the source from which or the means by which wisdom and revelation may be given. While the notion of "spirit" or "attitude" of wisdom has some merits, the context of the entire prayer implies Holy Spirit illumination about their identity, security, and victorious position with God. Moreover, we hear echoes of the "Spirit of wisdom" phraseology as in Exodus (31:3; 35:31) and Isaiah (11:2), where it refers to God's own Spirit. Such insight stands to bolster confidence, allay fears of malevolent forces, and engender befitting *modus vivendi* (1:15–23). Paul wishes that the church would become aware of the magnitude of God's power at work on its behalf, far beyond that

---

10   Fee, *God's Empowering Presence*, 667.
11   See the use of πνευματικός in adjectival function in 6:12. One cannot deduce the Holy Spirit or a particular evil spirit from the adjective itself.

of principalities and powers. Here, the triune God is collectively active in the enabling of the church.

1.4 Πνεῦμα in Reference to Satan in 2:2

Ephesians 2 transitions from assuring security in Christ to recounting the state of spiritual death in the readers' preconversion past marked by social, spiritual, and moral bankruptcy. Death and life metaphors are drawn from the Christ event in 1:15–23 to form an analogy with the condition of Christ followers. They were "dead in trespasses and sins," living (1) according to the age of this world, (2) according to ruler of the power of the air, and (3) in the flesh (2:1–3). Πνεῦμα in 2:2 refers to the "ruler of the power of the air" (Satan) who is the πνεῦμα currently responsible for instigating and engineering rebellion against God among unbelievers.[12] In other words, Satan exerts dominion over the world without Christ and in rebellion against God.[13] The Ephesians were once subject to evil spirits prior to the divine intervention that accorded them salvation in Christ. The gravity of the hopeless condition of their past sets the stage for appreciating God's salvific work (2:4–10).

1.5 Πνεῦμα in the Multiethnic Community in 2:18, 22

Salvation is born out of God's initiative and will to redeem a people who were hitherto subject to his own wrath. Through Christ, believers are brought near to have access in one πνεῦμα to the Father (2:18). The use of πνεῦμα here depicts the role of the Holy Spirit in kinship connection between God and members of his household (2:19). The phrase ἐν ἑνὶ πνεύματι implies that this access is either mediated by or takes effect in the realm of the Spirit. "Paul emphasizes that as one people of God in one Spirit we have access *into God's very presence*."[14] As a tabernacle (Exod. 40) and the temple (1 Kings 8) were filled with God's presence, so is he building the community through Christ to be a *holy* place in which he would be pleased to dwell by the Spirit (πνεῦμα; 2:22). The presence of the Spirit is akin to the presence of God. Paul does not conceive of a perfect church, but one that is growing to become a *holy* temple filled with the *Holy Spirit*.[15]

---

12 D.K. Darko, "The Ruler of the Power of the Air in the Salvific Story of Ephesians 2," *JBTS* 5, no. 1 (2020): 16.
13 A.G. Patzia. *Ephesians, Colossians, Philemon* (Peabody, MA: Hendrikson, 1984), 179.
14 Fee, *God's Empowering Presence*, 684.
15 Cohick, *Ephesians*, 199.

1.6 Πνεῦμα in the Unfolding Mystery in 3:5

Paul counts himself unworthy to be accorded the privilege of stewardship in the unfolding mystery, namely, the unification of Jews and Gentiles as one people of God. The mystery of Christ was concealed from previous generations, but it has now been revealed to the "holy apostles and prophets ἐν πνεύματι" (3:5 cf. 1 Cor. 2:6–12)). The phrase ἐν πνεύματι refers to the enabling of the Holy Spirit as in prophetic ministry. "This mystery is that the Gentiles are fellow heirs, members of the same body, and partakers of the promise in Christ Jesus through the gospel" (3:6, ESV). Paul counts himself among the apostles and prophets but as the very least among those who have been chosen, mandated and empowered by the Spirit to make the mystery known.

1.7 Πνεῦμα as an Empowering Agent in 3:16–17

Later, Paul petitions God in kinship parlance to aid in preserving his own honor in the household—implying a father whose honor is reflected by conditions of his household. The term "the riches of his glory" is an appeal to honor and shame sensibilities. Paul prays that God may strengthen the church with "power through his πνεῦμα (Spirit) in the inner man so that Christ may dwell in your hearts through faith" (3:16–17a). The Spirit is needed to empower members in the "inner person," namely, the unseen dimension of humans (cf. 2 Cor. 1:22), hoping that their hearts may be conducive for Christ to dwell therein. That πνεῦμα here refers to the Holy Spirit is not disputed. In a nutshell, Paul's prayer is for inner strength from the Holy Spirit, individually and collectively.

1.8 Πνεῦμα in the Paranesis of Ephesians

The paranesis in chapters 4–6 show an interplay of divine activity and human responsibility in the community's ability to live in ways appropriate to their calling. The ethical section features πνεῦμα as a designation for the Holy Spirit, evil spirits, and human spirit, as shown below.

1.8.1 The Unity of Spirit (Πνεῦμα) in 4:3–5

Generally, the paranesis draws from the preceding discourse to admonish members about the necessity of conducting themselves in a manner that befits their calling. Paul entreats them to exercise every ability to preserve the "unity of the Spirit (τὴν ἑνότητα τοῦ πνεύματος) in the bond of peace" (4:3). Unity of the Spirit is not an agenda to pursue but paramount in the makeup of the church. The Spirit accords authentication and manifests the presence of God in their midst. To disrupt the unity of the Spirit is to make the church unhabitable for God (1:13–14; 2:19–22). The notion of "fellowship of the Spirit" elsewhere in Paul echoes this concept of Spirit-enabled, Spirit-rooted, and Spirit connection among Christ followers (2 Cor 13:14; Phil 2:2). Paul further underscores seven commonalities underpinning their oneness, among which is the sharing of ἓν πνεῦμα (one Spirit [4:4–6]). It is noteworthy that Paul couches the essence of unity and commonalities shared by members in a trinitarian framework. Thus, the unity in question is partly rooted in the notion that they all share one Spirit, among other things.

1.8.2 Renewing the Spirit of the Mind in 4:23

Paul admonishes the church to "put off" their old humanity (outlook) and be renewed in τῷ πνεύματι τοῦ νοὸς ὑμῶν (4:23). Here, πνεῦμα refers to the mental attitude[16] or frame of mind that needs to be transformed in assuming a new outlook in the likeness of God in true righteousness and holiness (2:24; Rom 12:1–2). Most scholars concur that πνεῦμα here does not refer to the Holy Spirit, but this in no way precludes divine activity in the renewing of the mind. As Gordon Fee puts it, we must "be prepared also to recognize the Holy Spirit as hovering nearby, since in Paul's own theology, such renewal is indeed the work of the Spirit."[17] It is noteworthy that divine enabling of this kind is not unusual in the Pauline corpus (Rom 8 and Gal 5).

1.8.3 Grieving the Spirit (4:30)

The work of the Holy Spirit in sealing, empowering, or enabling members to counteract demonic influence is pivotal for a healthy church. Paul cautions the members to desist from vulgarity and other forms of vices in order not to grieve the *Holy* Spirit of God (τὸ πνεῦμα τὸ ἅγιον τοῦ θεοῦ [4:30]). The Holy Spirit is designated elsewhere as the Spirit of God (cf. 1 Cor 12:3), but this is the only place where the full ascription "the Holy Spirit of God" appears in the NT. Members are sealed by the Spirit "for the day of redemption" (1:13–14; 4:30); they are strengthened inwardly by the Spirit to make their hearts suitable for Christ to dwell therein (3:17); they are commanded to be enrobed in the likeness of God in true righteousness and holiness (4:24) and to be filled by the Spirit (5:18). As such, vices that stand to undermine the work of the holy God will grieve the *Holy* Spirit. As Cohick puts it, "putrid talk weakens the Christian community, and what diminishes God's temple grieves God's Spirit."[18] Paul had indicated previously that prolonged anger provides a topos for demonic influence (4:27). To grieve the Spirit[19] is to distress the holy God (cf. Isa 63:10; T. *Isaac*

---

16   Cohick, *Ephesians*, 288.
17   Fee, *God's Empowering Presence*, 712.
18   Cohick, *Ephesians*, 301.
19   The Holy Spirit of God is a person with emotion to grieve. Note also God's wrath in 2:3.

4.40). "The Spirit's presence now is the seal and assurance of the life and inheritance that Christians will possess fully in the end, and the very contemplation of that should lead them to purify their lives (1Jn. 3: 2–3)."[20] Apparently, spiritual influence on Christian character is not a matter of incertitude in Christian origins.

1.8.4   Be Filled with/by Ππνεῦμα in 5:18–21

The use of contrastive patterns to promote virtue was commonplace in ancient philosophy and in Ephesians 4–6. Paul utilizes old-new, darkness-light, and unwise-wise antitheses to promote desirable conduct. Additionally, he instructs his readers to abstain from drunkenness and be filled by πνεῦμα. The import of ἐν πνεύματι in 5:18 is a debated matter[21]—whether πνεῦμα is the antithetical counterpart to wine[22] or functions as the means by which the filling occurs. The limitations of the English language leave us with no easy choice. Two facts are indisputable: first, that πνεῦμα here refers to the Holy Spirit,[23] and second, that the focus is on community experience, not on the individual per se. Wallace argues in favor of πνεῦμα as a means and asserts that "the idea intended is that the believers are to be filled *by means of* the (Holy) Spirit."[24] If we accept this reading, then the content is unstated. Proponents of this view infer from 1:23 and 3:19 that the substance is the "fullness of God."[25] Conversely, a natural and plausible rendering is to interpret the passive expression as an instruction for the community to avail itself of the "full-filling" of/by the Spirit. The Spirit stands as an analogy to wine as the empowering agent that fills the church. In other words, the community is being entreated to be "filled *by* the Spirit" (cf. Acts 2) or "filled *with* the Spirit." They are to avail themselves of the filling[26] or effusion of the Spirit resulting in concrete acts of piety. Unlike the vices that accompany alcohol-induced inebriation, the effect of the Spirit's enabling is exemplified in qualities such as "addressing one another in psalms and hymns," singing, making melody, expression of gratitude, and mutual sub-

---

20   F. Foulkes, *Ephesians* (Grand Rapids: Eerdmans, 1989), 144.
21   Fee, *God's Empowering Presence*, 721–722. Translating the phrase as "with the Spirit" in ESV and NIV is ambiguous in this regard.
22   H.C.G. Moule. *Ephesians Studies* (London: Hodder and Stoughton, 1900), 275–276.
23   Fee. *God's Empowering Presence*, 721.
24   D.B. Wallace, *Greek Grammar beyond the Basics* (Grand Rapids: Zondervan, 1996), 375.
25   Wallace, *Beyond the Basics*, 375. Theologically, being filled with the "fullness of God" or the "Spirit" is a semantic issue when one conceives of acts of the triune God in concert to empower the church to be a witness to God's unfolding mystery to the world without Christ.
26   G.D. Fee. *Paul, the Spirit and the People of God* (Peabody, MA: Hendrickson, 1996), 99.

mission (5:19–21).²⁷ Fee puts it well in noting that the community must be one "whose life is so totally given over to the Spirit that the life and deeds of the Spirit are as obvious in their case as the effects of too much alcohol is obvious in the other."²⁸

1.8.5 Πνεῦμα in the Closing Statement of Ephesians

Whereas the first adjectival use of πνεῦμα appears at the opening, so the second is found in the closing remark of Ephesians—characterizing Christian living as a battle with evil *spiritual* forces: τὰ πνευματικὰ τῆς πονηρίας (6:12). Paul unambiguously contends that spiritual activities have an existential effect on the church's ability to stand firm. Ancient cosmology makes no distinction between the spirit world and the material world. The physical and metaphysical were perceived to be different dimensions of the same cosmos. They who are blessed with "every spiritual blessing" are also called to battle readiness to engage τὰ πνευματικὰ τῆς πονηρίας. These powers endeavor to uproot or weaken their standing with God, hence the call to stand firm. One of the weapons of God needed for the battle is described as "τὴν μάχαιραν τοῦ πνεύματος, which is the word (ῥῆμα) of God" (6:17). The word πνεύματος could be taken as genitive of source or possession, implying a sword of spiritual origin or one belonging to the Holy Spirit. The link of the spoken word (ῥῆμα) to spiritual activity (cf. 2 Tim 3:16–17) coupled with its function as an offensive weapon accentuates its potency in the battle between mere mortals and unseen spiritual forces. Paul concludes by requesting that the church pray unceasingly in the Spirit (ἐν παντὶ καιρῷ ἐν πνεύματι)—for all the saints and also for him to be able to proclaim the mystery of the gospel fearlessly (6:18–20). Praying ἐν πνεύματι is praying by the enabling of the Spirit or in the realm of the Spirit. The feature of the similar expression in 1 Cor 14:2, 14–16 is the reason some interpret it as a reference to speaking in tongues.²⁹ While we cannot exclude speaking in tongues or other spiritual gifts in its import, it is unlikely that Paul is primarily asking them to speak in tongues, given the itemized list of prayer requests and the absence of "tongues" in Ephesians (cf. 4:11–12).

---

27 See D.K. Darko, *No Longer Living as the Gentiles: Differentiation and Shared Ethical Values in Ephesians 4:17–6:9* (London: Bloomsbury, 2008), 56–66. I provide thorough analysis of the unwise-wise antithesis in Ephesians 5 that brevity of space here will not permit.

28 Fee, *God's Empowering Presence*, 721.

29 Fee, *God's Empowering Presence*, 731.

2 Πνεῦμα in Philippians

Philippians departs from the tone and tenor of Ephesians, specifically as it relates to πνεῦμα lexemes. As a circular letter to Asia Minor, Ephesians addresses regional concerns about "principalities and powers" versus the power of God at work on behalf of the saints through Jesus Christ and the Holy Spirit. Conversely, Paul seizes the opportunity to send a letter with an emissary from Philippi to encourage and warn the Philippians against internal and external threats to unity in the church. He refrains from discussing evil spiritual activities despite Luke's reference to such endeavors in Acts 16. It is noteworthy that Paul does not refer to the Third Person of the triune God with the full designation "Holy Spirit," nor does he employ πνεῦμα to describe an evil spirit in Philippians. The word πνεῦμα and its cognates appear five times in the letter. There are two references to πνεῦμα as human spirit/attitude (1:27; 4:23), one each as the "Spirit of Jesus Christ" (1:19), the "fellowship of the Spirit," (2:2) and the "Spirit of God" (3:3).

Paul assures his readers that his Roman imprisonment has not affected the advancement of the gospel; rather, it has contributed to its spread. He is confident that through prayer and God's supply of the πνεῦμα of Jesus Christ, he may be spared from shameful conduct so that Christ may be magnified in his body (1:19–20). The object of prayer is God, from whom Paul anticipates the help of the Spirit. Τοῦ πνεύματος Ἰησοῦ Χριστοῦ is a rare expression in the Pauline corpus.[30] The Spirit of Jesus Christ is the Holy Spirit in Rom 8:9. Elsewhere, he attributes the life he lives to Christ (Gal 2:20). That Paul as a Christ follower possessing the Spirit stands in need of the "supply" of "the Spirit of Jesus Christ" suggests an appeal to God's continued provision of divine strength or "gift of the Holy Spirit" (cf. Gal 3:5).[31] The trinitarian activity is instructive as one observes God, Jesus Christ, and the Holy Spirit in the phrase—in the incarcerated Paul's need for God's empowering presence. The strict untangling of their roles could be problematic in this regard.

The unwritten code of honor and shame in antiquity is later invoked in the admonition for members to conduct themselves as worthy adherents to the gospel of Christ (1:27–30). Paul hopes to see or hear that believers are standing firm in "one spirit." The phrase ἐν ἑνὶ πνεύματι (1:27) is followed by the necessity to strive to be μιᾷ ψυχῇ, denoting solidarity "in one spirit," "with one common purpose,"[32] or being "in one accord." The metaphorical use of "spirit" bespeaks

---

30 "Spirit of Christ" is found in Romans 8:9.
31 Fee, *God's Empowering Presence*, 740–741.
32 P.T. O'Brien, *The Epistle to the Philippians* (Grand Rapids: Eerdmans, 1991), 150–151.

oneness or being "of one mind" in a deeper relationship.³³ This reading is the one preferred by the translators of ESV, NLT, ASV and NKJV. Fee³⁴ is in the minority (with NIV) for rendering it as "in one Spirit" to imply the realm of the Holy Spirit. Pauline churches are Spirit endowed, filled, and empowered. One does not need to insert the Spirit where it is not self-evident to establish the presence of God in their midst.

The third mention of πνεῦμα features in 2:1–4, where Paul presents a string of relational qualities that would enhance solidarity and complete his joy. "Fellowship of the Spirit" is one of them. Here, πνεῦμα refers to the Holy Spirit (cf. 2 Cor 13:14). In Paul, members are connected to God by the Spirit and share the same Spirit with one another. Thus, κοινωνία πνεύματος (2:1) is fellowship or communion "brought about by,"³⁵ shared in, engendered, and permeated by the Holy Spirit they all share. Hansen captures this thought by translating κοινωνία πνεύματος as the "common sharing in the Spirit."³⁶ The practical outworking of true fellowship of the Spirit then would find expression where the Spirit permeates every aspect of life in the house churches. The Christ hymn in 2:5–11 follows to elaborate on the mental attitude (φρονέω) of Christ that is worthy of emulation.

In a critique of certain Judaizers and their emphasis on the "flesh," Paul contrasts them with those who perform their religious service (worship) by the "Spirit of God" (cf. Rom 7 and 8 and Gal 4 and 5). The "Spirit of God" is the presence and enabling power of God in the Hebrew tradition.³⁷ Elsewhere, Paul employs the "Spirit of God" phraseology interchangeably with the Holy Spirit (1 Cor 12:3). Similarly, the "Spirit of God" identifies the Holy Spirit as the identity marker of the people of God and the empowering presence of God.³⁸ John echoes this concept when he indicates that true worshipers are those who worship in Spirit and in truth (Jn. 4: 23–24). The final appearance of πνεῦμα is in the benediction, the very last sentence (4:23), where Paul expresses his final wish that the grace of Jesus Christ be with the (human) "spirit" of members of the church. Conceptually, this feature of πνεῦμα is not any different from Paul's customary wish for Christ to be "with you" (Gal 6:18; Phlm 25).³⁹ That this refers to the human spirit has widespread support, as evident in the ESV, NRSV, NIV, and NLT translations.

33 B. Witherington, *Paul's Letter to the Philippians: A Socio-Rhetorical Commentary* (Grand Rapids: Eerdmans, 2011), 102–103.
34 Fee, *God's Empowering Presence*, 746.
35 M. Silva, *Philippians* (Grand Rapids: Baker Academic, 1992), 90.
36 G.W. Hansen, *Philippians* (Grand Rapids: Eerdmans, 2009), 109–110.
37 Gen 1:2; 41:38; Exod 31:3; 35:31; Num 24:2; 1 Sam 11:6; 19:20; 2 Chron 15:1.
38 Rom 8:9, 14; 15:19; 1 Cor 2:11, 14; 3:16; 7:40. Cf. Matt 3:16.
39 O'Brien, *Philippians*, 555.

3 Conclusion

The study of πνεῦμα language in Ephesians and Philippians brings to the forefront the divine initiative pertaining to the nature of the church and the role of the Spirit as an identity marker, empowering agent, and the presence of God among God's people. The post-Enlightenment tendency to minimize the place of the Spirit and spiritual activity in church beliefs and praxis is incompatible with the findings from these two letters. Ephesians is unequivocal in noting that the human condition that prompted God's intervention in the salvific work of Christ was a state of spiritual death and subject to the "ruler of the power of air" (Satan)—the spirit that is currently at work in unbelievers (Eph 2:1–3). God has blessed the church "with every spiritual blessing" and has sealed them by the Holy Spirit to guarantee their inheritance with him (Eph 1:13). Consequently, their identity is not rooted in or associated with any pagan deity, and neither do they need any spiritual "blessings" from evil spiritual forces or folk religious entities. Through Christ, Jews and Gentiles have access to the Father in one Spirit (Eph 2:18). The presence of the Holy Spirit is akin to the presence of God in their midst (Eph 2:22). Moreover, the advancement of this good news is characterized as the mystery being revealed to the apostles and prophets by the Spirit, even as the word of God is "the sword of the Spirit" in the warfare against evil spirits (Eph 3:5 and 6:17). Paul prays that they might become fully aware of the power of God at work on their behalf in order to mitigate potential fears of diabolic influence (Eph 1:15–23). Philippians does not deal with evil spirits or some of the foundational issues pertaining to the Spirit/spirit but focuses more on the role of the Spirit in promoting unity in the community.

Philippians and Ephesians portray the Spirit as central to the functioning of the church. Paul expresses unity in the church as "fellowship of the Spirit" (Phil 2:1) and "unity of the Spirit" (Eph 4:3) respectively. Unity is not a mere human endeavour or creation, but one that is engineered, engendered, and permeated by the Holy Spirit. In Ephesians, members are admonished to recognize that believers share "one Spirit" (4:4). Paul indicts his Judaizing opponents in Philippi and argues that those who "worship" (λατρεύω) in the Spirit of God are the credible Christ followers (Phil 3:3). He also requests that intercession be made "in the Spirit" for him and for the church at large (Eph 6:18). The emotion of the Spirit is brought to bear when Paul instructs the church to desist from vulgarity in order not to grieve the Holy Spirit of God (Eph 4:30). Unlike Philippians, Paul characterizes Christian living as a battle against evil spiritual forces that requires the armor of God (6:10–17; cf. 2:2). In other words, spiritual realities require constant awareness of and divine enabling to flourish as a people of God.

It is noteworthy that the role of the Holy Spirit is not isolated from the work of God or Jesus Christ. The triune God works in concert in both letters to advance the mission of the church. This is also evident in the designation of the Holy Spirit as "the Holy Spirit of God" (Eph 4:30), "Spirit of God" (Phil 3:3), and "Spirit of Jesus Christ" (Phil 1:19). This observation is significant because Paul perceives the devil and evil spirits as spiritual agents that oppose the work of God. Ephesians refers to the "evil spirit" called Satan as "the ruler of the power of the air" (2:2) and "evil spiritual forces" as opponents (6:12). Both letters contain other references to "spirit" that are not designations for spiritual beings. Sometimes "spirit language" is employed anthropologically to refer to "human spirit/attitude" (cf. Eph 4:23; Phil 4:23) or the notion of being of one mind/common purpose (Phil 1:27).

The brevity of space in this essay did not allow for exhaustive treatment of the πνεῦμα lexemes. However, this cursory study reveals that Paul articulated the active and empowering presence of the Holy Spirit in the church on one hand, and the influence of evil spirits aiming to undermine the work of God on the other. The Spirit is not a theological concept but an active spiritual agent in the life and mission of the church. To reduce the Holy Spirit to an idea or exclude him from the day-to-day functioning of the church departs from what Paul espouses in these two letters. More so, to ascribe everything to the Holy Spirit to the neglect of human responsibility or to blame any misfortune on demonic activity are also incongruent with the referent or framework of πνεῦμα language in Philippians and Ephesians. The precedence from Christian origins is unequivocal: The Holy Spirit or spiritual activity was not a subject for philosophical theologizing but lived experience rooted in sound beliefs.

The Spirit in Colossians and Philemon: Love, Understanding, and Unity

Holly Beers

In Colossians πνευμα (S/spirit) and πνευματικος (spiritual, having to do with the S/spirit) appear only four times (though note the Ephesians parallels),[1] with 1:8 mentioning the Colossians' "love ἐν πνεύματι (in/through the S/spirit)."[2] Most see the Spirit rather than the "spirit" of the Colossians here, along with an instrumental use of ἐν, which together offer a translation such as "love empowered by the Spirit," a common Pauline notion.[3]

The word πνευματικος appears in the following verse when Paul stresses his prayers that God will fill them with "the knowledge of his will through all wisdom and understanding πνευματικῇ" (1:9; cf. Eph 1:17). Either the human or divine spirit could be in view, though in light of v. 8 and Jewish texts that connect the Spirit with wisdom and understanding (such as Exod 31:3; 35:31; Isa 11:2; Wis 9:17–18; Sir 39:6; 4 Ezra 14:22, 39–40; 1 Cor 2:6–16; 12:8), it is better to stress the Spirit's agency in stimulating these realities (cf. 2:23).[4] Significantly, the purpose of the Spirit's empowerment is so that their behavior may please the Lord (v. 10).

Later Paul mentions knowledge and warns against deception (2:2, 4), adding that though "absent in body, [he is] with them τῷ πνεύματι (in the S/spirit)" (v. 5; cf. Eph 3:3–5).[5] Some understand Paul to be referring to his own spirit,[6] though Paul's presence "in/through the Spirit" parallels his insistence that followers of

---

1 In Colossians the focus is on Christ, though for Paul, Christ and the Spirit are intimately related. See Nijay K. Gupta, *Colossians*, SHBC (Macon: Smyth & Helwys, 2013), 44; Vicky Balabanski, "The Holy Spirit and the Cosmic Christ: A Comparison of Their Roles in Colossians and Ephesians, or 'Where Has the Holy Spirit Gone?,'" *Colloquium* 42, no. 2 (Nov 2010): 173–187. Gordon D. Fee, *God's Empowering Presence* (Peabody: Hendrickson, 1994), 637–638, 643–645, connects "power" language in 1:11, 29 to the Spirit.
2 Authorship debates revolve partly around the few mentions of the Spirit, while scholars supporting Pauline authorship offer contextual reasons. See, for example, Fee, *Presence*, 636–638.
3 See, for example, Brian Wintle and Bruce Nicholls, *Colossians and Philemon*, Asia Bible Commentary Series (Carlisle: Langham, 2019), 33; Fee, *Presence*, 638–639.
4 James D.G. Dunn, *The Epistles to the Colossians and Philemon*, NIGTC (Grand Rapids: Eerdmans, 1996), 70–71; Wintle and Nicholls, *Colossians*, emphasize here the "personal and direct experience of God" (35).
5 Cf. 1 Cor 5:3; 1 Thess 2:17.
6 For example, Craig S. Keener, *The Mind of the Spirit* (Grand Rapids: Baker, 2016), 102n342, 103.

Jesus share and are united by the Spirit (for example, Eph 4:3–4; 1 Cor 12).[7] Also, πνευμα is written as a sacred name, rendering "Spirit," in the early manuscripts P[46] and ℵ.

Finally, πνευματικος appears in Col 3:16.[8] After stressing the need for "the word of Christ" to dwell in them as (or through the way) they "teach and admonish one another" (cf. 1:28), Paul mentions "singing psalms, hymns, and songs πνευματικαῖς to God."[9] The adjective may modify all three nouns or just "songs," the latter of which may be spontaneous and/or even glossolalic songs (cf. 1 Cor 14:15; T Job 48–50),[10] especially because of the parallel with Eph 5:18–19. Also worthy of note is the fact that women are apparently participants in these communal activities (including teaching and admonishing; cf. Nympha in 4:15; 1 Cor 14:26).[11]

In the letter to Philemon πνευμα appears only in a reference to the human (communal?!) spirit of Philemon and the assembly: "The grace of the Lord Jesus Messiah be with your (pl.) πνευμα" (v. 25; cf. Gal 6:18; Phil 4:23).[12] However, v. 6 may imply the Spirit's work in Philemon's "κοινωνία τῆς πίστεώς," possible translations for which include: "participation in [the] faith," "sharing produced by faith," and "faithful partnership" (cf. πνευμα and κοινωνια in 2 Cor 13:13; Phil 2:1). The Spirit is also likely empowering Philemon's ἐπιγνώσει (understanding, v. 6; cf. Col 1:9); his participation/sharing/partnership and understanding are both linked to Paul's request regarding Onesimus and how Philemon should welcome him (ἐπιγνώσει παντὸς ἀγαθοῦ [understanding all the good], v. 6; ἀγαθος [good deed], v. 14; κοινωνος [partner/sharer], v. 17).[13]

---

7   Gupta, *Colossians*, 88; Fee, *Presence*, 646. Cf. G.K. Beale, *Colossians and Philemon*, BECNT (Grand Rapids: Baker, 2019), 158.

8   See Fee, *Presence*, 646–648, for the Spirit's implied presence in Col 3:10, 15.

9   For syntactical discussion of how the elements are related (for example, order, means of, and so forth), see Dunn, *Epistles*, 211n14, 236–237. Beale, *Colossians*, 305–306, connects the psalms, hymns, and songs to Ps 66:1; 75:1 LXX and thus the ([re]new[ed]) temple and eschatological salvation of Gentiles.

10 Dunn, *Epistles*, 239; cf. Fee, *Presence*, 653, 654n71.

11 Leaders are not mentioned. See Fee, *Presence*, 649–650.

12 Kara Lyons-Pardue, "Philemon," in *Ephesians Colossians Philemon: A Commentary in the Wesleyan Tradition*, New Beacon Bible Commentary (Kansas City: Beacon Hill Press, 2019), 480. The second-century P[87] does not have πνευμα.

13 See Dunn, *Epistles*, 318–319; Lyons-Pardue, "Philemon," 450; Lloyd A. Lewis, "An African American Appraisal of the Philemon-Paul-Onesimus Triangle," in *Stony the Road We Trod* (Minneapolis: Fortress, 1991), 243.

The Spirit in 1 and 2 Thessalonians: The Function of the Spirit in Paul's Earliest Letters

Roji Thomas George

Understanding the character, role, and significance of the Holy Spirit in Paul's Thessalonian correspondence is to have a glance into his mind on the topic from his earliest writings. Paul does not offer systematic teaching on the Holy Spirit in these letters (as is the case with his other letters too!) rather, all the references to the Spirit in these letters are occasional in nature. His repeated reference to the Spirit's activity is functional in nature and pedagogical in intent to nurture and establish believers in their newfound faith (2 Thess 2:13, 15). The immediate context of the letters that Paul sent to the community in Thessalonica (ca. 50–51 CE) was of moral degradation and lack of integrity, encouraging and establishing the believers amid persecution from outside, and lack of teaching on eschatology.[1] Addressing the newly emerging situation in Thessalonica, Paul had sent the letters to his new converts in quick succession in order to instruct them on the matters of which they were as yet ignorant as believers in Christ. Hence, the apostle's earliest thoughts on the Holy Spirit must be considered against the historical background in Thessalonica. The intention of this article is not to provide an exhaustive account of the ongoing debate on Pauline pneumatology in the study of Thessalonians, for the available space does not allow an elaborate discussion on kernels of the apostle's earliest thought on the Holy Spirit as expressed in the letters and their fuller development in his later writings. Instead, it is to gain an overview of Paul's mind, based on his Thessalonian correspondence, on the Holy Spirit and the Spirit's role and function in the individual and corporate life-setting of the Thessalonian believers.

This article elaborates the three aspects of Paul's scattered thoughts on the Spirit in the Thessalonian correspondence. First, the persuasive and sanctifying

---

1 Roji T. George, *Called into the Mission of God: A Missional Reading of Paul's Thessalonian Correspondence* (Minneapolis: Fortress Press, 2020), 49–65. G.K. Beale, *1–2 Thessalonians*, IVP New Testament Commentary Series (Downers Grove, IL: IVP Academic, 2003), 31. For a short survey of views supporting the non-Pauline authorship of 2 Thessalonians see R. Wayne Stacy, "Introduction to the Thessalonian Correspondences," *Review & Expositor* 96, no. 2 (1999): 178; Robert Jewett, *The Thessalonian Correspondence: Pauline Rhetoric and Millenarian Piety*, Foundations and Facets (Philadelphia, PA: Fortress Press, 1986), 3–16.

function of the Spirit is discussed in the light of 1 Thessalonians 1:4–5, 4:1–8, and 2 Thessalonians 2:13. Second, the Spirit's emboldening function is considered based on the Spirit-inspired joy in Paul's readers as they stand firm amid persecution (1 Thess 1:6–7, 2:14–20). Finally, the charismatic function of the Spirit (1 Thess 1:5, 5:19–22) among the believers is studied.

1   Persuading and Sanctifying Spirit

In Paul's Thessalonian correspondence, he refers to two roles of the Holy Spirit in the spiritual life of a Christian: initiating spiritual rebirth at conversion and ethical formation. First, Paul mentions the role of the Holy Spirit in the Thessalonians' lives at conversion in 1 Thessalonians 1:5. Calling to mind his initial missionary activity in the city along with the cosenders of the letter, Paul says that his Spirit-inspired mission resulted in "deep conviction" (1 Thess 1:5). Though some have thought of "deep conviction" as referring to Paul's preaching ministry in Thessalonica,[2] Paul reminds the Thessalonians of how his ministry in the power of the Holy Spirit was carried out persuasively.[3] In other words, the "deep conviction" is the consequence of the Spirit's powerful activity in them through the apostle at the time of conversion. The Holy Spirit works within the preachers to speak words, unlike charlatans (1 Thess 2:2–6). The same Spirit's powerful activity induces "deep conviction" in the believers, enabling them to live out their faith exemplarily before others after their conversion (1 Thess 1:8–9). The Thessalonian believers were persuaded to accept the gospel "not as a human word, but as it actually is, the actual word of God" (1 Thess 2:13). Rightly, Fee concludes that "[h]is preaching was accompanied by the power of the Holy Spirit so as to carry great conviction, which finally was evidenced by their conversion."[4]

Second, in his second letter to the Thessalonians, Paul ascribes the function of sanctification of a believer in Christ to the Holy Spirit (2 Thess 2:13). For Paul, the Spirit is the divine catalyst in the process of their growing in holiness after they believed in the gospel of Christ (1 Thess 1:4–6; 2 Thess 2:13).[5] Menken

---

2   Charles A. Wanamaker, *The Epistles to the Thessalonians: A Commentary on the Greek Text*, New International Greek Testament Commentary (Grand Rapids, MI: Eerdmans, 1990), 79.
3   George, *Called into the Mission of God*, 122. See F.F. Bruce, *1 and 2 Thessalonians*, Word Biblical Commentary 45 (Waco, TX: Word Books, 1982), 14; Gordon D. Fee, *God's Empowering Presence: The Holy Spirit in the Letters of Paul* (Peabody, MA: Hendrickson Publishers, 1994), 44–45.
4   Fee, *God's Empowering Presence*, 45.
5   See Trevor J. Burke, "The Holy Spirit as the Controlling Dynamic in Paul's Role as Mission-

rightly states that "God's sanctifying work by the Spirit has precedence over the human activity of belief in the gospel."[6] This sanctifying role of the Spirit continues until he presents them "blameless and holy in the presence of our God and Father when our Lord Jesus comes with all his holy ones" (1 Thess 3:13; 5:23).

Why is the Spirit constantly at work sanctifying a believer? Paul believes that it is God's will that the Thessalonians be sanctified from their sins (4:3). The purpose of their call from their Gentile background (1 Thess 1:9) into this blessed faith in Christ is "to live a holy life" (4:7). Hence, they ought to pay close attention to pleasing the will of God by obeying the instructions he gave them by the authority of the Lord (4:1). Paul warns the Thessalonian believers that a rejection of the ethical instructions he gave them would mean that they are rejecting God, the giver of the Holy Spirit (4:8). The sanctifying role of the Spirit in a believer is implied in Paul's ethical warning and speaking about God as the one "who gives you his Holy Spirit" (4:8). According to Johnson, Paul's language in 4:8 refers to the ongoing activity of the Spirit in constantly energizing individual bodies to be ethically transformed in the Spirit-energized sanctifying lifestyle after conversion (cf. Gal 3:5; 5:16–18, 25).[7] So, responding to the sanctifying work of the Spirit in them, Paul exhorts the Thessalonians "to control your own body" (*skeuos ktasthai*) in a sanctifying and honorable manner (1 Thess 4:4). Paul's expression *skeuos ktasthai*, within the then Gentile cultic context, reminded the converts of the sexual sins that they must resist, for the Spirit given by God is at work in them.[8]

For Paul, the Holy Spirit initiates and enables ethical transformation in an individual according to the will of God. It is a continuous function of the Spirit in the life of a believer with an eschatological significance to present the individual blameless and holy before God the Father. The Thessalonian believers living in a morally degraded context ought to respond to God's election through the persuasive and sanctifying role of the Spirit in being ethically transformed according to the will of God.

---

ary to the Thessalonians," in *Paul as Missionary: Identity, Activity, Theology, and Practice*, ed. Trevor J. Burke and Brian S. Rosner (London: Bloomsbury T&T Clark, 2011), 153.

6   M.J.J. Menken, *2 Thessalonians*, New Testament Readings (London: Routledge, 1994), 121.

7   Andy Johnson, *1 & 2 Thessalonians*, Two Horizons New Testament Commentary (Grand Rapids, MI: Eerdmans, 2016), 115. Examining parallel thought in Galatians is important for understanding 1 Thessalonians 4:8 because, as I have argued elsewhere, Galatians was most probably written very close to Paul's Thessalonian correspondence between AD 50 and 52. See Roji T George, *Paul's Identity in Galatians: A Postcolonial Appraisal* (New Delhi: CWI, 2016), 115.

8   Karl P. Donfried, "The Cults of Thessalonica and the Thessalonian Correspondence," in *Paul, Thessalonica, and Early Christianity* (Grand Rapids, MI: Eerdmans, 2002), 29–31.

2   The Emboldening Spirit

Paul wrote the two letters to Thessalonians encouraging his readers to persist in faith amid intense persecution from others in the city (1Thess 1:6; 2:13–16; 3:2–5; 2Thess 1:4). In 1Thessalonians 1:6, Paul applauds them for receiving the gospel amid great suffering "*with* the joy *given by* the Holy Spirit" (emphasis added). Paul considers the Holy Spirit to be the source of the joy experienced by the believers in the face of persecution. The Spirit inspires joy, the fruit of the Spirit (cf. Gal 5:22), within a believer who stands firm in faith amid suffering. The unfavorable external circumstances are overcome within the community of God found in Christ through the enablement of the Spirit.

Paul speaks about two other explicit ways in which the Spirit-instilled "joy" in the Thessalonian believers is significant. First, they become not only coimitators of the Lord with other communities of God in suffering (1Thess 2:14–16) but also "a model to all the believers in Macedonia and Achaia" (1Thess 1:6–7). The Spirit-inspired joy modeled in them in the face of suffering had made them witnesses to the Lord's message before all ("The Lord's message rang out from you ... everywhere" 1:8). Second, it enables the persecuted group of believers to nurture the hope of eschatological rescue from the present suffering at the coming of Jesus Christ (1Thess 1:10; 2Thess 1:10). Interestingly, "joy" is the only emotion Paul uses to characterize his apostolic hope in the eschatological time standing before the Lord Jesus Christ (1Thess 2:19–20).

Further, the significance of the Spirit-inspired "joy" experienced by the Thessalonian believers amid persecution is that the Spirit is given by God who calls them into "his Kingdom and glory" (1Thess 2:12 cf. 2Thess 1:5). The term *kaleo* (1Thess 2:12) in the present tense "stresses the present and continuing nature of the event in which they now participate and which will be consummated in the future."[9] Paul has preached this message of the kingdom to them earlier with the power of the Spirit.[10] Now, the Spirit given to them by God inspires joy within them as they already share in the kingdom of God. A few years later, in Romans 14:17, Paul speaks explicitly about the kingdom of God as "joy" experienced by the believers, along with righteousness and peace, in the Holy Spirit. Such an explicit statement about the kingdom of God connected with the joy given by the Holy Spirit is absent in the letters to the Thessalonians. However, the Thessalonian believers already share in the kingdom of God and experience the joy of the Spirit. It warrants us to assume that a connection between

---

9   Karl P. Donfried, "The Kingdom of God in Paul," in *Paul, Thessalonica, and Early Christianity* (Grand Rapids, MI: Eerdmans, 2002), 241.
10   Donfried, "The Kingdom of God in Paul," 241.

the two was not absent in his mind when writing to the Thessalonians. Thus emboldened by the inner experience of "joy," the evidence of their sharing in the kingdom of God, the believers in Thessalonica boldly faced the hostility for the sake of their newfound faith.

In short, the Spirit sustains a redeemed community of God to face boldly the violent onslaught on them for the sake of their faith. The present emboldening ministry of the Spirit inspiring "joy" in the persecuted community of believers has both present and eschatological significances.

3 The Spirit and the Charismata

Paul believed that the Spirit had been active since the inception of his ministry in Thessalonica. The Spirit was active in their preaching ministry (1 Thess 1:4–5) and worship (1 Thess 5:19–22). What sort of activity of the Spirit is Paul speaking about in his Thessalonian correspondence? In 1 Thessalonians 1:5, Paul says that the gospel he preached at first in Thessalonica was not in words alone (*monon*) but was also accompanied by "power" (*dunamis*). The lack of "in" (*en*) before "deep conviction" (1:5) in several manuscripts has been best explained, by Fee and Weima, through possible scribal activity to be an epexegesis. So, the word "power" must be understood in the light of the expression "the Holy Spirit and deep conviction" in 1:5.[11] Then the term "power" refers to the powerful manifestations that were more than just words mediated by the Spirit in their ministry.

Wanamaker understands the word "power" in 1 Thessalonians 1:5 as referring to the "miraculous signs and wonders," a gift of the Spirit (cf. 1 Cor 12:8–10) that characterized Paul's initial preaching in the city.[12] Luke is silent about such a dynamic ministry of Paul in Thessalonica (Acts 17:1–9). The plausible reason may be that he related more to the apostle's ministry among the Gentile quarter of the population and the opposition he faced from Jews in Thessalonica. However, Luke does say that "a large number of God-fearing Greeks and quite a few prominent women" believed in the gospel, though he does not explain how and when he ministered among the Gentiles in Thessalonica during his very short

---

11 Jeffery A.D. Weima, *1–2 Thessalonians*, Baker Exegetical Commentary on the New Testament (Grand Rapids, MI: Baker Academic, 2014), 94; Fee, *God's Empowering Presence*, 40n5. Interestingly, even if "power," "the Holy Spirit," and "a deep conviction" are treated as three different terms explaining how the gospel has come to the Thessalonians, Johnson maintains that the latter two terms function "to clarify the phrase 'with power.'" Johnson, *1 & 2 Thessalonians*, 46.

12 Wanamaker, *Epistles to the Thessalonians*, 79. See George, *Called into the Mission of God*, 121–122; Fee, *God's Empowering Presence*, 45.

ministry in the city. We can assume that with Jews, Paul argued on the messiahship of Jesus in the synagogue. At the same time, his ministry among Gentiles was characterized by the signs and wonders performed through the Holy Spirit. Hence, Paul is sure that the Gentile believers in Thessalonica themselves can bear witness to the veracity of his claim.

In Romans 15:18–19, Paul reflects upon his ministry among the Gentiles. He says that his ministry was accompanied "by the power of signs and wonders, through the power of the Spirit of God." Paul mentions no exceptions in speaking about the ministry he has thus far carried out among the Gentiles, including those in Thessalonica. So based on Paul's own later words about his ministry in general and the internal clues to a charismatic ministry in Thessalonica, it is reasonable for us to assume that his ministry in Thessalonica was not an exception to his overall ministry among the Gentiles. A Spirit-empowered charismatic ministry of Paul in Thessalonica authenticated the content of the gospel he preached. It also distinguished him from other preachers who preached with ulterior motives (cf. 1 Thess 2:3–6).[13]

Further, in 1 Thessalonians 5:19–22, Paul commands them not to "quench the Spirit" but to continue to use the gift of prophecy with caution. Paul's negative command in 5:20 and the following positive command to "hold on to what is good" with caution based on the apostolic teachings (cf. 2 Thess 2:15) attests the significance Paul accords to the charismatic gifts of the Holy Spirit for the life of the church. The apostle's exhortation presupposes not only the exercise of charismatic gifts in the earliest Thessalonian Christian community but also the danger of treating "prophecies with contempt" in the context of possible misuse of them by some (cf. 2 Thess 2:2). Later in 1 Corinthians 12:31, he commands them to "eagerly desire the greater gifts" because God distributes them in the church "for the common good" (1 Cor 12:7). In the Corinthian context, Paul explains the threefold common good of the gift of prophecy—"strengthening, encouraging and comfort"—for the edification of the members in the church (1 Cor 14:3–4). So, learning how Paul held the charismatic gifts to be beneficial to the church's corporate life, the command not to quench the fire of the Spirit in Thessalonians underlines the importance he accorded them for the church.[14] Paul knows that the Thessalonians needed the Spirit-inspired prophetic words to withstand the hostility from outside the church and to wait in hope for the coming of the Lord Jesus.

To sum up, the pieces of evidence from Paul's Thessalonian correspondence prove that the Holy Spirit and his role in the individual and corporate life of the

---

13　Cf. Fee, *God's Empowering Presence*, 43–44.
14　George, *Called into the Mission of God*, 126–128.

Thessalonian believers were never absent in the apostle's mind. From the early stages of his ministry, Paul recognized the mediating role of the Spirit in a person's conversion, and he does so by reminding the Thessalonians of their very first instance of their conversion experience. For Paul, from that first moment, the Spirit is closely involved in their lives to sanctify them according to God's will. Thus, the Thessalonians are under the obligation to follow carefully the instruction Paul has given them. Further, amid persecution in Thessalonica, Paul understood the experience of joy in them, attesting to their participation in the kingdom of God as the work of the Spirit who emboldens them to suffer hostility standing firm. It nurtures the eschatological hope of rescue at the coming of Jesus in them as they become coimitators of the Lord and a model to other believers in suffering for their faith in Christ. Finally, the believers must not only recall the reception of the Spirit-powered gospel that came to them at first with charismatic expressions, but they must also hold fast to that which is good and reject the evil. They must keep the fire of the Spirit glowing in and among their community and never quench it or treat it with contempt.

The Spirit in the Pastoral Epistles: Inspiring, Gifting, Sanctifying Presence

Kenneth J. Archer

1 Timothy, 2 Timothy, and Titus are personal letters most likely written by the apostle Paul to Timothy and Titus, his beloved disciples and trustworthy co-workers in the Gospel.[1] Paul refers to them as his "true child[ren] in the common faith" (Titus 1:4 see also 1 Tim 1:2; 2 Tim 1:2).[2] The letters are canonically arranged by length and commonly referred to as the Pastoral Epistles (PE). The pneumatology of the PE appears at first glance to be rather limited.[3] The term *pneuma* occurs only seven times in the PE.[4] In the remaining essay, I will address the seven references in canonical order and then summarize the pneumatology of the PE.

1   1 and 2 Timothy

1 Tim 3:14–16 states what many consider to be the primary purpose of the letter. Paul is concerned about the way persons belonging to "the household of God," which is "the church of the Living God," are conducting themselves in his absence. 3:16 ends the extended discussion on godly household behavior via a hymn about Jesus that was most likely sung in the Christian communities. The phrase "who was manifested in flesh, vindicated/confirmed in spirit" has

---

[1] Paul is the implied author (1 Tim 1:1; 2 Tim 1:1; Titus 1:1), and minimally he has been recognized as the theological influence on these letters. On authorship, literary context, and canonicity, see Luke Timothy Johnson, *Letters to Paul's Delegates: 1 Timothy, 2 Timothy and Titus* (Harrisburg, PA: Trinity Press International, 1996), and Robert W. Wall with Richard B. Steele, *1 and 2 Timothy and Titus* (Grand Rapids, MI and Cambridge, UK: Eerdmans, 2012). When I refer to the author of the PE, I will use Paul.

[2] For Paul's relationship with Timothy see Acts 16:1–17:15, 18:5, 19:22, 20:4; Rom. 16:24; 1 Cor 4:17, 16:10; 2 Cor 1:1, 19, 2:22; Phil 1:1, 2:10, 22; Col 1:1; 1 Thess 1:1, 3:2, 6; 2 Thess 1:1, and Philemon 1:1. For Titus, see 2 Cor 2:13, 7:6, 7:13–14, 8:6, 16–17, 23, 12:18, and Gal 2:1, 3.

[3] See Frances Young, *The Theology of the Pastoral Letters* (New York and Cambridge: Cambridge University Press, 1994), 68–70, who specifically devotes less than three pages to the pneumatology.

[4] See Gordon Fee, *God's Empowering Presence: The Holy Spirit in the Letters of Paul* (Grand Rapids, MI: Baker Academic, 2011, first published by Hendrickson, 1994) for a comprehensive examination.

generated much discussion. The first part of the phrase may refer to the incarnation, the revelation of God through Jesus in human flesh. The second part of the phrase may then refer to his resurrection by the Spirit. Jesus manifests loving godliness (a key concern of the letter) for us on earth in the flesh as he made atonement for us. God further vindicated his life through resurrection by the Holy Spirit after Jesus endured the humiliation of crucifixion. The humiliation was not taking on flesh, not incarnation, but the manner of his death. God gave him over to death, but humanity crucified him (Acts 2:32). Jesus, fully human (and fully divine), is glorified bodily by the Spirit and is now in the same celestial realm as the Holy Spirit and angelic spirit beings.[5] Jesus is in the heavenlies (glory), but the Holy Spirit is present in and with the household of God, enabling her to live virtuously.

1 Tim 4:1 is a clear reference to the Holy Spirit being active in the communities. The Spirit is depicted as speaking, warning the communities that in these last times "deceitful spirits" (the plural form of *pneuma*) are at work among them, drawing some away from the faith to the point of apostasy. These "spirits" are most likely demons or fallen angels. Originally created good, they are now corrupted, fallen, and evil. The Holy Spirit uses various ways to speak to the community, with prophetic speech being the most common (see 1 Tim 1:18 and 1 Tim 4:14). Here the Spirit is working to remind the community of what Jesus had already said (see John 14–16). The Spirit is also making clear that before the return of Christ, believers will face demonic opposition, and the primary weapons of the demonic are deception through words, through false yet extraordinary counterfeit signs, and through immoral ways of living (2 Tim 2:16–17).

2 Tim 1:7 is about Timothy and the gift of God that is the Holy Spirit.[6] Paul challenges Timothy to "fan into flame" the "gift (*charismata*) of God" that came through Paul laying hands on him (2 Tim 1:6). This differs from 1 Tim 4:14, in which Timothy receives the gift through prophecy and the laying on of hands by the elders/presbyters but continues to confirm Timothy's calling through prophecies made about him (1 Tim 1:18). 1 Tim 1:18 and 4:14 are about Timothy's calling and gifting by the Holy Spirit for ministry. Paul is reminding Timothy and the communities in Ephesus that Timothy is called *by the Holy Spirit* and gifted *by the Holy Spirit* in ministering to the household of God. In 2 Tim 1:7 Paul

---

5 For the theological relationship of Jesus and God in the PE, see Young, *The Theology of the Pastoral Letters*, Chapter 3.
6 See Robert Menzies, "Subsequence in the Pauline Epistles," in *Pneuma* 39, no. 3 (2017): 342–363. Menzies argues that this verse as well as other Pauline verses demonstrate "the need for each believer to experience a post-conversion infusion of spiritual power for ministry."

states, "God did not give us a spirit (*pneuma*) of cowardliness but of love, power, and self-control." The verse presents a stark contrast between cowardliness and love, power, and self-control and thereby emphasizes the positive gift of God. Is Paul talking about the Holy Spirit as the source of love, power, and self-control, or is Paul saying that God gave to Timothy (his spirit or inner being) love, power, and self-control? Translators have rendered this verse both ways.[7]

Gordon Fee makes insightful comments on these passages. Fee makes a plausible argument that in 1 Tim 1:8 and 1 Tim 4:14, Paul is reminding Timothy and the established communities in Ephesus, especially the elders of which a few might be understood as teaching falsely, that Timothy has a "Spirit-initiated and Spirit-called ministry" that was attested to in the presence of the communities.[8] 2 Tim 1:7, qualified by subtle yet substantial grammatical differences, is referring to the gift of God that is the reception of the Holy Spirit. Fee argues that "elsewhere in Paul the Holy Spirit is expressively spoken of as *given* by God to be in believers (1 Thess 4:8; 1 Cor 6:19; 2 Cor 1:22)."[9] 2 Tim 2:7 is about receiving the Holy Spirit that is God's gift—the Spirit of love, power, and discernment.[10]

2 Tim 1:14 contains an imperative and a clear appeal to the Holy Spirit. Timothy is to "guard the deposit" by means of "the Holy Spirit that is in us." The deposit most likely refers to the previous discussion of sound teaching associated with the gospel (2 Tim 1:1–13). The Spirit is the source of truth, not of false teachings. In order to stand firm and care for the communities, Timothy can cooperate with the Holy Spirit, who will enable him to stay true to the faith. The Spirit is the present reality working powerfully in believers because of our Savior Jesus Christ.

2 Tim 3:16 is a favorite verse for evangelicals and pentecostals for they have always understood themselves as people of the Book.[11] "All Scripture is God breathed" (*theopneustos*).[12] Scripture is divinely inspired; hence, it has divine

---

7   The 2011 NIV translation reads, "For the Spirit God gave us does not make us timid, but gives us power, love and self-discipline." The NASB reads, "For God has not given us a spirit of timidity, but of power and love and discipline."
8   Fee, *God's Empowering Presence*, 772.
9   Fee, *God's Empowering Presence*, 787.
10 For an alternative understanding see W. Hulitt Gloer, *Smyth & Helwys Bible Commentary: 1 & 2 Timothy–Titus* (Macon, GA: Smyth & Helwys, 2010), 233. Gloer understands this to be referring to the human spirit. For the perspective that this is a subsequence experience to regeneration, the baptism in the Holy Spirit, see Menzies, "Subsequence in the Pauline Epistles."
11 See Kenneth J. Archer and Aaron Ross, "The Bible in Pentecostal Tradition," in *Your Word Is Truth: The Bible in Ten Traditions*, ed. J. Michael West and Gunar Mägi (WCC Publications and United Bible Society, 2018).
12 Also, see 2 Pet 1:21.

authority in that it is *useful for salvation*. Scripture (here referring to the OT) rightly interpreted in light of the gospel, in continuity with the received tradition and with the aid of the Holy Spirit, is "useful" for teaching and training in righteousness (1 Tim 1:8–9). Scripture is sanctified by the Spirit, hence put into service by God for the benefit of the church. These writings are set apart from and over all other useful writings. The community is birthed by the Spirit, not the *book* inspired by Spirit. The Book of all books that should be privileged and cherished in God's household is Scripture.[13]

2 Tim 4:22—"The Lord be with your spirit"—is referring to Timothy as a complete person rather than to some inner spiritual dimension. 2 Timothy is the most intimate of the PE; yet, Paul concludes this letter by reaffirming the presence of the collective community ("Grace be with you all"). Grace opens the letter, and grace closes the letter (2 Tim 1:2, 4:22). This reiterates that all aspects of salvation are experienced because of God's grace.

2   Titus

Titus 3:5 is an important text that ties together all the spirit passages in the PE. It is worth quoting in context:

> But when the kindness and love of God our Savior appeared, he saved us, not because of righteous things we had done, but because of his mercy. *He saved us through the washing of rebirth and renewal by the Holy Spirit*, whom he poured out on us generously through Jesus Christ our Savior, so that, having been justified by his grace, we might become heirs having the hope of eternal life.
>
> Titus 3:4–6, NIV, my italics

The Holy Spirit brings about regeneration or rebirth. The imagery of washing and renewal hints to water baptism and Spirit baptism but most definitely is talking about cleansing and purifying from contamination of sin (sanctification) and the demonic (deliverance). The Holy Spirit personally appropriates the atoning work of Jesus to those who respond to the gospel; therefore, "[t]he Spirit plays a crucial role in Christian conversion and ongoing Christian life."[14] This is because God is compassionate and merciful, desiring all to be saved

---

[13] Daniel Castello and Robert W. Wall, *The Marks of Scripture: Rethinking the Nature of the Bible* (Grand Rapids, MI: Baker Publishing Group, 2019).
[14] Fee, *God's Empowering Presence*, 757.

(1 Tim 4:10; Titus 3:4–5). The relationship between the Spirit and Jesus is intimately intertwined but not indistinguishable. God initiates salvation—it is the grace of God given through faith in Christ (2 Tim 3:15)—and God sustains believers in salvation through the gracious gift—the Holy Spirit and the gifts of the Holy Spirit. All are called to a holy life grounded in love and manifested in faithfulness or godliness (2 Tim 1:9). This generates hope and encourages holy endurance for God is for, among, and working in believers.

3 Summary

In sum, the PE reinforce the traditional systematic theological perspective of the role of the Spirit as active in revelation and the salvation process, and as empowering persons for service. The Holy Spirit is the main person of the Trinity actively working in eschatological salvation for all by bringing forth the fruit of holiness and working powerfully through the sufferings (1 Tim 3:12) of gifted persons. Salvation is possible because of God's gracious action in and through Jesus and the Spirit.

To be in covenant relationship with God is to be in the household of God which is the church (1 Tim 3:14–15). The Spirit, who vindicated Jesus, comes from God and is poured out on believers personally and corporately, and is working to instill loving holiness through the washing and renewing of the community. This includes maintaining sound tradition and proper teaching of Scripture, for through it we save ourselves and those who take heed (1 Tim 4:16). The church is to follow faithfully the leading of the Spirit in continuing the ministry of Jesus Christ; hence prophetic speech and other spiritual giftings aid her in the salvific journey. Godly virtue is the fruit of the Spirit manifested personally and publicly through faithful witness to Jesus Christ our Savior (2 Tim 2:19). By the Spirit, the household of God engages in spiritual warfare by manifesting love, power, and discernment for the sake of the world, especially humanity, whom God is saving (1 Tim 2:4, 5:15). In the words of Frances Young, the Spirit "empowers the life of the Christian … bearing fruit in the life of the Church, which lives between the 'epiphanies.'"[15] Far from being peripheral, the PE contributes richly to the pneumatology of the NT.

---

15 Young, *The Theology of the Pastoral Letters*, 70.

The Spirit in Hebrews: Guiding the Community to Further Truth

Cynthia Long Westfall

The letter to the Hebrews contains surprisingly few references to the Holy Spirit, although there are more than some may recognize.[1] The author of Hebrews is interested in moving the recipients on to maturity though advanced teaching, and he indicates that he does not want to review the fundamentals of the faith and Christian life with his recipients, but rather to build on those fundamentals (6:1–2). According to his line of reasoning, he believes that the recipients/hearers of the letter should be fully grounded in their communal life in the Spirit, but he is most interested in how the Holy Spirit is exhorting and guiding the community to further truth during their critical time of need. Therefore, his focus is the content of what the Spirit is currently communicating, and this content contains some of the most profound statements in the letter/sermon. There are possibly seven references to the Holy Spirit in Hebrews. Two of them are consistent with the early Christian traditions about the work of the Spirit: three of them concern the Holy Spirit's confrontation and communication to the recipients through Scripture, and two are disputed as references to the Holy Spirit, although, if they apply, they may reflect a perception of the divinity of the Spirit. The importance of the contexts in which the author mentions the Holy Spirit indicates a role for the Holy Spirit in the sermon/letter that extends beyond the texts in which the Spirit is directly referenced.

1 The Holy Spirit and Early Christian Traditions (2:4; 6:4)

The first reference to the Holy Spirit occurs at the end of the first passage of the letter/sermon (1:1–2:4), which presents Jesus as God's ultimate messen-

---

[1] The role of the Holy Spirit in Hebrews has been largely denied until recently; see, e.g., Barnabas Lindars, *The Theology of the Letter to the Hebrews* (Cambridge: Cambridge University Press, 1991), 56, and H.B. Swete, *The Holy Spirit in the New Testament: A Study of Primitive Christian Teaching* (London: Macmillan, 1910), 248–249. See Madison N. Pierce, *Divine Discourse in the Epistle to the Hebrews: The Recontextualization of Spoken Quotations of Scripture*, SNTS 178 (Cambridge: Cambridge University Press, 2020), 135–136n1, for an overview of works that have reexamined the pneumatology of Hebrews since 2003 as well as Pierce's chapter "Extra-Divine Discourse: The Holy Spirit Speaks to the Community," 135–174.

ger in contrast with all past messengers from God. At the point of departure, "God" signifies the relationship of the Father to the Son.[2] The passage concludes with an exhortation for the recipients to hang on to the things they have heard from Jesus that were confirmed to them by eyewitnesses (2:1, 3). The message Jesus announced is characterized as "so great a salvation." Not only was it confirmed by eyewitnesses, but God himself corroborated Jesus's message with "signs and wonders and various miracles, and by gifts of the Holy Spirit, distributed according to his will" (2:4).[3] The Old Testament has a number of references to "signs and wonders,"[4] but the triple formula of "signs, wonders and various miracles" was used in early Christianity (Acts 2:22; Rom 15:19; 2 Cor 12:12; 2 Thess 2:9).[5] The language about the gifts of the Holy Spirit distributed according to his will is consistent with Pauline teaching (1 Cor 12–14, cf. 12:7, 11),

---

2 Hebrews represents "God" as the Father and Jesus as the Son in 1:1–2, 5–6, 8; 3:6; 4:14; 5:5, 8–10; 6:6; 7:3, 28; and 10:29. This constrains the other references to God in Hebrews, with the exception of the vocative in 1:8, where God is depicted as addressing the Son as "God." See the substantial argument of Amy L.B. Peeler, *You Are My Son: The Family of God in the Epistle to the Hebrews*, LNTS (London: Bloomsbury T&T Clark, 2014). The thesis of the book is, "The familial imagery shapes the author's presentation of the three primary persons of the sermon: God, Jesus, and the humans in relationship with them, the author and his audience" (6).

3 The NRSV is cited except where the author's translation was used. A possible alternate reading is that God distributed the Holy Spirit, which takes "distributions of the Spirit" (πνεύματος ἁγίου μερισμοῖς) as an objective genitive construction. See Gareth L. Cockerill, *The Epistle to the Hebrews*, NICNT (Grand Rapids, MI: Eerdmans, 2012), 123. But also see Paul Ellingworth, *Commentary on the Book of Hebrews*, NIGTC (Grand Rapids, MI: Eerdmans, 1993), 142, who takes the genitive phrase as an objective genitive but renders it "of the gifts proceeding from the Holy Spirit … not of a distribution of the Holy Spirit himself." If the genitive phrase occurred without being modified by "according to his will," taking it as an objective genitive might be more compelling given that the gift of the Holy Spirit is associated with the reception of the gospel in Acts 2:38–39 and the accompanying signs (Acts 19:1–7). However, the plural noun "distributions" raises questions (as opposed to the singular "gift"), and since the phrase is modified with "according to his will," the entire phrase is more likely to have an intertextual connection with 1 Cor 12:11 of the Spirit's distribution of the gifts according to the Spirit's will that would be consistent with the teaching of the early church (ταῦτα ἐνεργεῖ τὸ ἓν καὶ τὸ αὐτὸ πνεῦμα, διαιροῦν ἰδίᾳ ἑκάστῳ καθὼς βούλεται). The focus of 2:4 is on the powerful confirmation of and testimony to the salvation announced by the Son, and understanding πνεύματος ἁγίου μερισμοῖς as a subjective genitive strengthens the testimony because it adds the Spirit's witness through action to that of the God (the Father).

4 The references to "signs and wonders" in the Old Testament refer to God's miraculous activity against Egypt, Pharoah, his household, and the people at the time of the exodus (Deut 4:34; 6:4; 7:19; 26:8; 29:3; 34:11; Neh 9:10; Psalm 135:9; Jer 32:20–21). The one exception is Isa 8:18, which in context refers to Isaiah and his disciples. Interestingly, Hebrews 2:12–13 cites Isa 8:17–18 as spoken by Jesus but omits the reference to signs and wonders.

5 However, the grammatical relationship between "power" and "signs" in Rom 15:19 is somewhat different from the other examples of the triple formula.

but the function of the gifts as confirmation of the gospel of salvation is consistent with conversion accounts in Acts. The community's manifestation of the gifts of the Spirit when they received the message was a matter of record.

The second reference to the Holy Spirit that is consistent with early Christian tradition is in 6:4, in the context of the warning against falling away. The author gives a stern warning to those who have become partners with the Holy Spirit.[6] While some try to argue that the description of the experiences in the Christian community in Hebrews 6:4–6 does not represent true conversion, the reference to being partners with the Holy Spirit indicates otherwise.[7] The author uses the word "partner" (μετοχός) to indicate being in an intimate salvific relationship with Jesus (3:1, 14). In the previous context, the author refers to the manifestation of the Spirit in the community (2:4), how the recipients had been taught "the basic elements of the oracles of God" (5:12), and how he wanted to move on from the "basic teaching" about Christ (6:1), including the "laying on of hands" (6:2). These references suggest that the Hebrews author considers the community to be well-founded in their pneumatology, as he moves forward to concentrate on his ground-breaking teaching concerning Jesus's high priesthood.

2 The Holy Spirit's Communication through Scripture (3:7, 9:8, 10:15)

The author refers to the Holy Spirit speaking through the citation of Scripture three times (3:7, 9:8, 10:15) and also describes Scripture as being spoken by God the Father (1:5, 6, 7, 8, 10, 13; 5:5, 6; 7:17, 21; 8:8; 13:5), by Jesus (2:12, 13a, 13b; 10:5), and even by "someone ... somewhere" (2:6).[8] It is not likely that the Holy Spirit

---

6   The author's translation, which is formal equivalent, takes μετοχός to be a substantive complement to "become" (γίνομαι), whereas the NRSV renders the phrase "shared in the Holy Spirit."

7   All four expressions in 6:4–5 are common idioms for genuine faith. See Koester's notes on the four expressions, Craig R. Koester, *Hebrews: A New Translation with Introduction and Commentary*, AB (New York: Doubleday, 2001), 313–315, as well as his concluding comment: "This section refers to an authentic experience of God's manifold grace" (321). There is significant evidence that suggests that the author was familiar with the Pauline corpus where there is an explicit connection between having the Spirit and being a child of God (Rom 8:1–17). The Hebrews' understanding of being a partner (μετοχός) with the Spirit explicitly signals a close relationship in comparison to the more generic "to have" (ἔχω) used by Paul.

8   "Someone has testified somewhere" in 2:6 introduces a citation of Psalm 8:4–6, which is a Davidic psalm. The only time Hebrews specifies a human author is in 4:7 where he specifies that God spoke Psalm 95 through David in order to establish the chronological context. Philo

is simply seen as the ultimate source of Scripture as has been commonly suggested, since God the Father is specified as the ultimate source of Scripture in the majority of the quotations.[9] The three Scripture passages attributed to the Holy Spirit differ from the quotations above because in each case they are directly applied to the present context of the recipients.[10] This suggests that the Hebrews author understands the Holy Spirit to be active in speaking directly through the current citation of Scripture to exhort and/or confront the recipients in creating a new understanding of a passage.

The introduction and citation of Psalm 95:7–11 in 3:7–11 is particularly interesting because the author represents the Holy Spirit, Jesus, God the Father, and David as speaking in, through, or within the psalm. Consistent with the author's point of departure in 1:1, in which God spoke through various messengers in the past, the author of Hebrews states that God was speaking through David when the psalm was written, which was particularly relevant when God set a certain day that was "today" in David's time (4:7).[11] In 4:3, God [the Father] is depicted as the one who spoke to the wilderness generation in the past in 3:10–11//Psalm 95:10–11, though he spoke through Moses and Aaron (Num 14:26–35). Consistent with 1:2, the author depicts Jesus as the one who is speaking in the present *within* the Holy Spirit's citation of the psalm. The preceding argument of Hebrews indicates that God is speaking through Jesus the Son "in these last days" (1:2), so it is Jesus's voice that the recipients would be hearing "as long as it is called 'today'" (3:13).[12] It is Jesus, who is God's apostle, as God's ulti-

---

also practiced indefinite references to human authors. Koester suggests this may reflect the idea that the OT is the word of God and that there is no need to cite particular biblical authors, Koester, *Hebrews*, 214.

9   Harold W. Attridge, *The Epistle to the Hebrews*, Hermeneia (Philadelphia: Fortress Press, 1989), 114.

10 The quotation of Prov 4:26 in 12:5–6 is also applied directly to the recipients without reference to the Holy Spirit: "And you have forgotten the exhortation that addresses you as children," which may reflect the gnomic nature of Proverbs that could be generally understood as a direct exhortation.

11 The statement in 1:1–2 says that in the past, God spoke through the prophets in many and various ways. "His voice" at the time of the wilderness generation was Moses, Aaron, and the angels, and David was "his voice" in Psalm 95.

12 In Heb 1:2, ἐλάλησεν is in the aorist tense, which is usually rendered in the past tense. However, the Greek verb does not establish temporal values, but rather tense grammaticalizes aspect. Temporal information is supplied by the context, which in 1:2 is "in these last days," which is depicted as the present, paraphrased by Riggenbach as translated by Ellingworth, "God has spoken in the present, and … this present is also the end time," Ellingworth, *Hebrews*, 93. The aorist tense depicts an action as complete and undifferentiated process, Stanley E. Porter, *Idioms of the Greek New Testament*, 2nd ed. (Sheffield: Sheffield Academic Press, 1994), 35.

mate messenger in these last days (1:2; 3:1). The recipients are therefore directly urged to listen to Jesus's voice in the quotation and repetition of "Today, if you hear his voice, do not harden your hearts as in the rebellion" in the following midrash (3:7–8a, 15//Psalm 95:7b-8). He is the one who continues to speak from heaven and must not be resisted (12:24–25). While the author is clear that God [the Father] is the ultimate source of the Davidic psalm, the introduction in 3:7 attributes the *citation* of the psalm in 3:7–11 to the Holy Spirit ("Therefore, as the Holy Spirit says").[13] The author is indicating that the Holy Spirit is applying the psalm to the recipients as an exhortation directed at their situation, and he is the one who is pleading for them not to harden their hearts if they hear Jesus's voice.[14]

The reference to the Holy Spirit in 9:8–9a also demonstrates that the Holy Spirit is communicating a contemporary message: "By this the Holy Spirit indicates the way into the sanctuary has not yet been disclosed as long as the first tent is still standing. This is a symbol of the present time." In other words, the author of Hebrews is saying that the way into the sanctuary that he is in the process of describing (4:16; 6:19–20; 10:19–22) is a new revelation by the Holy Spirit. As Attridge says, "The arrangements of the old cult signify ultimately its own inadequacy,"[15] but Second Temple interpretation did not have this evaluation of the arrangements for worship (Exod 25:10–26:37; 30:1–6; 36:8–37:29; Lev 16), nor is there evidence of this interpretation in the preceding early Christian tradition.[16] The context in Hebrews demonstrates an exegesis of the biblical description of the arrangements of the earthly tabernacle in 9:8 through a christological lens.[17] This lens includes not only the early traditions about

---

13   The author of Hebrews clearly speaks of "God" as the ultimate source of the psalm in 4:7, and the majority of the citations in Hebrews are divine utterances, as observed by Pam Eisenbaum in *The Jewish Heroes of Christian History: Hebrews 11 in Literary Context* (Atlanta: Scholars Press, 1997), 92. However, many commentators assert that Hebrews is simply identifying the Holy Spirit as the ultimate source of the Scriptures in 3:7, 9:8 and 10:15: e.g., Attridge, *Hebrews*, 114; F.F. Bruce, *The Epistle to the Hebrews*, NICNT (Grand Rapids, MI: Eerdmans, 1990), 95n23; Donald A. Hagner, *Hebrews*, NIBCNT (Peabody, MA: Hendrickson, 1990), 63; Celsus Spicq, *L'Epître aux Hebreux II* (Paris: Gabalda, 1952), 72.
14   As Martin Emmrich says, "When the Holy Spirit speaks the reader hears the divine viva vox that confronts head on in the here and now," "Pneuma in Hebrews: Prophet and Interpreter," *WTJ* 64, no. 1 (2002): 55–71, see 57.
15   Attridge, *Hebrews*, 240.
16   Emmrich, "Pneuma in Hebrews," 57–58.
17   Cockerill, *Hebrews*, 381, states, "What [the author] has to say is drawn from the plain biblical description of the old order understood in light of its fulfillment." That "fulfillment" would be disclosed through the christological lens that Jesus, the early Christian oral tradition, and the New Testament authors used to interpret the Old Testament.

Christ, but also what the author has already established: the high priesthood of Jesus (7:4–28), the heavenly tabernacle in which he serves (8:1–6), and the first covenant, which is "obsolete and growing old [and] will soon disappear" (8:13). The most intriguing part of his statement is that the way had not been disclosed "as long as the first tent is still standing." When did "the first tent," the holy place, cease to stand?[18] While the author of Hebrews limits his description and exegesis to the design and construction of the Mosaic tabernacle, the holy place continued to exist as a building and was functional in the first temple and the second temple, but it "ceased to stand" with the destruction of the second temple in 70 CE.[19] This suggests that "the present time" is the destruction of the first tent/holy place in 70 CE, or the imminent expectation of it in the preceding time during the Great Revolt that started in 67 CE, which is the time in which the author is writing the message from the Holy Spirit.[20] The destruction of the Jerusalem temple and the ending of the Levitical sacrificial system indicated that the First Covenant was obsolete and disappearing. In light of the loss, the Holy Spirit disclosed the way into the sanctuary by prompting the author to read the biblical description of the arrangements for worship in a new way as a symbol to understand the fuller significance of Jesus Christ's sacrifice.[21]

---

18 See Cockerill's convincing argument in *Hebrews*, 381–382, that the first tent was the holy place. However, he translates "as long as the first tent is still standing" as "while the First Tent still had validity" (371), but when στάσις describes a structure such as a tent or building, it refers to its physical/spatial position/condition. See Liddell and Scott http://www.perseus.tufts.edu/hopper/text?doc=Perseus%3Atext%3A1999.04.0057%3Aentry%3Dsta%2Fsis.

19 The temple also temporarily "ceased to stand" during the Babylonian Captivity, but that time period is clearly not in view.

20 Marie Isaacs makes a cogent argument for reading Hebrews in the light of the destruction of the Jerusalem temple in *Sacred Space: An Approach to the Theology of the Epistle to the Hebrews*, JSNTSup73 (Sheffield: Sheffield Academic Press, 1992). Similarly, Hooker writes, "If our author was writing after 70 AD, then the catastrophic events in Jerusalem could have provided the spark which led our author to think of Christ as replacing the cult." In Morna D. Hooker, "Christ, the 'End' of the Cult," in *The Epistle to the Hebrews and Christian Theology*, ed. Richard Bauckham et al. (Grand Rapids: Eerdmans, 2009), 207.

21 Cockerill, *Hebrews*, 381n45, states, "The Spirit who inspired Scripture enables the pastor to understand the meaning inherent in the text from the beginning." This appears to reflect an understanding of *sensus plenior*, which claims that a deeper meaning is in the Scripture (such as in messianic passages) that was intended by God but not understood by the human author, nor, arguably, by previous interpreters. As Hebrews is deemed to be inspired Scripture, the author is offering a ground-breaking understanding of Jesus's identity as High Priest, the heavenly tabernacle, the New Covenant, and the concluding effects of Jesus's once-for-all sacrifice. Some want to argue that the teaching of the author of Hebrews was already part of the Christian tradition. Setting aside the fact that the author flags the following section as new teaching in 5:11–14 and bases his argument on his own

The author has already attributed ultimate authorship of Jer 31:31–34 to God (the Father) in 8:8–12,[22] but in 10:15–17 he attributes an edited and slightly altered repetition of part of the passage to the Holy Spirit as part of a bigger message. The author states that the Holy Spirit is testifying that the Lord's promise of the new covenant in which the law will be written on hearts and minds in Jer 31:33 refers to how Jesus perfected for all time the people who are being sanctified with his one sacrifice (10:14). Furthermore, he claims the Holy Spirit is testifying that sacrifices for sins are no longer necessary because of the Lord's promise in Jer 31:34 that he will not remember the sins and lawless acts anymore. According to the author, the Holy Spirit is providing a fresh christological reading of Jeremiah and a theological understanding of the sacrifice of Jesus that has not been documented in the earlier Christian tradition. Furthermore, according to Acts, Jewish Christians in Jerusalem continued to relate closely to the Jerusalem temple (Acts 2:46; 3:1; 5:21, 42; 21:22–24), and even Paul participated in a purification ceremony that most likely included sacrifices for sin and atonement (Acts 21:22–24; cf. Num 6:1–21).[23] However, if the temple was destroyed and sacrifices had ceased (or was on the verge of destruction between 67 and 70 CE), the Holy Spirit would have been using the disaster and the cessation of sacrifices to prompt the interpretation of Jer 31:33–34 in a new way. The Holy Spirit revealed the fuller significance of Jesus's sacrifice in the once and for all provision that obviated the need for further sacrifice for sin for Jews who accepted Jesus as their messiah.

3   Disputed References to the Holy Spirit (9:14; 10:29)

There are two references to the S/spirit that have been taken traditionally to refer to the Holy Spirit beginning with patristic interpretation and that have been used to support a trinitarian theology. However, some modern scholars understand them as christological references rather than referring to the Holy Spirit.

---

close exegesis of Old Testament texts, several of the christological statements are unprecedented in the early Christian documents. Therefore, regardless of whether the statements originated with the author, the explicit claims would reflect a new development in interpretation and Christology in which the author claims that the Holy Spirit took a role.

22   As stated in n. 2, the author of Hebrews identifies God as the Father in relationship with the Son throughout the letter, and God is taken as the referent of "he" (αὐτούς) in 8:8 given the ongoing actions of God in the context.

23   The description of the four men's vow and purification rites in Acts 21:22–24 best fits the description of a Nazarite vow in Num 6:1–21, in which someone died suddenly in their presence (Num 6:9–12).

In describing the value of Christ's blood and its ability to cleanse the believer's conscience in 9:14, the author states that Jesus "through the eternal S[s]pirit offered himself without blemish to God." Attridge argues that the context of Jesus's offering is a spiritual locale and a spiritual offering, and that "it likely refers to Christ and to the interior or spiritual quality of his sacrificial act."[24] While one must recognize the christological focus of Hebrews 1:1–10:26, the author has not described the heavenly tabernacle, the sacrificial blood, or other aspects of the sacrifice as "spiritual," nor has he described the person or ministry of Christ with such terms.[25] Rather, he argues, these "unseen" heavenly realities past, present, and future consist of such profound substance that they cast a shadow that consists of the less substantial earthly tabernacle, services, and sacrifice established by the Law (8:5; 10:1). Therefore, it is more likely that this brief mention is meant to draw upon the recipients' experiences and knowledge of the Holy Spirit. If so, it would ascribe the divine attribute of eternality to the Holy Spirit and would depict the Spirit as working in conjunction with Jesus Christ and God Father in regard to Jesus's high priestly sacrifice.

In 10:29, the author warns that believers who willfully sin have "spurned the Son of God, profaned the blood of the covenant by which they were sanctified, and outraged the S/spirit of grace." Attridge suggests that this is "one of the results that flows from Christ's sacrificial act, its making available of divine favor."[26] However, this describes an entity who can be insulted and is very similar to descriptions of the Holy Spirit in the Pauline corpus.[27] Given the author's understanding of the recipients' background and experiences with the Holy Spirit, he could predict that they would link a brief reference to the "S/spirit" as part of their foundation upon which the new teaching is based unless the author clearly indicated otherwise.[28] If so, the immediate context places insult-

---

24 Attridge, *Hebrews*, 251.
25 Platonic dualism has "cast a shadow" over how Hebrews has been read, which has been convincingly challenged; such interpretations that assume a Platonic worldview must be reevaluated. See Cynthia Long Westfall, "Space and Atonement in Hebrews," in *So Great a Salvation: A Dialogue on the Atonement in Hebrews*, ed. Jon C. Laansma, George H. Guthrie, and Cynthia Long Westfall (London: T&T Clark, 2019), 228–248; cf. 230–232.
26 Attridge, *Hebrews*, 295.
27 Eph 4:30; 1 Thess 5:19. There are in Hebrews a number of links with the Pauline corpus that suggest that at least the author was acquainted with Paul's writings. Willful sin causes grief over a failed seal or quenches the Spirit's work also amounts to insulting the gift of grace given through the Spirit.
28 The author was knowledgeable and sensitized to what they had been taught and what was needed to build on their foundation (5:11–6:3). The teachings about the heavenly tabernacle, Jesus's function as a high priest, and the nature of the sacrifice were detailed, but there are no clear signals that "spirit" would be best interpreted as christological.

ing the Holy Spirit on a par with trampling the Son of God underfoot and treating his blood as if it were unholy.

4 Conclusion

The author of Hebrews describes a community that was established with the manifestations of the Spirit (2:4) and that was well-founded in its pneumatology (6:1–5). The three references to the Holy Spirit speaking through Scripture all involve the direct application of Old Testament passages to the current time and circumstances of the author and the recipients/hearers of the letter/sermon. In 3:7–11, Psalm 95:7–11 is spoken directly to the recipients as a message to them. In 9:8 and 10:15, the author depicts the Holy Spirit as communicating a fresh reading and interpretation of the biblical description of the arrangements of the Mosaic tabernacle and Jer 31:33–34 through a christological lens. His interpretations are unprecedented—there is no evidence of them in earlier Christian tradition. It is not absolutely necessary to accept that the context for Hebrews is the destruction of the Jerusalem temple and the Levitical sacrificial system, but such a scenario is consistent with how most scholars date Hebrews, and such catastrophic events generate the sort of profound theological reflection and openness to the communication of the Holy Spirit that we see in Hebrews. The author depicts the Holy Spirit as the dynamic source of new insight and guide in the ongoing hermeneutical task and the construction of theology that is relevant and meets contemporary needs. In view of the experiences of the recipients with the Holy Spirit, the current activity of the Holy Spirit that is depicted by the author, and the recipients' foundational pneumatology, the references to the S/spirit in 9:14 and 10:29 would most likely be understood as references to the Holy Spirit apart from further explanation and specific qualification by the author, as they have been understood in the history of interpretation until quite recently.

The Spirit in 1 Peter, 2 Peter, and Jude: Transformation and Transcendence

Rebecca Skaggs

1   Introduction

The Holy Spirit is central to the message of all three of these epistles. Although there are unique features in each, the basic idea is similar: the Holy Spirit is the means by which the believer is transformed in God and participates in the suffering and death of Christ. There is a long tradition of treating these three epistles together since they share important factors, such as a broad audience (rather than a particular church, as with the Pauline epistles). In the case of 2 Peter and Jude there is a considerable overlap in the text as well.[1]

2   The Role of the Holy Spirit in 1 Peter

The Holy Spirit is also the central component underlying the important concepts in 1 Peter.[2] His primary role as agent is first identified in the Introduction (1:2). As agent, he carries out the process of making holy. Indeed, it is the "sanctifying work of the Spirit" that enables the believers' relationship with God. 'Ἐν' should be considered instrumentally; by means of the activity of the Spirit, the believer as alien is brought into relationship with and relocated in God. Peter expands the concept further in 1:12. It is the activity of the Spirit that links the past prophecies (OT prophets) with the sufferings of Christ, providing continuity between the past prophecies, Christ's death, and the present preaching of

---

[1] In addition, since the time of Eusebius of Caesarea, ca. 260–340 CE, they are included in a group of seven epistles called the Catholic or general epistles, 1, 2, 3 John, James, 1, 2 Peter, and Jude. One of the unifying features of this group is that their authenticity has been challenged. Although 1 John and 1 Peter were accepted as authentic almost immediately, James, 2, 3 John, and Jude were deemed as possibly authentic. 2 Peter has always been seriously disputed even in current times (see Gerald Bray, ed., *James, 1–2 Peter, 1–3 John, Jude*, Ancient Christian Commentary on Scripture, NT Vol. 11 [Downers Grove: InterVarsity Press, 2000], xvii–xxi for details).

[2] See R. Bauckham, *Jude, 2 Peter* (Waco, TX: Word, 1988); J. Green, *1 Peter* (Grand Rapids, MI: Eerdmans. 2007); J. R Michaels, *1 Peter*, Word Biblical Commentary Series 49 (Waco, TX: Word, 1988).

the gospel by the apostles. In fact, this entire process is so awesome that even the angels desire to understand it (v. 12). In 1:11, Peter clarifies the relation of the Spirit to Christ by referring to the Spirit as the "Spirit of Christ," that is, the one who testifies to or belongs to Christ.

The role of the Spirit is expanded even further in 3:18–22, in that when Christ died, he was "made alive by the Spirit through whom also he went and preached to the spirits in prison who disobeyed long ago...." However this difficult passage is interpreted, it is clear that for Peter, the Spirit transcends not only time and space but even life and death. The Spirit transforms the believer from "alien" to a position of chosen by God, enabling the believer to participate in the very suffering and death of Christ. This passage has a lengthy tradition of discussion/debate on the nature of the relationship between baptism and salvation. In fact, many ancient writers interpret 1 Peter as linking the christological work of salvation with baptism by means of the Spirit.[3]

Finally, in 4:14, the "Spirit of glory" is the reward for suffering; when you suffer "for the name of Christ, you are blessed, because the Spirit of glory and of God rests upon you." The blessing comes as a result of the suffering but is on account of the Spirit and glory of God. Here, Peter associates the Jesus tradition (Matt 5:3–10; Luke 6:20–21) with that of Isaiah (Isa 11:2a, LXX), highlighting the Spirit as the means of the believer's participation in prophecy and the suffering of Christ as well as eschatological blessings. Peter underscores this connection by his use of the present tense ("rests") rather than Isaiah's future tense ("will rest"). This suggests that the prophecy has indeed been fulfilled, and the Spirit of glory presently exists in the experience of the believer as it was in the experience of Christ. Again, the Spirit functions as agent, bringing the blessing as the reward of suffering

3   The Role of the Holy Spirit in 2 Peter

The Greek word for Spirit ($\pi\nu\varepsilon\acute{\upsilon}\mu\alpha$) is only mentioned once, in 2 Peter 1:21: "For prophecy never had its origin in the will of man but men spoke from God, as

---

[3] See Rebecca Skaggs, *1, 2 Peter and Jude through the Centuries*, Wiley Blackwell Bible Commentaries (Oxford: Wiley-Blackwell, 2020), 96–97 for an overview of this discussion/debate through the centuries by the church fathers; for example, Augustine was ambiguous on the subject (Skaggs, *1, 2 Peter and Jude*, 99). Some of these writers link baptism with the descent of Christ into Hades (see J.A. MacCulloch, *The Harrowing of Hell* [Edinburgh: T & T Clark, 1930], 85–86), making the point that the Holy Spirit enabled the salvific work of baptism to apply to the righteous OT saints in Hades.

they were carried along by the Holy Spirit." This reference has a long history of scholarly debate about why this was written and what it means.[4] To seriously oversimplify the issue, the question is whether this was written as a rejection of the opponents in this church who asserted that OT prophecy was merely the ideas and interpretation of the prophets themselves rather than originating from God. Clearly the author is advocating that God is the source of prophecy, conveyed to the prophets as well as to future believers by the Holy Spirit. Perhaps we can see an echo of 1 Peter here, that the role of the Spirit is the agent who facilitates the process. The point is that since prophecy is God's direct word given and conveyed by means of the Spirit, it is by nature remarkably different from the false speech of the heretical teachers. Their speech is false and comprised of heresies, even about the sovereign Lord himself; moreover, their behavior is shameful, bringing disrepute on the truth.

It is tempting to equate the phrase "divine power" (θεία δυνάμεως) in 1:3–4 with the Holy Spirit (πνεύματος ἁγίου) (1:21). If the two are the same, the role of the Spirit in 2 Peter would mirror that of 1 Peter, namely, that the Holy Spirit is the agent for bringing transformation of the believer in God. In 2 Peter 1 there are more details: the Spirit conveys knowledge of the godly life including the virtues, and the precious promises. However, a careful consideration of the two terms suggests that there is a notable difference.[5]

4   The Role of the Holy Spirit in Jude

In this small epistle, Jude does not directly treat the topic of the Holy Spirit. Yet, it is central to his message. In fact, the Spirit is the key difference between his readers and the false teachers in the community who are opposing him. One of the main characteristics of the teachers, according to Jude, is that they "lack the Spirit" (v. 19). This is ironic, since they themselves claim inspiration by the Spirit, citing dreams and revelations (v. 8). Jude sharply judges them on their behavior that the Spirit does not produce lives of deception, self-centeredness (vv. 12–13), arrogance, and ungodliness (v. 15). Jude draws a marked contrast between the teachers and his readers, whom he urges to build themselves up in faith and prayer (v. 20), to keep themselves in the love of God (v. 21), and to show mercy to others (v. 22). The key to this life of faith, love, and mercy is prayer in

---

[4] For an overview on this debate, see Rebecca Skaggs, *Pentecostal Commentary: 1 Peter, 2 Peter, and Jude*, Pentecostal Commentary Series 17 (Sheffield, UK: Sheffield Academic Press, 2004), 108–111; for more details, see Bauckham, *Jude, 2 Peter*, 228–235.

[5] Bauckham, *Jude, 2 Peter*, 177.

the Spirit. This phrase "εν πνεύματι" often means "in the control of the Spirit" or "under the inspiration of the Spirit" in the New Testament and early Christian literature (for example, in Matt 22:43; Mark 12:36; Luke 2:27; 4:1; Acts 19:21; Rom 8:9; 1 Cor 12:3; Rev 1:10; 4:2; Barn 9:7; *Asc. Isa.* 3:19; Polycrates, *Ap.* Eusebius, *Hist. Eccl.* 5.24. 2. 5). Some scholars argue that references such as these indicate charismatic prayer in which the Spirit provides the words.[6] Some suggest that this kind of prayer might include speaking in tongues.[7] The significant point for Jude is that behavior indicates the presence of the Spirit; although the false teachers claim spiritual visions and prophetic utterances, their behavior shows otherwise. Indeed, according to Jude, they are "devoid of the Spirit" (v. 19).

5 Conclusion

Finally, these three small epistles are important to the study of the early church since they provide one of the main sources for a picture of the non-Pauline church of the late first century. Hence, they provide information for our understanding of the challenges and how the churches responded to the serious controversies of the late first century.[8] They clearly indicate that the Holy Spirit is indeed still central to the church.

---

6 James D.G. Dunn, *Jesus and the Spirit* (London: SCM Press, 1975), 239–240.
7 Dunn, *Jesus and the Spirit*, 25–46; see also Bauckham, *Jude, 2 Peter*, 113 for more details.
8 See Bray, *James, 1–2 Peter, 1–3 John, Jude*, xxi for details.

The Spirit in John's Apocalypse: Vision, Prophecy, Discernment

Melissa Archer and Robby Waddell

The common New Testament nomenclature "Holy Spirit" or "Spirit of God" never appears in the book of Revelation, which leads some interpreters to question whether the text contains an identifiable pneumatology. Despite the lack of unambiguous references to the Spirit, scholars have argued vigorously both for and against identifying some (though not all) of the occurrences of πνεῦμα as references to the Holy Spirit.[1] In the last couple of decades, a renewed interest in the Apocalypse—especially by pentecostal biblical scholars—has led to a fresh discovery of its pneumatology, among other insights.[2] This essay surveys the pneumatological components found in Revelation.

John uses πνεῦμα a total of twenty-five times along with a single use of its adverbial cognate πνευματικῶς. The clearest instances where πνεῦμα does *not* refer to the Spirit include three references to unclean or demonic spirits (16:13–14; 18:2). In Revelation 22:6, John refers to "the spirits (τῶν πνευμάτων) of the prophets," a reference most likely to human spirits.[3] Two occurrences of πνεῦμα are often translated as "breath"—at the resurrection of the two witnesses (11:11) and during the animation of the image of the beast from the sea (13:15). Giv-

---

[1] For a review of literature on the Spirit in Revelation, see David R. Johnson, *Pneumatic Discernment in the Apocalypse: An Intertextual and Pentecostal Exploration* (Cleveland, TN: CPT Press, 2018), 50–100.

[2] For the most recent examination of Revelation's pneumatology see John Christopher Thomas, "The Spirit in the Book of Revelation," in *The Oxford Handbook of the Book of Revelation*, ed. Craig Koester (Oxford: Oxford University Press, 2021), 241–255. See also studies focusing on discernment (Johnson, *Pneumatic Discernment in the Apocalypse*); worship [Melissa Archer, *"I Was in the Spirit on the Lord's Day": A Pentecostal Engagement with Worship in the Apocalypse* (Cleveland, TN: CPT Press, 2015)]; the use of universally inclusive language [Ronald Herms, *An Apocalypse for the Church and for the World: The Narrative Function of Universal Language in the Book of Revelation* (Berlin: de Gruyter, 2012)]; and the nature of Jewish-Christian relations [Philip L. Mayo, *"Those Who Call Themselves Jews": The Church and Judaism in the Apocalypse of John* (Eugene, OR: Pickwick, 2006)]. The most recent commentary from a pentecostal perspective is Jon K. Newton, *A Pentecostal Commentary on Revelation* (Eugene, OR: Wipf and Stock, 2021).

[3] *Contra* Mazzaferri who interprets this to be a reference to the Spirit of prophecy who is inspiring the prophets. Frederick David Mazzaferri, *The Genre of the Book of Revelation from a Source-Critical Perspective* (Berlin: de Gruyter, 1989), 301.

ing breath to the image of the beast is clearly not a reference to the Spirit, though the breath that entered the witnesses is described as the breath *of life from God*, which may suggest an allusion to the Spirit or conceivably a double entendre—breath/Spirit of life. The fact that the witnesses stand up on their feet when the breath enters them offers a contrast to the image of the beast, who merely speaks, implying (perhaps) a case of ventriloquism rather than life.

Revelation's pneumatology resides in the remaining references to πνεῦμα, which can be divided into four groups: (1) the seven spirits (1:4; 3:1; 4:5; 5:6), (2) John's claim to be "in the Spirit" (1:10; 4:2; 17:3; 21:10), and (3) references to the Spirit speaking (2:7, 11, 17, 29; 3:6, 13, 22; 14:13; 22:17). For example, all seven messages to the Asian churches end with the phrase, "whoever has an ear let them hear what the Spirit says to the churches." Later in the narrative, John records the direct speech of the Spirit (14:13; 22:17). Lastly, (4) the concept of "the Spirit of prophecy," which includes but is not limited to the explicit statement that "the Spirit of prophecy is the testimony of Jesus."[4]

1 The Seven Spirits

The seven spirits make four appearances in the Apocalypse. They are introduced within a trifold greeting of grace and peace "from the one who is, who was, and who is coming, and from *the seven spirits who are before his throne*, and from Jesus Christ, the faithful witness." At a later point, Jesus is said to hold in his hand the seven spirits of God and the seven stars. In the heavenly vision, the seven spirits—again before the throne—are depicted as seven flames of fire, and finally, in John's description of the Lamb, the imagery changes as the seven spirits of God are now said to be the seven horns and the seven eyes of the Lamb.[5] In each case, there appears to be a close relationship between the seven spirits and either God and/or Christ.

---

4 The reference to the Spirit of prophecy in 19:10 is disputed as evidenced in the English translations. Some translations use a lower case "s" when translating πνεῦμα, suggesting that the reference is not to the Holy Spirit. See Mark W. Wilson, "Revelation 19.10 and Contemporary Interpretation," in *Spirit and Renewal: Essays in Honor of J. Rodman Williams*, ed. Mark W. Wilson (Sheffield, UK: Sheffield Academic Press, 1994), 191–202.

5 It is possible that the seven spirits are associated solely with the seven eyes of the lamb and not its seven horns, though a potential allusion to Zechariah's prophecy suggests that the power of the Spirit is a corollary to the knowledge of the Spirit, imaged by John as horns and eyes, respectively (cf. Zech 4:6; 10b). Richard Bauckham, *The Theology of the Book of Revelation* (Cambridge: Cambridge University Press, 1993), 112.

God: the seven spirits who are before (God's) throne (1:4)
Christ/God: (Jesus) has the seven spirits of God and the seven stars (3:1)
God: before the throne burn seven torches of fire which are the seven spirits of God (4:5)
Christ/God: a lamb ... with seven horns and seven eyes which are the seven spirits of God sent out into all the earth (5:6)

Commentators, both ancient and modern, are divided over whether the symbolism of the seven spirits represents Jewish angelology or early Christian pneumatology.[6] The deciding factor appears to be which intertextual echoes the interpreter privileges. Oecumenius identifies the seven spirits in the greeting as seven angels and cites 1 Timothy 5:21 as support for his position: "In the presence of God and of Christ and of the elect holy angels."[7] Luke utilizes similar language: "For whoever is ashamed of me and my works, of him will the Son of Man be ashamed when he comes in his glory and the glory of the Father and the holy angels" (Luke 9:26). Victorinus, on the other hand, argues that the seven spirits represent the sevenfold traits of the Spirit of God (cf. Isa 11:2–3).[8] Andrew of Caesarea and Arethas acknowledge the possibility that the seven spirits may represent the seven operations of the Spirit, though they conclude—in agreement with Oecumenius—that the seven spirits are angels who are in no way to be counted within the Trinity.[9] However, all these early interpreters agree in their reading of Revelation 5:6 where they associate the seven spirits with reference to the Spirit of God from Isaiah 11.[10]

The modern interpreters offer a more consistent argument for an identification of the seven spirits as either angels or as the Holy Spirit. In attempts to avoid the anachronistic error of reading later trinitarian theology back onto the Apocalypse, numerous scholars dismiss the possibility that John references the Spirit with the symbolism of the seven spirits. R.H. Charles argues, "without hesitation," that the first reference to the seven spirits, placed between God the Father and Jesus, must be an interpolation, which he describes as a "grotesque conception."[11] In the entry on πνεῦμα in Kittel's *Theological Dictionary of the*

---

6   For a review of modern scholarship see Robby Waddell, *The Spirit of the Book of Revelation* (Blandford Forum, UK: Deo, 2006), 9–21.
7   Oecumenius, *Comm. Apoc.* 1.9; 2.11. Cf. Tob 12:15; 1 *En* 90:20–21.
8   Victorinus, Comm. *Apoc.* 1:4.
9   Andrew of Caesarea, *Apoc.* 3.7; Arethas, *Apoc. Comm.* 1.
10 Oecumenius, *Comm. Apoc.* 3.14, Andrew of Caesarea, *Apoc.* 4.12 and Arethas, *Apoc.* 12.
11 R.H. Charles, *A Critical and Exegetical Commentary on the Revelation of St John*, 1 vol. (Edinburgh: T & T Clark, 1920), lii, 11.

New Testament, Eduard Schweizer writes that "the decisive point" in understanding the pneumatology of the Apocalypse is to recognize that πνεῦμα is not the entity known as the "Holy Spirit," but rather, πνεῦμα is "no other than the exalted Lord Himself."[12] Drawing on verbiage from the Qumran literature in which the phrase "spirits of God" functions as synonyms for "angels." David Aune concludes that the seven spirits before the throne (1:4, 4:5) are identical to the seven angels who stand before God (8:2).[13] Craig Koester concludes that interpretating the seven spirits as seven angels is preferable—citing the close connection between the seven spirits, Jesus, and the seven stars, which are the seven angels of the Asian churches (1:20; 3:1). He also compares the symbolism of the flames of fire used for the seven spirits in Revelation with similar terminology found in the Psalms and Hebrews for angels (cf. Rev 4:5; Ps 104:4; Heb 1:7, 14).[14] John Christopher Thomas, however, notes that "the plural 'spirits' is never used for angels in the Hebrew Bible," though Psalm 104:4 may be an exception; nevertheless, on the rare occasions that "spirits" function synonymously for "angels" in the extrabiblical literature, the referents are typically malevolent spirits.[15]

The argument that the seven spirits are a symbol for the Holy Spirit rests on a couple of factors: the close relationship of the seven spirits with God and/or Jesus and a set of proposed allusions to Isaiah and Zechariah. The placement of the spirits between God the Father and Jesus in the introduction to the letter could indicate a reference to the Holy Spirit (1 Pet 1:2; cf. 2 Cor 13:13). Providing corroborative evidence for this position is that fact that the greeting of grace and peace derives exclusively from God and Jesus in the New Testament and never from an apostle or angel,[16] which is the primary reason Charles argued that the insertion of the seven spirits in the greeting was a later Christian interpolation.

Two passages from the Hebrew Bible have been identified as possible intertexts for John's symbol of the seven spirits—Isaiah 11 and Zechariah 3–4. As

---

12   Eduard Schweizer, "πνεῦμα," *TDNT* 6 (1968): 449. In a treatment of the pneumatology of the Johannine community, Gary Burge allotted only two paragraphs to the Apocalypse. It's not that Burge was excluding the Apocalypse from Johannine literature, but rather that he agreed with Schweizer that there simply wasn't a significant treatment of the Spirit in the text. Gary Burge, *The Anointed Community* (Grand Rapids, MI: Eerdmans, 1987), 176–177.
13   David Aune, *Revelation 1–5*, vol. 1 (Waco, TX: Word, 1997), 33–35. Cf. 4Q403 1 I 43; 4Q405 23 I 9–10.
14   Craig R. Koester, *Revelation* (New Haven, CT: Yale University Press, 2014), 216.
15   Thomas, "The Spirit in the Book of Revelation," 242.
16   Thomas R. Schreiner, *Magnifying God in Christ: A Summary of New Testament Theology* (Grand Rapids, MI: Baker Academic, 2010), 502.

mentioned above, the belief that John was referencing the sevenfold Spirit of God from Isaiah dates to the third century, though that identification has been criticized because the Hebrew text contains only six facets of the divine Spirit rather than the seven listed in the LXX.[17] Whether John's original readers would have detected such a variance is questionable. In any case, Isaiah is not the only allusion at play in Revelation's pneumatology.

Zechariah portrays the Spirit as a seven-pronged lampstand whose flames are identified as "the eyes of the Lord roaming throughout the earth" (4:2–10). John borrows this language in his depiction of the seven spirits, first as seven flames of fire (4:5) and then as the seven horns and seven eyes of the lamb sent out into all the earth, identifying the Spirit as the divine missionary agent of the Lamb's power and knowledge (5:6). "Since the seven spirits of God are embedded as the seven eyes of the Lamb," according to Thomas, "it would seem that they are an implied recipient when universal worship is rendered to the Lamb in 5:8–14, which again shows a divine identity and makes it plausible to interpret the seven spirits as a way to speak of God's Spirit. If this is correct, then Rev 5:6 is perhaps the only place in the NT where worship is rendered to the Spirit."[18] When John describes the seven flames before the throne, he omits a reference to a lampstand, perhaps because he has already employed that image as a symbol for the church. On earth, the seven flames illuminate each of the seven lampstands (which is to say, the seven churches of Asia). Shining with the light of Spirit, the churches play a vital role—participating in the ministry of the Lamb—as the primary location in which the horns and eyes of the lamb (that is, the Spirit) operate.[19] The role of the church as inspired witnesses comes into clearer focus in the prophecy about the two witnesses (11:1–13), which is discussed below in the section on the Spirit of prophecy.

From a history of religions perspective, Bogdan Bucur argues that the seven spirits are angelic beings, though he strikes something of a middle ground between the interpretations offered thus far, stating that "the seven angelic spirits of Revelation occupy an area of confluence between angelology and pneumatology" containing both "angelic imagery and pneumatological content" that "need not be viewed as mutually exclusive; rather, they can be fused

---

17　Jan Fekkes, III, *Isaiah and Prophetic Tradition in the Book of Revelation: Visionary Antecedents and Their Development* (Sheffield, UK: Sheffield Academic, 1994), 109.

18　Thomas, "The Spirit in the Book of Revelation," 244. Cf. John Christopher Thomas and Frank D. Macchia, *Revelation* (Grand Rapids, MI: Eerdmans, 2016), 492.

19　Richard J. Bauckham, *The Climax of Prophecy* (New York: T & T Clark, 1993), 165–166. The threat to remove the lampstand from the church in Ephesus becomes more severe once the connection is drawn between the Spirit and the lampstands (2:5b).

by appealing to the category of 'angelomorphic pneumatology.'"[20] The dualism of the Apocalypse, furthermore, provides support for an early Christian pneumatology given the parody between the dragon, the beast, and the false prophet vis-à-vis God the Father, the Lamb, and the Spirit.[21] Edmondo Lupieri, who describes Revelation's pneumatology as "some kind of (pre-) Trinitarian thinking," makes a similar argument, stating that the seven spirits contrast with the seven-headed demonic beast.[22]

2   Being in the Spirit

In addition to the seven spirits, the phrase ἐν πνεύματι ("in the Spirit") appears four times in Revelation. On the island of Patmos on account of the word of God and the testimony of Jesus, John testifies that he was "in the Spirit on the Lord's Day" when he receives a vision of the resurrected Christ (1:10). In the next portion of the narrative, John is taken to heaven "in the Spirit" and sees the One on the throne and the Lamb (4:2). Near the end of the narrative, John is taken "in the Spirit" by an angel—first to the wilderness where he sees Babylon, the Great Harlot, and then to a great mountain where he sees the descent of New Jerusalem (17:3 and 21:10, respectively). Each "in the Spirit" phrase is accompanied by a change in location: from Patmos, to heaven, to the wilderness, to a mountain. Each "in the Spirit" phrase is connected to something that John sees: the resurrected Christ, the heavenly throne room, Babylon, and New Jerusalem.[23]

The anarthrous construction of the phrase has led some scholars to argue that John is referring to an ecstatic state or an instance of spirit possession. For example, George Caird translates ἐν πνεύματι as "falling into a trance."[24]

---

20   Bogdan Bucur, *Angelomorphic Pneumatology: Clement of Alexandria and Other Early Christian Witnesses* (Leiden: Brill, 2009), 99.

21   David R. Johnson, "The Spirit of Prophecy and the False Prophet: Parody and Theology in the Apocalypse," in *The Spirit of Prophecy and Reconciliation*, ed. Robby Waddell and Chris E.W. Green (Sheffield, UK: Sheffield Phoenix Press, forthcoming).

22   Edmondo F. Lupieri, *A Commentary on the Apocalypse of John* (Grand Rapids, MI: Eerdmans, 2006), 136.

23   The revelatory activity of the Spirit for John in Revelation parallels the story in Ezekiel, who is transported in the Spirit and is shown visions in the Spirit (Ezek 2:2; 3:12, 14, 24; 8:3; 11:1, 24; 37:1; 43:5). Cf. Jean Pierre Ruiz, *Ezekiel in the Apocalypse: The Transformation of Prophetic Language in Revelation 16,17–19,10* (Frankfurt am Main: Peter Lang, 1989), 190–214.

24   George B. Caird, *A Commentary on the Revelation of St. John the Divine* (London: A & C Black, 1966), 19.

Schweizer equates John's phrase with his ecstatic visionary state (cf. Acts 11:5), though Luke's ἐν ἐκστάσει never appears in Revelation. However, as Thomas notes, "When compared with other forms of religious experience, John's seems to be more like that of a shaman than a medium, since he did not lose control of his own thoughts or awareness."[25] The phrase ἐν πνεύματι functions in at least three ways: (1) a claim to spiritual experience or enablement, (2) a reference to a liturgical context, and (3) a compositional marker of the narrative.

Richard Bauckham proposes that John is making a claim of authenticity when he declares that his prophecy was received when he was in the Spirit. He offers several parallel examples of being in the Spirit from Christian and Jewish literature. In the New Testament, the phrase can mean "in the Spirit's control" (cf. Matt 22:43, Luke 1:7; Acts 19:21 and 1 Cor 12:3). In the *Didache*, the phrase was apparently theologically neutral, for a prophet speaking in the Spirit would have to be tested according to his or her own behavior (11:7–9).[26] As Bauckham suggests, John never completely loses his volition though his normal consciousness is suspended and replaced by visions given by the Spirit. On this view, the Apocalypse ought not to be reduced solely to a literary convention, though both the Hebrew Bible and Jewish apocalyptic texts seem to have influenced his writing.[27] Thomas summarizes this position well: "the book of Revelation is the result of the 'dynamic convergence and intersection of all that is John's life,' experienced when he is 'in the Spirit.' Specifically, all that John is, his knowledge of the OT, the apocalyptic traditions, the Johannine Jesus tradition, his worshipping community, and the experience of revelation itself converges before his eyes and ears 'in the Spirit' to produce the text of the Revelation."[28]

John's initial experience of being "in the Spirit" in 1:9–10 has also been understood as a statement of worship. Being "in the Spirit *on the Lord's Day*" suggests a link between John's activity and the activity of the seven churches who would be worshipping on the Lord's Day.[29] If the Johannine churches understand worship to be "in the Spirit" (cf. John 4:24), then the hearers would understand John to be worshipping in or by means of the Spirit even though exiled on Patmos.

---

25 Thomas, "The Spirit in the Book of Revelation," 246.
26 Bauckham, *The Climax of Prophecy*, 151.
27 Koester, *Revelation*, 251–252.
28 Thomas, "The Spirit in the Book of Revelation," 248. Cf. John Christopher Thomas, *The Apocalypse: A Literary and Theological Commentary* (Cleveland, TN: CPT Press, 2012), 44–47.
29 Melissa L. Archer, *"I Was in the Spirit on the Lord's Day"*, 130.

This would affirm their own worship practices and reliance upon the Spirit (Rev 2–3). If the Spirit is linked to worship, then worship creates a context for the giving and receiving of visions and prophetic words.[30]

Further, the phrases suggest that the Spirit plays a key role as facilitator of John's vision, taking him here and there to view new scenes that extend the vision. The extraordinary nature of this is found in comparison to other visionary texts in which individuals are led throughout by angelic guides. Angels appear in abundance in Revelation, but John is rarely said to be directly guided by them even though such guidance is implied in 1:1. Thus, even though an angel tells John about the wilderness and the great mountain and what he will see from those vantage points, John is taken to both places "in the Spirit." More than a mode of visionary transportation, the Spirit is the agency through whom John and the churches are to discern the things he is seeing. The Spirit aids in the pneumatic discernment of the Apocalypse. That the "in the Spirit" phrases extend throughout the book indicates the pervasive presence of the Spirit throughout the Apocalypse.

Lastly, regarding the structure of Revelation, the phrase "I was in the Spirit" performs an influential role in the composition of the narrative.[31] After the prologue, the first occurrence of the phrase introduces the whole book as a narrative of John's visionary experience. The phrase recurs three times in the book, marking the major transitions within the vision. Based on this repetition, the text can be divided into six major sections:

Prologue (1:1–8)
"In the Spirit" on the Lord's Day (1:9–3:22)
"In the Spirit" in Heaven (4:1–16:21)
"In the Spirit" in the Wilderness (17:1–21:8)
"In the Spirit" on a Great Mountain (21:9–22:5)
Epilogue (22:6–21)

This outline has several things to commend it. The prologue and epilogue are easily identifiable, and it is generally agreed that the vision of Christ and the letters to the seven churches form the first major segment of the book. When John repeats that he was in the Spirit, he introduces a long and complex portion of the vision (4:1–16:21) that contains John's vision of the throne room and the series of seven seals, seven trumpets, and seven bowls, which are the only

---

30   Archer, *"I Was in the Spirit on the Lord's Day"*, 172.
31   Bauckham, *The Climax of Prophecy*, 1–37; Waddell, *The Spirit of the Book of Revelation*, 138–150.

enumerated groups of seven in the book. Based solely on the literary marker ἐν πνεύματι, the remainder of the book (17:1–22:21) consists of two final visions (17:1–21:8; 21:9–22:5).

3 The Spirit Speaks

The use of τὸ πνεῦμα ("the Spirit") is found in each of the seven prophetic messages (Rev 2–3), in 14:13, and in 22:17. In each of these narrative locations, the Spirit speaks. Given that the readers hear the voice of God and Jesus, the Christian reader should not be surprised to hear the voice of the Spirit, too. Each of these messages begins with a prophetic formula (τάδε λέγει), which echoes the common nomenclature of prophetic announcements in the LXX (cf. Acts 21:11, "thus says the Holy Spirit"). Each of the seven prophetic messages to the churches has in its concluding verses the phrase "let the one having ears hear what the Spirit says to the churches." What is most striking is that each of the seven messages purports to be the words of Jesus to the churches. This is made clear firstly, by the way the narrative identifies the speaker to each worshipping community with words and images first introduced in the inaugural vision of the resurrected Christ in Revelation 1:9–20, and secondly, by the use of "I" language in each message ("I know your deeds," "I know where you are living," and so forth). The hearing formula at the end of each message suggests that the Spirit and Christ speak in tandem.[32] The speaker is clearly identified as the risen Christ, and yet each church is admonished "to hear what the Spirit is saying to the churches."[33]

In identifying the words of Jesus as the words of the Spirit, the Apocalypse reveals a few interrelated concepts. First, as Jesus is *in the midst* of the churches (1:13), so is the Spirit; that is, Christ is present in the churches through the Spirit. Second, the Spirit speaks the words of Jesus to the worshipping communities. Johannine hearers would likely think of Jesus's teaching on the Spirit found in John 14–16, most notably that the Spirit comes from the Father and the Son (14:26; 15:26; 16:7), and the Spirit speaks what the Spirit hears (14:26; 16:13). Thus, the words of the Spirit are to be trusted since the Spirit is the Spirit of truth (John 14:17; 15:26; 16:13). Third, the words of Jesus given through the Spirit come to the churches as *prophetic* messages declaring the word of the Lord and call-

---

32 *Contra* Schweizer, "πνεῦμα," 449–450.
33 The hearing formula in Revelation echoes both the Hebrew prophets (for example, Isa 6:9–10; Ezek 3:27) and the words of Jesus in the Synoptic Gospels (for example, Matt 13:9, 43).

ing the communities to action. Fourth, the call to *hear* the words of the Spirit suggests the need for the community to engage in corporately discerning the words of Jesus, a task aided by the Spirit. Notice also that each church is to hear the words of the Spirit given to *all* the churches, expressing the expansive presence of the Spirit.

The final two appearances of τὸ πνεῦμα are in Revelation 14:13 and 22:17 and in each, the Spirit speaks. In 14:13, after the announcements of the three angels, John hears a voice from heaven saying, "Write: Blessed are the dead who die in the Lord from now on," to which the Spirit replies, "Yes so that they may rest from their labors, for their works follow after them." Because John hears the Spirit respond to the voice in heaven, the intimation is that the Spirit here and the "seven spirits" of God before the throne are identical. At the close of the Apocalypse, the Spirit speaks in tandem with the bride in calling for Christ to come as well as calling all who will to come to Christ (22:17).[34] Both 14:13 and 22:17 continue the theme of the Spirit's intimate connection with believers as the Spirit affirms both the sacred nature of the martyrs, those who die in the Lord (Rev 13), and the witness of the people of God—the bride—in their testimony to and about Jesus to those who are thirsty. This invitation mirrors the invitation extended in Revelation 21:6 by the one on the throne who is Alpha and Omega, the beginning and the end: "To the thirsty I will give water as a gift from the spring of the water of life." Because Jesus also identifies himself with these terms (22:13), the narrative establishes a tight connection between God, Jesus, the Spirit, and the bride in terms of their mission to the world. This closing invitation given by the spiritually inspired church reinforces the central message of the book that the people of God are to be a prophetic witness to the world (cf. Rev. 11:1–13).

4   The Spirit of Prophecy

If the references to πνεῦμα discussed thus far accurately represent the work of the Spirit, then the Spirit's role in the Apocalypse may best be defined as the Spirit of prophecy. At the end of his final two visions in the Spirit, John attempts

---

[34] Swete argues that πνεῦμα functions in this passage as shorthand for the spiritually inspired prophets. He writes, "*pneuma* is ... the Spirit of Prophecy, the Spirit of the prophetic order: 'the Spirit and the Bride' is thus practically equivalent to 'the Prophets and the Saints' (16:6; 18:24)." H.B. Swete, *The Apocalypse of St John* (London: Macmillan, 1907), 310. Bucur agrees that it makes "good sense to consider that πνεῦμα and 'bride' are collective terms for 'prophets' and 'saints.'" Bucur, *Angelomorphic Pneumatology*, 109.

to worship his angelic guide, who rejects adulation, stating: "Do not do that; I am a fellow servant of yours and your brothers and sisters who hold the testimony of Jesus; worship God! For the testimony of Jesus is the spirit of prophecy" (19:10; cf. 22:9). Debate has ensued as to whether the testimony of Jesus (ἡ μαρτυρία Ἰησοῦ) should be understood as an objective or subjective genitive. Both possibilities make sense. The prophecy is about Jesus, *and* Jesus is the faithful witness (1:5; 3:14), who bears this testimony (that is, "the words of this book"). Furthermore, John classifies his book as a work of prophecy and is himself associated with the prophets (1:3; 22:9).

The prophetic role extends to the community, if the two witnesses in Revelation 11 are understood as a symbol for the church. The witnesses are described as two olive trees and two lampstands. The olive trees, which echo a story in Zechariah 3–4, serve as a symbol of spiritual anointing, and the lampstands are a symbol that John has already used to refer to the church. If a reader wishes to interpret the witnesses as something or someone other than the church, then the burden of proof will lie with them and not with those who identify the witnesses as the church.

Represented as olive trees, the church in Revelation is anointed like Joshua and Zerubbabel in Zechariah to be priests and kings, though these witnesses prophesy. The notion that the Spirit of prophecy would be corporately available to the eschatological community of God's people can be traced through the Hebrew Bible (Num 11:29; Joel 3:1–5 [English 2:28–32]; Acts 2:16–21).[35]

Not unlike the story in Acts, the church represented by the two olive trees and the two lampstands is empowered by the Spirit to bear the prophetic witness of Jesus to the end of the earth (Rev. 11:4b//Acts 1:8). Thus, John is calling the church to engage in its prophetic role by bearing witness to Jesus via the power of the Spirit. As a priesthood of all believers, the church offers worship to God, but as a prophethood of all believers, the church bears the witness of God to the world.[36]

As the primary location in which the Spirit operates, the church plays a prophetic role in the accomplishment of the Lamb's victory. As they stand before the Lord of the earth, the witnesses (that is, lampstands) shine with the light of the Spirit.[37] Sharing a common echo from Zechariah 4:1–13, the images

---

[35] See Larry R. McQueen, *Joel and the Spirit: The Cry of a Prophetic Hermeneutic* (Sheffield, UK: Sheffield Academic Press, 1995).

[36] Waddell, *The Spirit of the Book of Revelation*, 193. See Roger Stronstad, *The Prophethood of All Believers: A Study in Luke's Charismatic Theology* (Sheffield, UK: Sheffield Academic Press, 1999).

[37] Bauckham, *The Climax of Prophecy*, 165.

of the seven spirits and the two witnesses are linked together. The role of the Spirit is to speak the words of Christ in the church and inspire the church to bear the testimony of Jesus to the world. The word of the LORD to Zerubbabel echoes clearly as the church is encouraged that, despite resistance in the world, the people of God will complete their eschatological mission, "not by might nor by power but by the Spirit of the LORD."[38]

Closely related to the theme of prophecy, the Spirit enables John and the churches to discern reality from the divine perspective. In Revelation 11:8, John is told that the dead bodies of the witnesses will lie in the street of the great city that is prophetically (πνευματικῶς) called Sodom and Egypt, where also their Lord was crucified.[39] The Spirit is the agent that enables readers of the Apocalypse to view the world through the eyes of the Spirit. "In the center of the Apocalypse, John places the story of the two witnesses, and in the center of this brief narrative, John describes the spiritual insight of the church discerning the reality of the great city."[40] David Johnson has produced the most comprehensive study on spiritual discernment in Revelation in which he suggests that discernment is the quintessential activity of the church.[41]

5   A Theophany of the Spirit

Ancient and modern scholars are divided over whether the mighty angel in Revelation 10 represents a Christophany or merely another angelic minister. The disagreement revolves around the divinelike characteristics that are ascribed to the angel. Most commentators—including the early interpretations of Oecumenius, Andrew of Caesarea, and Arethas—explain these features as representing the angel's origin; however, a significant minority, most of whom cite Victorinus for support, see in these allusions a veiled reference to the divine.[42] Like Christ, this angel arrives in a cloud (10:1; 1:7). Reminiscent of God's

---

38   Bauckham, *The Climax of Prophecy*, 163–164; G.K. Beale, *John's Use of the Old Testament in Revelation* (Sheffield, UK: Sheffield Academic Press, 1998), 105.

39   Contemporary versions vary significantly on their translation of πνευματικῶς. It is translated as symbolically, figuratively, allegorically, mystically, prophetically, and spiritually.

40   Waddell, *The Spirit of the Book of Revelation*, 183.

41   Johnson, *Pneumatic Discernment in the Apocalypse*, 348–392. See also Ronald Herms, "πνευματικῶς and Antagonists in Revelation 11 Reconsidered," in *The Book of Revelation: Currents in British Research on the Apocalypse*, ed. Garrick V. Allen, Ian Paul, and Simon P. Woodman (Tübingen: Mohr Siebeck, 2015), 133–146. Herms identifies πνευματικῶς as the essence of pneumatic interpretation.

42   Charles Gieschen, *Angelomorphic Christology: Antecedents and Early Evidence* (Leiden:

throne, a rainbow is over the angel's head (10:1; 4:3); its face shines like the sun (10:1; 1:16); its feet are pillars of fire (10:1; 1:15); and its voice is like a roaring lion (10:3; 5:5). Although space does not permit a thorough discussion, the mighty angel of Revelation 10:1–11 bears the markings of a theophany of the Spirit, a relatively novel idea in scholarship.[43] Not unlike the Fourth Gospel, the Spirit serves as another (ἄλλος) divine representative (cf. John 14:16). As argued above, the Spirit serves as John's primary agent of divine revelation.

Identifying the angel with the Spirit solves certain narrative critical issues in the story of the temple and the two witnesses (11:1–13). If the mighty angel in 10:1–11 is recognized as a pneumaphany, then the Spirit may be identified as the actor of the divine passives (ἐδόθη) in 11:1–2, which would indicate that the possessive that is, my two witnesses, (τοῖς δυσὶν μάρτυσίν μου) signals that the witnesses belong to and are commissioned by the Spirit (11:3). Indeed, the Spirit can be seen as the narrator of the complete prophecy 11:1–13. The Spirit may even speak of the death of Christ in the third person without difficulty (11:8).[44] No other character qualifies. Only the Spirit can possess attributes otherwise ascribed to God and Christ while at the same time narrating the prophecy in its entirety. With no indication of a change in speaker in this portion of the narrative, the best narrative option is to recognize the mighty angel as a theophany of the Spirit. Acknowledging that an undoubtable identification of the mighty angel remains elusive, it is nonetheless narratively plausible that given the explicit angelic imagery, this pneumaphanic interpretation may be categorized as an angelomorphic pneumatology.[45]

6 Conclusion

The Apocalypse unveils a rich pneumatology. Closely related to both God and Christ, the Spirit serves as the primary agent of revelation for John and the church. John is in the Spirit when he receives his visionary experience, and the

---

Brill, 1998), 256–260; Loren T. Stuckenbruck, *Angel Veneration and Christology* (Tübingen: Mohr Siebeck, 1994), 229–232; Robert Gundry, "Angelomorphic Christology in Revelation," *Society of Biblical Literature Seminar Papers* 33 (1994): 664; Heinrich Kraft, *Die Offenbarung des Johannes* (Tübingen: Mohr Siebeck, 1974), 147.

43 Waddell, *The Spirit of the Book of Revelation*, 157–163; Peter J. Leithart, *Revelation 1–11* (London: T & T Clark, 2018), 402.

44 Charles H. Giblin, "Revelation 11:1–13: Its Form, Function and Contextual Integration," *NTS* 30 (1984), 458n58.

45 Bogdan Bucur uses this phrase to define the seven spirits, though he interprets the mighty angel in Revelation 10 as an angel. Bucur, *Angelomorphic Pneumatology*, 94.

churches must hear what the Spirit is saying so they may conquer and receive their reward. The Spirit serves as the presence of God in the church represented as the seven flames that burn before the throne and upon each of the seven lampstands. The hearing formula at the end of each of the seven prophetic messages suggests that the Spirit speaks the words of Christ. Indeed, the Spirit serves as Christ's representative of power and knowledge symbolized as the seven horns and the seven eyes of the lamb, which are sent out into all the earth. The Spirit enlivens the church, fortifies her in her prophetic witness to the world, and aids her in the essential task of discernment.

AFTERWORD

From Bare Life to *Labash* Life: A Tribute to the Holy Spirit

Nimi Wariboko

> Cover me, cover me,
>   Extend the borders of thy mantle over me,
> Because Thou art my nearest kinsmen.
>   Cover me, cover me, cover me

∴

This popular song is based on Ruth 3:9. Ruth said to Boaz: "I am Ruth thine handmaid: spread therefore thy skirt over thine handmaid; for thou art a near kinsman." Engaging *The Spirit throughout the Canon: Pentecostal Pneumatology* is not a moment of reading, but of a movement, of the triple movement that extends our comprehension of the Holy Spirit, motivates us to worship God, and sets us to seek more of the covering, the clothing of the glory of God. If there is ever a case of a good biblical theology being a doxology, this is it. This collection or concert of essays comforts its readers with the deep knowledge that the triune God "who is able to do exceedingly abundantly above all that we ask or think, according to the power that works in us, to Him be glory in the church by Christ Jesus to all generations, forever and ever" (Eph 3:20–21).

The essays in this book are promissory notes, not ham-fisted conceptual claims and propositions that hide the provocation and summon of God's word in the Scriptures. When reading through them—and simultaneously ruminating on the place and work of the Holy Spirit—I became overshadowed with the redemptive power and presence of God the Spirit, the Spirit of Christ (Rom 8:9). In this moment and site of deep meditation, I felt the joy of the gift from our fellow Pentecostal brothers and sisters extending the borders of their scholarly wings over me. Their eloquent peroration was like a wind (spirit/*pneuma*) blowing in from the Upper Room, and I was caught in it with such a transport that I could not close the book. The wind of their intellectual gifts irresistibly propels me from cover to cover. This wind is what we call pneumatic luminosity. This reminds me of what Basil of Caesarea said about the sunbeam that illumines believers: "When a sunbeam falls on a transparent substance, the substance itself becomes brilliant, and radiates light from itself. So too Spirit-bearing souls, illumined by him, finally become spiritual themselves, and their grace is sent forth to others."[1]

For most of us who are not competent exegetes of the Bible, this group of scholars radiating intellectual light from their scholarship is our "nearest kinsman." In the hurly-burly world of the academia, they have extended the borders of their scholarly mantles to cover our hermeneutic deficiencies. They have taken us into the folds of their academic gowns, pressed us down to their bodies of scholarship, shaken off our calcified skills, and we rejoice in the fragrance of their erudition. Reading the 24 essays crafted by 26 scholars from almost all the continents is like receiving a special gift sent by the global body of Christ to me, a fragrant offering, a sacrifice acceptable and pleasing to God. The delicate odor of their *pure gift* is like the aroma of the captives in Christ's triumphal procession (2 Cor 2:14–17), the ones who are in a creative embrace with the Holy Ghost, who are saved, and among those who are spreading the fragrance of the knowledge of God everywhere. While perusing *The Spirit throughout the Canon: Pentecostal Pneumatology*, I had no greater joy than to gaze on the beauty of the Holy Spirit as illumined by brilliant scholarship, eagerly holding my special gift, and luxuriating in the radiance of his omnipresence. This book is such a sparkling display of human creativity that it must have moved you, the reader, to worship the Spirit in the beauty of holiness as it moved me. I expected it to open up a meditative space, a horizon of mystery and possibility, for you to re/encounter the divine. This space, I reasoned, might entice every reader to (again) invite the divine, the understanding, mystery, and possibility of God's Spirit, into their own lived experience. That was what reading this book achieved for me.

Thus, in exultation, I sang again: "Cover me, cover me ... Thou art my nearest kinsman ..." The Holy Spirit is Pentecostals' nearest kinsman in the tough, lonely, and tumbling world of the academia that has abandoned God, or of our nations that have lost faith. He covers and stands ready to cover us all the time. He clothes us with God's grace and glory. The Hebrew Bible uses the word *labash*—which means to clothe or cover—to describe the grace-giving, caring

---

[1] Basil the Great cited in Catherine Keller, "Theopoetics: A Becoming History," in *The Art of Anatheism*, ed. Richard Kearney and Matthew Clemente (London: Rowman and Littlefield, 2018): 29–41; quote, 30.

power of God's Spirit. The endless clothing, covering function of the Holy Spirit is always moving us from bare, naked, mere life to *labash* life, the redeemed, flourishing life in the spirit.

This special work of the Holy Spirit—the duty and gift of *labash*—in our lives can be discerned in five distinguishable but inseparable categories of *life-making, auteuring* life. God not only created all life, but he is also the sustainer of all living things. In filmmaking there is a view that considers the director as the primary creative force. This is the auteur theory. In lifemaking, the Holy Spirit plays such a defining role.

I have identified only five broad threads that the Spirit of God is always weaving over the eternal, divine loom to *make* our lives, to clothe our lives, to *labash* our exposed and vulnerable lives. I examine this Spirit's lifemaking in the immanent realm of creation through the metaphor of a coat of five colors. Through the humanly distorted lens of a garment of many colors, we would learn how the place and work of the Holy Spirit in the Biblical canon is a duty of care of the triune God, our nearest Kinsman-Redeemer, to cover all of us with grace. The place and work of the Holy Spirit in the Hebrew and Christian Bibles, the Old and New Testaments, is a narrative of the relentless pursuit of God's affection, grace, and love for us—and all created beings. The scrupulousness and wisdom with which our Pentecostal-Charismatic scholars have exposed this relentless pursuit are in themselves a testimony of the ongoing work of the Spirit, drawing us into deeper knowledge of God's redemptive and transformative plan for the whole of humanity.

The five "colors" that adorn the Spirit's lifemaking garment represent five spheres of human social existence: (a) creativity, (b) empowerment, (c) mindset, (d) common good, and (e) presence of God.

(a) *Creativity (auteuring life):* God fills Bezalel with the spirit of God which enabled him to craft special items for the tabernacle (Exod 31:3–5). "He could do what was humanly impossible, understanding just how to craft the specific items of the tabernacle that the Lord had revealed to Moses" (p. 337). Human beings do not wait to be endued with special divine spirit to execute their projects—they bear the image of Creator-God in them, and that is the ground and ideal of their creativity. I interpret the most fundamental Christian understanding of the nature of human beings—the image of God (Gen 1:27)—as creativity; that creativity is their *being*, the actualization of their potentiality ("essence") under the conditions of existence. The image of God is what connects human beings to their theonomous depth of existence. The creative freedom that founds and sustains the actualization of potentiality is an expression of God's power of creation and it connects the catholicity of ontological divine creativity to every human sociality.

(b) *Empowerment of existence*: "the Holy Spirit is the life-force of all created beings" (p. 341). The Spirit is the power of existence, ideal, and destiny of all human beings and enables the actualization of their modes of power of being in their concrete lives.

(c) *Mindset (moral vision)*: This is about the Spirit's ongoing function in a believer's life to guide them towards Christoformity. In other words, the Spirit functions in the life of believers "to enable them not to do whatever they wish to do ... One who submits to the Spirit's promptings walking in the moral pattern of the Spirit enjoys the guidance of the Spirit to bear fruits of the Spirit and to fulfill the law of Christ in love" (p. 507).

(d) *Common good*: The Spirit works for the redemption of the world, "salvation to the ends of the world" (Isa 49:6; Acts 1:8). The Spirit enables the church "to bear witness for Jesus in the face of opposition and persecution" (p. 436). Salvation in the broadest sense includes social transformation: conversion, regeneration and sanctification of individuals and communities. The baptism of the Holy Spirit is both soteriological and missional (p. 440).

(e) *God's presence*: This is the enveloping presence of God for all creation. In God we move, live, and have our being. God's presence refers to God's power, control, and style which gives each life or lifemaking its personal and unique style. The presence is particular and universal. God's presence is expressed by the immanent relationality of all created beings to God as the ground and destiny of all of them. Its relation to all created beings precedes the enactment, evolution, and deployment of any immanent relations between any two created beings. God's presence is transcendent in this sense: it is immanent to the totality of all presences (partial presences in comparison with God's presence) and permeates the whole of creation. And this totality is not controlled by any immanent relation between created beings or between it and any created being. The Holy Spirit re/presents this encompassing transcendental-immanent divine presence.

The five threads in the fabric of divine-human relationality, and when considered as a synecdoche, represent the total involvement of the Holy Spirit's lifemaking of humanity. Here, "lifemaking" is deployed in the double sense of *bio* and *zoe* as the Spirit is the ground, ideal, and destiny of our ontological and ontic life.[2] Simply, the Holy Spirit's lifemaking (life-poiesis) is both *biopoetics* and *zoepoetics* as the Spirit unites power and meaning in every concrete life. Pentecostal pneumatology as presented in this book speaks to this double function, the double helix, and is appropriately adorned by the five colors of the threads in the divine loom.

---

[2] I am alluding to Paul Tillich here.

The book presents a special gift to students of Pentecostal pneumatology and to the worldwide body of Christ that has no political, economic, or territorial tie. Neither an intellectual creed nor utilitarian, consumerist eisegesis, *The Spirit throughout the Canon: Pentecostal Pneumatology*, testifies to that enigmatic *something more* in every superior scholarship. It opens a third space—maybe, it stages or represents itself as a mysterious impossible possibility of Marion's *saturated phenomena*. Its evocative artistic brilliance is situated somewhere between van Gogh's peasant's shoes and Bernini's Ecstasy of Saint Teresa.

Indeed, the essays in this volume are affective, exhibiting both intellectual and theonomous depths. When read with attention, this writer caught the profound feeling that comes from inhabiting the presence of great minds. As I moved from the first essay to the last one, I was repeatedly reminded of the immense love and affection that the Spirit of God has for me and all God's children. While reading the collection, I dreamed I went to a city called Glory, so bright and so fair,[3] decorated with exquisite scholarship, and *Proverbs-8 Wisdom* was teaching and dancing in the streets. When I entered the gate, I bowed on my knees and cried,

> Come, Holy Spirit,
>   I need You;
> Come, sweet Spirit, I pray.
> Come in Your strength
>   and Your power.
> Come in Your own
>   gentle way.

---

3 I am riffing on Lari Goss's lyrics "I Bowed on My Knees and Cried Holy."

Subject Index

Apocalypse   1, 4, 209–212, 214–218, 220–221, 250

Baptism   60–63, 65–66, 68–71, 73–75, 77, 84, 90–92, 96, 105–106, 109–110, 130, 133, 140, 154, 194, 206, 226

Charismata   150, 155, 157–158, 186, 192
Community   24–27, 35, 42, 45, 47, 50, 55–56, 58–59, 66, 83–84, 86, 88, 101, 104–105, 125, 130–133, 136, 144–145, 148–150, 152–157, 172–173, 175–177, 180, 182, 185–188, 192, 194–196, 198, 204, 207, 215, 217–219, 240–241, 243, 246, 248
Covenant   4–5, 23–27, 40–41, 44, 47, 49–50, 58, 61, 63, 75–76, 89–90, 100, 136, 138–140, 147, 159, 161, 163, 195, 201, 203, 231, 234, 242
Creation   3, 5–6, 8, 23, 26–27, 29–30, 32, 34, 36–40, 42, 44, 50, 53, 55, 60, 107, 128, 142–143, 159, 168, 180, 225–226, 231, 233

Deposit   4, 159–160, 172, 193, 242
Deuteronomistic History   16, 230
Divine Anthropomorphism   47–48, 234
Divine Presence   226
Divinity of The Spirit   196, 248

Elect   37–38, 211, 233
Eschatology   182
Ethics   4–5

Formation   5, 36, 149, 152, 154, 156, 164, 168, 169, 183, 241
Former Prophets   16, 21

Holiness   4, 32–35, 46–47, 56–57, 137–138, 175, 183, 195, 224, 234, 245, 247

Illumination   150–151, 172

Judgment   9, 28, 36, 38–41, 43–44, 46–47, 51, 54–56, 61, 78, 84, 106, 124, 129, 156, 232, 234

Leadership   3, 11–14, 17–18, 20, 41, 44, 149, 157
Love   35, 39, 76, 140–141, 143, 148, 151, 155, 169, 189, 193–195, 207, 225–227, 246

Minor Prophets   3, 52, 235
Mystery   46, 151, 166, 174, 177, 180, 224

Obedience   27, 39, 60, 62–63, 65–66, 139–141, 146–148, 166

Pentecostal Theology   3, 229
Pastoral Epistles   191, 247
Pentateuch   2, 6, 228
Pneumatology   2–3, 5, 12, 14, 59, 86–87, 101, 104, 106, 129, 147, 150, 170, 182, 192, 195, 198, 204, 209, 210–214, 221, 223–224, 226–227, 229, 238–239, 247, 250
Power   3, 9, 11, 14–15, 21–23, 28–29, 32, 36, 38–39, 44–47, 54–55, 63, 65–67, 69–70, 72, 74–75, 79, 85–88, 97, 101, 104–105, 111, 137–139, 146–148, 150, 156–157, 172–174, 178–181, 183, 185–187, 193, 195, 207, 213, 219–220, 222–223, 225–227, 232, 238, 245
Prophetic   3, 12–14, 19–25, 27, 40–41, 44–45, 48, 54, 64, 75–77, 79, 81–89, 91–92, 94–98, 101, 104–105, 107, 131–133, 161, 174, 187, 192, 195, 208, 216–219, 222, 229, 234, 238
Purity   36, 132

Restoration   4, 24, 31, 39, 41, 43, 46, 51, 60, 88–90, 168, 234
Revelation   5, 10, 13, 45, 116–117, 123, 151–152, 156, 172, 192, 195, 200, 209, 211–221, 247, 250
Righteousness   39, 42, 57–58, 60, 62–66, 124, 129, 138, 141–142, 145, 148, 161, 167–168, 175, 185, 194

Sanctification   34, 105, 148, 183, 194, 226
Speech   13–14, 23–25, 27, 47, 50, 64, 71–72, 76, 80, 82–83, 86–87, 89, 92–96, 132–133, 192, 195, 207, 210, 234
Seal   4, 50, 159–160, 172, 176, 242
Seven Spirits   210–214, 218, 220, 250

Spirit of Prophecy   10, 82, 88–90, 95–97, 210, 213, 218–219, 250
Spirit of Yahweh   11, 29, 39, 46, 48–50, 54–58, 234
Suffering   3, 41, 43, 67, 73–74, 102, 143, 148, 185, 188, 195, 205–206, 245, 247, 249

Trinity   4, 16–17, 159, 162, 195, 211, 242, 247

Unity   124, 153–154, 159, 162–163, 174–175, 178, 180

Biblical Index

Gen
1	8
1:2	5, 6, 7, 8, 38, 55, 60, 179n37
1:3	38
1:6	38
1:9	38
1:11	38
1:14	38
1:20	38
1:24	38
1:26	38
1:26–27	37
1:27	225
2:2	8
2:5	38
2:7	29, 37, 60
3:8	6
3:24	46
4:8	55
6:3	6, 8, 29
6:17	6, 228
7:15	6
7:22	6, 29
8:1	6, 7, 8
12:3	167
26:35	6
35:23–26	81
41:8	6
41:38	6, 7, 8, 179n37
45:27	6

Exod
2:5	56
3:2	46
3:14	118
6:9	6
10:13	6
10:19	6
14:13	24
14:21	6, 7
15:8	6
15:6	90
15:10	6
19:14	146
19:16	46
19:19	46
20:18	46
20:21	46
25:9	9
25:10–26:37	200
25:18–22	47
25:40	9
26:1	47
28:3	6, 9, 11
29:5	18n9
29:8	18n9
29:30	18n9
30:1–6	200
31:3	6, 7, 8, 9, 26, 172, 179n37, 189
31:3–5	225
31:5	7, 9
33:19	35
35:21	6
35:31	6, 7, 8, 9, 26, 172, 179n37, 189
36:8–37:29	200
40	173
40:13–14	18n9

Lev
4:21	138n20
6:3–4	18
7:6–7	138n20
8:7	18
8:13	18
8:16	138n20
9:3	138n20
9:32	138n20
11:44	146
16	200
16:4	18
16:23–24	18
16:32	18
18:11	138n20
20:8	146
21:10	18
22:32	146
26:41	139

Num
4:30	44
5:14	6
5:30	6

Num (*cont.*)
6:1–21	202, 202n23
6:9–12	202n23
6:34	10
8:4	9
8:10	44
9	25
9:20	25
11	10, 12, 13, 82
11:17	4, 6, 10
11:17–29	6n2
11:24–30	4, 81, 82n22
11:25	6, 12, 14, 19n11, 81
11:25–26	10
11:26	6
11:29	4, 6, 13, 14, 18, 82, 83, 91, 100, 219
11:31	6
14:4	90
14:24	6, 10
14:26–35	199
15:25	90
16:22	6, 6n3, 9
20:26	18n9
20:28	18n9
24:1–2	10
24:2	6, 7, 179
24:16	6
24:18	6
27:16	6n3
27:18	6, 10, 18
31:8	10

Deut
2:30	6
4:12	46
4:15	46
4:33	46
4:34	197n4
4:36	46
5:4	46
5:22–26	46
6–8	46
6:4	197n4
6:14	90
7:19	197n4
10:4	46
10:16	139, 139n29
13:1–2	147

18:18	17
20:2–4	24
23:4	10
26:8	197n4
29:3	197n4
30:6	139
32:11	7
32:43	145n60
33:3	146
34:9	6, 9, 11, 18
34:11	197n4

Josh
2:11	16
3:9	20
3:13–17	20
5:1	16
6:26	21
13:22	10
24:9	10

Judg
3:10	4, 10, 17n6, 18, 24
3:11–14	21
3:18	21
4:9	21
4:11	21
4:15–23	21
4:18	21
6:34	10, 17n6, 18, 23
8:3	16n2
9:23	17n3
11	24
11:29	10, 17n6, 18
13:25	17n6, 18
14:6	10, 17n6
14:19	17n6
15:14	17n6
15:19	16n2

Ruth
3:9	223

1 Sam
1:15	16n2
3:13	156
10:6	17n6, 19
10:10	7, 17n6, 19
10:10–12	19

11:6	7, 17n6, 19, 179	21:5	16n2
13:14	21	21:27–29	22
15:23	21	22:1–40	25
16:13	19, 33, 41	22:19–23	22
16:13–14	17n6	22:21–23	17n3
16:14	19, 33	22:22–23	35
16:14–16	17n3	22:24	17n6
16:14–23	35		
16:15–16	7	**2 Kgs**	
16:23	7, 16n2, 17n3	1:9–15	19
17:47	24	2:9	17n6
18:10	7, 17n3	2:15	17n6
18:12	33	2:16	17n6, 20
19	19, 19n11	3:17	17n4
19:9	17n3	4:8–36	21n17
19:20	7, 17n6, 179	5:26	22
19:20–24	4	6:5–7	21n17
19:23	7, 17n6	6:15–17	22
24:5	22	9–10	21n15
30:12	16n2	13:21	21n17
		14:12–16	21n15
2 Sam		14:17–18	21n15
1:15	23n18	16:1–4	21n15
4:12	23n18	16:12	21n15
7:14	138	18–20	21
7:14–16	137	19:7	17n3
8:2	23n18	20:1–7	22
12:10–12	21	23:15	21n15
22:11	17n5		
22:16	17n5	**1 Chr**	
22:50	145n60	12:18	23
23:2	17n6	12:19	18, 23
		28:12	26
1 Kgs		28:19	26
1–2	21		
3:16–18	156	**2 Chr**	
6:23–29	47	15:1	7, 24, 179n37
8	173	15:2–7	24
10:5	16n2	18:1–34	25
11:29–39	21n15	18:23	25
12–16	21	20:1–4	24
12:15	21n15	20:14	24
12:22–24	21n15	20:15–17	24
13:1–5	21n15	24:20	7, 18, 24
16:34	21	24:22	25
18:12	17n6, 20		
18:45	17n4	**Ezra**	
19:11	17n4	6:14	26
19:24	12	14:22	189

Neh

8:8	26
8:13	26
9:5–37	25
9:10	197n4
9:13–14	26
9:20	25, 35
9:30	25
13:2	10

Esther

5:1	26

Job

26:13	60
27:3	30
29:14	18n8
33:4	8, 29
34:14–15	30
40:10	18n8
48–50	190

Ps

1:4	28
2:6–7	137
2:7	138
8:4–6	198n8
14:6	90
16:9	86n36
17:50	145n60
18	17n5, 35
18:3–21	35
18:10	35
18:15	28, 35
18:42	35
31:5	30n14
32:2	30n14
33:6	28, 29n7, 60
34:18	30n14
35:26	18n8
51	22n18, 31
51:1–9	31
51:10	31, 32
51:10–12	28, 31
51:11	28, 31, 32, 33n22, 34, 35
51:12	31, 34
51:13	22
66:1	190
75:1	190
76:12	28
77:3	30n14
77:6	30n14
78:8	28
78:39	28
84:4	145
89:26–27	138
89:26–33	137
93:1	18n8
95	198n8, 199n11
95:7–8	200
95:7–11	199, 204
95:10–11	199
104:1	18n8
104:3	29
104:4	29, 212
104:28–30	36
104:29	8, 28
104:29–30	29
104:30	5, 28
106:1	35
106:32–33	8
107:1	35
109:18	18n8
109:29	18n8
110:1	64n13, 72
117:1	145n60
118:1	35
132:9	18n8
132:16	18n8
132:18	18n8
135:7	29n7
135:9	197n4
135:17	29n7
137:5–6	45
136:1	35
139	34
139:1–6	34
139:7	28
139:7–12	34
142:3	30
142:5	30
143	35
143:3	35
143:4	30n14
143:5	35
143:7	30n14
143:8	35
143:10	28, 35

BIBLICAL INDEX

146:3–4	30n14
147:16–18	29n7
148:7–8	29n7

Prov

4:26	199n10

Son of Sol

17:26–37	78

Isa

3:19	208
4:4	78
6:9–10	217n33
7:13–17	40
8:17–18	197n4
8:18	197n4
11	43, 211, 212
11:1–5	42
11:2	14, 42, 173, 189, 206
11:2–3	211
11:2–4	78
11:3	11, 42
11:4	42, 78
11:6–9	42, 145
11:10	145n60
20:3	147
22:11	29
25:6–8	145
30	38, 40
30:1–2	40
30:3	38
31	40
32:15	39, 89n43
32:15–18	39
32:16	39
32:17–18	39
34	38
34:1–15	38
34:16	38
39:5–7	40
40–42	30n6
40:13	39, 152
42:1	42, 43
42:1–4	42, 62
42:2–4	43
42:3	43
42:4	43
42:5	30
44:1–5	43
44:3	39, 167
44:3–5	90
44:4–5	39
44:5	167
49:6	78n13, 82, 89, 89n43, 101, 226
51:9	18n8
53	43
59:21	40
61:1	41
61:1–2	79, 98
61:1–3	41
61:2	41, 80n15
61:2–3	41
61:4–7	41
61:10	18n8
63	39
63:1–6	39
63:7–9	39
63:10	9, 34, 39, 80n14, 162, 175
63:10–11	26n12
63:11	34, 37, 39
63:14	39
66:20	146, 146n64

Jer

4:4	139n29
31:31–34	32, 139, 161, 202
31:32–33	141
31:33	202
31:33–34	202, 204
31:34	202
32:30–21	197n4

Ezek

1	49
1:1	45
1:1–2	45n1
1:2–3	45n3
1:12	29, 46
1:20	29, 46
1:28–2:1	46
2:2	17, 47, 214n23
3:12	47, 214n23
3:14	45, 47, 214n23
3:22	45
3:23–24	46
3:24	17, 47, 47n13, 214n23
3:27	217n33

Ezek (*cont.*)
7:8	49
7:27	18n8
8:1	24n5, 45, 47, 48
8:2	48
8:3	20, 47, 48, 214n23
8:3–4	46
9:8	49
10:1	47n11
10:18–19	47
10:18–11:5	46
10:22–24	47
11:1	47, 214n23
11:4	47n13
11:5	47
11:16	47
11:19	139, 161
11:19–20	49, 50
11:22–23	47
11:23–24	46
11:24	7, 47, 214n23
16	49
16:60–63	49
20:8	49
20:41	146
23	49
28:25	146
30:15	49
34:25	49
36:18	49
36:24–27	5
36:25–27	5
36:25–29	50n17
36:26	50, 139
36:26–27	49, 90, 161
36:26–28	32
36:27	50, 141
37:1	45, 47, 47n13, 214n23
37:1–14	5, 28, 46
37:9	5
37:14	5, 9, 50
37:26–28	49
37:27	50
37:28	146
39:27	146
39:29	48, 49, 50
40–48	49
40:1	45
41:15	47
43:4–5 43:5	47, 214n23
47:1–12	50

Dan
2:1	53
2:3	53
2:35	53n4, 54
4:5–6	53, 53n5
4:15	53, 53n5
5:11–12	53, 53n5
5:14	53, 53n5
5:20	53, 53n5
6:4	53, 53n5
7:2	53n5, 54
7:14	54
7:15	53n5
8:8	54
11:4	54

Hosea
4:12	54
4:19	54
5:4	54
8:7	54
9:7	54
12:2	54
13:15	54

Joel
2:2–9	161
2:28	89, 101, 167
2:28–29	4, 5, 51, 54n13, 90, 100
2:28–32	83, 88, 89, 90, 91, 95, 98
2:32	88, 89
3:1–2	54
3:1–5	219

Amos
4:13	53n4, 53n6

Jon
1:4	55
4:8	55

Mic
2:7	8, 55, 55n17
3:8	55

BIBLICAL INDEX

Hab
1:11	53n4
2:19	53n4
11:13	139

Hag
1:13–14	56
2:5	56

Zech
2:6	56n20
2:10	56
3–4	212, 219
4:1–13	219
4:6	56, 210n5
4:10	210n5
5:9	56
6:5	56
6:8	56
7:12	56
12:1	56
12:10	56
13:2	56

Mal
2:15–16	57
4:5	21

Matt
1:1	60
1:18	60
1:20	60
1:22	64
2:5	64
2:15	64
2:17	64
2:23	64
3:7–10	61
3:11	60
3:12	61
3:15	62
3:16	59, 62n6, 69, 179n38
4:1	66n16
4:1–11	62
4:14	64
4:17	63
4:23–24	63
5:3–10	206
5:12	64
5:17	64
7:9–10	85n33
7:11	83
7:12	63
8:16	65
8:17	64
8:28–34	65
9:32–34	65
9:35–36	63
10	61
10:16–23	64n11
10:17–18	64
10:19–20	61, 64, 65
10:20	59
10:41	64n10
11:2–6	63
11:14	21
12:10	64n12
12:17	64
12:18	59
12:18–21	62
12:22–24	65
12:28	59, 62n6, 65
12:31	86
12:31–32	65
12:32	86
12:33–37	65
13:9	217n33
13:17	64n10
13:35	64
13:43	217n33
13:57	64
14:22–33	156
14:25–29	21n17
15:1–9	63
15:1–20	64n10
15:22–28	65
16:14	64
17:5	62
17:9	99n54
17:14–18	65
19:28	60
21:4	64
21:11	64
21:32	62n5
21:46	64
22:40	63
22:42–45	64n13
22:43	208, 215

Matt (*cont.*)

23:23	63
23:25–28	64n10
23:29	64n10
23:34	64, 64n11
24	20
24:9–14	65n
26:56	64
27:50	66n16
27:50–53	21n17, 66
27:66	172
28:18–20	61
28:19–20	65
28:20	61

Mark

1:1	67
1:2–13	67
1:7	70
1:8	67, 68, 72
1:10	67, 68, 69, 74
1:12	67
1:14–15	67
1:21–28	71
1:22	70
1:23	71
1:23–27	70
1:30–34	70
1:32	71
1:32–34	70
1:39	70
1:40–42	70
2:3–12	70
2:10	70
3:1–5	70
3:10	70
3:11	70
3:22–30	69
3:28–29	86
3:28–30	72
3:30	71
5:1–20	71
5:2	71
5:2–13	70
5:15	71
5:16	71
5:18	71
5:25–34	70
5:38–43	70
6:1–6	70, 79
6:2	70
6:5	70
7:25	71
7:26–30	70
7:32–35	70
8:22–26	70
9:17	71
9:25–27	70
10:36–40	73
10:46–52	70
11:15	69n6
11:27–33	70
12:36	72, 208
13:11	64n12, 73
14:23–25	73n11
14:36	73n11, 166
15:37	74
15:39	74

Luke

1:7	215
1:15	77
1:17	21, 77
1:35	77n9, 89n43
1:41	96n52
1:41–45	77
1:46–47	77
1:46–55	77n9
1:67	96n52
1:67–79	77
2:25–32	77
2:27	208
2:32	78n13
2:34	78, 91
3:16	76
3:16–17	77, 91
3:17	78
3:21	84
3:21–22	79, 86, 90
3:22	69, 79, 96n52
4:1	79, 80n14
4:4	80n14
4:8	80n14
4:12	80n14
4:14	79, 80n14, 96n52
4:16–30	79, 91, 97
4:17–19	79
4:18	79, 87

BIBLICAL INDEX

4:18–19	85, 96n52, 101	1:19	107
4:19	80n15	1:19–34	107
5:1	87n40	1:19–12:50	107
5:15	87n40	1:27	107
6:6	87n40	1:29	107
6:17–19	87n40	1:31	107, 109
6:20–21	206	1:32	107, 109, 119
7:11–15	21n17	1:32–33	107, 128, 130
9:1–2	87n40	1:33	108, 119, 121, 128
9:26	211	1:34	107
10:1	81, 82	1:38	123
10:1–16	81, 91, 102	1:49	109
10:16	81	2:1–11	109
10:19	85	2:21	118
10:21	86, 86n36	2:22	123
11:1	84	2:25	108
11:9	84, 85	3:1–16	128
11:9–13	83, 91, 92, 97	3:2	123
11:11–12	85, 85n33	3:3	108
11:13	76, 80, 83, 84, 85, 86, 89n43	3:4	109
11:14–28	85	3:5	109, 120
11:20	87	3:5–8	5, 50n17
12:2–9	86	3:6	110
12:9	86	3:7	110
12:10	64n12, 86, 87	3:8	110
12:11–12	64n12, 86, 91, 102	3:9	111
12:50	73n12	3:10	112
13:10	87n40	3:11	113
20:20–26	156	3:12	113
22:20	161n17	3:14–15	116
24:45–49	82	3:16	116
24:47–49	87, 89n43	3:17	117
24:48–49	88	3:18–21	117
24:49	87, 88, 89, 89n43, 91	3:21	117
24:50–51	87	3:22	109
24:52–53	87	3:26	131n55
		3:34	119, 121, 128
John		3:36	116
1:1	107	4:1	109
1:1–18	107	4:1–30	128
1:3	107	4:2	109
1:3–4	119	4:7	114
1:10–11	122	4:10	113, 116
1:12	120	4:11	114
1:13	110	4:12	114
1:14	107, 117, 122	4:13–14	115
1:15	107	4:14	120
1:16	107, 117	4:15	116
1:18	107	4:17	110

John (*cont.*)

4:20	116
4:21	116, 117
4:22	116
4:23	117, 119, 122, 179
4:23–24	120, 128, 179
4:24	21, 118, 128, 215
4:25	118
4:26	118
4:28–30	119
4:39–42	119
5:20	110
5:28	110
5:30	124
6:59	123
6:63	119, 128
7:14	123
7:15	110
7:21	110
7:28	123
7:33	124
7:35	123
7:37–39	120, 125, 127, 128
7:38–39	121
7:39	120, 121, 127
8:14	124
8:20	123
8:21	124
8:31	126
8:51	115
8:52	115
9:24	124
9:34	131n55
10:17–18	125
10:28	115
11:26	115
11:28	123
11:33	121n26
12:16	123
12:31	124
13:1–20:31	107
13:3	124
13:7	123
13:8	115
13:13	123
13:14	123
13:21	121n26
13:33	124
14–16	128, 192, 217
14:4	124
14:6	117, 119, 122
14:13–14	122
14:15–31	121
14:16	122, 128, 221
14:17	120, 122, 127, 128, 129, 130
14:26	122, 123, 128, 130, 217
14:28	124
15:26	123, 128, 129, 133, 217
15:26–16:4	127
15:27	128, 129
15:27–16:4a	123
16:4b–15	123
16:5	124
16:6	128
16:7	123, 127, 128
16:8	124
16:8–11	129
16:9	124
16:10	124
16:12–15	129
16:13	124, 217
17:5	127
18:20	123
19:26–27	125
19:30	66n15, 125
19:34	125, 133
20:16	123
20:19–23	125
20:21–23	127, 128
20:22	125, 127, 128, 128n50, 130
20:26	127
21:1–25	107

Acts

1–2	80
1:1	101
1:4	87, 88, 89, 91
1:4–5	78
1:4–8	82, 88, 89, 89n43
1:5	78n13
1:8	78n13, 87, 88, 89, 89n43, 101, 105, 219, 226
1:9	87
1:14	84n32, 87
1:21–22	103, 104
2	13, 22, 75, 82, 95, 176
2:1–21	51
2:3	78n13

BIBLICAL INDEX

2:4	84n32, 86, 88, 92, 93, 94, 95, 96, 96n52, 97	6:8	147
		6:10	102
2:4–11	94	7	156
2:5	92	7:31	99n54, 100n56
2:5–6	95	7:37	87
2:6	92	7:51	162
2:7–8	92	7:51–52	103
2:11	77, 92, 94	7:55	103
2:13	95	8:4–17	91, 92
2:14–41	98	8:12–17	90
2:15–17	95	8:14–17	82
2:16–21	219	8:14–19	93
2:17	80, 88, 99, 99n56, 101	8:15	84n32, 96n52
2:17–18	5, 82, 89, 89n43, 95, 96, 100, 104	8:16	76, 89
		8:17	84n32, 93
2:17–21	55, 82, 87, 88, 97, 98	8:18	96n52
2:17–22	100	8:26	20, 100n56
2:18	88, 95, 104, 105	8:26–29	100n56
2:19–20	100	8:39–40	20
2:21	89	9:10	99n54
2:22	100, 197	9:10–12	99n55
2:26	77, 86n36	9:12	99n54
2:32	192	9:15	137n16
2:33	87, 88, 89, 91, 95	9:16	103
2:33–36	93	9:17	84n32, 96n52
2:36	95	9:17–18	90
2:38	90, 91	9:17–19	93
2:38–39	88, 91, 197n3	9:20	96n52
2:39	87, 88, 89, 91	10:3	99n54, 99n55, 100n56
2:42–47	80n14	10:7	100n56
2:43	100	10:17	99n54, 99n55
2:46	202	10:19	99n54, 99n55, 156
3:1	202	10:22	100n56
3:15	102	10:38	79
3:22	87	10:42	138
4:8	96n52	10:42–43	96
4:12	102	10:42–48	95
4:19–20	102	10:43	96
4:30	147	10:44	90, 96
4:31	82, 85, 96n52, 104	10:44–48	82
4:31–36	80n14	10:45–46	96
5:11–16	80n14	10:46	86, 93, 94, 95, 96n52, 97
5:12	147	10:47	97
5:19	100n56	10:47–48	96
5:21	202	11:5	99n54, 99n55, 215
5:28	102	11:13	100n56
5:29–32	102	11:15	96
5:41–42	102	11:15–18	96
5:42	202	11:17	96

Acts (*cont.*)

12:7–23	100n56
12:9	99n54
13:9–10	96n52
13:47	78n13
14:3	147
15:12	147
16	178
16:1–17:15	191n2
16:6–7	100n56
16:9	99n54
16:9–10	99n53, 99n55
16:10	99n54
16:16–18	156
17:1–9	186
17:31	138
18:2	137
18:5	191n2
18:7	136
18:9	99n54
18:9–10	99n55
18:24–25	90
18:24–19:7	91, 92
19:1	89
19:1–7	82, 197n3
19:2	76, 85, 97
19:6	86, 93, 94, 95, 96n52, 97
19:21	208, 215
19:22	191n2
20:4	191n2
21:22	217
21:22–24	202, 202n23
22:6	137n16
22:11	137n16
22:14	137n16
23	156
26:11	87
26:13	137n16
27:23	100n56
28:31	103

Rom

1–4	147
1:3	137
1:3–4	137, 139, 147
1:4	146, 147n69
1:5	137n16, 146
1:5–6	137
1:7	145
1:9–10	146n62
1:10	135
1:11–12	146n62
1:13	135, 137, 137n16, 146n62
1:16	138, 146
1:16–17	139
1:18–3:29	139
2:10	145
2:15	143
2:17–20	140
2:26	139
2:27–29	161
2:29	139, 147
3:17	145
4:11	160n10
4:24–25	138
5–8	138, 147
5:1	140, 142, 145
5:2	140
5:5	137, 138, 140, 148
5:10	140
5:21	142
6:1	137
6:1–8:39	140
6:2–11	141
6:4	140
6:4–5	138
6:6	140
6:9	138
6:14–15	137n16
6:21–22	141
6:22	141
6:23	142
7	179
7:1	137n16
7:1–6	140
7:4	137n16, 138, 141
7:5	141
7:5–6	139
7:6	137, 140, 141, 148, 161
7:22–23	141
7:24	142
8	175, 179
8:1–17	198n7
8:2	137, 142
8:2–4	141
8:3	141
8:4	141, 160n8, 168
8:4–6	142

8:5	141	15:12	137
8:5–7	141	15:13	138, 145, 146, 147n69
8:6	141, 142, 145	15:14	135
8:7	142	15:15–16	137
8:8	142	15:16	138, 145, 146
8:9	76, 137, 142, 178, 178n30, 179n38, 208, 224	15:16–19	137n16
		15:18–19	187
8:9–11	142	15:19	138, 146, 147, 147n69, 148, 179n38, 197, 197n5
8:11	138, 142		
8:12–17	142	15:22	146n62
8:13	142	15:22–23	135
8:14	137, 142, 179n38	15:23–24	135, 146n62
8:15	137	15:24	135
8:15–16	76, 166	15:26–28	136
8:16	142	15:28	135, 160n9
8:17	143	15:28–29	146n62
8:18–25	143	15:30–32	146n62
8:20	168	15:31	136
8:23	143, 160n13	16:1	135n3
8:26–27	143	16:1–15	137
8:27–28	148	16:3	136, 137
8:28–30	143	16:4	135n3
8:30	142	16:5	135, 135n3
8:34	138	16:16	135n3
9–11	50, 147	16:23	135n3, 136
9:1	143	16:24	191n2
9:1–5	143		
10:9	138	**1 Cor**	
10:14–21	136	1–4	150
11:11–12	146	1:2	146
11:13	137, 137n16	1:4–9	137
11:13–36	136	1:5–7	150
11:25	146	1:14	136
11:29	19	1:17	137n16
11:33	151	1:20	151
12–15	141, 147	1:26	151
12:1–2	175	2:1–5	150
12:3	144	2:4	150
12:3–6	144	2:5	147n69
12:3–8	144, 148	2:6	151
12:6	144	2:6–12	174
12:6–7	144	2:6–16	151, 189
12:8	144	2:7–8	151
13:13	168	2:9	151
14:1–15:6	136	2:10	151
14:1–15:13	145	2:11	179n38
14:17	145, 185	2:12	151, 152n7
15:7–13	145	2:14	179n38
15:8	145	2:15	152n7

1 Cor *(cont.)*

3:1	152, 152n7
3:1–4	152
3:1–5	152
3:7	154
3:8	154
3:16	153, 179n38
3:16–17	152, 153
4:17	191n2
4:20	147n69
5:3	189n5
5:4–5	140
6:9–11	137
6:11	76, 146, 153
6:11–20	152
6:14	138
6:18	153
6:19	193
6:19–20	153
7:40	179n38
8–10	150
9:2	160n10
9:17	137n16
11:25	161n17
12	144, 157, 190
12–14	94, 150, 154, 197
12:1–3	131n57
12:3	144, 175, 179, 208, 215
12:4	157
12:4–6	157, 162
12:4–7	155
12:4–11	14, 154, 155
12:4–30	155
12:7	187, 197
12:8	189
12:8–10	155, 156, 157, 186
12:10	19, 94, 94n50
12:11	197, 197n3
12:12–13	154
12:13	105, 137, 152, 154
12:27–30	157
12:28	94n50, 155, 157
12:29–30	155, 157, 158
12:30	94, 94n51
12:31	187
13:1	94n51
13:1–3	155
13:1–13	155
13:8	94n50, 155
14	144
14:1–19	155
14:1–25	155
14:2	94n51, 177
14:3–4	187
14:4	94n51
14:6	94n51, 155
14:6–19	94
14:13	94n51
14:14	140
14:14–16	177
14:15	190
14:18	94n51
14:18–19	14
14:20–25	155
14:22	94n50
14:23	94n51
14:26	94n50, 155, 190
14:26–33	155
14:26–40	155
14:27	94n51
14:28	94
14:29	131n57
14:36–37	155
14:39	94n51
15:20	160n13
15:42–49	76
15:43	147n69
16:10	191n2

2 Cor

1:1	191n2
1:12–2:4	160
1:17	160
1:19	191n2
1:21	137
1:21–22	159, 160, 162, 172
1:22	140, 159n3, 160, 174, 193
2:13	140, 191n2
2:14–17	224
2:22	191n2
3	76, 159
3:3	137, 159n3
3:3–18	161
3:6	159n3, 161
3:7–13	159
3:8	159n3
3:17	137, 159n3, 161
3:18	159n3

4:2	168	5:18	142, 168
4:6	140	5:21	167
5:5	159, 159n3, 160, 172	5:22	145, 185
5:7	168	5:22–23	141, 169
5:14	140n32	5:25	168, 184
5:17–19	163	6:1	169
6:6	142, 159n3, 161	6:1–10	169
6:7	147n69	6:8	168
6:18	142	6:18	179, 190
7:3	140	15:18–21	167
7:6	191n2		
7:13–14	191n2	**Eph**	
8:6	191n2	1:3	170n2, 171
8:16–17	191n2	1:3–14	171, 172
8:23	191n2	1:13	160n9, 170n2, 172, 180
11:22	159	1:13–14	172, 174, 175
12:12	197	1:14	160
12:18	191n2	1:15–23	171, 172, 180
13:4	140n32	1:17	170n2, 172, 189
13:13	190, 212	1:23	176
13:14	159, 159n3, 162, 175, 179	2	173
		2:1–3	173, 180
Gal		2:2	170n2, 173, 180, 181
1:4	168	2:4–10	173
1:15–16	137n16	2:18	170n2, 173, 180
2:1	191n2	2:19	143, 173
2:3	191n2	2:19–22	174
2:20	165, 178	2:22	170n2, 173, 180
3–4	167	2:24	175
3:1	137, 165	3:3–5	189
3:1–5	165, 166n7	3:5	170n2, 174, 180
3:3	165	3:6	174
3:5	137, 165, 178, 179	3:16	170n2
3:14	137, 167	3:16–17	165, 174
3:16	167	3:17	175
3:26	166	3:19	176
3:29	167	3:20–21	223
4	179	4–6	174, 176
4:5–7	166	4:3	170n2, 174, 180
4:6	165, 166	4:3–4	190
4:7	167	4:4	170n2, 180
4:24–31	167	4:4–6	175
4:29	160n8, 166	4:11–12	177
5	176, 179	4:23	170n2, 175, 181
5:1–6:10	168	4:24	175
5:5	167, 168	4:27	175
5:16–18	184	4:30	8, 160n9, 170n2, 175, 180, 181, 203n27
5:16–6:10	168		
5:17	168	5	175

Eph (cont.)

5:18	162, 170n2, 175
5:18–19	190
5:19–21	177
6:10–17	180
6:10–20	171
6:12	170n2, 177, 181
6:17	170n2, 177, 180
6:18	170n2, 180
6:18–20	177

Phil

1:1	192n2
1:19	178, 181
1:19–20	178
1:27	178, 181
1:27–30	178
2:1	163, 179, 180, 190
2:1–4	179
2:2	175, 178, 191
2:5–11	179
3:3	161, 178, 180, 181
3:10	138
3:17–18	168
3:20	138
4:23	140, 178, 179, 181, 190
6:12	181

Col

1:1	191n2
1:8	189
1:9	189, 190
1:25	137n16
1:28	190
1:29	147n69
2:2	189
2:4	189
2:5	189
2:23	189
2:10	189
3:10	190n8
3:15	190n8
3:16	190
3:17	146

1 Thess

1:1	191n2
1:4–5	183, 186
1:4–6	183
1:5	137, 144, 147n69, 165, 183, 186
1:6	185
1:6–7	183, 185
1:8	185
1:8–9	183
1:9	184
1:10	185
2:2–6	183
2:3–6	187
2:4	137n16
2:12	185
2:13	183
2:13–16	185
2:14–16	185
2:14–20	183
2:19–20	185
3:2	191n2
3:2–5	185
3:6	191n2
3:11–13	140n31
3:13	184
4:1	184
4:1–8	183
4:4	184
4:7	194
4:7–8	139n20
4:8	184, 184n7, 193
4:13	168
5:19	203n27
5:19–22	183, 186, 187
5:20	187
5:20–21	131n57
5:23	184

2 Thess

1:1	191n2
1:4	185
1:5	185
1:10	185
1:11	147n69
2:2	187
2:9	197
2:13	160n13, 182, 183
2:15	182, 187
2:16–17	140n31
2:17	146, 189n5
3:5	140n31

BIBLICAL INDEX 245

1 Tim

1:1	191n1
1:2	191
1:8	193
1:8–9	194
1:18	192
2:4	195
3:12	195
3:14–15	195
3:14–16	191
3:15	142
3:16	191
4:1	192
4:10	195
4:14	192, 193
4:16	195
5:15	195
5:21	211

2 Tim

1:1	191n1
1:1–13	193
1:2	191, 194
1:6	192
1:7	192, 193
1:9	195
1:14	193
2:7	193
2:16–17	192
2:19	160n10, 195
3:15	195
3:16	193
3:16–17	177
4:22	194

Titus

1:1	191n1
1:4	191
3:4–5	195
3:4–6	194
3:4–7	162
3:5	194

Philm

1:1	191n2
1:6	190
1:14	190
1:17	190
1:25	190

Heb

1:1	199
1:1–2	197n2
1:1–2:4	196
1:1–10:26	203
1:2	199, 199n12, 200
1:5	198
1:5–6	197n2
1:6	198
1:7	198, 212
1:8	197n2, 198
1:10	198
1:13	198
1:14	212
2:1	197
2:3	197
2:4	196, 197, 198, 204
2:6	198
2:12	198
2:12–13	197n4
2:13	198
3:1	198, 200
3:6	197n2
3:7	198, 200, 200n13
3:7–8	200
3:7–11	199, 200, 204
3:10–11	199
3:13	199
3:14	198
3:15	200
4:3	199
4:7	198n8, 199, 200n13
4:14	197n2
4:16	200
5:5	197n2, 198
5:6	198
5:8–10	197n2
5:12	198
6:1	198
6:1–2	196
6:1–5	204
6:2	198
6:4	196, 198
6:4–6	198
6:6	197n2
6:19–20	200
7:3	197n2
7:4–28	201
7:17	198

Heb (*cont.*)
7:21	198
7:28	197n2
8:1–6	201
8:5	203
8:8	198
8:8–12	202
8:13	201
9:8	198, 200, 200n13, 204
9:8–9	200
9:14	202, 203, 204
9:15	161n17
10:1	203
10:5	198
10:14	202
10:15	198, 200n13, 204
10:15–17	202
10:19–22	200
10:29	197n2, 202, 203, 204
12:7	197
12:11	197
12:24–25	200
13:5	198
13:8	16

1 Pet
1:2	205, 212
1:11	206
1:12	205
3:18–22	206
4:14	206

2 Pet
1:3–4	206
1:21	21, 193n12, 206
2:15	10

1 John
1:3	132
1:7	132
2:1	132
2:2	132
2:6	132
2:12	132
2:14	132
2:20	129, 130, 131
2:22–23	132
2:24	130
2:27	130, 131
2:28–29	132
3:2–3	176, 132
3:5–6	132
3:7	132
3:24	131, 133
4:1–3	132
4:1–6	131
4:2	133
4:6	133
5:6	133
5:7–8	133
5:8	133

2 John
1:7	133
1:9	129, 130n55

Jude
1:8	99, 207
1:12–13	207
1:15	207
1:19	207, 208
1:20	207
1:21	207
1:22	207

Rev
1:1	216
1:1–8	216
1:3	219
1:4	210, 211, 212
1:5	219
1:7	220
1:9–10	215
1:9–20	217
1:9–3:22	216
1:10	208, 210, 214
1:13	217
1:15	221
1:16	221
1:20	212
2–3	216, 217
2:7	210
2:11	210
2:14	10, 130n55
2:17	210
2:29	210
3:1	210, 211, 212
3:6	210

3:13	210	11:3	221
3:14	219	11:4	219
3:22	210	11:7–9	215
4:1–16:21	216	11:8	220, 221
4:2	208, 210, 214	13	218
4:2–10	213	14:13	210, 217, 218
4:3	221	17:1–21:8	216, 217
4:5	210, 211, 212, 213	17:1–22:21	217
5:5	221	17:3	210, 214
5:6	210, 211, 213	19:10	21, 219
5:8–14	213	21:6	218
8:2	212	21:9–22:5	216, 217
10:1	220, 221	21:10	210, 214
10:1–11	221	22:6	209
10:3	221	22:6–21	216
11	219	22:9	219
11:1–2	221	22:13	218
11:1–13	213, 218, 221	22:17	210, 217, 218

www.ingramcontent.com/pod-product-compliance
Lightning Source LLC
Chambersburg PA
CBHW021807220426
43662CB00006B/208